AF830743

The Business of Health

This book offers a discussion about the dramatic development of healthcare business around the world during the twentieth century. Through a broad range of cases in Asia, Europe and the US, it shows how health was transformed into a fast-growing and diversified industry.

Health and medicine have developed as one of the fastest growing sectors of the economy around the world during the twentieth century. However, very little is known about the conditions of their transformation in a big, globalized business. This book discusses the development of health industries, tackling the various activities in manufacturing (drugs, biotechnology, medical devices, etc.), infrastructure (hospital design and construction) and services (nursing care, insurances, hospital management, etc.) in relation to healthcare. The business history of health carried out in this book offers a systemic perspective that includes the producers (companies), practitioners (medical doctors) and users (patients and hospitals) of medical technology, as well as the providers of capital and the bodies responsible for regulating the health system (government).

The chapters in this book were originally published as a special issue of the journal *Business History*.

Pierre-Yves Donzé is Professor of Business History at Osaka University, Japan, and Visiting Professor at the University of Fribourg, Switzerland. He is co-editor of the journal *Business History*. His research focuses on the history of the global dynamics of industries (hospitals and medtech, watchmaking, fashion and luxury).

Paloma Fernández Pérez is Professor of Economic and Business History at Universitat de Barcelona. She is former co-editor of the journal, *Business History* and co-editor of the *Journal of Evolutionary Studies in Business*. Fernández Pérez is an expert in history of entrepreneurship in industries and services. Her most recent book is *The Emergence of Modern Hospital Management and Organization in the World 1880s–1930s* (2021).

The Business of Health

New Approaches to the Evolution of Health Systems in the World

Edited by
Pierre-Yves Donzé and
Paloma Fernández Pérez

Routledge
Taylor & Francis Group
LONDON AND NEW YORK

First published 2022
by Routledge
2 Park Square, Milton Park, Abingdon, Oxon OX14 4RN

and by Routledge
605 Third Avenue, New York, NY 10158

Routledge is an imprint of the Taylor & Francis Group, an informa business

© 2022 Taylor & Francis

All rights reserved. No part of this book may be reprinted or reproduced or utilised in any form or by any electronic, mechanical, or other means, now known or hereafter invented, including photocopying and recording, or in any information storage or retrieval system, without permission in writing from the publishers.

Trademark notice: Product or corporate names may be trademarks or registered trademarks, and are used only for identification and explanation without intent to infringe.

British Library Cataloguing in Publication Data
A catalogue record for this book is available from the British Library

ISBN: 978-1-032-18739-6 (hbk)
ISBN: 978-1-032-18741-9 (pbk)
ISBN: 978-1-003-25598-7 (ebk)

DOI: 10.4324/9781003255987

Typeset in Myriad Pro
by Newgen Publishing UK

Publisher's Note
The publisher accepts responsibility for any inconsistencies that may have arisen during the conversion of this book from journal articles to book chapters, namely the inclusion of journal terminology.

Disclaimer
Every effort has been made to contact copyright holders for their permission to reprint material in this book. The publishers would be grateful to hear from any copyright holder who is not here acknowledged and will undertake to rectify any errors or omissions in future editions of this book.

Contents

Citation Information vii
Notes on Contributors ix
Acknowledgement x

1 Introduction: Health Industries in the Twentieth Century 1
Pierre-Yves Donzé and Paloma Fernández Pérez

2 Learning from giants: Early exposure to advanced markets in the growth and internationalisation of Spanish health care corporations in the twentieth century 20
Paloma Fernández Pérez, Nuria Puig, Esteban García-Canal and Mauro F. Guillén

3 Thriving in the shadow of giants: The success of the Japanese surgical needle producer MANI, 1956–2016 45
Ken Sakai

4 Challenging the Problem of 'Fit': Advancing the Regenerative Medicine Industries in the United States, Britain and Japan 72
Maki Umemura

5 'Importance of Germany to Countries around and to World Economy makes it impossible to ignore' – The Rockefeller Foundation and Public Health in Germany after WWII 97
Sabine Schleiermacher

6 Socialisation of healthcare demand and development of the French health system (1890–1938) 114
Jean-Paul Domin

7 China: The development of the health system during the Maoist period (1949–76) 134
Roser Alvarez-Klee

8 Architects and knowledge transfer in hospital systems: The introduction of Western hospital designs in Japan (1918–1970) 154
Pierre-Yves Donzé

9 The genesis, growth and organisational changes of private health insurance companies in Spain (1915–2015) 174
Jerònia Pons-Pons and Margarita Vilar-Rodríguez

Index 196

Citation Information

The chapters in this book were originally published in the journal, *Business History*, volume 61, issue 3 (2019). When citing this material, please use the original page numbering for each article, as follows:

Chapter 1

Health Industries in the Twentieth Century
Pierre-Yves Donzé and Paloma Fernández Pérez
Business History, volume 61, issue 3 (2019), pp. 385–403

Chapter 2

Learning from giants: Early exposure to advance markets in the growth and internationalisation of Spanish health care corporations in the twentieth century
Paloma Fernández Pérez, Nuria Puig, Esteban García-Canal and Mauro F. Guillén
Business History, volume 61, issue 3 (2019), pp. 404–428

Chapter 3

Thriving in the shadow of giants: The success of the Japanese surgical needle producer MANI, 1956–2016
Ken Sakai
Business History, volume 61, issue 3 (2019), pp. 429–455

Chapter 4

Challenging the Problem of 'Fit': Advancing the Regenerative Medicine Industries in the United States, Britain and Japan
Maki Umemura
Business History, volume 61, issue 3 (2019), pp. 456–480

Chapter 5

'Importance of Germany to Countries around and to World Economy makes it impossible to ignore' – The Rockefeller Foundation and Public Health in Germany after WWII
Sabine Schleiermacher
Business History, volume 61, issue 3 (2019), pp. 481–497

Chapter 6

Socialisation of healthcare demand and development of the French health system (1890–1938)
Jean-Paul Domin
Business History, volume 61, issue 3 (2019), pp. 498–517

Chapter 7

China: The development of the health system during the Maoist period (1949–76)
Roser Alvarez-Klee
Business History, volume 61, issue 3 (2019), pp. 518–537

Chapter 8

Architects and knowledge transfer in hospital systems: The introduction of Western hospital designs in Japan (1918–1970)
Pierre-Yves Donzé
Business History, volume 61, issue 3 (2019), pp. 538–557

Chapter 9

The genesis, growth and organisational changes of private health insurance companies in Spain (1915–2015)
Jerònia Pons-Pons and Margarita Vilar-Rodríguez
Business History, volume 61, issue 3 (2019), pp. 558–579

For any permission-related enquiries please visit:
www.tandfonline.com/page/help/permissions

Notes on Contributors

Roser Alvarez-Klee, Department of Economic History, Institutions, Policy and World Economy, University of Barcelona, Barcelona, Spain.

Jean-Paul Domin, Regards EA 6292, Université de Reims Champagne-Ardenne, CEPN UMR 7234, UFR de sciences économiques, sociales et de gestion, Reims, France.

Pierre-Yves Donzé, Graduate School of Economics, Osaka University, Osaka, Japan.

Paloma Fernández Pérez, Departament d´Història i Institucions Econòmiques, Facultat d´Economia i Empresa, Universitat de Barcelona, Barcelona, Spain.

Esteban García-Canal, Department of Business Administration, Universidad de Oviedo, Oviedo, Spain.

Mauro F. Guillén, The Wharton School, University of Pennsylvania, Philadelphia, PA, USA.

Jerònia Pons-Pons, Facultad de Ciencias Económicas y Empresariales, Departamento de Economía e Historia Económica, University of Seville, Seville, Spain.

Nuria Puig, Universidad Complutense de Madrid, Madrid, Spain.

Ken Sakai, Graduate School of Economics and Management, Tohoku University, Sendai, Japan.

Sabine Schleiermacher, Forschungsschwerpunkt Zeitgeschichte, Institut für Geschichte der Medizin, Charité – Universitätsmedizin Berlin, Berlin, Germany.

Maki Umemura, Cardiff Business School, Cardiff University, Cardiff, UK.

Margarita Vilar-Rodríguez, Departamento de Economía Aplicada I, University of A Coruña, Facultad de Economía y Empresa, A Coruña, Spain.

Acknowledgement

Research of Paloma Fernández has been sponsored by Spanish Project PGC201S8-093971-B-I00 granted by the Ministry of Science and Innovation Programme for Knowledge Generation project PGC 2018-093971-B-100, funded by MCIU/AEI/FEDER, UE.

INTRODUCTION

Health Industries in the Twentieth Century

Pierre-Yves Donzé and Paloma Fernández Pérez

ABSTRACT
This article is the introduction to the special issue' Health Industries in the Twentieth Century'. It offers a broad literature review of scholarly works about the history of health and medicine, and stresses the opportunities for business historians to tackle the field of healthcare.

Healthcare has experienced a deep transformation characterised by significant growth in expenditures during the twentieth century. Today, it represents one of the fastest growing sectors of the economy.[1] While estimates of health expenditures indicated about 1% of a country's total GDP in 1900, OECD statistics put that proportion at 4–6% in 1970 (5.2% in France; 5.7% in Germany; 4.4% in Japan; 4% in the UK; and 6.2% in the US) and on a steady increase through to the present day. In 2015, health expenditures accounted for 11% of GDP in France, 11.1% in Germany, 11.2% in Japan, 9.8% in the UK, and 16.9% in the US.[2] Moreover, this phenomenon is not limited to developed countries. Emerging countries also follow the same trend, with health expenditures that went from 4% to 6% of GDP in China and 4% to 5% in India between 1995 and 2014, for example.[3] Worldwide, endless growth of health expenditures has led to financial concerns for governments of all kinds. Scholars have also engaged in public debate, trying to provide evidence to explain this development. The mechanisms of the growth of health expenditures led to the emergence of a new academic field in the 1960s—health economics, whose main objectives are to evaluate the most economically efficient systems to take care of people's health and to measure the impact of new technologies on health expenditures.[4]

Health industries stand as one of the cornerstones of the welfare system, and the regulation of market access to the corresponding products and services represents a major battlefield in political debates in OECD countries. In referring to 'health industries', we consider the various activities in manufacturing (drugs, biotechnology, medical devices, etc.), infrastructure (hospital design and construction) and services (nursing care, insurances, hospital management, etc.) in relation to healthcare. We use the plural term 'industries' rather than 'industry' to emphasise the broad variety of sectors engaged in healthcare. Although health has become a fast-growing sector of global economies, the foundations of the welfare system, and one of the major reasons for progress in the Human Development Index worldwide during the twentieth century, very little is known about the conditions shaping the transformation of health industries from small, local, personal services into big, globalised, high-tech businesses.

The heterogeneous nature of the health industries may account in part for the relative scarcity of related studies from a historical perspective. The World Health Organization, as well as the OECD official statistics about healthcare, tackle medical activities and measure human capital that includes physicians, nurses, and pharmacists. *Forbes* and *Fortune* analyse medical and drug corporations, among them large manufacturers and distributors. National governments consider the wholesale and retail distribution of drugs and medical services via public and private institutions as entities that provide products and services related to healthcare. Health economics scholars concentrate the bulk of their research on studies financed and used by health insurance companies to analyse risk and health spending. The specialised literature reveals a clear divide. On the one hand are approaches from health economics, which tend to tackle current problems (such as growing costs, the organisation of the health market, the role of insurance providers, and the financial impact of new technology) with little, if any, historical perspective. On the other hand, approaches from the history of medicine and public health field focus more on social, cultural, and gender issues (such as the personal experiences of patients, the professionalisation of nurses, social control through health policies, and the international expansion of Western medicine within the context of imperialism).

The bibliometric analysis of the vast number of publications related to the history of health, history of hospitals, and history of medicine using the Web of Science, Scopus, and Mendeley, over the last 15 years, below, reveals that the field has expanded enormously and is therefore difficult to summarise or analyse (see table 1). Pressure for academic productivity and the effects of the internet era in expanding the possibilities of cooperative research and publications may help explain the fact that there are more than one million references to the history of health, hospitals, and medicine alone.

Works by health economists have helped shed light on the workings and challenges of current health systems. Nevertheless, they do not explain why or how medicine and health have transformed from local services into fast-growing and largely globalised businesses during the last century. What were the driving forces of transformation and growth in this sector? Which companies and entrepreneurs engaged in building new kinds of businesses to improve the population's health and answer the needs of medical doctors and patients? What were their incentives, and what possible alternative choices and pathways were available to them during the modernisation of the healthcare business of the twentieth century? How did a financial system take shape, operating on a foundation of insurance providers and state interventionism, to support the growth of the system? Answering such questions is essential to achieving a proper understanding of the historical development of health. Despite the sector's tremendous record of development during the twentieth century, however, very few scholars have analysed health from a systemic perspective adopting an approach of business and economic history.[5] Numerous scholars have addressed the history of medicine and health, but they often opted for inquiries into specific, fragmented parts of the health market.

Hence, the objective of this special issue is to employ a longitudinal, business history-centric approach in analysing and understanding the complex context in which the construction of health industries and services took place—via a variety of pathways—throughout the world since the 1900s. This volume first illustrates the role of path dependence and the

Table 1. Bibliometric analysis History of Health, Hospitals and Medicine. 2000–2016 Web of Science, Scopus, Mendeley.

2000–2016	WOS				SCOPUS					Mendeley
Key Words	Total	Article	Proceedings	Review	Total	Article	Proceedings	Review	Social Sciences	
History Hospitals	**31,707**	29,620	1599	1072	**561,547**	402,268	12,166	93,289	22,715	
"History Hospitals"	**0**				**81**	54	3	9	14	
"History of Hospitals"	**17**				**415**	221	12	81	97	13
"History of Hospital"	**80**	78	2	1	**415**	221	12	81	97	190
History medicine	**16,430**	12,249	967	2253	**1,11,5791**	756,719	29,340	2,08330	80,642	
"History medicine"	**31**	13	1	1	**423**	174	3	101	128	
"History of medicine"	**1887**	1240	89	225	**42,368**	18,765	1606	11,782	6031	6566
History Health	**59,443**	52,229	3105	4332	**864,932**	586,984	25,628	147,344	126,650	
"History health"	**142**	108	6	5	**1863**	1168	38	338	483	
"History of health"	**210**	151	11	12	**1451**	805	32	296	410	601

Source: Paloma Fernández´s own elaboration with technical assistance of Jaime López. From Web of Science, access 13/10/2016. Scopus, access 13/10/2016. Mendeley, access 14/10/2016.

diversity of the models that different countries followed in transforming locally embedded health services into fast-growing globalised businesses. Secondly, the articles in the special issue emphasise the impact of the diverse institutional frameworks that helped define national health systems. Thirdly, the issue aims to shed new light on the emergence of new therapeutic agents and new frames of care and culture, as well as the influence of new actors and changing organisations. Finally, the influence of entrepreneurship, together with different types of ownership and management styles, is a subject of analysis for both fostering a deeper understanding of the complexities in each country and exploring the branches of the health industry for establishing incentives, obstacles, and opportunities in the creation of technological and scientific innovations and the transfer thereof from firms to society.

1. Literature review

This volume builds on a rich and diversified literature in the history of medicine, pharmacy, and general science and technology pertaining to health. Numerous works have examined particular aspects of this transformation, but, unlike the articles in this issue, very few offer an inclusive perspective that establishes a dialogue with the diverse factors that have had and continue to have a key role in the construction of our national health systems: institutions, medical technology, and private and public healthcare companies.

The most relevant literature can be classified in three major fields. First is the history of health system organisation and funding.[6] These works emphasise the evolution of public health systems and the funding structures of hospitals, addressing elements like the involvement of the state and insurance providers, the roles of local communities, the relative decline of philanthropy and charity in the Western world. These works, however, lack a focus on new medical technology and the action of private companies, which are vitally important in the diverse experiences of Japan, the United States, and some European areas like Catalonia and Madrid in Spain. Secondly, there are publications in the history of medical technology that have shed light on the process of innovation in health and medicine and demonstrated the role of social networks in the diffusion of new technology.[7] However, these seldom embrace the analytical perspectives of business and economics and rarely account for the role of enterprises and market structures. Thirdly, the pharmaceutical industry has generated several studies employing a business history approach.[8] They follow a perspective that analyses the competitiveness of firms relative to organisational capabilities, industrial organisation, and markets. The existing research does not usually consider the organisation of health systems and the interactions with other actors within them (governments, insurance companies, and medical doctors) as determinants of change, though, and our special issue aims to contribute to the discussion on that point.

Hence, there has been relatively little analysis of the construction and management of public and private hospitals and clinics, first of all, and the factors that created opportunities or obstacles for those entities in transferring modern, life-saving technologies and knowledge to real patients—to society. We also know relatively little about the construction of health insurance companies or the process through which, in some countries, periods of coexistence or private and public health insurance came about in order to finance the population's access to scientific and technological modern healthcare innovations. Entrepreneurship and innovation among latecomers in regions of the world that were far from the leading pioneers in Germany, France, the United Kingdom, the United States, Switzerland, and Japan, too, remain relative unknowns. How, when, and why did life-saving drugs or knowledge make their way to 'the rest of the world'? In which subfields of the healthcare industries has 'the rest of the world' innovated and transferred technological, scientific, and organisational developments into their public and private healthcare institutions? How can innovative entrepreneurs and small enterprises in the healthcare businesses grow and become medium or large corporations in markets increasingly dominated by oligopolies headquartered in a few pioneering countries? Through which possible mechanisms, in which context, and under which obstacles and incentives can these changes take place? We know extremely little about the history and typologies of historical regulatory systems affecting the volume and prices of drugs and medical services in our countries. Today, when so much is at stake, when we are witnessing the transitions and crises of national health systems created in the latter half of the twentieth century, we believe that business historians have a responsibility to integrate dispersed, isolated methodologies and approaches into a historical overview of the historical construction of our national health systems.

Given the scope of that goal, this special issue cannot fully cover all the aspects of the institutional and business dimensions of health systems. This introduction concentrates on a few relevant topics: medical professions, innovation and new medical technologies, and the creation, management, and growth mechanisms of healthcare firms and corporations. It then provides a general model for historical analysis of the construction and development of health systems worldwide.

2. Medical professions

Since ancient times, Greek, Roman, Chinese, Arab, South American, and African practitioners created and preserved knowledge about remedies and techniques to prevent illnesses, safeguard against epidemics, and heal and treat the sick with varying degrees of centralised control and funding. The commercial revolution of the fifteenth century onward brought unprecedented changes in political systems worldwide, along with wars and upheavals both social and demographic, all of which had consequences on the world's diverse healthcare institutions. Asia and the Middle East maintained ancient systems of religious provision of care for the poor and sick in large, centralised buildings and temples where religion and local healing traditions prevailed. Meanwhile, the Western world witnessed a more dramatic change from the Middle Ages and well into the sixteenth and seventeenth centuries—a long period of darkness during which authorities disregarded and abandoned advanced Greek, Roman, and Arab medical knowledge and institutions and yielded control of public healthcare to religious authorities and charitable institutions. According to those in control, illness was a consequence of sin, as was the study of the human body. The sixteenth-century Protestant revolution and seventeenth-century scientific revolution were transformations that elevated the medical profession to a higher social status in some Western European countries, as the anatomic analysis of the body was no longer a condemned pursuit and the regulation of scientific studies started to take shape. The biological study of plants and the exploration of medical drugs of organic origin, which had started in a scattered, informal way as curious individuals from a variety of professional origins in other parts of the world delved into inquiry, received a more institutionalised form of acknowledgment in the eighteenth century in most of the Western world; royal institutes, royal associations, and specialised books and journals lent that brand of research more legitimacy.[9] 'Imperial science' during the nineteenth century contributed to marginalising ancient medical knowledge from non-Western civilizations and also spreading to and imposing on distant parts of the world Western academic knowledge and medical institutions and practices relating to biology, chemistry, and medicine thanks to new rotary printing machinery, continuous paper production, new mass media, and, of course, the revolutions in communication and transportation stemming from the first wave of globalisation.[10] Since the mid-nineteenth century, until the end of the two World Wars, most countries in the Western world had established new, centralised national sanitary legislation and governmental agencies that slowly took control of the business of health away from religious, philanthropic, or local institutions. Closely linked to the new role of governments in taking control of health problems, particularly epidemics (many related to the processes of mass migration and industrialisation of the world), countries set up new national educational institutions and plans to train members of the medical profession—now in urgent demand—through new faculties and schools of medicine, pharmacy, biology, and chemistry. The number of graduates of medicine, pharmacy, and chemistry programmes increased in the last decades of the nineteenth century, as records of existing student registers at European universities and the preserved records of local and provincial doctors' associations reveal.[11]

International statistics that take account of the expansion of the medical profession and the construction of Western-style hospitals started to emerge after World War I in a fragmented, experimental way. The figures that came from numerous European, American, Asian, and African countries have only recently come under scholarly scrutiny, with researchers examining the pioneering efforts at transferring knowledge of the modern organisation of large hospitals.[12] Statistical collection only became a systematic, significant process after the creation of international associations focusing on healthcare after World War II. The World Health Organization and OECD provide relatively reliable and representative information for a large sample of countries since the 1960s and particularly after the 1990s. As the OECD statistics in Tables 2, 3, and 4 illustrate below, only a handful of countries with high concentrations of professionals— Germany, the United States, Japan, Spain, Italy, and the United Kingdom—have substantial amounts of data before the crisis in the 1970s. These professionals were physicians, nurses, and pharmacists. Considering the numbers of professionals per 1000 inhabitants, nurses have clearly been the segment most available to the sick.

3. Innovation and the history of new medical technologies

The various works on the history of the organisation and funding of hospitals emphasise that the introduction of modern management practices from the private sector and the diversification of financial resources were key conditions for enabling the growth of the sector during the twentieth century. Yet, organisational scholars very rarely analyse the reasons and the necessity to develop and grow. In brief, the literature on the subject does not tackle the issue of change in external conditions, the new social and political demand for health services in liberal societies and traditional developing countries with accelerated urbanisation and immigration, or the pressure to develop medical innovations to meet the new challenges.

Table 2. Density of physicians by country (per 1000 people).

	Country	1960	1970	1980	1990	2000	2010	2013
Practising physicians	France	..	..	..	..	..	..	3.1
	Germany	..	..	..	..	3.26	3.73	4.05
	Italy	..	..	..	..	..	..	3.9
	Japan	1.03	1.09	1.27	1.65	1.93	2.21	..
	Spain	**..**	**..**	**1.84**	**2.05**	**3.16**	**3.76**	**3.81**
	United Kingdom	0.85	0.94	1.32	1.62	1.96	2.7	2.77
	United States	..	..	..	..	2.29	2.43	2.56
Professionally active physicians	France	..	..	..	3.02	3.26	3.27	3.33
	Germany	..	2.08	2.82	3.76	3.58	4.08	4.43
	Italy	..	..	..	..	4.16	4	4.19
	Japan	..	..	1.32	1.7	2	2.28	..
	Spain	**..**	**..**	**..**	**2.24**	**3.41**	**4.01**	**4.1**
	United States	..	..	..	..	2.45	2.57	2.7
Physicians licensed to practice	Germany	..	..	..	..	4.49	5.37	5.83
	Italy	..	1.08	2.62	4.7	6.07	6.27	6.37
	Spain	**1.17**	**1.34**	**2.3**	**3.83**	**4.45**	**4.8**	**4.99**
	United Kingdom	..	..	..	..	3.43	3.61	3.72
	United States	..	1.63	2.06	2.47	2.88	3.19	3.31

Source: Paloma Fernández´s own elaboration with technical support of Jaime López at the University of Barcelona, from data accessed on 22 Jan 2016 from OECD.stat http://stats.oecd.org/.

Table 3. Density of nurses by country (per 1000 people).

	Country	1980	1990	2000	2010	2013
Practising nurses	Germany	..	..	10.52	12.16	12.96
	Japan	..	..	..	10.11	..
	Spain	2.1	2.68	3.57	5.15	5.14
	United Kingdom	..	..	9.01	9.52	8.18
Professionally active nurses	France	..	..	6.66	8.45	9.39
	Italy	..	..	..	..	6.14
	Japan	..	..	..	10.67	..
	Spain	..	2.87	3.79	5.35	5.39
	United States	..	..	10.17	10.94	11.14
Nurses licensed to practice	Italy	..	..	5.48	6.32	6.88
	Spain	3.24	3.92	4.92	5.48	5.54

Source: Paloma Fernández´s own elaboration with technical support of Jaime López at the University of Barcelona, from data accessed on 22 Jan 2016 from OECD.stat http://stats.oecd.org/.

Table 4. Density of pharmacists by country (per 1000 people).

	Country	1980	1990	2000	2010	2013
Practising pharmacists	France	..	..	..	..	1.06
	Germany	..	..	0.58	0.62	0.64
	Japan	0.54	0.73	1.13	1.54	..
	Spain	..	..	0.72	0.92	1.12
	United Kingdom	..	..	..	0.65	0.8
Professionally active pharmacists	France	..	0.94	1.01	1.13	1.12
	Germany	..	..	0.65	0.72	0.76
	Italy	..	..	..	0.87	0.97
	Spain	..	..	0.82	1.03	1.26
	United States	..	..	0.75	0.87	0.91
Pharmacists licensed to practise	Germany	..	..	..	0.96	1.01
	Italy	..	0.97	1.1	1.37	1.47
	Spain	0.62	0.94	1.26	1.38	1.43

Source: Paloma Fernández´s own elaboration with technical support of Jaime López at the University of Barcelona, from data accessed on 22 Jan 2016 from OECD.stat http://stats.oecd.org/.

Studies of the history and sociology of medical technology can thus help us better understand the conditions of innovation in medicine and their relations with the healthcare system. In this field, the influence of social constructivism was very important. In the wake of groundbreaking books by Bruno Latour and Steve Woolgar,[13] as well as Thomas Hugues, Wiebe Bijker, and Trevor Pinch,[14] many authors tackled cases of medical innovation from a social history perspective. Stuart Blume studied the example of medical imagery,[15] while Thomas Schlich focused on surgery,[16] and Julie Anderson, Francis Neary, and John V. Pickstone analysed hip replacement technology.[17] All these works made the argument that medical innovation was not a 'natural' phenomenon. They highlighted the major roles of social networks in bringing an innovation into the public eye—on a global scale—and professional use. In this sense, medical innovation can be approached as a social construction: what innovation literature has labelled as innovation through 'communities of knowledge' or what entrepreneurial scholars have described as 'collective entrepreneurship'.[18] The articles in this special issue are especially important in contributing new empirical evidence about the complex social, political, and educational professional contexts in which medical innovative knowledge and management can and must develop.

However, the sociology and social history of medical technology has usually overlooked the establishment of connections with business and the relevant economic context, a trend that this special issue aims to change. Analyses of innovation in medicine must address the pertinent relationships with hospital finances, the effects of market regulation, and the roles of health insurance. As in other economic sectors, innovation in medical technology occurs within organisations (universities, R&D centres, and enterprises) within a given market; therefore, business conditions have a major impact on the way medical innovation comes about. The pharmaceutical and drug industry appears here as a specific case, as pharmaceuticals represent one of the very few medical technologies to have been the subject of special analysis by business historians. Most of the studies focus, however, on the first phase of drug innovation, running from the development of aspirin in the early twentieth century to that of beta-blockers in the 1960s. Innovation in the drug businesses followed different waves, of course, aligning closely with the product life-cycle theory. The development of cell biochemistry in the 1970s and insights into molecular structure since 2000 have led to the emergence of new players, mostly start-ups, which followed various paths of development (transformation into global companies, absorption by established multinational enterprise, and decline, for instance). The dynamics of the drug industry since the 1970s are still under-addressed by scholars, while they have a growing impact on healthcare consumption.

4. The creation, management, and financing of healthcare corporations and organizations

Hospitals, manufacturers of medical technologies and drugs, and wholesale and retail distributors of technologies and drugs are the main players in the business of healthcare industries and services. Large hospitals were well-known since antiquity in the Middle East; there have also been large charitable hospitals in the Western world since the fifteenth century, mostly in the largest urban centres of Europe and the Americas. Large hospitals, in their modern form, began emerging slowly in the late nineteenth century and then in an accelerated way in the mid-twentieth century. In ancient and early mediaeval times, hospitals were often financed by charitable religious organisations, local institutions, and pious sponsors, with non-professional voluntary entities with little or no professional medical or administrative knowledge responsible for hospital management in nearly all cases. The primary objective of these hospitals centred on taking care of and controlling the poor and marginal sectors of society. Their original goal was, in many cases, to take away sick poor people and their illnesses (or deaths) from the eyes of society at large. It was industrialisation and the rapid urbanisation of the Western world first—and the rest of the world shortly thereafter—that increased the speed in the growth of the poor and sick populations, transforming what was once a charitable action into an urgent social problem of public healthcare; that transformation gradually prompted local and national authorities to realise the need to organise and control the situation, which after the nineteenth century became a problem of civil order, in a more centralised, civil way relative to the former administrations of religious institutions and specific individuals. It was impossible for the church or for pious individuals to finance and manage enough buildings to accommodate the millions of people migrating from the countryside into the industrialised cities of Europe or the East Coast cities of the United States after the mid-nineteenth century. It was also a problem for large commercial cities in the East, like Hong Kong, to deal with the massive waves of migration they witnessed in the nineteenth century, which brought with them epidemics and illnesses. During the late nineteenth century, the effects of expanding Latin American metropolises, the construction of the Panama Canal, and the Spanish-American Wars of the late nineteenth century revealed how inefficient traditional hospitals for the poor were in treating and healing an ballooning number of wounded and sick people as the imperial powers and foreign multinationals—together with the urban pull from the countryside—drove millions to large cities in the region.[19] From the mid-nineteenth century onward, the world's large cities, industrialised countries, and urban centres where the economic powers dealt in trade and logistics reformed or created brand-new, larger centralised hospitals. Mechanisms combining public money and private funding also established themselves as the key most efficient approaches on a global scale. The medical and managerial organisation of new large hospitals and the underlying philosophical and political basis of the societies and institutions in which the hospitals operated varied greatly in Asia, Western and Eastern Europe, North and South America, and Africa and Australia. Despite that variety, facilities expanded across the board, and a transnational process for disseminating organisational and medical ideas took place well before World War II, with the exchange and movement of technologies, human capital, funds, and ideas picking up speed rapidly after the 1940s.[20]

Hospitals had to be built, organised, and managed by administrative staff accountable for the funds supplied by the authorities, provided with hospital equipment, supplied with drugs, and connected to the regular-salaried services of the new class of professionals in medicine and pharmacy who were graduating by the thousands at the end of the nineteenth century from European and North American universities.

Most of the studies on the historical evolution of management and finances of hospitals have tackled American and British cases, although there is ongoing research on digitalised account books and commemorative books with historical accounts and data on hospital organisations at the hospitals of France, Germany, Spain, Italy, Hong Kong, China, Egypt, Colombia, Argentina, Mexico, Peru, Brazil, Chile, Russia, Canada, Scandinavian countries, Central and Eastern Europe, India, and Australia, among others.[21]

In the United States, there were strong pressures seeking the modification and modernisation of the country's fragmented, poor hospital system in the second half of the nineteenth century. With the deaths of legions of soldiers in the American Civil War, the casualties of the Spanish-American Wars in Cuba and the Philippines in the late nineteenth century, and the rapid immigration and urbanisation on the East and West Coasts since those years, the unprecedented problem of managing the wounded and addressing epidemics affected the country both at home and abroad in its international operations. The pressure led to an organisational and managerial revolution in US hospitals that science and business historians have only superficially tackled thus far. New research reveals that there were two driving actors in the modernisation of American hospitals in this context of change from the demand side during the late nineteenth century and the first half of the twentieth century: the Army and the Navy, on one hand, and the influence of industrial ideas from Taylorism and Fordism in hospital management, on the other.[22] The wars made the medical services of the US Army and Navy realise the poor conditions in which thousands of their wounded soldiers received medical attention at home and abroad, first of all. In addition, the wars exposed the urgency of not only improving the endowment of medical products and professionals for the soldiers but also organising new, large, centralised buildings, managed with new logistics to move provisions more efficiently and standardised medical resources from one place to another, to save more lives and improve the psychological and physical conditions of the sick and wounded at hospitals. In parallel to the new hospitals organised by the US Army and Navy, new hospitals in East- and West-Coast metropolises were built, or old ones were moved to new locations with expanded facilities. Scale and scope in the new hospitals were chief concerns, and the owners of the new hospitals embraced the new industrial organisational ideas of the new large corporations from the start in the hope of organising or reorganising hospital resources and designs and also managing the facilities.[23] One must stress the influence of Alfred D. Chandler, to whom several historians of medicine explicitly have referred, on the literature about the subject. For example, Neil Larry Shumsky argued as early as 1978 that 'the world of contemporary medicine is one of structure, bureaucracy, and organisation',[24] and explained the development of the municipal clinic of San Francisco based on Chandler's work on large enterprises. Barbara Bridgman Perkins, meanwhile, asserted that American hospitals reorganised during the years 1900–1930 through the introduction of management methods from the industrial sector (essentially division of work and hierarchy), which gave way to the establishment of medical specialities.[25] However, the most influential work in this field is undoubtedly Joel Howell's seminal book on New York Hospital and Pennsylvania Hospital.[26] Based on a study of patient files from the two hospitals between 1900 and 1925, he showed how medical technology, such as X-ray equipment and laboratories, became central to hospital administration. Howell's primary contribution lay in demonstrating that the development of hospitals relied as much on organisational and managerial issues as on medical innovation itself. According to sociologists Marc Berg and Stefan Timmermans, the standardisation of hospital infrastructure during the beginning of the twentieth century in the United States was the first step of a general trend that reached the entirety of medical practice during the 1980s and 1990s, characterised by the generalisation of a so-called "evidence-based medicine" that relies on international standardised norms.[27]

Some other scholars focused on the issue of financing hospitals, and more broadly health systems, from a historical perspective. Here, too, the most important works came from

Anglo-Saxon countries. Steven Cherry published extensively on the evolution of hospital funding in the United Kingdom, stressing the shift from philanthropy to other sources (public funding, patients, and insurance providers).[28] In the US, one can cite the research of Stephen Kunitz on the emergence of health insurance in the early twentieth century,[29] and, more recently, of Christy Chapin on the development of insurance to the present day.[30] As financing health and medicine had become a major political issue throughout Western countries in the 1990s, many scholars undertook historical studies on the historical development of funding for health in countries such as Germany,[31] Spain,[32] France,[33] and Switzerland.[34]

Hospitals had to have sufficient supplies of medico-technical equipment and drugs, the latter of which also served outpatients. During the end of the nineteenth century and the first six decades of the twentieth century, new firms and corporations appeared, first in developed pioneering countries, and eventually in other latecomer countries, to fill the expanding needs for new products: drugs, medical machinery, medical technology, and precision devices. In the pharmaceutical and chemical industries, the pioneering firms first established new scientific and technological knowledge and learning bases between the 1870 s and the 1930s; after World War II and through the 1990s, the pioneers then established solid entry barriers to fend off competitors at home—and particularly abroad—in the markets they were creating with disruptive new products and services. Only from the end of the 1990s onward did global competition from challengers begin to erode the competitive basis of some of the industry's first-comers.[35] This chronology explains well the establishment of leaders like Bayer, Ciba Geigy, and Sandoz in the United States, Germany, France, the United Kingdom, Switzerland, and Japan. In latecomer countries, many of these innovative products and services arrived quickly due to early nineteenth-century contact between scientists and the leading pioneering centres and corporations, as well as via the efficient networks that faculties of medicine and pharmacy in Europe, America, and Asia had established among themselves to communicate knowledge of innovations swiftly and efficiently.

Regarding the manufacture and distribution of hospital equipment, in Europe, North America, Latin America, and Asia, small and medium companies with scientist-entrepreneurs soon started to register their mercantile activity in order to take advantage of the expanding market opportunities as millions of sick patients congregated in the industrialised cities that began to grow in tandem with industrialisation and globalisation after the mid-nineteenth century. Studies on trademarks and corporate monographs have revealed the coexistence of multiple pathways of this multiplication of small entrepreneurship in the production of chemical drugs and medicines that appeared in the mid- and late nineteenth century. Some grew serving the military needs of their armies (Nobel in Russia, Behring in Germany, Abbott and Baxter in the United States); some transformed into large multinationals in the food industry in the twentieth century (like Nestlé, Danone, and Coca Cola); some developed via government support to cover large population needs (CSL in Australia); some changed headquarters due to war pressures and enjoyed successes in becoming large multinationals on other continents (Danone moved from Spain to France, for example, while Andrómaco shifted from Spain to the United States and then to Central and Latin America). Of the litany of small laboratories that existed before the 1920s, however, very few remained intact after the 1950s; many did not survive the two World Wars and the collapse of global trade in the interwar period.[36]

After World War II, there was a decline in the number of small and medium family-owned companies in Western Europe, particularly in the United Kingdom, and a concentration of the chemical and pharmaceutical and medical drugs business into larger corporations.[37] North American corporations were particularly well placed to assume leadership in the new world order, including in the healthcare industries covering the manufacturing and distribution of hospital equipment and drugs. As the need for complex technologies and medical drugs expanded with population growth in the postwar period, and as hospitals grew in number to serve the increasing number of potentially sick people, hospitals faced the need to purchase diagnostic instruments, pharmaceuticals, and laboratory equipment like sterilisers, masks, gloves, and microscopes. During the late nineteenth century in the US, as was the case in Europe, there were many small manufacturers of such items: the Gendron Wheel Chair Company (founded in 1872), Davol Rubger Company (1874), American Sterilizer Company (1894), Beckton, Dickinson and Company (1897), and Bard-Parker Company Inc. (1915) are several examples. In the pharmaceutical industry, Merck and Company, Abbott Laboratories, Cutter Laboratories, and Mead Johnson and Company were all founded between 1883 and 1900. However, most manufacturers had to sell their products directly to thousands of hospitals across the country, and the transaction costs involved were high. The American Surgical Trade Association, founded in 1902, had attempted in vain to organise the industry. Then, a talented medical supplies salesman named Foster McGaw emerged and, in 1921, founded the American Hospital Supply Corporation—which would go on to be one of the world's largest wholesale distributors of hospital supplies through 1985.[38] The reasons behind their success were the new competencies developed in connecting distant manufacturers, establishing price convergence across distant hospitals within the given country and abroad, and organising of a professional sales force trained specifically for the products that they had to sell. This 'Chandlerian' corporation would be difficult to imitate in other countries until the late 1980s. In Western Europe, particularly in Germany and German-speaking countries, the same type of concentration took place in a different context. Around twenty local manufacturers and distributors were taken over during World War I by the X-ray equipment producer Reiniger, Gebbert & Schall, a company that was based in Erlangen and founded in 1887. In 1921, a holding company called Industrie-unternehmungen AG (INAG) took control of the group to provide all the technical equipment that hospitals and independent doctors needed. A few years later, in 1924, Siemens & Halske purchased INAG and established itself as a leader in the hospital equipment business.[39] This leadership grew even stronger and extended to emerging countries after WWII, when Siemens engaged in hospital building.[40]

OECD statistics again prove useful in understanding the dynamics of hospital systems and healthcare business in various countries over the last thirty years (see Tables 5 and 6 below). The availability of beds per hospital is a simple variable that indicates the concentration of professionals, drugs, and services that have implemented healthcare among populations across countries; the figures demonstrate the United States' dominance in total number of hospital beds, followed by Japan and Germany. When one considers the number of hospital beds per 1000 population in each country, the power of the United States becomes less pronounced, and Japan appears as the best-served country in that different statistical context. Moreover, the numbers express the existence of a broad variety of systems (the high density of small hospitals in Japan versus the presence of a small group of large hospitals in Western Europe) with a major impact on the diffusion of medical technology and the consumption of healthcare.

Table 5. Hospitals by country (number).

Country	1980	1990	2000	2010	2013
France	..	..	3120	2707	3382
Germany	..	..	3635	3301	3183
Italy	..	1757	1321	1230	..
Japan	..	10,096	9266	8670	8540
Spain	1084	820	771	765	764
United States	6965	6649	5810	5754	..
Hospitals by country (Per million people)					
France	..	..	51.35	41.76	51.48
Germany	..	..	44.22	40.37	39.47
Italy	..	30.98	23.2	20.75	..
Japan	..	81.67	73	67.7	67.09
Spain	28.95	21.11	19.15	16.42	16.39
United States	30.65	26.64	20.59	18.6	..

Source: Paloma Fernández´s own elaboration with technical assistance from Jaime López at the University of Barcelona, from data accessed on 22 Jan 2016 from OECD.stat http://stats.oecd.org/.

Table 6. Total hospital beds by country (number).

Country	1960	1970	1980	1990	2000	2010	2013
France	..	..	..	..	484,279	416,710	413,206
Germany	..	..	..	..	749,473	674,473	667,560
Italy	450,539	568,513	542,260	410,026	268,057	215,980	..
Japan	..	..	..	..	18,64,008	17,30,215	16,95,114
Spain	..	157,598	201,035	165,897	148,081	145,199	138,153
United Kingdom	..	..	..	..	24,13,31.8	18,38,48.55	17,67,88.8
United States	16,58,000	16,16,000	13,65,000	12,13,000	983,628	941,995	..
Total hospital beds by country (Per 1000 people)							
France	..	..	..	..	7.97	6.43	6.29
Germany	..	..	..	..	9.12	8.25	8.28
Italy	8.97	10.56	9.61	7.23	4.71	3.64	..
Japan	..	..	..	..	14.69	13.51	13.32
Spain	..	4.66	5.37	4.27	3.68	3.12	2.96
United Kingdom	..	..	..	..	4.1	2.93	2.76
United States	9.18	7.88	6.01	4.86	3.49	3.05	..

Source: Paloma Fernández´s own elaboration with technical assistance of Jaime López at the University of Barcelona, from data accessed on 22 Jan 2016 from OECD.stat http://stats.oecd.org/.

5. For a business history of health

The literature on the management of hospitals and the social history of medical technology offers an important basis for building and developing a new approach to considering the transformation of health into a fast-growing business during the twentieth century. A business history of health requires a systemic perspective that includes the producers (companies), practitioners (medical doctors), and users (patients and hospitals) of medical technology, as well as the providers of capital and the bodies responsible for regulating the health system (government). Figure 1 illustrates the organisation of a healthcare system.

Business historians can employ this model as an analytical tool for discussing the development of health in various countries through different examples and sources. Of course, it is not always possible to consider all five actors with the same importance in any case study. Some scholars may give more attention to relations between two of the actors (insurance providers and government, practitioners and patients, or technology producers and investors, for example). They should, however, be aware of the existence of and roles played by other actors in the health system to provide a comprehensive view of the business history of health.

The articles in this special issue focus particularly on one or two of these actors but explain the interactions with other actors to offer a fuller understanding of how given health systems developed, either nationally or globally. The perspective of the producers of medical technology is the framework for the three first articles, which analyse various cases of development and growth of small and medium enterprises in a sector dominated by large, multinational enterprises. Paloma Fernández Pérez, Nuria Puig, Esteban García-Canal, and Mauro F. Guillén demonstrate that the successful internationalisation of small and medium enterprises in a developing economy (the plasma laboratory Grifols and the pharmaceutical company Ferrer, both from Spain) relied not only on the internalisation and transfer of knowledge from US and German first movers but also on the local institutional environment, a system of innovation that encouraged the collaboration of scientists, politicians, and entrepreneurs in modernising and transforming local healthcare businesses. The Barcelona district of biomedical scientists gave the entrepreneurs the opportunity to build the learning bases necessary for launching cooperative efforts with large foreign companies. For example, the roots of Grifols go back to a small clinical laboratory that doctors from the University of Barcelona's Faculty of Medicine opened in 1910. During the following decades, members of the Grifols family studied medicine and pharmacy and acquired scientific knowledge from both Germany and the US after World War II. The subsequent expansion of these family firms in Europe, the US, and Japan resulted from cross-border mergers and acquisitions that allowed them to acquire knowledge and develop their R&D facilities.

The article by Ken Sakai on Mani, a Japanese surgical needle manufacturer, during the second part of the twentieth century is another example of how a small company in a country with a seemingly weak, uncompetitive pharmaceutical industry managed to grow. Mani's technological development was achieved through cooperation with large private companies, like Toshiba, and semi-governmental organizations such as the Atomic Energy Research Institute. Moreover, the company's growth tied into a fast-expanding hospital market, then the company started to expand abroad since the 1990s, when the number of hospitals in Japan started to stagnate then to decline. This example thus reflects the impact of regulation

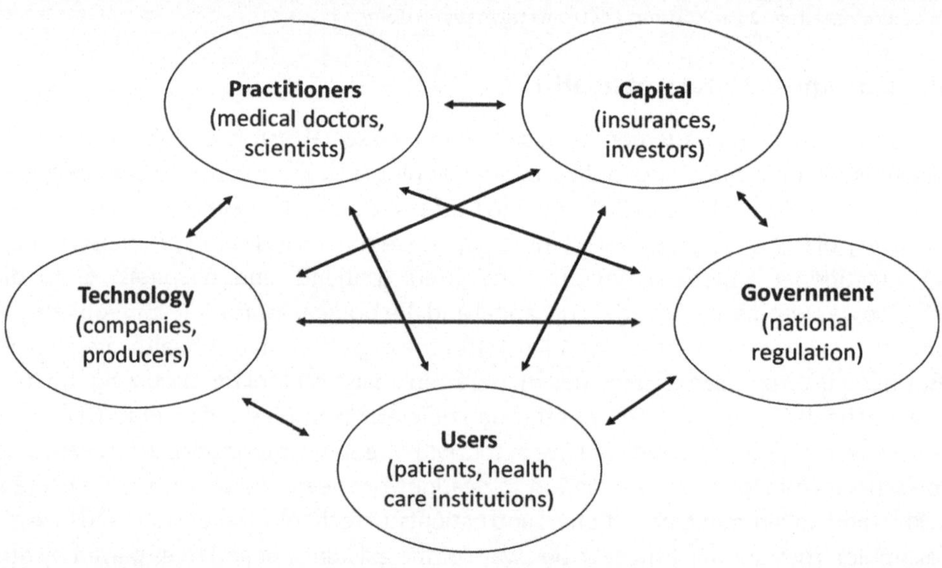

Figure 1. Organisation of the health care system.
Source: drafted by Pierre-Yves Donzé.

in the healthcare market on medical technology firms: the lack of interventionism on the part of the Japanese government, which led to the opening of numerous hospital beds (about 700,000 in 1960 and more than 1.6 million in 1990), represented an opportunity for many small companies like Mani because it offered a large market for medical devices.

The third paper on medical technology firms, by Maki Umemura, compares firms in regenerative medicine since the 1970s in the US, UK, and Japan. She argues that this specific sector was shaped by more than just technological issues related to cell-based therapies, regardless of how undoubtedly complex the issues may be. She details the relations between scientist-entrepreneurs and investors, the latter of which were impatient to transform firms into highly profitable businesses and sometimes withdrew their investments. The connection between capital and medical technology shines through in Umemura's incisive analysis. Another dimension that comes to light through the paper's international comparison is the importance of regulation. R&D and the consumption of biotechnology products are subject to legal frameworks that differ between countries—and that regulatory environment has a deep impact on innovation.

Next, three articles analyse the perspectives of the organisation and regulation of healthcare markets. Sabine Schleiermarcher focuses on the attempts of the Allied forces in Germany to restore medical care and public health service immediately after World War II. She also looks at how, in the context of the European Recovery Programme, the Rockefeller Foundation organised grants, visitation programmes, and a school of public health. The article shows how the North American initiative underestimated the strength and endurance of pre-World War II traditions of public health organisation and also miscalculated the medical profession's resistance to adopting outside models of medical care and service.

The article by Jean-Paul Domin tackles state interventionism in France between 1890 and 1938, an effort to implement a public insurance system that would support the access of the population to healthcare—what the author calls the 'socialisation of healthcare demand'. The interventionism relied both on assistance (free medical assistance for the poor, introduced in 1893) and insurance (workers' health costs due to work accidents, covered by employers in 1898, and social insurance for all citizens, enacted in 1928–1930). Regulated competition following state interventionism led medical professions to organise themselves and adopt common fees for government-supported patients, as free competition would result in decreasing revenues. The important outcomes of this policy were increasing insurance coverage (from less than 5% of the population in the late nineteenth century to 46% after 1930) and rapid development of the hospital market—due to growing guarantees of revenues by patients. The state organised the competition, but the business management of medical doctors and hospitals was autonomous.

Roser Álvarez studies the important changes that took place in the Chinese public healthcare system during the Maoist period (1949–1976), confirming the general increase in health resources in those years. The study also reveals a decrease in infectious diseases, a reduction in mortality rates, and an increase in life expectancy. However, she also uses provincial data for the Henan Province to uncover a strong provincial inequality in the allocation of health resources, an imbalance that may have accounted for the gaps in the provincial and regional health indicators she presents. Her study illustrates the transformation and endurance of traditional healthcare services like the rural medical agents that took shape in years and regions where large hospitals could not be built.

The users of medical technology are the main subject of the article by Pierre-Yves Donzé, who tackles a case study of the transnational experiences of knowledge transfer from the

West to the East: the introduction of Western hospital designs to Japan between 1918 and 1970. The paper demonstrates the influence and relevance of studying hospital design and architecture. Neither factor is a simple, short-term decision with minimal significance; after all, hospitals are enduring service infrastructures that, on average around the world, serve millions of people over periods lasting more than a century. Making the right decision on an efficient design that accounts for the needs of the population, the costs involved in maintenance and repairs, and the human capital that must coexist and manage the hospital efficiently is of paramount importance—yet historians of medicine and business have tended to overlook the topic. Donzé describes the transformation in Japan from prewar models of small hospitals in urban areas to the large public hospitals of the post-war era, explaining how the main drivers of the new hospitals were architects with knowledge of large Western hospitals who had the support of local authorities to introduce foreign designs in dealing with new local needs. The article details some of the pioneering new Japanese hospitals, the architects behind them, and the context that helps elucidate the introduction and hybridisation of Western concepts of hospital design in Japan.

Finally, this special issue includes an article by Jerònia Pons and Margarita Vilar on private providers of capital for healthcare in Spain during the last century: private health insurance companies. The authors assert that the private insurer community is not a new outcome of the current welfare crisis in Europe but rather an old actor that has been part of the healthcare system for a century, flexibly adapting to changing external institutional and economic conditions. Private insurance companies have transformed not only their internal organisations and strategies but also their external relationships with foreign competitors and the state.

Notes

1. Ortiz-Ospina and Roser, 'Financing Healthcare.'
2. OECD, Health expenditures and financing, retrieved from: http://stats.oecd.org/index.aspx?DataSetCode=SHA# (accessed 4 October 2016).
3. Database of the World Health Organization, http://apps.who.int/nha/database/ViewData/Indicators/en (accessed 4 October 2016).
4. Sherman, Goodman & Stano, *The Economics of Health and Healthcare.*
5. Based on the case study of Japan, see for example Donzé, *Making Medicine a Business.*
6. Rosner, *A once charitable enterprise*, Labish & Spree, *Krankenhaus-Report 19. Jahrhundert*, Gorsky & Sheard, *Financing medicine*, Domin, *Une histoire économique de l'hôpital.*
7. Löwy, *Medicine and Change*, Howell, *Technology in the Hospital*, Stanton, *Innovations in Health and Medicine*, Schlich, *Surgery, Science and Industry*, Boersma, 'Structural ways to embed a research laboratory into the company.'
8. Vagelos & Galambos, *Medicine, science and Merck*, Cramer, 'Building the 'World's Pharmacy.'
9. Porter, *Health, Civilization and the State.*
10. Colli, *Dynamics of International Business.*
11. Porter, *Health, Civilization and the State.*
12. Fernández Pérez, *The Revolution of Hospital Management in the World, 1900s–1930s.*
13. Latour & Woolgar, *Laboratory life.*
14. Bijker, Hugues & Pinch, *The Social Construction of Technological Systems.*
15. Blume, *Insight and Industry.*
16. Schlich, *Surgery, Science and Industry.*
17. Anderson, Neary & Pickstone, *Surgeons, Manufacturers and Patients.*
18. Fernández Pérez and Rose, *Innovation and Entrepreneurial Networks in Europe.*

19. Fernández Pérez, *The Revolution of Hospital Management in the World, 1900s–1930s.*
20. Fernández Pérez, *The Revolution of Hospital Management in the World, 1900s–1930s.*
21. Fernández Pérez, *The Revolution of Hospital Management in the World, 1900s–1930s.*
22. Fernández Pérez, P. *The Revolution of Hospital Management in the World, 1900s–1930s.*
23. Fernández Pérez, P. *The Revolution of Hospital Management in the World, 1900s–1930s.*
24. Shumsky, 'The municipal clinic of San Francisco.'
25. Perkins, 'Shaping institution-based specialism.'
26. Howell, *Technology in the Hospital.*
27. Berg & Timmermans 2003, *The Gold Standard.*
28. Cherry, 'Accountability, Entitlement, and Control Issues and Voluntary Hospital Funding c1860-1939,' Cherry, 'Before the National Health Service,' Cherry, 'Hospital Saturday, Workplace Collections and Issues in late Nineteenth-Century Hospital Funding,' Gorsky & Sheard, *Financing medicine.*
29. Kunitz, 'Efficiency and reform in the financing and organization of American medicine in the progressive era.'
30. Ford Chapin, *Ensuring America's Health.*
31. Spree, 'Krankenhasuentwicklung und Sozialpolitik in Deutschland während des 19. Jahrhunderts,' Labisch & Spree, *Krankenhaus-Report 19. Jahrhundert.*
32. Pérez Castroviejo, 'La formación del sistema hospitalario vasco.'
33. Domin, *Une histoire économique de l'hôpital.*
34. Donzé, *L'ombre de César.*
35. Chandler *Shaping the Industrial Century.*
36. Fernández Pérez 'Andrómaco,' Colli, *Dynamics of International Business*, Torres, *Cien empresarios españoles del siglo XX.*
37. Colli, Fernández, Rose, 'National Determinants of Family Firm Behaviour.'
38. Stuyrdevant, *American Hospital Supply Corporation.*
39. Feldenkirchen, *Siemens 1918–1945*, 311–313.
40. Donzé, 'Siemens and the Construction of Hospitals in Latin America.'

Funding

This work was supported by Japan Society for the Promotion of Science [grant number Grant-in-Aid for Scientific Research, (C) 17K03839].

References

Anderson, J., F. Neary, and J. Pickstone; Surgeons. *Manufacturers and Patients: A Transatlantic History of Total Hip Replacement*. Basingstoke: Macmillan, 2007.

Berg, M., and S. Timmermans. *The Gold Standard: The Challenge of Evidence-Based Medicine and Standardization in Health Care*. Philadelphia: Temple University Press, 2003.

Bijker, W., T. Hugues, and T. Pinch, eds. *The Social Construction of Technological Systems: New Directions in the Sociology and History of Technology*. Cambridge, MA: M.I.T. Press, 1987.

Blume, S. *Insight and Industry. On the Dynamics of Technological Change in Medicine*. Cambridge: MIT Press, 1992.

Boersma, F. K. "Structural Ways to Embed a Research Laboratory into the Company: A Comparison between Philips and General Electric 1900–1940." *History and Technology* 19, no. 2 (2003): 109–126.

Chandler, A. D. *Shaping the Industrial Century: The Evolution of the Modern Chemical and Pharmaceutical Industries*. Cambridge: Harvard University Press, 2005.

Cherry, S. "Accountability, Entitlement, and Control Issues and Voluntary Hospital Funding c1860–1939." *Social History of Medicine* 9, no. 2 (1996): 215–233.

Cherry, S. "Before the National Health Service: Financing the Voluntary Hospitals, 1900–1939." *The Economic History Review* 50, no. 2 (1997): 305–326.

Cherry, S. "Hospital Saturday, Workplace Collections and Issues in Late Nineteenth-Century Hospital Funding." *Medical History* 44, no. 04 (2000): 461–488.

Colli, A. *Dynamics of International Business: Comparative Perspectives of Firms, Markets and Entrepreneurship*. London: Routledge, 2016.

Colli, A., Fernández Pérez, P, Rose M.B. "National Determinants of Family Firm Behaviour?." *Enterprise and Society* 119, no. 1 (2003): 18–31.

Cramer, T. "Building the "World's Pharmacy": The Rise of the German Pharmaceutical Industry, 1871–1914." *Business History Review* 89, no. 01 (2015): 43–73.

Domin, J.-P. *Une Histoire Économique de L'hôpital, XIXe-Xxe siècles*, 2volumes. Paris: CHSS, 2008–2013.

Donzé, P.-Y. *L'ombre de César. Les Chirurgiens et la Construction du Système Hospitalier Vaudois (1840-1960)*. Lausanne: BHMS, 2007.

Donzé, P.-Y. "Siemens and the Construction of Hospitals in Latin America, 1949–1964." *Business History Review* 89, no. 03 (2015): 475–502.

Donzé, P.-Y. *Making Medicine a Business: X-ray Technology, Global Competition, and the Transformation of the Japanese Medical System, 1895–1945*. Singapore: Springer, (2018).

Feldenkirchen, W. (1995). *Siemens 1918–1945*. Columbus: Ohio State University Press.

Fernández Pérez, P., & M. B. Rose, eds. *Innovation and Entrepreneurial Networks in Europe*. New York: Routledge, 2010.

Fernández Pérez, P. "Laboratorios Andrómaco. Origins of the First Subsidiary of a Spanish Pharmaceutical Company in the United States (1928–1946)." *Journal of Evolutionary Studies in Business* 1, no. 2. Retrieved from http://revistes.ub.edu/index.php/JESB/article/view/j019.

Fernández Pérez, P. The Revolution in Hospital Management in the World. Bingley, UK Emerald Publishers, forthcoming.

Ford Chapin, C. *Ensuring America's health: The public Creation of the Corporate Health Care System*. Cambridge: Cambridge University Press, 2015.

Gorsky, M., and S. Sheard, eds. *Financing Medicine: The British Experience since 1750*. London: Routledge, 2006.

Howell, J. *Technology in the Hospital: Transforming Patient Care in the Early Twentieth Century*. Baltimore: Johns Hopkins University Press, 1995.

Kunitz, S. "Efficiency and Reform in the Financing and Organization of American Medicine in the Progressive Era." *Bulletin of the History of Medicine*, 55 (1981): 497–515.

Labisch, A. and R. Spree, eds. *Krankenhaus-Report 19. Jahrhundert. Krankenhausträger, Krankenhausfinanzierung, Krankenhauspatienten*. Frankfort: Campus Verlag, 2001.

Latour, B. W. S. *Laboratory Life: The Social Construction of Scientific Facts*. London: Sage Publ, 1979.

Löwy, I., ed. *Medicine and Change: Historical and Sociological Studies of Medical Innovation*. Paris: INSRM and John Libbey Ltd, 1993.

Ortiz-Ospina, E., and M. Roser. *Financing Healthcare*. London: ourworldindata.org, 2019. Retrieved from https://ourworldindata.org/financing-healthcare.

PérezCastroviejo, P. M. "La Formación del Sistema Hospitalario Vasco: Administración y Gestión Económica, 1800–1936." *Transportes, Servicios y Telecomunicaciones* 2002 (2002): 73–97.

Perkins, B. B. "Shaping Institution-Based Specialism: Early Twentieth-Century Economic Organization of Medicine." *Social History of Medicine*, 10, no. 3 (1997): 419–435.

Porter, D. *Health, Civilization and the State. A History of Public Health from Ancient to Modern Times*. London: Routledge, 1999.

Rosner, D. A. *Once Charitable Enterprise. Hospitals and Health Care in Brooklyn and New York, 1885–1915*. Cambridge: Cambridge University Press, 1982.

Schlich, T. *Surgery, Science and Industry. A Revolution in Fracture Care, 1950s–1990s*. Basingstoke: Palgrave Macmillan, 2002.

Sherman, F., A. C. Goodman, and M. Stano, eds. *The Economics of Health and Health Care*. Basingstoke: Macmillan, 1993.

Shumsky, N. L. "The Municipal Clinic of San Francisco: A Study in Medical Structure." *Bulletin of the History of Medicine* 52 (1978): 542–559.

Spree, R. "Krankenhasuentwicklung und Sozialpolitik in Deutschland Während des 19. Jahrhunderts." *Historische Zeitschrift* 19 (1995): 75–105.

Stanton, J., ed. *Innovations in Health and Medicine. Diffusion and Resistance in the Twentieth Century*. London: Routledge, 2002.

Stevens, R. *In Sickness and in Wealth: American Hospitals in the Twentieth Century*. New York: Basic Books, 1999.

Stuyrdevant. American Hospital Suppply Corportation, 1975.

Torres, E. *Cien Empresarios Españoles del siglo XX*. Madrid: LID, 2000.

Vagelos, P. R., and L. Galambos. *Medicine, Science and Merck*. Cambridge: Cambridge University Press, 2004.

Learning from giants: Early exposure to advanced markets in the growth and internationalisation of Spanish health care corporations in the twentieth century

Paloma Fernández Pérez, Nuria Puig, Esteban García-Canal and Mauro F. Guillén

ABSTRACT
This article examines the influence of early exposure to advanced markets of the United States and Germany in the growth and internationalization of health care firms from Spain, a late industrialised country. Based on the case studies of the Spanish corporations Grifols and Ferrer, the study shows that early exposure to advanced markets helped them grow in their national markets, and in the world health care industry. It shows further that the specific capabilities developed by both firms were determined by path-dependent networks with scientists and institutions, on the one hand; and strategic alliances, acquisitions and mergers with German and US corporations on the other.

Introduction

Over the last four decades accelerated growth and globalisation have shaped the health care industries in Europe, the United States and Japan.[1] Their technological and scientific innovations have contributed significantly to increase life expectancy at birth worldwide.[2]

The successful development of American multinationals, the globalisation of old European groups after World War II, and the oligopolistic structure of the health care industry have influenced our perception of this industry in general and the growth and internationalisation of the first movers in particular.[3] According to Alfred D. Chandler Jr, a relatively small number of first movers in the most developed countries defined one century ago the evolving pathways of learning in the pharmaceutical industry, creating barriers to entry, strategic boundaries and limits to growth. The barriers set by first movers would have been so high that, according to Chandler after the 1920s, in the group of the 30 largest pharmaceutical companies he identified in the most developed markets, no new pharmaceutical enterprise was able successfully to enter their industry.[4] The first movers grew in scale and scope, and their size and their control of new learning bases in the industry, therefore, allowed them to dominate global health care markets for a century, and contributed to prevent new challengers, and new scientific findings, changing the bases of the industry.[5]

Small players from late industrialised countries would have therefore faced huge disadvantages that may have hampered their opportunities to challenge the supremacy of traditional global leaders from the most developed markets. And yet there are some examples of firms from these countries that, somehow, have been able to thrive in this environment, climbing to leadership positions. Obviously, the rise of global leaders from emerging and middle-income countries is not a phenomenon exclusive to health care, but to all industries.[6] However, the huge internal path-dependent differences in capabilities for growth and internationalisation within the health care industries, as compared to other industries, as demonstrated for the case of the pharmaceutical industry,[7] make the study of the mechanisms of entry of small players from latecomer markets in the health care industries extremely interesting.

There is a wealth of published research about how innovative small firms become big firms in developed countries, but not much about this process in developing economies.[8] Following this line of thought, this article seeks to contribute to the scarce literature that exists, in the business history research field, about how knowledge-intensive small companies from the periphery can become global leaders.[9]Our research aims to shed new light on the growth and globalisation of small players in the health care industries born in late industrialised countries, asking how small companies in this environment, with weak or unstable institutional support, have been able to enter the major league of the health care industries, and rise to the top levels. Our hypothesis is that, in the health care industries, early exposure to advanced markets, and alliances with first movers, may provide these firms with capabilities to grow and cross entry barriers in developed markets.

We use in-depth case studies to test this hypothesis and provide arguments which future research may extend to understand the globalisation of knowledge-intensive small firms in other developing economies. We examine in this article, more specifically, the long-term transformation of two small Spanish companies into global players: Grifols and Ferrer. Both companies were selected in order to test the hypothesis because they operated in different specialised branches of the health care industries, but until the 1990s in a similar institutional local environment.

Grifols ranks third among the top corporations in the world plasma industry, and Ferrer ranks fifth in Spain and 65th in Europe in the pharmaceutical industry. The Grifols family started a clinical institute in 1910, and a clinical laboratory in 1940. Ferrer started actvities in 1925, and a pharmaceutical firm in 1953. The plasma industry's key asset is the ownership of high-quality raw material and manufacturing and distribution processes, whereas the pharmaceutical industry's key asset is the ownership of brands, licences, and patents of a vast portfolio of products and processes.

The analysis of their growth and internationalisation strategies in the second half of the twentieth century in this article concludes that despite the differences in specialisation, their early exposure to pioneering and leading corporations helped organize their firms in a way that allowed them to be leaders in their industries from the very beginning. This helped them take long-term strategic decisions to, helping them take strategic decisions to: first, achieve scale and scope; second, develop their own learning bases to innovate; and third, change their management to cross entry barriers into the global health care markets.

The empirical analysis of this process also provided evidence, as indicated before, about the usefulness of Chandler's proposed chronology of the dynamics of the growth and modernisation of the first movers in the most developed markets, in the pharmaceutical and chemical industries, in the twentieth century. With a different environment, size and organisational complexity, the small labs in Spain studied for this article, as we will see, seemed to replicate, on a smaller scale, and for different reasons, the key chronological periods and major changes indicated by Chandler to explain the shaping of modern leaders in the Western European and US chemical and pharmaceutical corporations. According to Chandler, between the late nineteenth century and early 1920s firms created their integrated learning bases in production and marketing; in the inter-war years and during World War II companies strengthened their capabilities and grew in parallel with the 'therapeutic revolution' and the cascade of discoveries linked to penicillin, sulfa drugs, and other health care products developed in wartime. In the 1960s and 1970s the most enduring companies concentrated in their core businesses to expand production and sales at home and abroad. Their growth set entry barriers in their industries and markets to new challengers. After the 1970s new scientific findings in molecular biology and medical engineering, together with new managerial approaches, created a new wave of new startups, building new learning basis and entry barriers.[10]

There is no comprehensive study about the modernisation of the health care industries in developing economies comparable to the one published by Chandler about chemical and pharma corporations in the developed economies of the world. There is, therefore, no such comprehensive analysis about the history of the growth and internationalisation of Spanish health care industries, only fragmented historical case studies or sectoral studies, with few resources like a recent database about the international operations of the Spanish pharmaceutical corporations since the late 1980s.[11] This database shows that, as observed in other latecomer multinationals, in the last decades the most dynamic ones seem to have followed a dual path in their international expansion. On the one hand, they expanded into more developed countries with the aim of upgrading their capabilities and catching up with their more advanced competitors. On the other hand, they looked for less developed countries to exploit their experience and intangible assets. For the last three decades, for Spanish pharma companies, entering into an advanced country was associated with being a more active player in the international arena than those not entering into these countries.[12] Not only would firms investing in advanced countries have undertaken more international operations; they would have also had a higher propensity to expand aggressively (i.e. without partners) than the firms not entering into these countries.

This article provides archival evidence from in-depth case studies which suggest that this dual path of growth is not only a contemporary trend of dynamic Spanish pharmaceutical corporations, as believed, but also a century-old feature of some dynamic Spanish health care corporations that include pharmaceutical and also biomedical, clinical and hospital equipment manufacturing and sales. The article argues that networks and alliances with health care leaders of pioneering German and US corporations encouraged early imprinting of strategic capabilities needed to grow and be a global firm, particularly scientific, organisational and market knowledge.

The evidence presented in this article indicates that this was not a straightforward process, and that there were many difficulties within the firms, and in the relationship of the firms with the external institutional environment and their competitors. The history of the international expansion of Grifols and Ferrer in advanced markets shows that it was preceded by a decades-long process of networking, technology transfer and capability building.

In the following sections we first provide a synthetic view of the long-term evolution of the Spanish health care industries, within the historical framework proposed by Alfred D.

Chandler.[13] Then we examine the processes of imprinting and internationalisation of Grifols and Ferrer in each of the three 'Chandlerian' stages (1880s–1920s, 1930s–1980s, 1990–present). Finally, a concluding section summarises the main findings of our comparative exercise.

Dynamics of the health care industries in the twentieth century for small firms: The case of Spain

From a technological and institutional perspective, the foundations of the health care industries are more than a century old. Chandler identified three big waves of technological and scientific therapeutic revolutions under the lead of a handful of corporations from the United States and Western Europe: the first movers. These waves are briefly characterised in Figure 1. How did firms raised outside the historical core of large and innovative corporations build their capabilities and go international?

Recent studies on the pharmaceutical and biomedical industries in peripheral markets suggest that neutrality during the two world wars and the technological convergence that took place during the golden age accelerated the transfer of old and new scientific and technological innovations to the rest of the world.[14] The demographic growth was a particularly good opportunity to invest in innovation and growth. There was a rapid demographic growth in developing economies in the mid 1960s, and the institutional conditions protected the access of the population to health care products and services through public and private insurance and medical companies.

There was, however, an unfavourable context for the growth of small firms in the health care industries in Spain between the mid-1930s and the late 1970s. After the end of the Spanish Civil War in 1939 the state changed the rules of the game for the health care industries in the country until the late 1970s. During those decades the various governments created: (1) a new mandatory public health insurance for all Spaniards in 1942 (the Seguro Obligatorio de Enfermedad); (2) new central public agencies like the Instituto Nacional de Previsión or the Ministerio de Sanidad to regulate medical and pharmaceutical services and products that increased public health spending (with the construction of new large centralised hospitals); (3) regulations fixing the number of new pharmacies that could open in the market; and (4) regulations fixing pharmaceutical profits, by keeping the cost of many old

Stages	First movers' main growth strategies
Stage 1 (1880s-1920s)	Pioneering firms from Western Europe establish new scientific and organizational bases. US and Japanese firms catch up after WWI. Full exploitation of economies of scale and scope.
Stage 2 (1930s-1980s)	First movers continue to exploit economies of scale and scope and increase international activity. They build entry barriers yet the emergence of a post WWII international technological market facilitate technological transfer and strategic alliances within and outside advanced economies.
Stage 3 (1990s-present)	First movers meet growing industrial, financial and regulatory challenges by either strengthening core business or diversifying into other businesses.

Figure 1. Growth strategies of the first movers.

drugs almost unchanged at 1963 prices, and allowing relatively free pricing for new products not regulated between 1963 and 1975.[15] This situation led to large profits, and incentives for innovation and investments in health care firms, including pharmaceutical firms, health insurance companies, engineering and construction firms (to build or renovate large central hospitals), and manufacturers and distributors of hospital products. Forces from the demand and supply side grew together in a favourable regulatory context. Until the late 1970s, the health care market became concentrated in the hands of a few big national producers and large foreign US and Western European multinationals.[16]

Small firms in the 1950s and 1960s lacked scale and scope, and capabilities to influence regulatory public agencies, to be competitive in the public bids in Spain, and take advantage of the expanding demand for health care. Many remained small despite the incentives in the market. However, some innovative firms had room for growth. The comparison of the two Spanish laboratories Grifols and Ferrer shows that two key mechanisms for growth among small knowledge-intensive firms in this context were: specialisation in new products and technologies and, if they had entrepreneurial vision and ambition and networks abroad, the establishment of alliances with giants from developed markets. Some small and medium-size health care firms in Spain borrowed extensively and learnt from the first movers, particularly from the two countries that were leading the second wave of industrialisation (Germany and US) between the 1880s and 1980s, through four major channels: foreign trade; Spanish subsidiaries and joint venture links with research centres; and the post-World War II cooperative environment and US technical assistance.[17]

These four channels helped build bridges and networks in both directions with the most advanced health care corporations in developed economies. The connection was first established to import goods and knowledge which was very scarce and expensive to obtain in Spain from the end of the nineteenth century until the late 1980s.[18] The professionalisation of the management of the small laboratories took place in the 1980s, closely following German and US models of management of large corporations in leading health care corporations, which helped imprint the managerial knowledge necessary to achieve scale and scope, and the globalisation, of both corporations between the 1980s and the first years of the twenty-first century. Foreign multinationals did not aim to transfer strategic knowledge that allowed for the import substitution strategies of their Spanish partners, but the accumulation of knowledge and networks inevitably provided such knowledge, particularly when the results were profitable to both sides, as it was the case in the history of Grifols and Ferrer.[19] This is the process analysed in the following sections, and summarised in Figure 2, that follows the Chandlerian chronology of the evolution of modern pharmaceutical and chemical corporations from leading economies. The important finding, that maybe future research will help expand to other case studies and developing countries, is that small firms exposed from the late nineteenth century to advanced markets were able to develop the learning bases of the new scientific and engineering knowledge, by combining the resources obtained from local and regional systems of innovation with capabilities provided through alliances and networks established with first movers from Germany and the United States.

Grifols and Ferrer are good examples of this process. They were two typical small labs that followed this path of growth to become global firms. They were family businesses in the mid-twentieth century, small firms at a disadvantage in the Spanish health care market of the Francoist state. Foreign currency to pay for imported raw materials or equipment was not easily available to them until the late 1960s, and public bids for the construction or

Stages	Grifols and Ferrer
Stage 1 (1880s-1920s)	Company founders develop learning scientific and organizational bases by combining resources from existing local networks (in the Barcelona area) and first movers' Spanish subsidiaries and import agreements. Spanish neutrality during WWI and rising living standards improve business environment.
Stage 2 (1930s-1980s)	Heirs engage in knowledge transfer from leading centers through personal relations and trips, business alliances (Grifols-Dade-AHS) and acquisitions (Ferrer-Trommsdorff). Growth goes hand in hand with sound reorganization, professionalization and internationalization.
Stage 3 (1990s-present)	Subsequent generations seize worldwide opportunities to become global leader in the plasma industry (Grifols) and increase international activity (Ferrer). Whereas Grifols resorts to acquisitions to integrate backwards and adopts global organization, Ferrer consolidates worldwide commercial network based on regulatory knowhow, licencing in and out and cooperative research, keeping corporate and research base in Barcelona.

Figure 2. Growing outside the historical oligopoly.

supply of the new large hospitals were often won by larger domestic companies with privileged connections in Madrid, the centre of regulating agencies. Both were founded in Barcelona, in close connection with the local Faculties of Medicine and Pharmacy that had traditional links with leading researchers and centres in Germany, France, the United Kingdom, Switzerland, Italy and the Scandinavian countries. They were different, though. Grifols specialised in blood products and in hospital and clinical equipment, and Ferrer in pharmaceutical drugs that were usually sold under medical prescription. Whereas the plasma industry depends on stable and large supplies of high-quality raw materials, the pharmaceutical industry needs to invest heavily in marketing and patented/licensed innovation.[20] For these reasons, in the last 25 years Grifols has relied on mergers and acquisitions in its internationalisation process far more than Ferrer, which has resorted to strategic alliances in the research and marketing areas.

The resources and skills both companies used to expand abroad had a long history of creation, and originated in a similar environment, which fits broadly speaking Chandler's proposed chronology of the evolution of modern corporations in other more advanced economies.

The early exposure to advance markets in Barcelona and the early imprinting of strategic capabilities, 1880s–1920s

The Spanish health system experienced remarkable progress in the early decades of the twentieth century, laying the foundation of modern public health policy and institutions.[21] This modernisation effort was supported by knowledge originating in the advanced European nations as well as by the International Health Board of the Rockefeller Foundation, among others.[22] Barcelona was a city where demographic, industrial and scientific changes had combined to create an advanced health care district in Spain between the 1880s and the early 1930s. In this favourable local context small enterprises in the clinical analysis activity, in the production of pharmaceutical drugs, and in private surgical activity appeared and flourished, led by professionals from the local Medical and Pharmaceutical Faculties.[23]

Our two firms participated in this dynamic environment in different ways. Grifols in the creation of outward-looking clinical laboratories (in 1910 and 1940) and the first civil Spanish blood bank (1945); Ferrer in the creation of outward-looking pharmaceutical laboratories (1925).

The Grifols archive preserves newspapers, books and conference papers from the late 1920s and early 1930s and 1940s which show the persistent activity of learning updated news of German, French, Italian and British scientists in the field of clinical analysis. Josep Antoni Grifols Morera graduated in Medicine from the University of Barcelona in 1889, and his son, José Antonio Grifols Roig, would study Medicine too. Upon his graduation in 1909, he worked in Danzig and Munich, where he specialised in pathology and lab practice. Back in his home town, he founded a small clinical laboratory – Instituto Central de Análisis Clínicos – with colleagues from the Faculty, doctors Celis, Moragas and Gordan. The German imprinting and transfer of scientific knowledge and clinical practice continued in the small Grifols firm until the 1950s, with German staff arriving in 1925 (Helmut Hempel) and with them German scientific journals and clinical know-how. The two sons of Grifols Roig, Victor and above all José Antonio Grifols Lucas, read and spoke German and French and were avid consumers of scientific publications obtained through friends and contacts. With their private collection they organised a private library for consultation in their lab, with specialised newspapers, conference reports and books. Aware that 'no man is an island', they decided to share news with the profession, and created a newsletter and specialised courses distributed for free, upon request, among physicians and clinical practitioners in Spain, thus increasing the reputation and good name of the family lab, in the difficult times of scarcity after the Spanish Civil War, between the 1930s and the 1950s.[24]

In contrast with the 'Germanic' Grifols lab, the origins of Ferrer provide an example of a firm more locally embedded into the commercial and industrial atmosphere of Barcelona. Medir, Ferrer y Cía, Ferrer's forerunner, was founded in 1925.[25] It was one of the many partnerships established at the time to seize the opportunities of importing drugs from the most advanced countries and serving the growing Spanish urban population. International networking and modern marketing were to play a relevant role in the development of Ferrer International.

At this stage both small labs were run by outward-looking entrepreneurs with scientific education, fluent in foreign languages, and with an embedded strategy of keeping informed about news from leading centres and companies in their different market niches of clinical analysis and pharmaceutical over-the-counter drugs.

New organisational and commercial knowledge from the United States and Germany and growth in scale and scope, 1930s–1990s

In this second stage both labs had to adapt to a cycle of collapse and slow reconstruction and late international integration in their traditional activities in their home markets due to the Spanish Civil War (1936–1939), Franco's dictatorship (1940–1975) and the international orientation of the new democratic governments after 1975, which imposed a long period of strict limitations to foreign trade and knowledge transfer, and therefore a common framework of difficulties to maintain former links with European firms. After World War II both labs struggled to maintain contacts with European firms and scientific institutes and congresses, and would focus their scarce resources on importing knowledge, and establishing alliances, with firms and centres from the three economies that seemed to be dominating innovation and world markets in the most knowledge-intensive products and processes: Germany, the United States and Japan.

The changing environment, and the new contacts, required organisational changes in both labs, in order to develop and design new strategies for internationalisation. In the case of Grifols, during World War II a German Jewish doctor, Dr Oppenheimer, who had escaped from Nazi Germany, came to work at the Grifols laboratory. The German staff continued to help Grifols keep up to date with the latest discoveries in microbiology and blood testing. Using Chandler's terminology, Grifols would have pioneered the biological drive of the health care industries in Spain following the German influence, in contrast with other local labs concentrated in the manufacturing and sale of old nutritional products and simple pharmaceutical remedies and vaccines in the pre-penicillin and sulpha era. The civil war in Spain (1936–1939) provided the Grifols family with a new and unexpected learning experience. The sons of Grifols Roig, Victor and José Antonio Grifols Lucas, students of Medicine and Pharmacy, had to become soldiers in the civil war, and in the midst of the disaster, had the fortune to work in the battlefield with the Spanish pioneer in blood transfusion and collection Dr Duran Reynalds, learning new methods of blood preservation for transfusion. Back home, the young sons convinced their father to start leaving aside the old business of nutritional products created by their grandfather Grifols Morera in 1910, due to scarcities in raw materials, and concentrate the core business on the new field of blood transfusion, collection and later manufacturing of blood derivatives. Laboratorios Grifols was founded in 1940 with Grifols Roig and his wife, to be joined soon by their two sons and their daughter and after 1946 by a local businessman (Alfons Brasó) completely unrelated to the family business but with much-needed money in times of scarcity.[26]In 1946 Grifols Roig's son Victor Grifols Lucas went to England to study penicillin production and visit two of his father's exiled Catalan friends, Dr Trueta in Oxford and Dr Duran in Manchester. His main goal was to meet executives from the British subsidiary of a US multinational to invite them to consider the Grifols project of a joint partnership, intended to establish a factory to produce penicillin in Spain, at a time when there was expanding demand and no major penicillin producer in the country. The proposal was rejected by the US multinational, due to lack of financial resources of Grifols, which at the time had a good reputation but was only a very small firm with little money to invest.

Despite the unsuccessful attempt at their first joint venture with a US corporation, 1946 must be considered a major historical landmark. It was the first time the small family firm showed that they had abandoned Germany as their source of innovation and knowledge transfer after World War II, and demonstrated their excellent information about where the future of the health care industries was pointing, towards the other side of the Atlantic, to the United States of America. Grifols had no tangible resources to consolidate a joint venture with US corporations in 1946, but started negotiations with them, and in this process an early exposure to US styles of doing businesses in the health care industries was integrated and embedded in the small family firm, that would remain for decades, until the present.[27]

The relative opening of the Spanish economy to the US multinationals in the 1950s seemed the right time to try again to find British and US partners. Grifols Lucas found it first in Dr Robert Race of the Lister Institute (established in London in 1891). Race, who had established the structure of the human chromosome related to the RH system, was invited to Barcelona and he agreed to cooperate with Grifols on analysis-related matters. Grifols sought to enter the specialised market niche of plasma fractionation, which they achieved in 1956. Given Spain's poor international reputation, it was very difficult for Grifols to sell plasma outside the Spanish market. The company found a way: selling it under the customer's brand. Swiss, Swedish and German firms bought small volumes of plasma from Grifols sent in small glass containers by airplane. Through the attendance of Grifols at international conferences the Spanish lab had a good international reputation and foreign firms trusted the quality procedures. Payments were made through bank transfers.[28] Sales within Europe in the 1950s and 1960s were basically of the same type as they had been within Spain in the late 1940s and early 1950s, *maquila* style: Grifols sold to other labs with prestigious names (vaccines and penicillin to Sociedad General de Farmacia and gamma globulin to Hubber in Spain, blood to the Swiss Red Cross, gamma globulin to the Swedish Kabi), and those labs added their brand names to the products before they reached the final client. During the mid-1950s, and particularly after the association with Dade Reagents and with the American Hospital Supply Corporation, exports of plasma to the United States followed strict transparency rules which allowed for greater visibility of the Grifols brand and products in the US market, and in the Food and Drugs Administration. This increased sales, and reputation.

For serums and reagents, friendship with a Barcelona pharmacist, Dr Roca Vinyals, helped connect Laboratorios Grifols and their Blood Bank with the North American company Dade Reagents Inc., to export plasma and import their reagents. Dade Reagents had been established in Miami in 1949 by John Elliott, one of the pioneers in blood banking and the business of blood derivatives in the United States. Grifols established contact with the managers through previous commercial contacts maintained with them by the Barcelona pharmacist Roca Vinyals.[29] In January 1958 J.M. Potts, Dade Reagents' Vice President, sent a letter to J.A. Grifols Lucas, Director of Grifols Blood Bank. In that letter Potts said that Dade Reagents needed to buy human plasma to make tissues, and that they were interested in buying plasma from the Grifols Blood Bank if their price was 'more reasonable' than the price of the plasma available in the United States. Potts said they needed 20–25 monthly units of 250 c.c. per unit of sterilised human plasma of any blood group. For him, the price was the most important determining factor to close the deal. Correspondence with Dade Reagents in 1958 and 1959 in the Grifols Archive show they reached that deal, with a price per unit of US$7.80.[30] Again, as in the 1946 trip to London, this time the most important thing for the future was, again, that the negotiation involved in how to prepare the product, how to send it and how to pay for it, and how to be in continuous communication in another language with the US client, represented a learning process, and an early exposure to US models of management of international operations. The process was not easy for Grifols; the correspondence shows they had to adjust and adapt administrative, financial and organisational routines. But they did a good job, and provided a good product on a satisfactory basis, and this paved the way for their first successful alliance with a US corporation. Dade's president and vice president Dr Griffitts and Mr Potts suggested incorporating a joint venture company, Dade Grifols, half owned by Dade Reagents, and half owned by Roca de Vinyals and the Grifols family. Negotiations started in 1959 and the company was registered in 1960, despite the sudden death of Roca de Vinyals. Without sons, the widow and niece of Roca de Vinyals would remain very active in the new company, along with the Grifols family. Dade Grifols, whose archive was almost completely lost when Baxter bought Dade Reagents in the 1980s, became the most profitable company of the Grifols informal business group composed of Laboratorios Grifols, Grifols Blood Bank, Gri-Cel and Dade Grifols. New products much in demand in the Spanish health system (cardiovascular products and lab equipment particularly), with the new capital and managerial advice contributed by the North American partners, and on-site training at the North American factories opened up a new period in the history of the labs.[31] Three women would play a very relevant role in launching initiatives that would consolidate the scientific reputation of Dade Grifols: María Cristina Cadira (co-manager of Dade Grifols, sister of Roca de Vinyals' widow), Julia Mas (director of the immunohaematology lab) and Montserrat Vinyals (chemistry graduate, technical director of Dade-Grifols, and wife of Grifols' top commercial manager between the 1950s and the 1970s, Antonio Ruiz).[32] It was the beginning of new times, the alliance in 1960 of a small biopharmaceutical company of Barcelona with a North American pioneering giant in the clinical laboratories industries. Grifols imported reagents and exported plasma, and adjusted internal organisational routines to the requirements of the US client. In this way the small firm learnt by doing and introduced incremental organisational innovations that prepared the way for future alliances and more ambitious projects with US firms and markets.

The mid-1950s until the early 1980s were therefore decades of fruitful cooperation of the small Grifols lab with North American partners, first Dade Reagents (1957/1960–1965) and, when Dade was absorbed by American Hospital Supply Corporation, with American Hospital Supply Corporation (1966–1982). A prestigious Cuban doctor specialised in clinical diagnosis of tropical diseases and quality control methods, named Guillermo Anido, who, with his family, went into exile in Miami after the Cuban revolution in 1961, had started working in the innovation department of Dade in 1961, the same year Victor Grifols travelled for the first time to Miami after the constitution of Dade Grifols in 1960, to meet the new partners and see their manufacturing installations and routines. Anido and Grifols were the only two Spanish-speaking persons in Dade Reagents in 1961, and both they and their families became close friends. The friendship of two Spanish-speaking scientists helped the transfer of US routines from Dade, and later from American Hospital Supply, to the Spanish family firm.

New products, new routines in manufacturing, administration and organisation, played key roles in the survival of the Grifols family firm, when the Spanish state decreed the prohibition of blood exports (1965), and Dade Grifols (50% shares owned by AHS and 50% by the Grifols group) helped the Grifols shareholders diversify into the expanding business of the distribution of (US) hospital supplies to the new large Spanish centralised hospitals. In 1965, the Spanish government prohibited the export of blood, to 'nationalise' and protect the Spanish plasma manufacturing industry. Plasma exports collapsed. Grifols' exports sharply declined from 3.3 million Spanish pesetas in 1965 to 917,000 pesetas in 1966. The domestic market had to be the solution to survive, in a compulsory reconquest of Spanish markets, with sales increasing from 875,000 pesetas in 1965 to 2.2 million pesetas in 1966. The US partnership Dade Grifols decisively helped in this reconquest, providing new exclusive products for hospital consumption, and training in US managerial practices typical of a large Chandlerian corporation. Sales and profits account for the great support provided by the joint partnership. Quantitatively speaking, in 1966 the sales (59.2 million Spanish pesetas) of this joint partnership with a US corporation were approximately 30 times bigger than the sales of the other two firms in the Grifols group, Laboratorios Grifols (2.2 million pesetas) and Gri-Cel (less than 1 million), that same year.[33]

Grifols not only survived, but increased sales. The profits helped the company reinvest and self-finance with its own resources growth in the former core business of blood products, by integrating forward the manufacturing of plasma derivatives with its own Grifols brand, thus substituting imports and developing plasma manufacturing capabilities.[34] Grifols felt confident enough to send its own patents to be considered for exploitation in the US market, and to export plasma and plasma technology to the United States.[35] Profits of Dade Grifols were around three to eight times the average profits of Laboratorios Grifols and Gri-Cel during the first three years of the 1970s, the only ones for which information is available after the loss of the Dade Grifols archive when it merged with Baxter Travenol in the mid-1980s.[36]

There were a few weaknesses during the years of transformation of the small lab and blood bank into an industrial holding, between the mid-1950s and the mid-1970s. On the productive side: lack of productivity; accumulation of stocks for lack of coordination between production and the commercial network of sales agents; expenses and costs to train technical staff in labs and in the sales network; lack of security in infrastructure (a fire in September 1967 in the chemistry lab); informal supply of machinery and other elements needed to maintain the buildings and organise post-sales service. On the distribution side: lack of specialised and standardised training of the sales network; difficulties of planning sales abroad due to changes in the regulatory framework (prohibition of blood exports in 1965, regulation of prices by the Spanish Ministry of Health in the 1970s–1990s); lack of internal sales statistics to coordinate with production departments and avoid accumulation of stocks. In management: a disorganised sales network and lack of experience in coordinating production departments and the sales network.[37] The external context of rampant inflation in the country during the 1970s increased expenses in human resources, raw materials, services and reduced profit margins on the sales. Some products had constant losses but were maintained to preserve reputation and avoid losing clients. The excellent development of the sales was, therefore, not a good indicator of what was going inside the company in these years of growth.[38]

The solution came with scale and scope following US factory models. The Grifols family decided to build a brand-new US-style factory in Parets del Vallés (land was bought in 1966, a factory was built in 1970) with plenty of space to create a large standardised building that met all the requirements of the US Food and Drug Administration in order to be a manufacturing centre whose products could one day be registered in the US market, to compete with US corporations. It was an ambitious dream, and it would be American Hospital Supply Corporation, a pioneering company in hospital equipment, with which Dade Reagents merged in the mid-1960s, that would help Grifols with an alliance. From the mid-1960s until the mid-1980s AHS Corp. was to be not just a commercial partner for the Grifols firms, but also a business school of good practices in the health industries in order to learn how the best corporations produced and sold in the US and the global markets. AHS staff would greatly help in the planning, design, construction and layout of the new building. Several trips to the different centres of AHS in the United States followed: to Miami in 1961 by Victor Grifols Lucas, Victor Grifols Roura in 1974 and other technical managers travelled in 1978 to Miami, Houston, Chicago, Evanston, Philadelphia and Washington.[39] The partnership with AHS allowed the Grifols company to learn about new layouts, new financial and technical practices, and establish contacts with relevant authorities, like the Secretary of Health Mr O'Keffe in March 1978. Sales and profits multiplied as well. Profits rose from €7.3 million in

1975 to €286 million in 1986, the golden age of the partnership of Grifols with AHS Corp. Americans had helped the Spaniards to acquire the strategic resources in terms of creation, and management, of a large corporation in the health industries, and also the long-term, stable capital that the Grifols needed to overcome the serious weaknesses the lab had had during the 1950s and 1960s.

A new generation participated in the new times. Victor Grifols Roura had joined the company's commercial department in 1973, and learnt from AHS, and from his father and the technical staff, how to run the US-style Parets factory. He had been travelling to the United States and supervised the launch of the internationalisation of the company, with the establishment of exports to China in 1983–1985, the first subsidiaries in Portugal in 1988, and in Argentina, Chile and Mexico in the early 1990s. He was well acquainted with the problems of the global health industries, and trained in business administration at high-quality local institutions. Grifols Roura, as the internal bulletins testify, was a tough manager who was determined to impose the highest standards of quality and professionalism at all levels of the group, in close coordination with the North American, Japanese and Spanish shareholders and staff. When in December of 1985 he joined the Board, taking on all the responsibilities formerly held by his father, he was well prepared to start a long period of complex and ambitious acquisitions in Europe, Asia and above all the United States.[40]

Like Grifols, Ferrer had its beginnings in the industrial and scientific milieu of early twentieth-century Barcelona and was strongly influenced by the talents, background and social networks of its founders and managers, basing its growth on alliances with leading international companies. The company's origins in the commercialisation of imported chemical and pharmaceutical products would determine the focus and capabilities of Ferrer. The Ferrer family had seized control of Medir, Ferrer y Cía SRC at the death of the senior partner, and created two new companies, Manuel y Francisco Ferrer SL (1940) and Laboratorios Ferrer SL (1953), to take advantage of post-war Spain's nationalistic industrial policy. By then the second generation, second cousins Carlos Ferrer Salat and Jordi Ferrer Batlles, a chemical engineer and a pharmacist respectively, had taken over. The company continued to manufacture under foreign licences and to represent foreign multinationals, but it also diversified into the food industry.[41] From the 1960s Ferrer Salat became deeply involved in the modernisation of the Spanish economy, playing a major role in the democratisation of Spanish employers' associations, and lobbying for Spain's full integration into Europe and the dissemination of free market economics and social dialogue in post-Franco Spain.[42]

The growth and internationalisation of Ferrer would be nurtured by this context. The most decisive change took place in the 1970s.[43] Jordi Ferrer sold his share of the company (40%). Lacking sufficient purchasing power himself, Ferrer Salat turned to another cousin, the financier Josep Vilarasau, to the new local industrial banks (Banco Industrial de Cataluña, founded in 1968, and Banco Catalan de Desarrollo, founded in 1964), and to a few private investors, all of them connected with Ferrer Salat's institutional initiatives. This type of investment network had been common in Catalonia since the beginning of industrialisation.

In 1974, Ferrer Salat asked Rafael Foguet to replace him as CEO. Foguet was a chemist whose entire career had been spent with a leading Spanish chemical group, Cros. His experience at Cros had been highly formative: in the building of an industrial group and in the lessons he learned from Cros' international partners Hoechst, Wacker Chemie, Occidental-Hooker, Standard Oil, Shell, ICI, Dupont and Progil[44]: German and North American know-how about organisation and international operations. As in Grifols, these partners transferred much more than products, they transferred managerial and organisational models of production, commercialisation typical of large pioneering corporations in knowledge-intensive industries.

At Cros, Foguet had relentlessly promoted the diversification characteristic of industrial groups through the acquisition of firms working in more technologically advanced fields and the establishment of three research centres. Foguet demanded abundant financial resources and a hierarchical organisation. It was no easy task. Foguet found himself saddled with a family-run firm that was still digesting the recent acquisition of another family-run firm, Robert, and 'a daring mini-presence abroad' in three countries: Peru and Mexico, where Ferrer had established subsidiaries (dedicated mainly to product packaging under the brand name Novag) in 1961 and 1967, respectively; and Germany, where Ferrer had just acquired the pharmaceutical laboratory Trommsdorff.[45] In terms of research, Ferrer had little more than 'a laboratory of incremental R&D that had achieved some recognition for producing esters and salts that improved the therapeutic properties of certain active ingredients'.[46]

As in the case of Grifols, transforming Ferrer into an industrial group and promoting innovation called for the exploitation of synergies and modernisation of the company's laboratories and production facilities.[47] The new CEO replaced the existing, very informal, structure with a pyramidal and centralised model, with himself in control of the areas of finance, human resources and research, with periodic meetings with the department heads. The new structure required a legal change (incorporation), a new name (Ferrer Internacional) and the long-term objective of consolidation, something that would not be achieved until 1996. Between 1975 and 1996, Ferrer Internacional experienced exponential growth based on new products of chemical and pharmaceutical research, developed individually or jointly; new process and product technology; the adaptation of products to international norms; advances in safety and environmental issues; internationalisation; diversification of activities into similar or complementary areas; and the training of management staff by area. In 1978 Ferrer had become a group in technical, legal and administrative terms. By closely controlling research from the top, Foguet had subordinated innovation to commercialisation. Diversification would involve the acquisition of companies working in fine chemistry, diagnostics, food products, dermopharmacy, nutriceuticals and specialities. New activities such as food, aromas and diagnostics required their own facilities and development laboratories, as well as specific methods of production, control and distribution. Diversification reached the research area, which was structured into six specific R&D centres, five of them in the Barcelona area.

Acquisitions provided organisational knowledge for the renewal of the production facilities, and the management organisation, but also commercial platforms for global markets, as in Grifols. The purchase of Trommsdorff by Ferrer was a great opportunity identified by Ferrer Salat during one of his many international trips. Founded in 1795 in Erfurt and rebuilt in Aachen after World War II, Trommsdorff was a small yet highly respected company. In 1970 Trommsdorff was controlled by the Fossen and Hüllen families, who were coping with falling sales (from 20 million to 3–4 million DM) due to the recent discovery of negative side effects in its leading product, the stomach protector *Rabro*. Ferrer Salat purchased 50% of Trommsdorff in exchange for 20% of Ferrer. As Trommsdorff's financial situation continued to worsen, Ferrer, already an active board member, set the stage for Ferrer's 100% acquisition of the German firm. In less than a decade, Ferrer had engaged in a dual path of internationalisation. According to Foguet, Ferrer aimed to integrate Trommsdorff into the group's new structure as a means of achieving internationalisation in markets which were more demanding, but also more stable, than those of Latin America.

As with Grifols, Spain's poor international reputation and country image posed a problem. The company decided to 'hide' its Spanish background behind a German brand, but hired Spanish managers at Trommsdorff. Trommsdorff experienced remarkable growth, doubling its staff to around 250 and increasing its productivity to twice that of Ferrer's Barcelona facilities. The German subsidiary became focused on four therapeutic areas: cardiovascular, anti-bacterial, dermatological and pneumological. Although Trommsdorff's research centre was small and more oriented toward development than research, Ferrer sought from the very beginning to widen its activities by establishing collaborations with German research centres.

As in the case of Grifols' early exposure to German and US markets, Ferrer's early exposure to the German market provided valuable lessons for its international expansion over the next four decades.[48] Ferrer, like Grifols, learnt that advanced markets required dealing with regulatory, technical and commercial issues; that they might be difficult to enter, but were a safer bet in the long run. Further they learnt that industrial subsidiaries in countries such as Germany benefited from both their industrial tradition and the prestige of the country, which provided an export platform. Finally, as with Grifols, Ferrer realised that to maintain a uniform group strategy, foreign subsidiaries must be effectively controlled through the group CEO and the director of the international division. This is the model that Ferrer tried to implement in the over 20 international subsidiaries established before 1996. Having a German laboratory in the heart of Europe did allow Ferrer to create commercial subsidiaries all over the continent (Greece, Italy, Portugal, Belgium and Ireland), to gain access to the Austrian market, to establish a subsidiary in Hong Kong and, most crucially, to gain knowledge about advanced markets and acquire a solid global vision.

Concerted research, still unusual in Spain in the 1970s, replaced the traditional scheme of a sovereign researcher that had characterised Ferrer since the 1950s.[49] In addition, the new research centre, staffed by about 50 people, half of them university graduates, was kept separate from the factory and managed through a system of weekly meetings with the CEO and reports from each department of Ferrer Internacional. Foguet quickly sought to establish enduring relations with Spain's public and private research institutions and, in 1982, with the Massachusetts Institute of Technology (MIT).[50] A medical doctor by training, Dr Ortiz had worked for Sandoz and Hobson and Infar Natterman and helped design Spain's new regulatory framework before joining Ferrer.[51]

Over the next three decades, the size of the research centre tripled. Most projects would be conducted in cooperation with researchers specialised in clinical pharmacology or with hospitals to test particular drugs before obtaining their official medical registration.[52] A familiarisation with foreign systems of research and registration did facilitate internationalisation in all of its dimensions (licensing in and out). The hierarchical organisational model implemented in 1975 included 'a precise, dynamic system of follow-up, with objective parameters and indicators and controlled by the company's decision-makers'.[53] Finally, since 1984 the Ferrer Research Foundation and the Severo Ochoa Award for Biomedical Research have helped to give visibility to Ferrer inside and outside Spain.[54]

In both cases, the early imprinting of knowledge obtained in the first stage was maintained in the second stage of growth, but changed the scale and scope between the 1930s and 1990s. The growth of national and international demand of healthcare products unfolded in a common context of institutional change and strong foreign competition on the Spanish market. Both firms could have disappeared, as many other small labs did, in this second stage of development of their businesses, in face of the difficulties, but both labs had managers and owners who foresaw a possible option: alliance with foreign giants, instead of just surviving in increasingly smaller market niches in the national market. Their dialogue with German and US leaders interested in entering the Spanish market was negotiated in such a way that both labs used it to improve capabilities and competitiveness in their organisation, their structure and their strategies. They learnt from the world giants to become giants at home and slowly abroad in neighbouring markets like Portugal or France. This stage was, therefore, a period when the early imprinting of the previous period was carried on to a more grown up mature stage.

Expansion in developed markets after the 1990s: mergers and acquisitions (Grifols) and strategic alliances (Ferrer)

After the 1990s, Grifols and Ferrer were, like many other labs, able to grow by a range of new possibilities to buy abroad. It was a period of frenzy in mergers and acquisitions, which privileged investments in advanced markets in Western Europe and the United States.

From the 1990s Grifols' goal has been to integrate backwards and forward at a global scale, by controlling the global supply of its raw materials (high-quality plasma proteins), and in this way the most dynamic and profitable global markets in its market niche (plasma protein derivatives). With this strategy in mind, Grifols accelerated acquisitions in the United States in the early decades of the twentieth century.[55] The alliance with the Green Cross Corporation, the Japanese leader in plasma products, and with Alpha Therapeutic Corporation (GCC's North American subsidiary) provided a technological basis that increased sales in foreign markets to 25% of total income, and exports, multiplying by four since 1992. The subsidiaries provided further experience in international accounts, payments and the export of health and pharmaceutical products: Portugal was the first one in 1988, the Czech Republic in 1990, Slovakia 1999, the Miami Pexaco Intl Corp to distribute to Central and South America (except Brazil until 1998) in 1990, Chile in 1990, Argentina 1991, Mexico in 1993, Brazil in 1998. A qualitative step forward came with the opportunity to buy ATC's subsidiaries in Germany, Italy and the United Kingdom in mid-1997: safety problems had destroyed the financial future of these subsidiaries, and the Japanese GCC offered Grifols the option of purchase of its subsidiaries in these markets previously closed to Grifols by Alpha's commercial interests in Europe. The subsidiary in France came in 1999 and in 2003 the acquisition of Alpha's assets in the United States led Grifols to establish headquarters in the US in Los Angeles, where Alpha had had central offices and plants. The Singapore office opened in 2000, and the acquisition of Alpha's assets in 2003 led to merging with the subsidiaries in Malaysia and Thailand, serving 15 countries in Asia. In 2001 Grupo Santander Central Hispano became a shareholder of Grifols in order to help buy Seracare, a leading plasma supplier in the United States, in 2002. It was the first step in the acquisition of companies that had donation centres in the United States, to integrate horizontally, and control the quality of plasma in the manufacturing plants. The family Grifols retained 30%, and the corporation became listed on the Spanish stock exchange in 2006. In 2005, three investment funds led by Morgan Stanley replaced Banco Santander Central Hispano and Deutsch Bank as the main financial partners. The third international expansion started with subsidiaries in Japan in 2006, in 2009 in China and Switzerland, and In the Nordic countries and Colombia in 2010. The core acquisitions after this year concentrated in the US market with Talecris and assets from Novartis Diagnostics in 2011 and 2014.[56] Today the most important market, and manufacturing plants, of the corporation are in the United States, and only 6% of sales go to the Spanish market. Grifols has more than 70% of its employees in the United States, where it has totalled investments for €6400 million (acquisitions and expansion of current installations combined), and of the €3935 million in sales in 2015 more than 60% were obtained in the North American market.[57]

In the case of Ferrer, the group consolidated accounts and organisation in 1996, but maintained ownership and management under the Ferrer family, with a clear strategy of increasing its international presence in leading advanced markets. The preference was Western Europe, in contrast to Grifols' dominant strategy of acquisitions in the United States. After Carles Ferrer Salat's sudden death in 1998, his son Sergi took over. Two years later, Dr Ortiz was succeeded by Dr Joan Fanés as R&D director. As for Rafael Foguet, he maintained his central role until 2004, being replaced by Dr Jordi Ramentol. Forty years after its sound transformation, Ferrer is still a chemical, pharmaceutical and food product group which is vertically integrated, highly diversified and strongly commercial (licensing in and out), but with a more centred R&D strategy and a more selective and stable system of alliances. To understand the group's growth strategy one has to pay special attention to Ferrer's four major partners as of 2016: Centro Nacional de Investigaciones Cardiovasculares (CNIC), Alexza, Histocell and Janus Developments.[58] Alexza is an American pharmaceutical company specialising in research, development and commercialisation of innovative products to treat acute and intermittent disorders such as asthma or schizophrenia. This alliance allows Ferrer to participate in the development and marketing of Staccato and Adasuve systems, owned by Alexza. As for Histocell, it is a Spanish biopharmaceutical company developing cell therapy and tissue engineering products for regenerative medicine.[59] This alliance has two ongoing projects. The first project, aimed at developing a new cell therapy medication for the treatment of traumatic spinal cord injuries, marks a completely new strategy for the use of adult stem cells. The second focuses on the development of a new drug from the patient's adult stem cells and a new biomaterial for clinical application in articular cartilage injuries. Janus Developments is an incubator for biotech start-ups that facilitates collaboration between academic research, industry and investors, created in 2009 with the support of Ferrer, Enantia and Caixa Manresa.[60] Finally, in September 2016 Ferrer launched an alliance with the public research centre IBEC/Instituto de Bioingenieria de Catalunya (Bioengineering Institute of Catalonia) and the private company Mind the Byte, both based in Barcelona, devoted to the computational development of therapeutic molecules to fight cancer metastasis.

Grifols and Ferrer Internacional remain deeply rooted in the biomedical and chemical-pharmaceutical cluster of Barcelona, with slight differences. Grifols has strong connections with the research centres of the city, but has concentrated most of the scientific staff outside Spain due to mergers and acquisitions in Europe, America and Asia and the concentration of donor centres and clients in the United States. On the other side, Ferrer has a strong marketing and commercial component located in Barcelona, and a very high percentage of its team trained in Catalan universities. Ferrer preferably resorts to Spanish scientists to form scientific committees. Today Ferrer's international network, with 27 subsidiaries, is one of the most extensive of Spanish-funded laboratories, even though Ferrer has only two industrial subsidiaries, Mexico and Alsdorf. Their function is strictly instrumental: to provide support to and increase European and American sales of products which are developed in Barcelona. This is coherent with the company's historical trajectory and with the fact that sales are concentrated in Europe (66%) and Latin America (21%). Ferrer's international sales account for nearly 50% of the group's total sales. The R&D activity of the foreign subsidiaries is very modest. However early and daring, Ferrer's internationalisation remains essentially commercial in nature and, much as it was in the 1970s, a drive to widen markets in order to sustain innovation, which takes place in Barcelona. In Grifols, with 96% of its sales outside Spain, and sales and employment concentrated in the United States, the R&D of foreign subsidiaries is strategic and is concentrated in or around its extensive network of donor centres in the United States, and the connected factories. Grifols' internationalisation is essentially productive in nature, in search of very stable and large high-quality markets of raw materials derived from human plasma.

Both companies started small, but grew large in many ways because of their early ties with leading giants from Germany and the United States. The small companies from a backward country specialised in an industry which required initially high-quality knowledge and networks. Both firms accumulated this initial knowledge at home in the Barcelona cluster of biomedical scientists born in the late nineteenth century. Both firms were able to grow, following Chandler's chronology, after the 1930s, but for different reasons to those posited by Chandler: not by establishing barriers to competitors, but by establishing networks and alliances with giants who did not see the Spanish labs as a threat, but as a target. Once the alliance yielded results, in terms of scale and scope and internationalisation via foreign trade, the Spanish companies used organisational knowledge from those giants to launch, in a favourable period after the 1990s, their foreign direct investment into the US or Germany, where old labs were being sold, or were near bankruptcy. In this way, after a century of learning from giants, the small firms joined the reduced group of giants in their industry, and started to try to establish, as Chandler indicated, entry barriers for other potential followers.

Lessons from history: final remarks

The oligopolistic structure of the modern pharmaceutical industry did not stop small firms based in late industrialised countries from developing their own organisational and innovation capabilities throughout the twentieth century and going global since the 1990s. Early exposure to advanced markets, particularly Germany and the United States of America, accelerated a learning process and the imprinting of new capabilities in knowledge-intensive industries from advanced countries. Personal and institutional networks played a crucial role in the long and effective learning strategies of both multinationals.

Six conclusions emerge from our comparative exercise. First, both Grifols and Ferrer established early contacts with incumbents from more developed countries, contacts which provided knowledge, networks and entrepreneurial attitudes oriented to embed innovative strategies and structures in their small companies in the early twentieth century. The Grifols travelled, studied or worked in German clinical labs in the first three decades of the twentieth century, keeping in touch in those early years with the most modern techniques to organise clinical labs for diagnosis that would develop in the world after World War II. Ferrer's internationalisation in pharmaceutical products started with a close link with German markets, also learning German organisational routines in the pharmaceutical Industry in the 1960s. In both companies import activities and distribution of products of corporations from developed economies, leaders in innovation, contributed to their learning and training with international players. A large share of the profits of Grifols and Ferrer from the 1950s until the 1970s came from the import and distribution in Spain of specialities from advanced countries, a crucial activity to achieve and sustain international competitiveness over time.

Second, in both companies leading scientists of the founding family institutionalised innovative scientific routines in their companies before the 1970s, and in both companies a change took place after the 1970s when professional managers with a German and/or American background occupied CEO positions and led an accelerated era of foreign investments and exports: Victor Grifols Roura in Grifols and Rafael Foguet in Ferrer.

Third, both corporations made this transition from a science-managed firm to a business-oriented global corporation with culturally hybrid entrepreneurs and managers.[61] Culturally hybrid entrepreneurs and managers possessed a rare, valuable intangible experience: they had a good command of how to combine organisational knowledge of late developed markets with organisational knowledge of developed markets. In Grifols there were several family members with this intangible asset difficult to find in Spain before the 1980s (the founder, the sons and the grandsons) and members of their social network (the Cuban-American Guillermo Anido innovation manager in the US Dade Reagents and American Hospital Supply Corp, and Hikosuke Yorihiro, the Japanese CEO of Alpha Therapeutic Corporation). In Ferrer, it was the founder Ferrer and Rafael Foguet. Grifols accumulated these networks and knowledge through travel, scientific conferences, and import activities with France and Germany before the 1940s, the United Kingdom in the second half of the 1940s, and above all with the US since the 1950s, and the US and Japan after the 1980s.

Fourth, the stage of development in which the transformation of a small lab into a vertically integrated industrial group took place had profound and lasting effects on corporate development and R&D. It is important to underline the relationship between internationalisation and innovation, with the former always serving the latter in the two cases. The long training received by Grifols during the alliances and joint ventures with three North American corporations between the late 1950s and 1998 was essential to understand the company's self-confidence and the speed of mergers and acquisitions in the world after the 1990s. Similarly, Ferrer's history of enduring strong embeddedness in the Barcelona biomedical cluster was and remains the key to the company's international competitiveness.

Fifth, investments in Europe, in the 1970s by Ferrer and the 1980s–1990s by Grifols, provided the two companies with organisational knowledge about international operations, a fundamental resource to increase industrial, commercial and regulatory capabilities within and outside Europe. Trommsdorff's acquisition served well the objective of allowing a modest Spanish pharmaceutical firm to access mature markets and increase its industrial, commercial and regulatory capabilities. Grifols' acquisition of the European subsidiaries of the North American Alpha Therapeutic Corporation transformed a Spanish-based company into a European corporation that became visible as a new global player in the plasma industry after the 1990s.

Sixth, private family ownership has not prevented Grifols and Ferrer from going international and innovating. Self-financing and strategic alliances have always played a major role in both since the mid-twentieth century, but Grifols resorted to the local bank Sabadell in the 1970s–1980s and to a variety of other Spanish and international banks, the stock market and international investors since the 1990s. In contrast, Ferrer, which remains a closely held group, resorted to three related local banks to fund its ambitious growth plans.

And finally, the accumulation of social networks useful to expand the market niche of the two case studies must be underlined to understand the long-term resilience of the two health care companies. Both companies were founded by Catalan entrepreneurs very connected to centres of scientific excellence at the local and international level from their early beginnings until today. Both created enduring social networks within their different market niches, without which the transformation of small labs into global corporations could not have taken place. Throughout the twentieth century Grifols formed close networks with the local and global scientific community in its two market niches. Ferrer led and participated actively in the creation of networks with the local and European elites. In both cases the leadership in the creation and participation of networks helped them to participate in the design of strategic rules of the game, in the Spanish pharmaceutical industry in the case of Ferrer, and in the global plasma industry in the case of Grifols.

Early exposure to advanced markets helped them grow outside, but in dialogue with, the oligopolistic structure of the world health care industry. It shows further that the specific capabilities developed by both firms were determined first of all by personal and institutional networks that linked them to advanced research centres since the 1920s; and, second, by their acquisitions, mergers and strategic alliances, which gave them access to advanced organisational and global commercial knowledge from leading German and American companies from the 1960s. Future research may help provide additional case studies that could expand the lessons from these two firms to other processes of modernisation of health care companies from developing economies.

Notes

1. CGCOM, *Informe sobre el sector farmacéutico*; OECD, Statistics 2016.
2. Prados de la Escosura, "World Human Development."
3. Galambos and Sewell, *Networks of Innovation*, pp; Galambos and Sturchio, "Pharmaceutical Firms"; Vagelos and Galambos, *Medicine, Science, and Merck*; and Chandler, *Shaping the Industrial Century*.
4. Chandler, *Shaping the Industrial Century*, 9.
5. Data from public health care corporations listed in Nasdaq, one of the leading world markets for these industries, show that at the end of 2016 the largest major pharmaceutical corporation in the US (Johnson and Johnson) has a market capitalisation which is six times the capitalisation of the next follower (Abbott Laboratories) in this subsector of the health care industries, see https://www.nasdaq.com/screening/companies-by-industry.aspx?industry=Health%20Care&marketcap=Mega-cap#ixzz4TN36thM5Na
6. Guillén and García-Canal, "American Model of the Multinational."
7. Chandler, *Shaping the Industrial Century*, 9.
8. Fernández Pérez and Colli, *Endurance of Family Business*; Guillén and García-Canal, *Emerging Markets Rule*; Fernández Pérez and Lluch, *Evolution of Family Businesses*.
9. Campins and Pfeiffer, "La importancia de las redes sociales" for the Argentinian pharmaceutical industry, and Fernández Pérez, "Laboratorios Andrómaco" for a case study of the US subsidiary of the Spanish pharmaceutical multinational Andrómaco between 1928 and 1946.

10. Chandler, *Shaping the Industrial Century*, 9.
11. Guillen and García-Canal, "La expansion internacional," 23–34. For the purposes of this research, the original database has been updated to 2014, following the same methodology of search and codification.
12. We consider advanced countries those hosting the headquarters of world leading firms in the industry, namely US, UK, France, Germany, Switzerland and Japan.
13. Guillén and García-Canal, "American Model of the Multinational."
14. Sjögren, "Family Capitalism"; Puig, "The Global Accommodation"; Puig, "Networks of Opportunity"; Chauveau, "Quelle historie de l'hôpital"; Colli, "Patterns of Innovation"; Zamagni, "The Rise and Fall"; and Donzé, "Siemens and the Construction."
15. Pons and Vilar, *Seguro de salud privado y público*; Chaqués, "Políticas públicas y democracia en España."
16. Pons and Vilar, *Seguro de salud privado y público*; Chaqués, "Políticas públicas y democracia en España."
17. Puig and López, "Chemists, Engineers and Entrepreneurs," 345–59; Fernández Pérez, "Laboratorios Andrómaco," 266–75.
18. *Estadística del comercio exterior de España*. Madrid, Dirección General de Aduanas/Ministerio de Hacienda 1905–1980, and Ministerio de Economía y Competitividad for 2005.
19. Puig, *Constructores de la química Española*; Cilingiroglu, *Transfer of Technology*.
20. Grifols i Lucas, *Vivències* d'un *empresari de postguerra*; Grifols, *When a Dream Comes True*, pp.
21. Pérez Moreda, Reher, and Sanz, *La Conquista de la Salud*.
22. Rodríguez and Martínez, *Salud Pública en España*.
23. Catalán, "El círculo virtuoso"; and Fernández Pérez, "Laboratorios Andrómaco."
24. Historical Archive Museu Grifols in Barcelona. Library Catalog and Journals Catalog. Also Grifols i Lucas, *Amb un suro*; Grifols, *When a Dream Comes True*.
25. Cabana, *Carles Ferrer Salat*.
26. Historical Archive Museu Grifols in Barcelona. Actas Laboratorio Grifols 1940–1964 (Ref. 6864); and notarial documents of constitution and changes in the family firm (Escrituras de constitución y ampliación de capital).
27. Historical Archive Museu Grifols in Barcelona. "Memoria sobre el viaje a Inglaterra realizado por Victor Grifols del 12 de julio al 22 de Agosto de 1946." Ref. 05898. Grifols Lucas had an interview with an executive of the British subsidiary of the US firm Hayden looking for an agreement on technical cooperation and investment with them. Hayden replied that they would be positive provided Grifols guaranteed the joint firm would have exclusive rights of manufacturing of penicillin in Spain, strong protection against imports, and a joint investment of 10 million pesetas. He also met representatives of Burroughs Welcome and Co. and Ashe Laboratories Ltd for nutritional products. Grifols arranged with a Catalan contact in London named Pedro Gilabert to have an agent providing commercial and information services to Grifols. In 1948 the Spanish government regulated the monopoly of the production of penicillin in Spain, that would benefit two large business groups, and would mean a de facto exclusion of small entrepreneurs like Grifols that were working hard to contact leading penicillin producers to try to break in to the business of penicillin. This legal exclusion was the first one in the history of Grifols that made the company take the decision to diversify in order to survive. The other important legal landmark in this regard would come in 1965 with the legal prohibition on exporting blood in Spain, which de facto benefited once again a few large plasma manufacturers like Hubber that were integrating the business and needed to control Spanish raw materials for their new large firms, again damaging the interests of small labs like Grifols, which had been exporting blood to Scandinavian countries, Germany, Switzerland and the US, among others, in the first years of the 1960s. This prohibition, again, made Grifols diversify, going into the expanding business of the distribution of hospital equipment, for which they entered into an alliance and partnership with the leading US company, American Hospital Supply Corporation.
28. 'Spain had a poor reputation in the world and it was almost impossible to sell anything abroad ... we began to sell plasma to a German lab, but under its own brand' (Grifols i Lucas, *Amb un suro*, 110).

29. Interview with Alfonso Vidal Ribas Cadira, Roca Vinyal's nephew by the phone with Paloma Fernández, January 26, 2015. Roca Vinyals had no sons when he died in 1960, only nephews, and the widow María Dolores Cadira continued his businesses after he died.
30. Historical Archive Museu Grifols in Barcelona. Correspondence Hemobanco and Dade Reagents Inc., Ref. 2331 to 2374, 1958–1969.
31. Historical Archive Museu Grifols in Barcelona. Private correspondence and Notarial Records 1957–1966.
32. Historical Archive Museu Grifols in Barcelona. Agreement with American Hospital Supply Corporation; and Grifols 2011:113. On Antonio Ruiz and these three women, and Interview with Montserrat Vinyals Vallesta (Ruiz's wife) by Rosa Avella from the Grifols Archive on 4 May 1999 (transcript in the Grifols archive).
33. Historical Archive Museu Grifols Ref. 06316.
34. Historical Archive Museu Grifols in Barcelona. Interview with Guillermo Anido by Rosa Avella in 1999, transcript; Interview with Victor Grifols Roura by Paloma Fernández, February 13, 2015; and Shareholders Agreements and Notarial Constitution of Companies in Grifols Archive years 1960 to 1985.
35. Historical Archive Museu Grifols in Barcelona. Ref. 06316.
36. Historical Archive Grifols in Sant Cugat del Vallés. Ref 05878c and 05878b.
37. Historical Archive Museu Grifols in Barcelona. Ref. 2176 Actas Laboratorio Grifols Caja 92, June 15, 1965, Junta General ordinaria de accionistas, and Juntas for June 15, 1966, June 20, 1967, June 7, 1968, June 18, 1973, June 5, 1974.
38. Historical Archive Museu Grifols. Ref 2176. Actas Laboratorio Grifols 1965–1987.
39. Historical Archive Museu Grifols in Barcelona. Ref 05626 and Conference in Miami (1994) and Boletín Informativo Grupo Grifols May 1980 in Ref 05659.
40. Victor Grifols Roura, interviewed February 13, 2015.
41. Cercle d'Economia, *Cercle d'Economia 1958–1983*; Maluquer de Motes, *El Largo Camino a Europa*.
42. See note 5 above; and Ferrer Salat, *Europa y España*.
43. Ferrer Salat, "Hacia una Política Industrial."
44. Foguet, *Solemne discurso de investidura*.
45. Bank of Spain, Historical Archive, Deed of Conversion, 1975.
46. Historical Archive Museu Grifols in Barcelona Reference 05626; and Conference in Miami (1994) and Boletín Informativo Grupo Grifols May 1980 in Historical Archive Museu Grifols in Barcelona Reference 05659.
47. Ibid., 128–9.
48. Ibid., 138–9.
49. Foguet, *Investigación concertada*.
50. Ibid., 134–5.
51. Accessed July 2016. https://www.jaortiz.info/index.html
52. Historical Archive of the Bank of Spain, IEME Files, Deed of Conversion, 1975.
53. See note 39 above, 135.
54. Accessed July 2016. https://www.ferrer.com
55. Acquisitions of Grifols in the US: https://www.grifols.com/portal/es/grifols/origens; https://www.belinked.es/exito(March2015);https://openaccess.uoc.edu/webapps/o2/bitstream/10609/13101/1/GRIFOLS%20Factores%20Competitividad%20a%20Largo%20Plazo.pdf (March 2015); https://www.elexportador.com/062003/digital/empresas_huellas.asp (about the Probitas operation, March 2015). Also Rich, "'La historia de…"
56. Grifols, Historical Archive Grifols in Barcelona. Revista Cosmos; http://www.grifols.com.
57. Grifols, http://www.grifols.com and *La Vanguardia*, Saturday July 9, 2016.
58. Accessed September 2015. http://www.Ferrer.com
59. Accessed May 2016. http://www.histocell.com
60. Accessed May 2016. http://www.spheriumbiomed.com
61. Fernández Pérez, "Acerinox."

Disclosure statement

No potential conflict of interest was reported by the authors.

Funding

This work was supported by Fundación BBVA [I Ayudas a la Investigación en Socioeconomía FBB].

References

Cabana, F. *Carles Ferrer Salat. Biografía*. Barcelona: RBA, 2015.

Campins, M., and A. Pfeiffer. "La importancia de las redes sociales en los orígenes de la industria farmacéutica argentina. El caso de los catalanes en Argentina." *Revista de Historia Industrial* 47 (2011): 17–50.

Catalan, J. "El círculo virtuoso de Grifols 1909-2013: I+D+i, éxito global desde el cluster médico farmacéutico de Barcelona." *Revista de Historia de la Economía y de la Empresa* 8 (2014): 27–64.

Cercle d'Economia. *Cercle d'Economia 1958-1983. Una trajectòria de modernització i convivencia.* Barcelona: Cercle d'Economia, 1983.

CGCOM (Consejo General de Colegios Oficiales de Médicos de España)/ OMC (Organización Médica Colegial). *Informe sobre el sector farmacéutico*. Madrid: CGCOM, 2014. www.cgcom.es

Chandler, A. D. *Shaping the Industrial Century: The Remarkable Story of the Evolution of the Modern Chemical and Pharmaceutical Industries*. Cambridge, MA: Harvard University Press, 2005.

Chaqués, L. "Políticas públicas y democracia en España. La política farmacéutica del franquismo a la democracia." Unpublished doctoral dissertation, Universitat de Barcelona, 1999.

Chauveau, S. "Quelle histoire de l'hôpital aux XXe et XXIe siècles ?" *Les Tribunes de la santé* 4, no. 33 (2011): 81–89.

Cilingiroglu, A. *Transfer of Technology for Pharmaceutical Chemicals. Synthesis Report on the Experience of Five Industrialising Countries*. Paris: Organization for Economic Cooperation and Development, 1975.

Colli, Andrea. "Patterns of Innovation, Strategies and Structures in the Italian Chemical Industry, 1973-2003." In *Innovation and Entrepreneurial Networks in Europe*, edited by P. Fernández Pérez and M. B. Rose, 99–117. New York, NY: Routledge, 2010.

Donzé, P.-Y. "Siemens and the Construction of Hospitals in Latin America 1949-1964." *Business History Review* 89, no. 3 (2015): 475–502.

Fernández Pérez, P. "Acerinox. A Successful Japanese Joint-Venture in Southern Europe in the Second Half of the Twentieth Century." *Entreprises et Sociétés* 80 (2015): 57–83.

Fernández Pérez, P. "Laboratorios Andrómaco. Origins of the First Subsidiary of a Spanish Pharmaceutical Multinational in the United States (1928-1946)." *Journal of Evolutionary Studies in Business* 1, no. 2 (2016): 266–275.

Fernández Pérez, Paloma, and Andrea Colli, eds. *The Endurance of Family Businesses. A Global Overview*. Cambridge: Cambridge University Press, 2013.

Fernández Pérez, Paloma, and Andrea Lluch, eds. *Evolution of Family Businesses. Continuity and Change in Latin America and Spain*. UK.: Edward Elgar Publishers, 2016. Original version in Spanish published in 2015 as *Familias empresarias y grandes empresas familiares en América Latina y España*. Bilbao: FBBVA.

Fernández Pérez, Paloma, and Nuria Puig. "Dynasties and Associations in Entrepreneurship: An Approach through the Catalan Case." In *The Determinants of Entrepreneurship: Leadership, Culture, Institutions*, edited by José L. García-Ruiz, and Pier A. Toninelli, 105-125. New York: Pickering & Chatto, 2010.

Ferrer Salat, C. *Europa y España: La lucha por la integración*. Barcelona: Discurso de ingreso en la Real Academia de Ciencias Económicas y Financieras, 1993.

Foguet, R. *Investigación concertada en el campo de la química fina y farmacéutica*. Barcelona: Boletín de la Sociedad Catalana de Ciencias Físicas, Químicas y Matemáticas, 1983.

Foguet, R. *Solemne discurso de investidura Dr.H.C.* Barcelona: Univesitat de Barcelona, 2010.

Galambos, L., and J. E. Sewell. *Networks of Innovation: Vaccine Development at Merck, Sharp&Dohme and Mulford, 1895–1995*. Cambridge: Cambridge University Press, 1995.

Galambos, L., and J. L. Sturchio. "Pharmaceutical Firms and the Transition to Biotechnology: A Study in Strategic Innovation." *Business History Review* 72, no. 2 (1998): 250–278.

García-Canal, E., M. Guillén, and A. Valdés. "La internacionalización de la empresa española. Perspectivas empíricas." *Papeles de Economía Española* 132 (2012): 64–81.

Grifols. *When a Dream Come True*. Barcelona: Grifols, 2015.

Grifols i Lucas, V. *Amb un suro i un cordill. Vivències d'un empresari de postguerra*. Barcelona: Grifols, 2009.

Guillén, M., and E. García-Canal. "La expansión internacional de la empresa española: una nueva base de datos sistemática." *Información Comercial Española. Revista de Economía* 839 (2007): 23–34.

Guillén, M. F., and E. García-Canal. "The American Model of the Multinational Firm and the "New" Multinationals from Emerging Economies." *Academy of Management Perspectives* 23, no. 2 (2009): 23–35.

Guillén, M., and E. García-Canal. *Emerging Markets Rule: Growth Strategies of the New Global Giants*. New York: McGraw-Hill, 2012.

Guillén, M., and E. García-Canal. *The Rise of the New Multinationals*. Bilbao: BBVA-OpenMind, 2015. https://www.bbvaopenmind.com/wp-content/uploads/2015/04/BBVA-OpenMind-The-Rise-of-the-New-Multinationals-business-innovation.pdf.

Malerba, F., and L. Orsenigo. "The Evolution of the Pharmaceutical Industry." *Business History* 57, no. 5 (2015): 664–687.

Maluquer de Motes, J. *El largo camino a Europa. Cincuenta años del Círculo de Economía 1958-2008*. Barcelona: Centro editor PDA, 2008.

Pérez Moreda, V., D. Reher, and A. Sanz. *La conquista de la salud. Mortalidad y modernización en la España contemporánea*. Madrid: Marcial Pons, 2015.

Pons, J., and M. Vilar. *El seguro de salud privado y público en España. Su análisis en perspectiva histórica*. Zaragoza: PUZ, 2014.

Prados de la Escosura, L. "World Human Development 1870–2007"." *Review of Income and Wealth* 61, no. 10 (2014): 220–247.

Puig, N. *Constructores de la química española. Bayer, Cepsa, Puig, Repsol, Schering y La Seda*. Madrid: LID, 2003.

Puig, N., and S. López. "Chemists, Engineers and Entrepreneurs. The Chemical Institute of Sarria's impact on Spanish Industry (1916-1922)." *History and Technology* 11 (1994): 345–359.

Puig, Núria. "The Global Accommodation of a Latecomer: The Spanish Chemical Industry Since the Petrochemical Revolution." In *The Global Chemical Industry in the Age of the Petrochemical Revolution*, edited by Louis Galambos, Takashi Hikino and Vera Zamagni, 368–400. Cambridge: CUP, 2006.

Puig, Núria. "Networks of Opportunity and the Spanish Pharmaceutical Industry." In *Innovation and Entrepreneurial Networks in Europe*, edited by Paloma Fernández and Mary Rose, 164–183. UK: Routledge, 2010.

Rich, G. "La historia de … Grifols en Estados Unidos." *Tribuna Norteamericana* 17 (Dec 2014): 1–16.

Rodríguez Ocaña, E., and F. Martínez Navarro. *Salud pública en España. De la Edad Media al siglo XXI*. Sevilla: Junta de Andalucía, 2008.

Sjögren, H. "Family Capitalism Within Big Business." *Scandinavian Economic History Review* 54, no. 2 (2006): 161–186.

Vagelos, R., and L. Galambos. *Medicine, Science, and Merck*. Cambridge: Cambridge University Press, 2004.

Zamagni, Vera. "The Rise and Fall of the Italian Chemical Industry, 1950s-1990s." In *The Global Chemical Industry in the Age of Petrochemical Revolution*, edited by Louis Galambos, Takashi Hikino and Vera Zamagni, 347–367. Cambridge: Cambridge University Press, 2006.

Archives

Museo Grifols, Barcelona. Historical Archive and Library.
Grifols Corporation, Sant Cugat del Vallés, Barcelona.
Archivo General de la Administración, Madrid.
Banco de España (Madrid). Historical Archive and Library.

Websites

https://www.ferrer.com, accessed September 2015 and July 2016
www.grifols.com, accessed 2014, 2015 and 2016
https://www.jaortiz.info/index.html, accessed July 2016
www.histocell.com, accessed May 2016
www.spheriumbiomed.com, accessed May 2016

Interviews

Eduardo Herrero, 9 December 2013. By Paloma Fernández.

Rosa Avella, interviewed 2013-2015. By Paloma Fernández.
Nuria Pascual, various interviews 2013-2015. By Paloma Fernández.
Alfonso Vidal Ribas Cadira, 26 May 2015. By Paloma Fernández.
Victor Grifols Roura, 13 February 2015. By Paloma Fernández.
Francesc Cabana, 11 November 2015. By Nuria Puig.
Rafael Foguet, 14 December 2015. By Nuria Puig.

Thriving in the shadow of giants: The success of the Japanese surgical needle producer MANI, 1956–2016

Ken Sakai

ABSTRACT

Large companies have a clear presence in the medical instruments industry, but in their shadow, many small and medium-sized enterprises (SMEs) have successfully carved out and defended niches. This article examines one of these enterprises in detail: MANI, a Japanese company that manufactured the world's first stainless steel surgical needles and remains among the top three producers of these needles today. This article explains the company's success using the 'dynamic imbalance' framework; this framework helps map MANI's development of a sustainable competitive advantage as the result of internally driven and repeated processes rather than externally driven and specific technological inventions.

Introduction

This article examines the historical development of MANI, Inc. (hereafter, MANI), a Japanese medical instruments company that was created in 1956 when Masao Matsutani (1911–2003) started producing and selling surgical needles.[1] The company name was changed from Matsutani Seisakujo to MANI in 1996 for the purpose of global expansion,[2] but in this article, MANI is used throughout for simplicity.

Initially, MANI was a small metalworking shop in the Tochigi prefecture located in the Kanto region on the island of Honshu, Japan. Today, it is among the top global producers of surgical needles and is competing for third position in the world market with B. Braun from Germany, trailing only the market leader Johnson & Johnson (which is a part of the Johnson & Johnson family of companies, Ethicon) and number two, Covidien from Ireland, which in 2015 became part of Medtronic.[3] MANI has also gained a significant share in a dental care product market and in the ophthalmologic knife product market.[4] In 2016, MANI's sales totalled approximately 16.5 billion Japanese Yen (150 million US dollars). Moreover, its 2016 sales to operating income ratio was approximately 27%.[5] My main interest here is to understand the process involved in this dramatic transformation into a growing and competitively successful firm.

My investigation of MANI's growth process will contribute to clarifying a broader issue for business historians: how small or medium-size enterprise (SME) survives and succeeds in an industry dominated by large companies. Medical instruments is one of the most significant industries in the world. Its revenues reached approximately 228 billion US dollars in 2014, up from 164 billion US dollars in 2010. Johnson & Johnson is the leading medical instruments company, with revenues of 28.7 billion US dollars, followed by General Electric, with revenues of 18.1 billion US dollars, and Medtronic, with revenues of 17.1 billion US dollars.[6] Considered together, the top 20 global companies generated 156.4 billion US dollars in revenues in 2014.[7] However, there are many SMEs in this industry, reflecting the large number of small products. According to Pullen, Weerd-Nederhof, Groen, and Fisscher,[8] approximately 80% of companies in the medical instruments sector are SMEs. How have they emerged and held their own among large competitors? Because MANI can be considered one of the most successful SMEs in the industry, it provides an excellent case for examining this question.

Although the success of SMEs in the medical instruments sector has been an object of debate, two arguments can be confirmed. The first has stressed the efficacy of the dense network or industry cluster and its complementarity. For instance, Pullen et al. insisted that multiple network characteristics, including 'goal complementarity,' are the key success factors for SMEs in the medical instruments sector.[9] Additionally, a Russian case study by Zemtsov, Barinova, Bukov, and Eremkin confirmed the existence of an industrial cluster of medical instrument SMEs in Russia.[10] The same argument can be found in studies about Japanese medical instruments SMEs. Donzé investigated the beginning of the Japanese medical instruments industry (from 1880 to 1937) and revealed that almost all SMEs were located in Tokyo and represented an industry cluster because there were many doctors and wholesalers of medical instruments in Tokyo.[11] According to the study, in the dense cluster, SMEs relied on internal joint research activities aimed at the sharing of knowledge between craftsmen and doctors. Additionally, Takeuchi[12] showed that the concentration of the SMEs in Tokyo continued even in the 1970s.

By contrast, some previous studies have stressed the importance of early internationalisation and intensive competition in the global market for medical instrument SMEs. For instance, according to Hall, Lotti, and Mairesse, international competition fosters R&D intensity among Italian SMEs, especially in high-tech industries including medical instruments, and firm size and R&D intensity enhances the likelihood of creating both process and product innovation.[13] Similarly, Sass[14] revealed that successful Hungarian SMEs in the medical instruments industry can be characterised by continuous innovative activity accompanying high-level competitiveness and internationalisation.

These two arguments appear to be different, but there are also common points. First, both of them emphasise R&D or technological innovation activity. However, except for limited studies (e.g. Sass[15]), these arguments have not stressed the importance of continuity and repetition of the activity. Second, whether the network or the competition, the two arguments tend to consider that the driving-forces of the R&D or innovative activity are external to the SME, i.e. inter-organisational relationships.

Although the previous studies provide important insights, repetitive, long-term and internally driven dynamics also must be taken into consideration. MANI is an appropriate and typical case for considering these points. First, MANI realised technological innovations not as one-shot activity but through a repeated and long-term process. Second, at least in the initial stage, there was not remarkable external force driving MANI's innovative activity. MANI started and grew in a rural area, where there is no dense network such as an industry cluster. In addition, although MANI participated in the international market as it grew, in the beginning, MANI was only a local SME and did not face global competitions. Thus, an investigation into MANI will enrich our understanding of the success of SMEs in the medical instruments sector.

To date, however, the studies of MANI have been insufficient. For example, Yanagawa and Matsutani and Yanagawa described several characteristics of the firm's mission, technology, and corporate governance, but they did not investigate its growth process in detail, primarily because of a lack of historical perspective.[16, 17] The Japan Finance Corporation for Small and Medium Enterprises,[18] and the Nikkei Top Leader,[19] have also mentioned MANI. Although these studies insisted that MANI's strength is its technology, such descriptions are superficial.

To consider the growth process in depth, this article uses multiple sources of data to improve validity through triangulation.[20] In terms of written documents, a nearly complete set of magazine and newspaper articles concerning MANI's history was obtained using the National Diet Library collections in Tokyo and the Tochigi Prefectural Library. Furthermore, I documented sections of MANI's homepage and added them to the data for analysis. In addition, five oral-history interviews were conducted with the following individuals: (i) Kanji Matsutani, the company's former president; (ii) Masamitsu Matsutani, the company's former vice-president who was in charge of sales (both Kanji Matsutani and Masamitsu Matsutani are sons of MANI's founder, Masao Matsutani); (iii) Akira Sakai, the senior managing director of Matsuyoshi & Co., Ltd. (hereafter, Matsuyoshi), one of MANI's most important wholesalers, and two users of MANI's surgical needles; (iv) Kazuhiko Hagane, a veteran surgeon; and (v) Ieko Nomoto, a veteran nurse at a hospital in Tochigi prefecture. Finally, on February 22, 2016, the author received a brief explanation of the history of MANI from Kanji Matsutani, based on confidential lecture material that was used for in-house training.[21] All of these sources were arranged in chronological order and then analyzed. Both the written sources and the range of interviewees counter balanced the risk of an overly 'heroic' account based on the actions of the founder and his sons.

Based upon this evidence, I reconstructed the mechanism and the driving force behind MANI's growth utilising the so-called dynamic imbalance framework.[22] This framework considers imbalance to be a useful management tool. The imbalance could be either between business goals (or projects) and existing competencies or among components of a technological system. This imbalance leads the company to focus on an area in which resources should be invested, thereby generating further investment and growth. This means that the dynamic processes for solving this imbalance contribute to the development of organisational competencies and ultimately create competitive advantage. The dynamic imbalance framework is particularly appropriate for analysing the growth of SMEs. In general, SMEs are poorer in resources than large companies and cannot afford to invest in every possible project equally. Therefore, they typically focus their investment on a single project. Outstanding success in one project encourages SMEs to invest in the next undeveloped project. As Hirschman discusses,[23] a chain-reaction of investments expands the possibilities of growth for have-nots such as SMEs.

An advantage of this framework is that it can prevent a reversion to fatalistic or deterministic perspectives while highlighting how the internal agency of entrepreneurs creates and corrects imbalances. Preoccupation with fatalistic or deterministic perspectives affords little insight from which future entrepreneurs could learn. Therefore, it is necessary to consider the function of entrepreneurs' agency as a developmental phenomenon. Using the dynamic balance framework, I analyze historical changes in extant capabilities, goals, and dynamic processes. I focus on the technological capabilities and goals of MANI because, as noted, previous studies on SMEs in the medical instruments sector emphasise the importance of technology, and previous studies on MANI also suggest that technology is one of its strengths.[24] Consequently, a chronological description of these elements will help vividly illustrate the history of MANI.

Nonetheless, this framework poses an issue. Namely, it may favour interview data that support entrepreneurs' positions, which might result in an account rooted in heroism. To minimise this narrative risk, I verified the validity of the interview data by cross-referencing information with written sources, which provided contextual data.[25] Consequently, I revised the heroic recollection of an entrepreneur who typically claims that he formed a nearly complete expectation of future demand. After completing this revision to increase validity, the dynamic imbalance framework became more appropriate to account for the growth of an SME such as MANI.

The remainder of this article is organised as follows. Section 2 provides a brief overview of MANI's current products. Section 3 presents a detailed history of MANI since 1956. Section 4 clarifies the mechanisms driving MANI's growth from the perspective of the dynamic imbalance framework and summarises this study's findings and its contribution to the broader literature.

MANI's products today

As shown in Figure 1, MANI has achieved high levels of sales growth and operating income. Today, MANI's sales mainly derive from three products: surgical needles, dental care products, and ophthalmologic knives.[26] In 2016, sales of surgical needles totaled approximately 4.2 billion Japanese Yen (40 million US dollars, 16.5% of total product sales). Sales of dental care

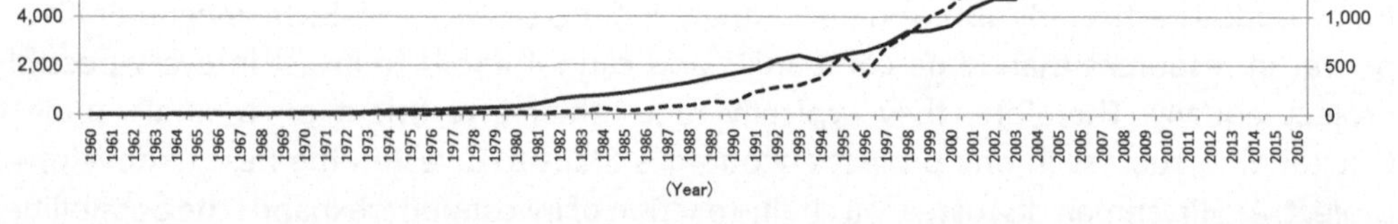

Figure 1. Long-term trends in sales and operating income of MANI. Source: MANI. 'Yukashoken Hokokusho 2014' [Securities Report 2014]; MANI. 'Yukashoken Hokokusho 2015' [Securities Report 2015]; MANI. 'Yukashoken Hokokusho 2016' [Securities Report 2016]; Personal interview with Kanji Matsutani (January 15, 2016; February 22, 2016); Personal memo from Kanji Matsutani during the interview.

products totaled approximately 8.3 billion Japanese yen (79 million US dollars, 50.3% of total product sales). An approximately 43% increase in the sales of dental care products occurred because of mergers and acquisitions with German dental care companies in 2015. Sales of ophthalmologic knives totaled 4.0 billion Japanese Yen (38 million US dollars, 24.2% of total product sales).[27] In the worldwide dental care product market, MANI's dental reamer, a dental care instrument, has the largest share (estimated 50% in 2013), and the ophthalmologic knives are estimated to constitute a 30% share in 2014.[28] It is believed that the ophthalmologic knives products division exceeded the market share of Alcon, a large global eye care company, in 2015 to become the global market leader.[29]

Despite the significant success in the dental care and ophthalmologic knife products, this account mainly focuses on surgical needles because they are the most important products for explaining MANI's history of growth. MANI was founded in 1956, when the late Masao Matsutani started producing and selling surgical needles in Tochigi prefecture.[30] MANI entered the dental care product market only in 1976,[31] and in 1998 entered the ophthalmologic knives market by employing technological capabilities in the microfabrication of hard stainless steel that the company had developed through its surgical needle business.[32]

Surgical needles are MANI's main products and are used in surgeries today. Most such needles have an arc shape.[33] Today, MANI produces more than 10,000 types of surgical needles;[34] this wide variety is because surgical needles possess varying attributes (e.g. in terms of length, diameter, and strength) that correspond to the human body part being operated on and the doctor's preferences.[35] Accordingly, because of the nature of this particular segment, economies of scale do not apply, and SMEs such as MANI have an opportunity to enter the market. Although few SMEs succeed because of the high level of competition in this segment, MANI has been highly successful.[36]

As Table 1 shows, the surgical needles that MANI produces today can be classified into approximately three types. The first type is surgical eyed needles, which are used to install pre-surgery sutures in hospitals.[37] This type of needle used to be one of MANI's main products, but now it represents only 4–5% of MANI's sales.[38] The second type is eyeless needles, which are semi-processed goods for surgical needle-equipped sutures.[39] These needles are delivered from MANI to other manufacturers, which transform them into surgical needle-equipped sutures by adding a suture. Eyeless needles, substitutes for surgical eyed needles, accounted for approximately 20% of MANI's total sales in 2016 (the share of total sales account for by surgical eye needles decreased by approximately 10 percentage points from 2014 because of mergers and acquisitions with German dental care product companies in 2015).[40] The third type is needle-equipped sutures. While MANI sells eyeless needles to other companies, it also manufactures needle-equipped sutures in-house by procuring and adding a suture.[41]

MANI's share of the worldwide market for eyeless needles, which are the main products manufactured by the surgical needles division, was estimated at 10% in 2014,[42] approximately 3.7 billion Japanese Yen, 34 million US dollars,[43] and the company nearly tied with B. Braun for market share.[44] These two companies have been vying for third position in the market. Although the market share of Covidien, which is estimated as the number two company by market share, is unclear, Johnson and Johnson (Ethicon), which has been the leading manufacturer of eyeless needles, has been estimated to own more than 60% of the market in recent years.[45] Its sales were estimated to be approximately 190 million US dollars. Thus, Johnson and Johnson (Ethicon) is clearly a giant in the market. Nevertheless, MANI

Table 1. The characteristics of MANI's surgical needle products.

Types	Product Overview
Eyed Needles	Traditional surgical needle There is a hole for threading at the tip of the body Although the conventional material of eyed needles was iron MANI made them from stainless steel MANI sells it to primary wholesalers At hospitals, nurses antisepticise eyed needles and thread the needles
Eyeless Needles	They are semi-processed goods of surgical needle-equipped sutures It has a hole at the cross section to equip the suture It MANI sells it to surgical needle manufacturers
Eyeless Needles with Suture (Needle-equipped Suture)	Relatively new type of surgical needle It is equipped with a suture It is already antisepticised at the manufacturing companies

Source: Furuhashi and Sasamoto, Zusetsu Shujutsu Kikai [Everything about Surgical Instruments]; Personal interview with Kanji Matsutani (January 15, 2016; February 22, 2016).

has maintained high levels of sales growth and operating income (see Figure 1), and it can therefore be said that MANI has been thriving in the shadow of giants.

History of MANI

Next, I provide a detailed overview of the history of MANI, subdivided into four periods. For each period, I examine how MANI developed new products and related technological capabilities by addressing various challenges in a step-by-step manner, gradually building a lasting competitive advantage.

Origins and entry into the surgical needle supply chain (1926–1956)

The founder of MANI is Masao Matsutani, who inherited a metalworking business from his father. According to newspaper articles, a book, and oral-history interviews sources,[46] during World War II (1939–1945), he successfully constructed strong bombers and machine guns from chrome steel at two factories in Tokyo and Yamanashi prefecture and accumulated knowledge about metal materials and metalworking. However, most of these factories were destroyed by US Air Force bombing, and when World War II ended, military demand abruptly ceased. Therefore, Masao Matsutani closed his factories, dispersed his employees, moved to Takanezawa (Tochigi prefecture), where his wife had been born and to where his wife and two sons had been evacuated during the war, and following advice from an acquaintance who worked for the Welfare Ministry, decided to manufacture medical instruments. The main reason for this bureaucrat's advice was that technological conversion from military to civilian applications using technologies that had been developed during World War II was a fundamental government policy.[47] Additionally, (1) the strong necessity for rapidly developing the medical and welfare industry and (2) the suitable characteristics of Tochigi prefecture for the surgical needle industry were important. Let us discuss these two reasons in detail.

First, the strong necessity for rapidly developing the medical industry was due to the extremely low performance of the industry. As shown in Figure 2, while there were 4,858

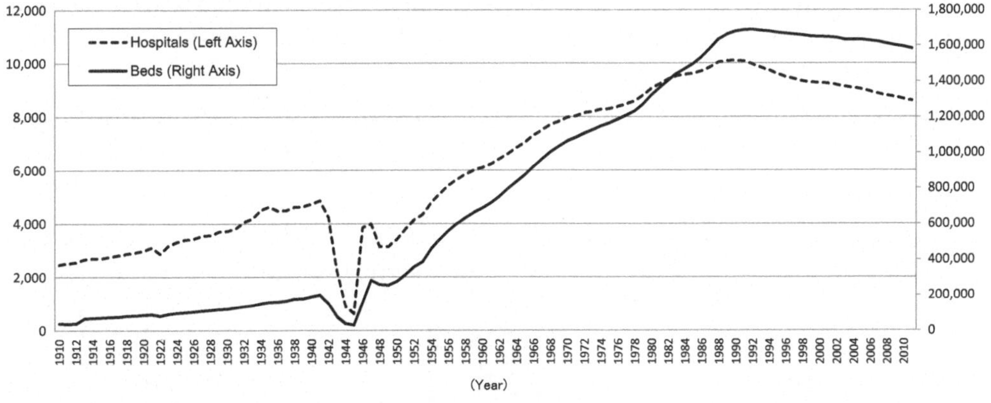

Figure 2. Long-term change in the number of hospitals and beds in Japan. Source: Statistics and Information Department, Minister's Secretariat, Ministry of Health, Labour and Welfare, 'Byosho no Shuruibetsu Byoinbyoshosu' [Hospital Beds by Kind 1910–2004]; Statistics and Information Department, Minister's Secretariat, Ministry of Health, Labour and Welfare, 'Byoin no Shuruibetsu Byoinsu' [Hospitals by Kind 1910–2004]; Fukunaga, Nihon Byoinshi [The History of Japanese Hospitals], 346.

hospitals and 199,831 beds in 1941 in Japan, only 645 hospitals and 31,766 beds remained in 1945 because of fires. Although the number of hospitals and beds increased in 1946, these hospitals were insanitary and lacked basic equipment such as soap, fuel, and bandages.[48] For instance, even in the Saiseikai Utsunomiya hospital, one of the most well-known hospitals in Tochigi, surgical procedures were conducted in offices.[49] In addition, no catering facilities were available, so many families of patients cooked with charcoal in hospital corridors.[50] The large number of starvation victims in 1945 and 1946 indicates the seriousness of the food situation.[51]

Similar to the hospitals, the Japanese surgical instruments industry was in a rudimentary condition.[52] This condition resulted from not only the ravages of World War II but also the technological immaturity in the field since before World War II. For example, Toru Sakakibara (1899–1992), who performed the first cardiac surgery in Japan, recorded in 1936 that the surgical needles available in Japan were inadequate to perform cardiac surgery. Although he repeatedly tried to sew cardiac wounds, he could not do so smoothly.[53]

Therefore, immediately after World War II, Crawford F. Sams (1902–1994), Colonel of the Medical Corps and Chief of the Public Health and Welfare Section of General Headquarters (GHQ), learned of the serious and unsanitary conditions in Japanese hospitals. He began implementing reforms of the Japanese medical system (e.g. medical education and the organisation of hospitals) modelled after the United States.[54] Consequently, the Welfare Ministry, which was under the control of the GHQ, wanted to encourage the development of national medical instruments manufacturers.

Second, suitable characteristics of Tochigi prefecture for the surgical needle industry included the ease of visiting Tokyo and of finding blacksmiths. Tochigi prefecture is landlocked and is approximately 100 km from Tokyo prefecture, the capital of Japan.[55] Tochigi had developed as a supply source for crops because of its terrain, climate, and proximity to Tokyo. In fact, even in 1955, the percentage of farmers in Tochigi was 51.8%.[56] Thus, blacksmiths for farm tools also emerged in Tochigi. For instance, in 1955, Tochigi had the largest market share (over 70%) of straw cutters in Japan and approximately 400 blacksmiths.[57]

For these reasons, in 1956, Masao Matsutani began manufacturing surgical needles with a concrete stable and one blacksmith, and this was the beginning of MANI.[58] Figure 3 summarises the supply chain for surgical needles at the time. The coloured box in Figure 3 indicates MANI's position in the chain. In the 1950s, and 1960s, this industry comprised not

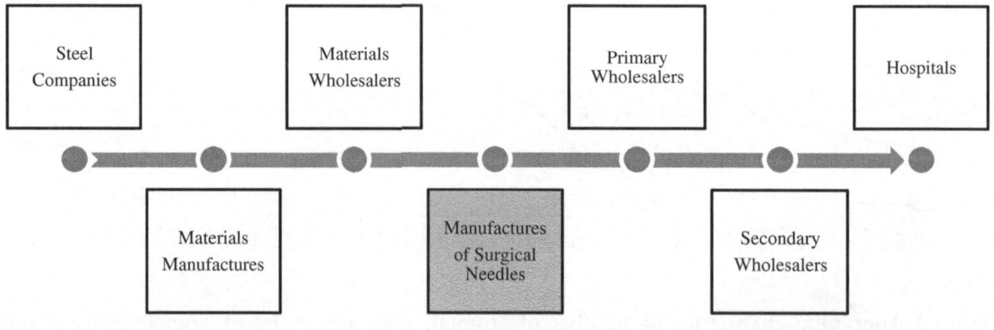

Figure 3. The supply chain for surgical needles. Source: Fujikeizai, Ryutsu Mappu [Overview of Distribution in 1977]; Personal Interview with Matsutani, K (January 15, 2016; February 22, 2016), Matsutani, M. (March 22, 2016), Sakai, A. (February 17, 2016).

formal companies but small shops run by craftsmen.[59] MANI was a small shop run by Masao Matsutani; at the time, there were approximately 100 similar small shops.[60] These shops bought metal wire rods from wholesalers located in the upper reaches of the supply chain, manufactured surgical needles from those materials, and sold the products to primary wholesalers of medical products. These primary wholesalers sold the products (in most cases small medical instruments such as surgical needles, they were sold under the wholesalers' brand name) to smaller and more locally based secondary wholesalers scattered throughout Japan. These wholesalers would in turn sell the products to hospitals.[61]

Based on Fujikeizai,[62] there were approximately 30 primary wholesalers, less than the number of surgical needle manufacturers and secondary wholesalers. The primary wholesalers fulfilled the functions of warehousemen and domestic vendors, distributing various medical instruments including surgical needles. Most primary wholesalers were located in Tokyo's Hongo district. For small medical supplies, including surgical needles, the 'top three' large-scale primary wholesalers were Fujimoto, Morikawa Iryoki, and Matsuyoshi. According to historical records, in 1977, Fujimoto had 660 employees and sales of 14.4 billion Japanese Yen, Morikawa Iryoki had 180 employees and sales of 4.5 billion Japanese Yen, and Matsuyoshi had 118 employees and sales of 3.9 billion Japanese Yen. Moreover, according to Akira Sakai, [63] who was a top manager of Matsuyoshi, the company had approximately 30 sales employees in 1946. In addition to these 'top three companies', five relatively powerful primary wholesalers generated more than 1 billion yen in sales. There were also six primary mid-level wholesalers in 1977.[64]

Because a small number of larger primary wholesalers such as Matsuyoshi had built distribution channels across a wide area, these wholesalers' influence was immense.[65] This structure gave these larger wholesalers power over other companies. Therefore, manufacturers such as MANI were original instruments manufacturers (OEMs) for the wholesalers and had to obey their orders.[66]

MANI's First challenge: Making surgical needles from stainless steel (1957–1965)

According to Freidin and Marshall, Furuhashi and Sasamoto, and two oral histories,[67] in those early days, 'eyed' surgical needles made of iron treated with surface plating predominated. At that time, it was commonly accepted that although austenite stainless steel (hereinafter referred to as stainless or stainless steel) was less likely to rust, it was too flexible to be used as a raw material for surgical eyed needles because they require hardness as an indispensable characteristic.[68] Therefore, whereas stainless was used as the raw material for most medical instruments that did not require hardness, the raw material used for surgical eyed needles remained iron treated with surface plating. Accordingly, Masao Matsutani also started to make iron surgical needles with surface plating.[69] Although MANI had insufficient funds to make the necessary investment, it could use public financing from Tochigi prefecture, which offered a low interest rate for developing local start-ups.[70]

Based on multiple oral histories and Furuhashi and Sasamoto, however, because iron surgical needles with surface plating tend to become rusted over the short term, it was difficult for nurses to treat the needle before surgical operations.[71,72] Nurses had to select unrusted needles of the appropriate type for the surgery to be performed. Through this selection process, approximately 70%–80% of iron needles were thrown away. Next, nurses would wipe oil from the needle's surface and disinfect the surface to prepare for surgery. After surgery, the nurses would again spread oil on the needles.

Whereas such complicated quality controls had once been taken for granted, Masao Matsutani realised their inefficiency and expected an increased demand for difficult-to-rust-surgical needles.[73] Therefore, he decided to develop stainless surgical eyed needles, while continuing to manufacture iron surgical eyed needles, by investing money earned from the sale of iron surgical eyed needles into the development of stainless steel surgical eyed needles.[74] However, the development process was quite difficult. There were numerous problems developing stainless steel surgical eyed needles related to (1) the innovation of stainless steel as the raw material and (2) processing problems with the new stainless steel.[75] Masao Matsutani and his son, Kanji Matsutani, met these challenges not simultaneously but successively.

The first subject was the innovation of stainless steel as a raw material.[76] Because the most important drawback of using stainless steel as the material for surgical needles was its lack of hardness, the initial technological goal was to increase the hardness of stainless steel. To do so, it was necessary that he make a connection with a material wholesaler positioned in the upper stream of the supply chain, inform the material wholesaler of the necessary quality level for the materials to be produced by the manufacturers, and ask for that quality level.[77]

Kanji Matsutani, who is a son of the founder Masao Matsutani and was a student of Chiba University's engineering department, took the role of the negotiator because Masao Matsutani was engaged in the management.[78] Based on the oral history sources,[79] Kanji Matsutani expected stainless steel to be harder from drawing a wire through a small hole without the annealing process. If the goal was simply to make slim stainless steel, the annealing process was both indispensable and rational, but the calorification associated with the annealing process makes the stainless steel flexible. Therefore, the hard stainless steel that Kanji Matsutani requested could not be made through the annealing process.

Although at first, the materials manufacturers and the materials wholesalers resisted Kanji Matsutani's suggestion because they believed that wire drawing through a small hole without the annealing process would tear the materials to pieces, they changed their view through a series of repetitive negotiations.[80] First, the materials manufacturers introduced a method of drawing the stainless wire through a small hole in a washing powder in order to improve the slipperiness without the annealing process. Second, to increase the hardness still more, they lowered the factory temperature by confining the manufacturing period to cold winter days. To reduce manufacturing costs, the use of air conditioners was avoided. However, because the second remedy (depending upon the natural temperature) would destabilise the manufacture of surgical needles, they decided to secure three months' stock of materials. This stock did not cause cash-flow problems because the material cost represented only approximately 2 to 3% of all manufacturing costs,[81] as most of the manufacturing cost resulted from processing.[82]

Thus, the second subject was to improve the processing, and its main problem was the lack of capacity to process the hard stainless material ultra-finely.[83] When the material acquired its astonishing hardness, the ease of its processing was lost. When MANI succeeded in producing the worldwide prototype for stainless steel surgical needles in 1961,[84] it was a deficit product because of the hand-worked processing.[85] Therefore, to resolve the imbalance between innovative stainless material and old-fashioned processing, MANI launched a radical and innovative microfabrication project.[86] In 1965, Kanji Matsutani became a senior managing director of MANI and assumed the central role in the project because his father, Masao Matsutani, was busy with his responsibilities as top manager.[87]

According to Kanji Matsutani,[88] there were three difficult points in the processing; sharpening, punching for suturing, and curving. Although these difficulties were the result of the hardness of the stainless material, a method of heating the material to make it flexible could not be chosen because flexibility would be meaningless if the hardness was lost.

First, the problem of the sharpening process was solved by developing a new, cautious way to shave the material. In the case of traditional iron-eyed needles, the sharpening process is completed with three round-trip grindings per needle. However, because such shavings increase the material's heat, that option could not be selected. Eventually, Kanji Matsutani invented a device to gradually shave the stainless material, avoiding the generation of heat by conducting 60 round-trip grindings per needle.[89]

Second, the extremely difficult problem of punching was solved.[90] At first, although a way to punch the material using a hard punching machine was attempted, that machine was chipped in short order. Kanji Matsutani then changed the material of the punching machine, but it still did not work. However, he realised that the idea that the material should be punched in a single step was incorrect. Therefore, he invented a device to make a dent in the material once, invert it, and make a second dent. The process generated shear fracture between the dented parts and the intact parts. Next, the device thrust a rod into the dent and removed the residue. After the device was invented, the production of stainless eyed needles increased dramatically.[91]

Third, the problem of the curving process was resolved by inventing a new device.[92] As mentioned above, the curved shape is an important characteristic of surgical needles in terms of convenience for surgeons.[93] Previously, to curve a metal wire, it was generally necessary to immediately coil the wire around a shaft. However, because hard stainless steel material had great rigidity, the simple curving process did not work. After innumerable trial-and-error processes, Kanji Matsutani realized that the idea of immediately coiling the wire around a shaft could be changed; he invented a new device to gradually coil the wire around a shaft through a shifting belt.[94]

MANI obtained some patents on the process, which contributed to its competitive advantage, especially in the domestic market for stainless surgical needles from the 1970s to the 1980s.[95] Because MANI did not obtain patents on the hard stainless material, its competitors were able to acquire the material. However, MANI's competitors could not make stainless surgical eyed needles because they could not imitate MANI's processing technologies. In this regard, Kanji Matsutani noted:[96]

> Other companies did not make stainless-steel surgical eyed needles at that time because they could not process the hard stainless material. The harder the materials become, the more difficult they are to process. We made the materials hard as best we could. It was a serious problem for competitors.

In this way, MANI succeeded in creating stainless eyed needles that were not only resistant to rust but also hard.[97] By a rough estimate, the price per needle was approximately 11 yen, whereas the price per iron eyed needle was approximately 8 yen. A 3-yen difference per eyed needle did not represent a serious cost issue for most hospitals (particularly large ones).[98] Furthermore, hospitals could expect the price difference to decrease as stainless needles became more widely available. In addition, MANI's stainless eyed needles could solve the quality problems experienced by hospitals using iron eyed needles.[99]

However, despite the notable tendency associated with the high growth of the Japanese economy toward an increasing number of Japanese hospitals and beds (see Figure 2), the stainless steel eyed needles did not diffuse as rapidly as MANI expected (see Figure 1), primarily because most surgeons and nurses did not feel a need for them.[100] Because of the quality control requirements of medical instruments, including iron surgical needles, and the other countless tasks in support of doctors, even in the 1960s, nurses were working under harsh employment conditions and often could not allocate sufficient resources to nursing.[101] Therefore, throughout Japanese hospitals, they fought for higher wages and more paid leave in 1960 and 1961.[102] Their movement did not achieve significant results, however, because of strong resistance from hospital management,[103] and a lower class consciousness related to gender and nursing. Most nurses, who were women, were subordinated for cultural reasons.[104]

Therefore, general nurses did not recognize the need for improvements such as high quality, efficient surgical needles because they tended to believe that their work was naturally difficult. Even if they recognised it, they could not argue about the need for stainless eyed needles because they did not have the power to assert their opinion to the doctors.[105] Surgeons did not appreciate the quality problems related to the iron eyed needles because those needles were removed from the supply by nurses,[106] so surgeons typically did not see rusted surgical needles. Therefore, although some advanced surgeons who were originally interested in innovative surgical products began buying the stainless steel eyed needles following the product description by MANI (e.g. a surgeon at the Self-Defence Forces Central Hospital in Tokyo became interested in the stainless eyed needles), most doctors did not.[107]

Second challenge: Adding sutures to stainless steel eyeless needles (1966–1967)

In addition to the poor sales of MANI's stainless steel eyed needles, because Kanji Matsutani was not satisfied with MANI's subcontractor position and wished to focus on autonomous research and development related to surgical needles,[108] his passion for innovation in surgical needles did not diminish.[109] Because of the influence of the industrial structure,[110] MANI had to obey the orders of the primary wholesalers downstream in the supply chain. Indeed, MANI had to sell the innovative stainless surgical eyed needles not under MANI's original brand name but under a wholesaler's brand name because the wholesalers insisted that the stainless surgical eyed needles were merely an improved version of iron eyed needles, which were sold under the wholesalers' brand names. MANI had to comply with the wholesalers' demand and had to ask the wholesalers' opinion whenever it wanted to improve the stainless surgical needle.[111]

A breakthrough occurred when MANI sold its stainless eyeless needles with sutures under its own brand name, preventing any interference from wholesalers because the eyeless needle with suture was clearly different from the existing stainless needles. The world's first stainless surgical eyed needle, which MANI developed in the early 1960s, was not integrated with sutures in MANI's factory. Therefore, these needles had to be installed with sutures in each hospital.[112] However, around that time, iron eyeless needles with sutures were gradually becoming more widely used in the United States due to their hygiene and convenience. After learning about the situation in the United States through magazines and newspapers,

[113] Kanji Matsutani decided to make the eyeless needles with sutures from stainless steel by investing money from MANI's existing business, i.e. iron and stainless steel surgical eyed needles. This challenge could be divided into three parts[114]: (1) the method of integrating the needle part and the suture; (2) the method of sterilising the stainless eyeless needle with a suture; and (3) the method of selling the stainless eyeless needle with sutures.

The first problem for manufacturing the stainless eyeless needles was how to integrate the needle part and the suture. Initially, there was experimentation with an idea to drill the end of the needle part to make holes in which to screw the sutures, it was soon abandoned because the manufacturing cost was very high as a result of the drill's high wear rate. Next, a method of fitting a pipe to the end of needle and screwing the suture into the pipe with an adhesive agent was tried. However, the second method was also rejected due to vulnerability at the junction. Finally, another method was adopted: first a pursed pipe was made, a suture with a knot was screwed into the pipe, and the pipe was integrated with the suture. The integration issue was thus solved, at least for a time.[115]

The next technological problem was how to sterilise the stainless eyeless needle with a suture. Unlike surgical eyed needles, eyeless needles with a suture had to be sterilised at the time of shipment from the factory.[116] It was quite difficult to sterilise eyeless needles in hospitals because the suture was made from natural materials such as silk or sheep (or cow) gut,[117] and it tended to change the nature of heat sterilisation, which was the standard sterilisation process in hospitals.[118] Even if MANI purchased sterilised sutures, contamination by bacteria was inevitable because of the integration process with stainless needles. However, MANI did not have any knowledge and capability related to sterilisation because, since its founding, its domain had been metalworking.

Considering the literature on sterilisation, sterilisation through gamma ray irradiation was considered.[119] MANI developed a sterilisation process for the stainless eyeless needle with sutures using gamma ray irradiation through a collaborative study with the Japan Atomic Energy Research Institute, who became interested in the idea because it was seeking peaceful uses of radiation.[120] In 1966, a joint-development contract between MANI and the institute was signed and a stainless eyeless needle with sutures was completed.[121] In 1967, MANI launched the product under its original brand name[122] and almost simultaneously, Kanji Matsutani inherited MANI's top management position from his father.[123]

Key challenge: Increasing sales at home and abroad (1968–2016)

Based on two other oral histories,[124] against the wish of MANI, the wholesalers did not actively engage in sales of the stainless eyeless needle with sutures because it competed with the eyed needles sold under the wholesalers' brand names. Moreover, in those days, most Japanese surgeons were unfamiliar with eyeless needles with sutures.[125] Therefore, MANI's sales did not increase even after it developed the stainless eyeless needles with sutures. MANI tried to overcome this difficulty by collaborating with the Nihonshoji Corporation (Nihonshoji) based in Osaka, Japan (now part of Alfresa Holdings Corporation), which was not only a domestic but also an international trading and manufacturing company of medical instruments, with both a commercial and a manufacturing department.[126]

Although Nihonshoji began to develop eyeless needles at almost exactly the same time as MANI, they asked MANI to supply stainless needles and to jointly develop eyeless needles with sutures because they did not have the ability to make stainless eyeless needles and sterilise them using gamma ray irradiation, and as a result, their products experienced a rusting problem during alcohol sterilisation. There were two reasons MANI accepted these requests. First, the stainless eyeless needles with sutures suffered from low sales. It was therefore a sound deal for MANI to have Nihonshoji purchase only the stainless eyeless needle part. Second, Nihonshoji had both a manufacturing and a commercial department, and so MANI could expect that Nihonshoji would sell MANI's stainless eyeless needles with sutures worldwide.[127]

A new type of stainless eyeless needles that MANI developed was suitable for mass production by collaborating with Nihonshoji's manufacturing department. The main characteristic of this collaboration was the method of integrating the eyeless needle part and the suture. Whereas simple fitting was used to integrate the previous version of the product, resistance welding was utilised in the new version. The development of this integration process increased the production of stainless eyeless needles with sutures. Therefore, Nihonshoji found this new type of product profitable and deepened its relationship with MANI.[128]

Because Nihonshoji's stainless eyeless needles with sutures were soon diffused in Japanese hospitals through the efforts of Nihonshoji's sales force, it was natural that Kanji Matsutani felt that the product had the potential for overseas expansion and asked Nihonshoji's commercial department to collaborate in this. However, its reaction was not positive, and so he asked Nichimen Enterprise (Sojitz Corporation, today) to sell the stainless eyeless needle part. As a result, MANI sold its eyeless stainless needles to a medical device manufacturer in the United States. As MANI's sales volume increased because of its deal in the United States, the commercial department of Nihonshoji asked MANI to sell the stainless eyeless needles.[129] In the 1960s, most sutures were made from sheep or cattle gut,[130] and so there were many surgical suture manufacturers in Brazil, Argentina, Australia, and Mexico, all of which were famous for stock farming. As the commercial department of Nihonshoji promoted MANI's stainless eyeless needle part to surgical suture manufacturers,[131] the product was exported to various countries.[132] The foundation for MANI's high foreign sales to total sales ratio today was established during this period (e.g. even in 1985, the ratio was slightly below 60%;[133] in 1996, it exceeded 60%;[134] in 2007, it was 68%[135]).

Exporting its products also helped MANI to improve. Approximately three years after the beginning of its collaboration with Nihonshoji, a vulnerability in the welded parts in the body of the stainless eyeless needle and the pipe was reported from a Brazilian surgical suture manufacturer. Although MANI conducted sampling inspections, it had not detected this vulnerability. As a result, the integration method between the needle part and the pipe part was radically reconsidered, returning to the question of how to make a hole in the body of the stainless needles.[136] Kanji Matsutani described his feelings at the time thus:[137]

> The conjugation of two parts inevitably creates some defects. In architectural structures, there are many parts of conjugation. If one of the parts of conjugation had something wrong, the other parts can support the entire structure. However, in the case of surgical needles, there is only one part of conjugation. Therefore, we cannot fail... if there were any defects, serious problems will occur in surgery. That is why we had to seek a way to dig a hole in one material.

The technological target was to make a 30-μm hole in the stainless needle body,[138] but MANI's drilling device could only drill a hole approximately 0.4 mm deep (400 μm).[139] Therefore, an alternative method of drilling was sought, and focus centred on laser technology.[140] Eventually, in 1971, the problem was solved by utilising the laser technology of

Toshiba,[141] which was one of the leading technology companies in Japan.[142] The price of the device was approximately 7 million Japanese Yen (based on the consumer price index; this sum would be 21 million Japanese Yen, or 189,000 US dollars, in 2016).[143] According to Kanji Matsutani, some executives of MANI's local competitors (SMEs) derided his decision to purchase such an expensive device for the production of low-priced surgical needles.[144] However, the laser device's cutting technology increased not only the quality but also the production of MANI's stainless eyeless needle. Because MANI's local competitors could not immediately buy the same machine because it was too expensive in comparison to the size of their businesses,[145] MANI was able to enjoy a first-mover advantage.

Starting in the 1970s, the challenge of entering new product markets was pursued. First, although MANI entered the general surgical knife product market in the early 1970s, it was defeated in technological competition with knife manufacturers skilled at sheet metal working. MANI could not use its core capability in the microfabrication of stainless steel wire in the general surgical knife product market.[146] Thus, in 1976, MANI developed the dental broach, a small, dental root canal treatment instrument, taking advantage of its capability in the microfabrication of stainless steel wire and thereby entering the dental care product market.[147] MANI subsequently entered other dental care product markets one after another. MANI introduced the dental reamer, a spiral-shaped dental care instrument, in 1979, the paste carrier in 1984, and the diamond-coated stainless steel bar for removing decay in 1989.[148] MANI also developed a technology to coat various tooth cutting tools with diamond material in 1991.[149] These entrances into the dental market further contributed to the firm's growth.[150] In 1998, MANI entered the ophthalmologic knife market because the technological capabilities of the microfabrication of hard stainless steel that MANI had previously developed could be applied to the manufacturing of small ophthalmologic knives.[151] These capabilities contributed to increases in sales and operating income (see Figure 1).

Moreover, in the 1980s, a change in part of Japan's social structure boosted the sales of MANI's stainless needles: the empowerment of nurses in hospitals. In the past, Japanese hospital nurses had accepted their low status and endured difficult tasks such as managing iron surgical needles that rust easily.[152] In 1978, however, the Japanese Nursing Association began lobbying for improvements in nurses' working conditions.[153] Nurses also benefitted from an unintended consequence of a 1985 law that was passed requiring prefectures to prepare medical plans. Because the law curtailed hospitals' right to change the number of hospital beds beginning in 1987, it triggered a last-minute increase in the number of hospitals.[154] From 1986 to 1988, the number of hospital beds increased by 100,422,[155] and the number of nurses increased by 55,063.[156] Although the compound annual growth rate of the number of nurses in that period (4.21%) exceeded the growth rate of beds (3.22%),[157,158] most nurses felt that the disparity between the number of beds and number of nurses was becoming seriously strained.[159] As Table 2 shows, the nurse-to-bed ratio, indicating the number of nurses per hospital bed, was clearly lower in Japan than in other developed countries.

As a result of the surge in beds, the shortage of nurses became more serious, and nurses complained and became angry. For instance, the Japan Federation of the Medical Worker's Unions started to fight for improvement in nurses' conditions, collecting 76,635 signatures in 1988.[160] According to a nurse with a great deal of experience, these dynamics improved nurses' position in hospitals in the 1980s.[161]

Table 2. Comparison of nurse-to-bed ratios among developed countries (headcounts).

Country	Japan	Canada	France	Germany	Italy	United States
Nurse-to-Bed Ratio	0.43	1.00	0.58	0.66	1.11	1.12
Year	1988	1988	1997	2000	2003	1991

Source: Statistics and Information Department, Minister's Secretariat, Ministry of Health, Labour and Welfare. "Byosho no Shuruibetsu Byoinbyoshosu" [Hospital Beds by Kind 1910-2004]; Statistics and Information Department, Minister's Secretariat, Ministry of Health, Labour and Welfare. "Iryo Kankeisyasu" [Medical Care Personnel 1874-2004]; Quandl, "Canada, Canada, total hospital beds, nurse to bed ratio"; Quandl, "France, total hospital beds, nurse to bed ratio"; Quandl, "Germany, total hospital beds, nurse to bed ratio"; Quandl, "Italy, total hospital beds, nurse to bed ratio"; Quandl, "United States, total hospital beds, nurse to bed ratio".

Note. The data for France, Germany, Italy, and the United States were the oldest available data. Data for the United Kingdom were not available. The number of nurses in Japan includes assistant nurses (the share of assistant nurses in 1988 was approximately 38.4%).

The improvement in the nurses' position increased the demand for readily controlled stainless surgical needles (i.e. stainless surgical eyed needles or stainless eyeless surgical needles with sutures), for which MANI had various technological capabilities. The increasing demand for stainless eyed and eyeless needles weakened the primary wholesalers' negotiating power over MANI; they now had no choice but to purchase MANI's products.[162] In this manner, the dynamics of the nurses' social position in Japanese hospitals and the success of MANI's overseas expansion changed the industrial structure of the surgical needle business and resulted in a notable increase in MANI's sales from the late 1980 to the 2000s (see Figure 1). In 1985, MANI's domestic market share of surgical needles production reached approximately 60%, and its export market share reached approximately 90%.[163] Its market share of dental care products in the Western Bloc was approximately 17% in 1988,[164] and in the domestic market, its share was approximately 30% in 1993.[165] Although the number of employees in 1988 was 120,[166] it reached 140 in 1990.[167]

From the late 1980s to 1990s, MANI continued investing in cutting-edge research and innovation. In 1988, MANI employed one researcher who learned microfabrication techniques in graduate school.[168] Because Kanji Matsutani was commended by the Japanese government for implementing innovative technologies for microfabrication,[169] and the well-equipped R&D department of MANI was already known among microfabrication researchers,[170] MANI could attract skilled human resources for R&D, despite its location and small size. That year, MANI spent 7.2% of its sales on research and development.[171] In 1991, these investments led to the development of a new stainless steel material for surgical needles with greater hardness,[172] and a surgical stapler that used specialised staples to close skin wounds for the United States and European markets.[173] Also in 1991, MANI developed the smallest surgical needles in the world for brain surgery. These needles measured 27 µm in diameter.[174] MANI drastically reduced its manufacturing costs and the price of its surgical needles. The manufacturing cost of surgical eyed needles decreased by 30% in 1994 by fostering communication between the R&D and production departments, introducing new technology in the processing operation,[175] and building a new factory for surgical needles.[176] The price of surgical needles for export was discounted by 35% from the conventional average price in the world in 1995.[177] Thus, MANI developed both the highest product quality in the world,[178] and sold it at the lowest price, two accomplishments that were difficult for competitors to match. The number of employees reached 220 in 1996.[179] In 2003, this number increased to 300 (of these, approximately 30 were microfabrication researchers), and R&D expenditure increased to 8.5% of sales.[180]

During this period, MANI promoted global expansion because, as the tendency to decrease the numbers of hospitals and beds in 1990s indicated (see Figure 2), the domestic market was shrinking. As a result, MANI became a global company. There were 58 export destination countries even in 1985,[181] and this number increased to over 60 in 1994.[182] Additionally, manufacturing subsidiaries were established in Vietnam in 1996,[183] and Myanmar in 1999,[184] and the overseas production ratio reached 6.7% in 2003.[185] The number of consolidated employees reached 2,555 in 2011 (287 non-consolidated employees).[186] Sales subsidiaries were established in Vietnam in 2010 and in China in 2012.[187] MANI was listed in the first section of the Tokyo Stock Exchange in 2012. In 2015, all shares and ownership of Schütz Dental GmbH and GDF Gesellschaft für dentale Forschung und Innovationen GmbH in Germany were acquired by MANI to extend the dental care product division.[188]

Discussion and conclusion

In the medical instruments sector, a bi-polar structure can be observed. At one end of the spectrum are the 'giants,' global companies such as Johnson & Johnson. At the other end are numerous SMEs. In this context, MANI is an example of a group of specialised SMEs. MANI has become one of the most successful SMEs by developing from a small metalworking workshop and maintaining a strong position in the shadow of the giants.

This article has explained MANI's success beyond a simplistic story focused on R&D, technological inventions and innovation, which has been the predominant narrative in the existing literature on SMEs. The explanation presented here attends to long-term dynamics and repeated processes rather than a one-shot phenomenon – processes that involved the formation of an imbalance and subsequent, emergent strategic solutions to overcome the imbalance by tackling each problem in turn.

Masao Matsutani and Kanji Matsutani incessantly worked on the formation of imbalances. These imbalances can be categorised into the following two types: (1) those between the Matsutanis' vision of high-level conceptual technological targets and the company's existing technological capabilities[189]; and (2) those between the various components required to manufacture the new products.[190] For example, while MANI originally manufactured only iron surgical eyed needles (it was received wisdom that the raw material for surgical eyed needles should be iron), Masao Matsutani developed a bold vision that MANI would manufacture stainless steel surgical eyed needles. This was the first imbalance. Kanji Matsutani then divided the technological gaps between the goals and the existing substantive technological capabilities into sub-problems. For instance, for the initial stainless surgical eyed needle project, he first broke down the problems into a material issue and a processing issue. He then solved the material problem first by creating an innovative stainless material, which resulted in a technological gap between the materials and the current method of processing. This was the second imbalance.

MANI attempted to resolve the imbalances in turn by mobilising the necessary resources through various channels. For example, the company mobilised the necessary money from public financing and existing businesses. It also improved its technological capabilities through collaborations with outside organisations, i.e. the Atomic Energy Research Institute and Toshiba. The development of capabilities to correct imbalances produced unique technological resources,[191] in particular, the microfabrication of stainless steel, that MANI's competitors could not easily imitate.

Four main critical factors explain why MANI was able undertake this long-term process. First, the initial technological challenges regarding surgical needle manufacturing created MANI's original core capabilities of microfabrication, which supported the company's overall growth. These capabilities enabled MANI to create highly competitive and profitable products. Its good reputation as a high technology company also attracted the necessary R&D human resources. A second factor concerns the leadership of top management with a strong motivation to expand MANI's operations. Leadership at MANI has never been satisfied with the existing situation and has continued to identify new goals one after another and to invest in the required resources to attain these goals. Although the influence of individual leadership should not be overestimated in historical description, it also should not be underestimated when analysing SMEs' continuous growth from the perspective of the dynamic imbalance mechanism. Third, MANI has been a small organisation since its foundation. Small organisations tend to pursue an innovative goal relatively quickly and to stretch toward the achievement of that goal compared with large companies because the organisational structures of SMEs are less rigid and institutionalised than those of large companies.[192] Therefore, the top leaders of SMEs may find it relatively easy to pursue a fairly new and different goal. A fourth factor is the influence of historical contexts. For example, the expanding hospital market in Japan during a period of high-economic growth supported MANI's confidential investment practices. As discussed, the social structural change concerning the position of nurses also influenced MANI's growth. With improvements in the position of nurses in Japanese hospitals, Japanese nurses were no longer required to manage the inefficient use of iron surgical needles because they preferred MANI's stainless surgical needles. They were able to assert their preferences.

Now, we can return a broader issue: how an SME survives and succeeds in an industry dominated by large companies, such as the medical instruments sector. Overall, this account provides a contribution to the advancement of this research. First, unlike many previous studies, this article illuminates the dynamic and repetitive processes employed by a resource-starved company to establish and maintain a competitive advantage. Although SMEs might swing for the fences, many small efforts can lead SMEs to incredible achievements. Second, whereas previous studies have focused on external influences from a dense network (industry cluster) or intensive competition, this article sheds light on an internally driven dynamic imbalance process. Indeed, the help of others, pressure from competition, and structural change can boost the success of SMEs. However, internal driving forces, i.e. the agency of entrepreneurs, is indispensable to realise the dynamic and repetitive processes of SMEs. Additional historical studies may reveal whether the dynamic imbalance framework proves equally useful in explaining the growth and success of other SMEs.

Notes

1. 'Tsuisoroku: Matsutani Masao' [Reminiscences of Masao Matsutani].
2. 'Matsutani Seisakujo Intanetto' [Promotion by the Internet].
3. Matsutani, K., Personal Communication via E-mail (May 8, 2017).
4. Noguchi, 'Seicho e no Sekkeizu' [Blueprint for Growth]; The Stock Research Center, 'Horisutikku Kigyo Repoto' [Holistic Corporate Report].
5. MANI, Homepage of MANI. Accessed May 8, 2017. http://www.mani.co.jp/
6. Cunningham et al., 'Medical Device Sectoral Overview'.
7. Ibid.

8. Pullen, et al., 'Open Innovation in Practice'.
9. Ibid.
10. Zemtsov, et al., 'Uncovering Regional Clustering'.
11. Donzé, 'Japanese Medical Instruments Industry'.
12. Takeuchi, 'Tokyo ni Okeru Iryo' [Regional Structure of Medical].
13. Hall, et al., 'Innovation and productivity'.
14. Sass, 'Internationalisation of innovative SMEs'.
15. Ibid.
16. Yanagawa, 'MANI Kabushikigaisha' [Mani Inc].
17. Matsutani and Yanagawa, 'MANI Matsutani Kanji' [Interview to Kanji Matsutani].
18. Japan Finance Corporation for Small and Medium Enterprises, *Hasso to Gijutsu* [Innovative Companies].
19. Nikkei Top Leader, *Kiseki no Seizogyo* [Miracle Manufacturing Companies].
20. Kipping et al., 'Analyzing and Interpreting Historical'.
21. Matsutani, K., Brief Explanation of MANI (February 22, 2016).
22. Hirschman, *The Strategy of Economic Growth*; Itami and Roehl, *Mobilizing Invisible Assets*; Rosenberg, 'The Direction of Technological Change'.
23. Hirschman, *The Strategy of Economic Growth*.
24. Japan Finance Corporation for Small and Medium Enterprises, *Hasso to Gijutsu* [Innovative Companies]; Nikkei Top Leader, *Kiseki no Seizogyo* [Miracle Manufacturing Companies].
25. Kipping et al., 'Analyzing and Interpreting Historical'.
26. MANI, Homepage of MANI. Accessed on May 8, 2017. http://www.mani.co.jp/
27. MANI. 'Yukashoken Hokokusho 2016 [Securities Report 2016]'.
28. The Stock Research Center, 'Horisutikku Kigyo Repoto' [Holistic Corporate Report].
29. Matsuzaki, 'Eigyo Riekiritsu 34%' [Operating Profit Rate is 34%].
30. 'Tsuisoroku: Matsutani Masao' [Reminiscences of Masao Matsutani].
31. 'Kenkyu Kyoten o Miru' [Observation for Research]; 'Shikayo Daiya Bar' [MANI Entered the Dental].
32. Matsutani, K., Brief Explanation of MANI (February 22, 2016).
33. Freidin and Marshall, *Illustrated Guide*.
34. 'Fukyo ni Makenai' [Against the Recession].
35. Furuhashi and Sasamoto, *Zusetsu Shujutsu Kikai* [Everything about Surgical Instruments].
36. Nikkei Top Leader, *Kiseki no Seizogyo* [Miracle Manufacturing Companies]; Oguchi, 'Ningen Hakken 1' [The President of MANI Vol. 1].
37. Freidin and Marshall, *Illustrated Guide*; Furuhashi and Sasamoto, *Zusetsu Shujutsu Kikai* [Everything about Surgical Instruments].
38. Matsutani, K., Brief Explanation of MANI (February 22, 2016).
39. Freidin and Marshall, *Illustrated Guide*; Furuhashi and Sasamoto, *Zusetsu Shujutsu Kikai* [Everything about Surgical Instruments].
40. MANI. 'Yukashoken Hokokusho 2014' [Securities Report 2014]; 'Yukashoken Hokokusho 2015' [Securities Report 2015]; 'Yukashoken Hokokusho 2016' [Securities Report 2016].
41. MANI. 'Yukashoken Hokokusho 2016' [Securities Report 2016].
42. The Stock Research Center, 'Horisutikku Kigyo Repoto' [Holistic Corporate Report].
43. MANI. 'Yukashoken Hokokusho 2014' [Securities Report 2014].
44. Matsutani, K., Personal Communication via E-mail (May 8, 2017).
45. Ibid.
46. 'Habataku Bencha' [Successful Venture]; Japan Finance Corporation for Small and Medium Enterprises, *Hasso to Gijutsu* [Innovative Companies]; Matsutani, K., Personal Interview (January 15, 2016; February 22, 2016); Matsutani, M., Personal Interview (March 22, 2016); Oguchi, 'Ningen Hakken 2' [The President of MANI Vol. 2].
47. Miyamoto et al., *Nihon Keieishi* [Japanese Business History].
48. Fukunaga, *Nihon Byoinshi* [The History of Japanese Hospitals].
49. Saiseikai Utsunomiya Hospital, *Soritsu 15 Shunen Kinen* [The Memorial 15th Anniversary].
50. Fukunaga, *Nihon Byoinshi* [The History of Japanese Hospitals].
51. Ibid.

52. Saiseikai Utsunomiya Hospital, *Soritsu 15 Shunen Kinen* [The Memorial 15th Anniversary].
53. Sakakibara, *Tabu ni Mesu* [Surgeon Broke the Taboo].
54. Shimazaki, *Nihon no Iryo* [Japanese Medical Care].
55. Tochigi Prefecture, *Tochigi Prefecture*.
56. Tochigi Shimbunsha, *Tochigi Nenkan 1957* [Yearbook of Tochigi Prefecture 1957].
57. Tochigi Shimbunsha, *Tochigiken Shoko Yoran* [Commerce and Industry Handbook].
58. 'Tsuisoroku: Matsutani Masao' [Reminiscences of Masao Matsutani].
59. Sakai, Personal Interview (February 17, 2016).
60. Matsutani, K., Personal Interview (January 15, 2016; February 22, 2016); Matsutani, M., Personal Interview (March 22, 2016).
61. Fujikeizai, *Ryutsu Mappu* [Overview of Distribution in 1977]; Matsutani, M., Personal Interview (March 22, 2016); Sakai, Personal Interview (February 17, 2016).
62. Fujikeizai, *Ryutsu Mappu* [Overview of Distribution in 1977].
63. Sakai, Personal Interview (February 17, 2016).
64. Fujikeizai, *Ryutsu Mappu* [Overview of Distribution in 1977].
65. Fujikeizai, *Ryutsu Mappu* [Overview of Distribution in 1977]; Matsutani, K., Personal Interview (January 15, 2016; February 22, 2016); Matsutani, M., Personal Interview (March 22, 2016); Sakai, Personal Interview (February 17, 2016).
66. Matsutani, K., Personal Interview (January 15, 2016; February 22, 2016); Matsutani, M., Personal Interview (March 22, 2016); Sakai, Personal Interview (February 17, 2016).
67. Freidin and Marshall, *Illustrated Guide*; Furuhashi and Sasamoto, *Zusetsu Shujutsu Kikai* [Everything about Surgical Instruments]; Nomoto, Personal Interview (March 18, 2016); Sakai, Personal Interview (February 17, 2016).
68. Furuhashi and Sasamoto, *Zusetsu Shujutsu Kikai* [Everything about Surgical Instruments]; Morino, 'Shugyoku no Chusho Kigyo' [Excellent Small].
69. Matsutani, K., Personal Interview (January 15, 2016; February 22, 2016); Sakai, Personal Interview (February 17, 2016).
70. Matsutani, K., Personal Interview (January 15, 2016; February 22, 2016).
71. Hagane, Personal Interview (March 18, 2016); Matsutani, K., Personal Interview (January 15, 2016; February 22, 2016); Matsutani, M., Personal Interview (March 22, 2016); Nomoto, Personal Interview (March 18, 2016).
72. Furuhashi and Sasamoto, *Zusetsu Shujutsu Kikai* [Everything about Surgical Instruments].
73. 'Tsuisoroku: Matsutani Masao' [Reminiscences of Masao Matsutani].
74. Matsutani, K., Personal Interview (January 15, 2016; February 22, 2016); Matsutani, M., Personal Interview (March 22, 2016).
75. 'Habataku Bencha' [Successful Venture]; 'Tsuisoroku: Matsutani Masao' [Reminiscences of Masao Matsutani].
76. Matsutani, K., Personal Interview (January 15, 2016; February 22, 2016); Morino, 'Shugyoku no Chusho Kigyo' [Excellent Small].
77. Morino, 'Shugyoku no Chusho Kigyo' [Excellent Small]; 'Tsuisoroku: Matsutani Masao' [Reminiscences of Masao Matsutani].
78. Matsutani, K., Personal Interview (January 15, 2016; February 22, 2016); Oguchi, 'Ningen Hakken 2' [The President of MANI Vol. 2].
79. Matsutani, K., Personal Interview (January 15, 2016; February 22, 2016).
80. Ibid.
81. 'Kitakanto no Seichokigyo' [A Growing Company].
82. 'Tochigiken Kigyo' [A Company in Tochigi].
83. 'Habataku Bencha' [Successful Venture]; 'Kenkyu Kyoten o Miru' [Observation for Research]; Noda, 'Keieisha Intabyu' [CEO Interview].
84. 'Habataku Bencha' [Successful Venture].
85. Matsutani, K., Personal Interview (January 15, 2016; February 22, 2016).
86. 'Habataku Bencha' [Successful Venture]; 'Kenkyu Kyoten o Miru' [Observation for Research]; Morino, 'Shugyoku no Chusho Kigyo' [Excellent Small].

87. Matsutani, K., Personal Interview (January 15, 2016; February 22, 2016); Noda, 'Keieisha Intabyu' [CEO Interview].
88. Matsutani, K., Personal Interview (January 15, 2016; February 22, 2016).
89. Matsutani, K., Personal Interview (January 15, 2016; February 22, 2016); Morino, 'Shugyoku no Chusho Kigyo' [Excellent Small].
90. 'Habataku Bencha' [Successful Venture].
91. Matsutani, K., Personal Interview (January 15, 2016; February 22, 2016).
92. Ibid.
93. Furuhashi and Sasamoto, *Zusetsu Shujutsu Kikai* [Everything about Surgical Instruments].
94. Matsutani, K., Personal Interview (January 15, 2016; February 22, 2016).
95. 'Kenkyu Kyoten o Miru' [Observation for Research]; 'Habataku Bencha' [Successful Venture].
96. Matsutani, K., Personal Interview (January 15, 2016).
97. Morino, 'Shugyoku no Chusho Kigyo' [Excellent Small]; 'Tsuisoroku: Matsutani Masao' [Reminiscences of Masao Matsutani].
98. Hagane, Personal Interview (March 18, 2016); Nomoto, Personal Interview (March 18, 2016); Sakai, Personal Interview (February 17, 2016).
99. Ibid.
100. Hagane, Personal Interview (March 18, 2016); Nomoto, Personal Interview (March 18, 2016).
101. Ishihara, *Kango 20 Nenshi* [Twenty Years of Nursing History]; Nomoto, Personal Interview (March 18, 2016).
102. Hashioka, 'Sengo no Kango Rodo' [What Labor Movements]; Ishihara, *Kango 20 Nenshi* [Twenty Years of Nursing History].
103. Hashioka, 'Sengo no Kango Rodo' [What Labor Movements].
104. Kameyama, *Kangofu to Ishi* [Nurses and Doctors].
105. Hagane, Personal Interview (March 18, 2016); Nomoto, Personal Interview (March 18, 2016).
106. Furuhashi and Sasamoto, *Zusetsu Shujutsu Kikai* [Everything about Surgical Instruments].
107. Matsutani, K., Personal Interview (January 15, 2016; February 22, 2016); Sakai, Personal Interview (February 17, 2016).
108. Matsutani, K., Personal Interview (January 15, 2016; February 22, 2016).
109. Noda, 'Keieisha Intabyu' [CEO Interview]; Oguchi, 'Ningen Hakken 3' [The President of MANI Vol. 3].
110. Porter, *Competitive Strategy*.
111. Matsutani, K., Personal Interview (January 15, 2016; February 22, 2016); Sakai, Personal Interview (February 17, 2016).
112. Furuhashi and Sasamoto, *Zusetsu Shujutsu Kikai* [Everything about Surgical Instruments]; Hagane, Personal Interview (March 18, 2016); Nomoto, Personal Interview (March 18, 2016); Sakai, Personal Interview (February 17, 2016).
113. Matsutani, K., Personal Communication via E-mail (May 8, 2017).
114. Matsutani, K., Brief Explanation of MANI (February 22, 2016); Matsutani, K., Personal Interview (January 15, 2016; February 22, 2016).
115. Ibid.
116. Hagane, Personal Interview (March 18, 2016); Matsutani, K., Personal Interview (January 15, 2016; February 22, 2016); Nomoto, Personal Interview (March 18, 2016).
117. Freidin and Marshall, *Illustrated Guide*.
118. Hagane, Personal Interview (March 18, 2016); Matsutani, K., Personal Interview (January 15, 2016; February 22, 2016); Nomoto, Personal Interview (March 18, 2016).
119. Matsutani, K., Personal Interview (January 15, 2016; February 22, 2016).
120. Ibid.
121. MANI, Homepage of MANI. Accessed May 8, 2017. http://www.mani.co.jp/
122. Matsutani, K., Personal Interview (January 15, 2016; February 22, 2016); Sakai, Personal Interview (2016, February 17).
123. Matsutani, K., Personal Interview (January 15, 2016; February 22, 2016).
124. Matsutani, K., Personal Interview (January 15, 2016; February 22, 2016); Sakai, Personal Interview (February 17, 2016).

125. Freidin and Marshall, *Illustrated Guide*; Furuhashi and Sasamoto, *Zusetsu Shujutsu Kikai* [Everything about Surgical Instruments].
126. Matsutani, K., Brief Explanation of MANI (February 22, 2016).
127. Matsutani, K., Brief Explanation of MANI (February 22, 2016); Matsutani, K., Personal Interview (January 15, 2016; February 22, 2016).
128. Ibid.
129. Ibid.
130. Freidin and Marshall, *Illustrated Guide*.
131. Matsutani, K., Personal Interview (January 15, 2016; February 22, 2016).
132. 'Habataku Bencha' [Successful Venture].
133. Ibid.
134. 'Matsutani Seisakujo Intanetto' [Promotion by the Internet].
135. Porter prize, 'MANI Kabushikigaisha' [MANI Inc.].
136. Matsutani, K., Brief Explanation of MANI (February 22, 2016); Matsutani, K., Personal Interview (January 15, 2016; February 22, 2016).
137. Matsutani, K., Personal Interview (February 22, 2016).
138. 'Habataku Bencha' [Successful Venture]; Japan Finance Corporation for Small and Medium Enterprises, *Hasso to Gijutsu* [Innovative Companies]; 'Kenkyu Kyoten o Miru' [Observation for Research].
139. Matsutani, K., Personal Interview (January 15, 2016; February 22, 2016).
140. Oguchi, 'Ningen Hakken 3' [The President of MANI Vol. 3].
141. Ibid.
142. Shimoda, *Reiza to Butsuri* [Razer and Physics].
143. Matsutani, K., Personal Interview (January 15, 2016; February 22, 2016); Oguchi, 'Ningen Hakken 3' [The President of MANI Vol. 3].
144. Matsutani, K., Brief Explanation of MANI (February 22, 2016); Matsutani, K., Personal Interview (January 15, 2016; February 22, 2016).
145. Ibid.
146. Oguchi, 'Ningen Hakken 4' [The President of MANI Vol. 4].
147. 'Shinkojo o Kansei Sogyo' [MANI Has Completed a New Factory].
148. 'Shikayo Daiya Bar' [MANI Entered the Dental].
149. 'Mushiba o Daiya' [Coating Technology].
150. 'Shikayo Daiya Bar' [MANI Entered the Dental].
151. Oguchi, 'Ningen Hakken 4' [The President of MANI Vol. 4].
152. Kameyama, *Kangofu to Ishi* [Nurses and Doctors]; Nomoto, Personal Interview (March 18, 2016).
153. Tanaka, 'Kangoshi no Seikatsu' [Life and Labor of Nurses].
154. Ibid.
155. Statistics and Information Department, Minister's Secretariat, Ministry of Health, Labour and Welfare. 'Byosho no Shuruibetsu Byoinbyoshosu' [Hospital Beds by Kind 1910–2004].
156. Statistics and Information Department, Minister's Secretariat, Ministry of Health, Labour and Welfare. 'Iryo Kankeisyasu' [Medical Care Personnel 1874–2004].
157. Ibid.
158. Statistics and Information Department, Minister's Secretariat, Ministry of Health, Labour and Welfare. 'Byosho no Shuruibetsu Byoinbyoshosu' [Hospital Beds by Kind 1910–2004].
159. Tanaka, 'Kangoshi no Seikatsu' [Life and Labor of Nurses].
160. Ibid.
161. Nomoto, Personal Interview (March 18, 2016).
162. Matsutani, K., Personal Interview (January 15, 2016; February 22, 2016); Sakai, Personal Interview (February 17, 2016).
163. 'Habataku Bencha' [Successful Venture].
164. 'Kagicho no Chumoku Hatsumei' [Science and Technology Agency].
165. 'Shika Chiryoki Innai Kansen' [Preventing Hospital Infections].
166. Noda, 'Keieisha Intabyu' [CEO Interview].
167. 'Kitakanto no Seichokigyo' [A Growing Company].

168. Noda, 'Keieisha Intabyu' [CEO Interview].
169. Ibid.
170. 'Kenkyu Kyoten o Miru' [Observation for Research].
171. Noda, 'Keieisha Intabyu' [CEO Interview].
172. 'Shinsozai Tsukai Hogoshin' [New Material Surgical Needles].
173. 'Hochikisu' [Suture Stapler].
174. 'Sekai Saisho no Hogoshin' [The Smallest Surgical Needle].
175. 'Iryokiki no Matsutani Seisakujo' [MANI Will Reduce Manufacturing Costs].
176. 'Shin Kiyohara Kojo' [The Construction of the New Kiyohara Factory].
177. 'Tochigiken Kigyo' [A Company in Tochigi].
178. Nikkei Top Leader, *Kiseki no Seizogyo* [Miracle Manufacturing Companies].
179. 'Tobidasu Chiho Kigyo' [Progressive Local Company].
180. 'Fukyo ni Makenai' [Against the Recession].
181. 'Habataku Bencha' [Successful Venture].
182. 'Iryokiki no Matsutani Seisakujo' [MANI Will Reduce Manufacturing Costs].
183. 'Tobidasu Chiho Kigyo' [Progressive Local Company].
184. 'Shin Wagasha no Senryaku' [Our New Corporate Strategy].
185. 'Fukyo ni Makenai' [Against the Recession].
186. Noguchi, 'Seicho e no Sekkeizu' [Blueprint for Growth].
187. Takeda, 'MANI Tsugi no Suteji' [MANI toward the Next Stage].
188. 'Doku Shika Chiryo' [MANI Acquired All Shares]; MANI, 'Yukashoken Hokokusho 2015' [Securities Report 2015].
189. Itami and Roehl, *Mobilizing Invisible Assets*.
190. Rosenberg, 'The Direction of Technological Change'.
191. Barney, 'Firm Resources'; Barney, *Gaining and Sustaining*.
192. Leonard-Barton, 'Core Capabilities and Core Rigidities'.

Acknowledgements

I would like to thank the editor Pierre-Yves Donzé and two anonymous reviewers for their valuable comments and suggestions. I am also grateful to Matthias Kipping for his constructive feedback on earlier versions of this article.

Disclosure statement

No potential conflict of interest was reported by the author.

ORCID

Ken Sakai http://orcid.org/0000-0003-2359-1408

References

Barney, J. "Firm Resources and Sustained Competitive Advantage." *Journal of Management* 17, no. 1 (1991): 99–120. doi:10.1177/014920639101700108

Barney, J. *Gaining and Sustaining Competitive Advantage* 2nd ed. Upper Saddle River, NJ: Pearson Education, 2002.

Cunningham, J., B. Dolan, D. Kelly, and C. Young. (2015). *Medical Device Sectoral Overview, Galway City and County Economic and Industrial Baseline Study*. Galway: Whitaker Institute for Innovation & Societal Change - NUI Galway, 2015 Accessed May 8, 2017. http://galwaydashboard.ie/publications/medical-sector.pdf

"Doku Shika Chiryo Kigu Meika Nisha o Baishu: MANI [MANI Acquired All Shares of Two German Dental Products Manufacturers]." 2015. *The Nihon Keizai Shimbun*, March 19.

Donzé, P. Y. The beginnings of the Japanese medical instruments industry and the adaptation of western medicine to Japan, 1880–1937. *Australian Economic History Review* 56, no. 3 (2016):272–291. doi:10.1111/aehr.12095

Freidin, J., and V. Marshall. *Illustrated Guide to Surgical Practice*. London: Churchill Livingstone, 1984.

Fujikeizai. *77 Ryutsu Mappu No. 9: Iyakuhin Iryohin Hen Higashinihon* [Overview of Distribution in 1977: Medical Instruments, East Japan] Tokyo: Fujikeizai, 1977.

Fukunaga, H. *Nihon Byoinshi* [The History of Japanese Hospitals]. Tokyo: Pilar Press, 2014.

"Fukyo ni Makenai Kocho Kigyo Keieisha Intabyu [Against the Recession: Interview of Successful Company Executives]." 2003. *Shimotsuke Shimbun*, January 10.

Furuhashi, S., and E. Sasamoto *Zusetsu Shujutsu Kikai no Subete 1 Kisoteki Kikai* [Everything about Surgical Instruments, No.1, Basic Instruments]. Tokyo: Ishiyaku Publishers, 1968.

"Habataku Bencha: Hogoshin de Sekai Ichi no Za Matsutani Seisakujo [Successful Venture: The Best in the Surgical Needle Market: MANI]." 1985. *The Nihonkeizai Shimbun*, July 20.

Hall, B. H., F. Lotti, and J. Mairesse Innovation and productivity in SMEs: Empirical evidence for Italy. *Small Business Economics* 33, no. 1 (2009): 13–33. doi:10.1007/s11187-009-9184-8

Hashioka, T. "Sengo no Kango Rodo Undo ga Shimeshita Mono [What Labor Movements of Nurses after World War II Indicated]." In *Kensho: Sengo Kango no 50 Nen* [Verification: 50 Years of Nursing after World War II], edited by Nihon Kango Rekishi Gakkai [Japan Society of Nursing History], 174–194. Tokyo: Medical-Friend, 1998.

Hirschman, A. O. *The Strategy of Economic Growth*. New Haven, CT: Yale University Press, 1958.

"Hochikisu Gata no Hifu Hogogu: Matsutani Seisakujo [Suture Stapler: MANI]." 1990. *The Nihon Keizai Shimbun*, May 3.

"Iryokiki no Matsutani Seisakujo: Ninenkan de Seizogenka Hangen [MANI Will Reduce Manufacturing Costs by 50% in the Coming 2 Years]." 1994. *The Nihon Keizai Shimbun*, March 5.

Ishihara, A. *Kango 20 Nenshi* [Twenty Years of Nursing History]. Tokyo: Medical-Friend, 1967.

Itami, H., and T. W. Roehl. *Mobilizing Invisible Assets*. Cambridge, MA: Harvard University Press, 1991.

Japan Finance Corporation for Small and Medium Enterprise. *Hasso to Gijutsu ga Umareru Kaisha: Saisentan o Iku Business Frontier 20 Sha* [Innovative Companies: Business Frontier 20]. Tokyo: Chukei Publishing Company, 1989.

"Kagicho no Chumoku Hatsumei, Matsutani Seisakujo no Shikayo Konkan Sessaku Sochi o Sentei [Science and Technology Agency Selected the Dental Root Canal Treatment Instruments of MANI as a Notable Invention]." 1988. *The Nihon Keizai Shimbun*, April 22.

Kameyama, M. *Kangofu to Ishi* [Nurses and Doctors]. Tokyo: Domesu Publishers, 1984.

"Kenkyu Kyoten o Miru: Matsutani Seisakujo Gijutsuka, Seimitsu Bisai Gijutsu ni wa Teihyo [Observation for Research and Development Base: Technology Division of MANI Has an Established Reputation]." 1989. *The Nihon Keizai Shimbun*, February 28.

Kipping, M., R. D. Wadhwani, and M. Bucheli "Analyzing and Interpreting Historical Sources: A Basic Methodology." In *Organizations in Time: History, Theory, Methods*, edited by M. Bucheli and R. D. Wadhwani, 305-329. Oxford: Oxford University Press, 2014.

"Kitakanto no Seichokigyo Matsutani Seisakujo [A Growing Company in the North Kanto Region: MANI]." 1990. *The Nihon Keizai Shimbun*, March 11.

Leonard-Barton, D. "Core Capabilities and Core Rigidities: A Paradox in Managing New Product Development." *Strategic Management Journal* 13, no. S1 (1992): 111-125. doi.10.1002/smj.4250131009

MANI. 2017. "Yukashoken Hokokusho 2014 [Securities Report 2014]." MANI. Accessed August 28. http://www.mani.co.jp/ir/library3.html

MANI. 2017. "Yukashoken Hokokusho 2015 [Securities Report 2015]." MANI. Accessed August 28. http://www.mani.co.jp/ir/library3.html

MANI. 2017. "Yukashoken Hokokusho 2016 [Securities Report 2016]." MANI. Accessed August 28. http://www.mani.co.jp/ir/library3.html

Matsutani, K., and T. Yanagawa. "MANI Matsutani Kanji Kaicho Intabyu [An Interview to Kanji Matsutani, CEO of Mani Inc]." *Hakuoh University Daigakuin Keiei Kenkyu* [Hakuoh University Graduate School Management Research] 10 (2010): 247–287.

"Matsutani Seisakujo Intanetto de Eigyosuishin [MANI: Sales Promotion by the Internet]". 1996. *The Nihon Keizai Shimbun*, March 6.

Matsuzaki, Y. "Eigyo Riekiritsu 34%, Koshueki Kigyo MANI o Sasaeru Gijutsuryoku: Ganka Naifu de Sekai Shea Shui e [Operating Profit Rate Is 34% Based on the Technology: The Profitable Company MANI Is about to Obtain the World's Number One Share in the Ophthalmologic Knife Products Market]." (2015). Kaisha Shikiho Online, March 29. Accessed August 28, 2017. http://shikiho.jp/tk/news/articles/0/64612

Miyamoto, M., T. Abe, M. Udagawa, M. Sawai, and T. Kikkawa *Nihon Keieishi*, 2nd ed. [Japanese Business History]. Tokyo: Yuhikaku, 1995.

Morino, S. "Shugyoku no Chusho Kigyo: File. 3 Shujutsuyo Hogoshin [MANI Excellent Small and Medium Companies: Chapter 3 Surgical Needle from MANI]." *Nikkei Monozukuri*, no. 669 (2010)June: 69-71.

"Mushiba o Daiya de Kezuru Chiryoyo Cotingu: Matsutani Seisakujo Kireaji Taikyusei Nibai ni [Coating Technology of Dental Care Tools to Reduce Tooth Decay: MANI Doubled the Sharpness and the Durability Compared to Conventional Products]." 1991. *Nihon Keizai Shimbun*, January 27.

Nikkei Top Leader. *Kiseki no Seizogyo: Tsuburenai Kaisha o Tsukuru tameno Itsutsu no Nouhau* [Miracle Manufacturing Companies: Five Hints on How to Create a Sustainable Company]. Tokyo: Nikkei BP, 2011.

Noda, M. 1988. "Keieisha Intabyu: Asu o Tsukuru, Matsutani Seisakujo Shacho Matsutani Kanji Shi [CEO Interview: Creating Tomorrow, MANI CEO Kanji Matsutani]." *The Nikkei Sangyo Shimbun*, June 10.

Noguchi, H. 2011. "Seicho e no Sekkeizu MANI Matsutani Masaaki Shacho: Kanja, Ishi no tameni Kaizen [Blueprint for Growth by MANI CEO Masaaki Matsutani: Kaizen for Patients and Surgeons]." *Shimotsuke Shimbun*, November 3.

Oguchi, M. 2012. "Ningen Hakken Matsutani Kanji San: Iryokigu no Chisana Kyojin 1 [The President of MANI, Kanji Matsutani: Small Giant in the Medical Instruments Industry Vol. 1]." *The Nihon Keizai Shimbun (evening)*, June 18.

Oguchi, M. 2012. "Ningen Hakken Matsutani Kanji San: Iryokigu no Chisana Kyojin 2 [The President of MANI, Kanji Matsutani: Small Giant in the Medical Instruments Industry Vol. 2]." *The Nihon Keizai Shimbun (evening)*, June 19.

Oguchi, M. 2012. "Ningen Hakken Matsutani Kanji San: Iryokigu no Chisana Kyojin 3 [The President of MANI, Kanji Matsutani: Small Giant in the Medical Instruments Industry Vol. 3]." *The Nihon Keizai Shimbun (evening)*, June 20.

Oguchi, M. 2012. "Ningen Hakken Matsutani Kanji San: Iryokigu no Chisana Kyojin 4 [The President of MANI, Kanji Matsutani: Small Giant in the Medical Instruments Industry Vol. 4]." *The Nihon Keizai Shimbun (evening)*, June 21.

Porter, M. E. *Competitive Strategy: Techniques for Analyzing Industries and Companies*. New York: The Free Press, 1980.

Porter Prize. 2016. "MANI Kabushikigaisha 2008 Nendo Dai 8 Kai Pota Sho Jusho, Kogatairyoyokigu Seizogyo [MANI, Inc. 2008 8th Porter Prize Winner, Medical Tool Manufacturer]." Accessed January 30. http://www.porterprize.org/pastwinner/2008/12/02111040.html

Pullen, A. J. J., P. C. de Weerd-Nederhof, A. J. Groen, and O. A. M. Fisscher. "Open Innovation in Practice: Goal Complementarity and Closed NPD Networks to Explain Differences in Innovation Performance for SMEs in the Medical Devices Sector." *Journal of Product Innovation Management* 29, no. 6 (2012): 917–934. doi:10.1111/j.1540-5885.2012.00973.x

Quandl. 2017. "Canada, Total Hospital Beds, Nurse to Bed Ratio (Head Counts)." Accessed August 22. https://www.quandl.com/data/OECD/HEALTH_REAC_HOPITBED_NURRAT_CAN-Canada-Total-Hospital-Beds-Nurse-To-Bed-Ratio-Head-Counts

Quandl. 2017. "France, Total Hospital Beds, Nurse to Bed Ratio (Head Counts)." Accessed August 22. https://www.quandl.com/data/OECD/HEALTH_REAC_HOPITBED_NURRAT_FRA-France-Total-Hospital-Beds-Nurse-To-Bed-Ratio-Head-Counts

Quandl. 2017. "Germany, Total Hospital Beds, Nurse to Bed Ratio (Head Counts)." Accessed August 22. https://www.quandl.com/data/OECD/HEALTH_REAC_HOPITBED_NURRAT_DEU-Germany-Total-Hospital-Beds-Nurse-To-Bed-Ratio-Head-Counts

Quandl. 2017. "Italy, Total Hospital Beds, Nurse to Bed Ratio (Head Counts)." Accessed August 22. https://www.quandl.com/data/OECD/HEALTH_REAC_HOPITBED_NURRAT_ITA-Italy-Total-Hospital-Beds-Nurse-To-Bed-Ratio-Head-Counts

Quandl. 2017. "United States, Total Hospital Beds, Nurse to Bed Ratio (Head Counts)." Accessed August 22. https://www.quandl.com/data/OECD/HEALTH_REAC_HOPITBED_NURRAT_USA-United-States-Total-Hospital-Beds-Nurse-To-Bed-Ratio-Head-Counts

Rosenberg, N. "The Direction of Technological Change: Inducement Mechanisms and Focusing Devices." *Economic Development & Cultural Change* 18, no. 1, Part 1, Part 1 (1969): 1-24. http://www.jstor.org/stable/1152198

Saiseikai Utsunomiya Hospital. *Soritsu 15 Shunen Kinen Shi* [The Memorial 15th Anniversary Magazine]. Tochigi: Saiseikai Utsunomiya Hospital, 1957.

Sakakibara, N. *Tabu ni Mesu o Ireta Gekai* [A Surgeon Broke the Taboo]. Tokyo: The Mainichi Newspapers, 1993.

Sass, M. "Internationalisation of innovative SMEs in the Hungarian medical precision instruments industry." *Post-Communist Economies* 24, no. 3 (2012): 365–382. doi:10.1080/14631377.2012.705470

"Sekai Saisho no Hogoshin Kaihatsu: Matsutani Seisakujo [The Smallest Surgical Needle: MANI]." 1991. *The Nihon Keizai Shimbun*, June 13.

"Shika Chiryoki Innai Kansen o Boshi: Matsutani Seisakjo [Preventing Hospital Infections via Dental Care Instruments: MANI]." 1993. *The Nikkei Sangyo Shimbun*, October 28.

"Shikayo Daiya Bar ni Shinshutsu: Matsutani Seisakujo Raigetsu kara Honkaku Seisan [MANI Entered the Dental Diamond Bar Products Market and Will Begin Production Next Month]." 1989. *The Nihon Keizai Shimbun*, March 13.

Shimazaki, K. *Nihon no Iryo: Seido to Seisaku* [Japanese Medical Care: Institutions and Policy]. Tokyo: University of Tokyo Press, 2011.

Shimoda, K. *Reiza to Butsuri Kyoiku: Hikari no Naka o Ayunde* [Razer and Physics Education: Walking in the Light]. Tokyo: Center for Academic Publication Japan, 1981.

"Shin Kiyohara Kojo ga Kansei: Matsutani Seisakujo [The Construction of the New Kiyohara Factory is Complete: MANI]." 1995. *The Nihon Keizai Shimbun*, July 7.

"Shinkojo o Kansei Sogyo o Kaishi, Matsutani Seisakujo [MANI Has Completed a New Factory and Started Operation]." 1975. *The Nikkei Sangyo Shimbun*, September 22.

"Shinsozai Tsukai Hogoshin: Matsutani Seisakujo Rainen kara Ryosan [New Material Surgical Needles: MANI Will Mass-produce in the Next Year]." 1990. *The Nihon Keizai Shimbun*, April 3.

"Shin Wagasha no Senryaku: MANI Matsutani Kanji Shi [Our New Corporate Strategy: MANI, Kanji Matsutani]." 2007. *Shimotsuke Shimbun*, June 7.

Statistics and Information Department, Minister's Secretariat, Ministry of Health, Labour and Welfare. 2017. "Byoin no Shuruibetsu Byoinsu [Hospitals by Kind 1910-2004]." Accessed August 22. http://www.stat.go.jp/data/chouki/24.htm

Statistics and Information Department, Minister's Secretariat, Ministry of Health, Labour and Welfare. 2017. "Byosho no Shuruibetsu Byoinbyoshosu [Hospital Beds by Kind 1910-2004]." Accessed August 22, 2017. http://www.stat.go.jp/data/chouki/24.htm

Statistics and Information Department, Minister's Secretariat, Ministry of Health, Labour and Welfare. 2017. "Iryo Kankeisyasu [Medical Care Personnel 1874-2004]." Accessed August 22. http://www.stat.go.jp/data/chouki/24.htm

Takeda, T. 2015. "MANI Tsugi no Suteji e [MANI toward the Next Stage]." *The Nihonkeizai Shimbun*, October 15.

Takeuchi, A. "Tokyo ni okeru Iryokikaikogyo Shudan no Kosei [The Regional Structure of Medical Instrument Industry in Tokyo]." *Japanese Journal of Human Geography* 26, no. 6 (1974): 658–673. doi:10.4200/jjhg1948.26.6_658

Tanaka, S. "Kangoshi no Seikatsu to Rodo [Life and Labor of Nurses]." In *Nihon no Kango no Ayumi* [The History of Japanese Nursing], edited by Nihon Kango Rekishi Gakkai [Japan Society of Nursing History], 27-42. Tokyo: Japanese Nursing Association, 2014.

The Stock Research Center. 2017. "Horisutikku Kigyo Repoto MANI: 7730 Tosho Ichibu [Holistic Corporate Report on MANI: Security Code 7730, First Section of the Tokyo Stock Exchange]." Accessed August 28. http://www.holistic-r.org/c_info/7730/7730140718.pdf

"Tobidasu Chiho Kigyo Tochigiken: MANI Kawase Risuku Kaihi e Genchika [Progressive Local Company: MANI Has Improved Localization to Avoid Exchange Rate Risk]." 1996. *The Nikkei Sangyo Shimbun*, June 11.

Tochigi Prefecture. 2017. "Tochigi Prefecture." Department of Industry, Labor, and Tourism. International Affairs Division. Accessed May 10. http://www.pref.tochigi.lg.jp/english/documents/2016_english.pdf

Tochigi Shimbunsha. *Syowa 30 Nen Ban Tochigiken Shoko Yoran* [Commerce and Industry Handbook of Tochigi Prefecture in 1955]. Tochigi: Tochigi Shimbunsha, 1955.

Tochigi Shimbunsha. *Tochigi Nenkan 1957* [Yearbook of Tochigi Prefecture 1957]. Tochigi: Tochigi Shimbunsha, 1957.

"Tochigiken Kigyo 21 Seiki e no Chosen: Dai 2 Sho Kakaku Kakumei, Matsutani Seisakujo [A Company in Tochigi Prefecture Challenging the 21st Century: Chapter 2 Price Revolution, MANI]." 1995. *The Nihon Keizai Shimbun*, August 1.

"Tsuisoroku: Matsutani Masao San [Reminiscences of Masao Matsutani]." 2003. *The Nihon Keizai Shimbun*, December 26.

Yanagawa, T. "MANI Kabushikigaisha Chiho Hatsu no Chokogyoseki Warudo Kanpani [Mani Inc., the World-Wide Company with Super High Performance Located in Tochigi Prefecture]." *Hakuoh University Daigakuin Keiei Kenkyu* [Hakuoh University Graduated School Management Research] 6 (2006): 73–156.

Zemtsov, S., V. Barinova, D. Bukov, and V. Eremkin. "Uncovering Regional Clustering of High Technology SMEs: Russian Case." *Mediterranean Journal of Social Sciences* 6, no. 6 (2016): 309–320. doi:10.5901/mjss.2015.v6n6s7p309

Challenging the Problem of 'Fit': Advancing the Regenerative Medicine Industries in the United States, Britain and Japan

Maki Umemura

ABSTRACT
This article follows the evolution of biopharmaceutical firms as they bore great uncertainty and risks in their endeavours to commercialise new therapies – through the regenerative medicine industry in the United States, Britain and Japan. Despite its beginnings in the 1970s, regenerative medicines have yet to become a widely accepted form of medicine. A large part of the problem lay with the lack of 'fit' with the broader health context. This article illustrates how the trajectory of the sector was shaped, not only by the nature of the technology, but also by the complex contexts in which firms were embedded.

Introduction

This article is part of a special issue that explores histories in the business of health. In line with the aim of this issue, this contribution looks to develop a richer understanding of how context influences the business of medicine. It considers how distinctive national contexts shaped the evolution of regenerative medicine firms in the United States, Britain and Japan. While regenerative medicines have held tremendous therapeutic promise, they posed a problem of 'fit' with the existing health context owing to their difference from conventional therapies. Even in the United States, with its academic entrepreneurs, well-developed capital markets and private healthcare system, regenerative medicine firms faced enormous difficulty in commercialisation. In Japan and Britain, the lack of 'fit' between regenerative medicine and the existing institutional arrangements was even greater.

In considering the question of 'fit' between existing health contexts and novel therapies, it may be useful to think of health contexts as similar to a computer operating system, and novel therapies as similar to new applications. New applications will not function, regardless of their merits, if they are incompatible with the existing operating system. If partially compatible, the application may function, but not in an optimum fashion.

The importance of the issue of novel therapies and their 'fit' with the broader health contexts can be illustrated by the case of the American biotechnology firm Dendreon. When the Federal Drug Administration (FDA) in the United States approved the firm's prostate cancer drug Provenge in 2010, the product was heralded as a breakthrough. However, the firm became bankrupt within four years. A large part of the firm's failure lay in the incompatibility of its business model with the broader American healthcare context. The therapy's price tag of $93,000 for a few extra months of life, was neither affordable to the vast majority of cancer patients nor considered cost-effective by American insurance providers.[1]

Moreover, cell-based therapies, which involve living cells, were much more difficult to administer than existing (i.e. chemical- or protein-based) therapies, and led to limited use by physicians. Across three of the countries discussed in this article, the business of regenerative medicine has struggled to survive, partly as most of the therapies do not fit the existing healthcare contexts. This lack of 'fit' – in regulation, reimbursement, clinical delivery and beyond – is related to the problem of path dependence; a phenomenon widely discussed by economic historians concerning the challenge of introducing novel technologies.[2]

Regenerative medicine refers to therapies that seek to generate 'living, functional tissues to repair or replace tissue or organ function lost owing to age, disease, damage or congenital defects'.[3] There are two principal types of regenerative medicine: tissue engineering and cell therapy. Tissue-engineering treats ailments by creating and applying functioning tissue that is created from scaffolds, cells and biologically active materials.[4] In comparison, cell therapy treats ailments by administering (usually live) cells.[5] Both aim to provide treatment that is 'curative', rather than 'symptomatic'.[6]

Unlike existing therapies, regenerative medicine is novel in its technological base of cells. It involves the cultivation and handling of perishable, live cells whose scientific mechanism is immensely complex. Living cells are also expensive to handle at every stage of the value chain – from R&D, production, distribution, to delivery. The cells used for these treatments may be mass-produced from another body (allogeneic) or may come from the individual patient (autologous).

This article compares the regenerative medicine industries of three countries – the United States, Britain and Japan – for several reasons. First, the three countries represent the main locations for research and industry development concerning regenerative medicines in North America, Europe and Asia, respectively. Second, while the three countries share long life expectancies and growing health expenditures,[7] they differ in their healthcare contexts. The United States, while a public–private hybrid system, is nevertheless a largely fragmented, market-oriented healthcare system where patients are highly sensitive to the cost of therapies. In comparison, Britain is largely a unified, publicly administered system, where patients are largely insensitive to cost. The Japanese system is situated in between the United States and Britain in terms of private–public orientation, unity vs. fragmentation, and patient sensitivity to the cost of therapies. Government–industry relations are much closer in Japan than in Britain or the United States. The United States offers much greater access to venture capital compared with Britain or Japan. In view of these differences, a comparison of the three countries allows us to explore how the broader health contexts shaped industry development.

While all regenerative medicine firms experienced significant challenges in developing their therapies, the paths of firms in the three countries varied. For example, the regenerative medicine industry has been more dynamic in the United States and less so in Britain, with Japan situated between the two. The dynamism in the United States resulted from factors such as: a stronger tradition of academic entrepreneurship; a more vibrant venture capital market; and the lack of a universal healthcare system. The absence of universal healthcare in the United States is relevant to explaining why the regenerative medicine industry is stronger in the country, because single-payer systems often adopt stronger cost control measures that disadvantage firms that seek payment for novel therapies that have yet to demonstrate cost-effectiveness. After all, novel therapies are rarely cost-effective options, and require second order innovations to reach more effective dosages, concentrations, and lower cost.[8]

Health contexts in the United States, Britain and Japan

Existing literature, such as the systems of innovation scholarship,[9] has shown how the institutional environment in which firms are embedded, shapes innovative capacity.[10] In the varieties of capitalism literature, the conventional view is that in liberal market economies such as the United States and Britain, firms engage in radical, nonlinear forms of innovation. By contrast, coordinated market economies such as Germany and Japan are considered to support firms' engagement in incremental, linear forms of innovation.[11] Owing to institutional complementarities that generate path dependence, the broader institutional environment has not changed significantly over time. In this context, American and British regenerative firms, which have institutional environments that support radical innovation, may be considered conducive to the development of new therapies in regenerative medicine. Yet caution must be taken to avoid over-simplistic assessments, as the cultivation of known, live cells for novel therapies takes advantage of the precise strengths of the Japanese institutional environment that build upon tacit, firm-based knowledge and incremental innovation.[12]

Close attention should be paid to the specific institutions considered to support the biopharmaceutical industry. For instance, Henderson et al. argued that the American firms' global leadership in this industry was due to the distinct institutional environment in the United States. These features included: extensive the public support for basic research; strong intellectual property protection; robust procedures for drug development and approval; as well as sound pricing and reimbursement policies.[13] Furthermore, the closer links in the United States between university and industry; a regulatory framework that supported academic entrepreneurship; and vibrant capital markets helped realise the ambitions of the early firms.[14] Such differences in the American, British and Japanese health contexts are presented in Table 1 and examined in the main discussion, following a discussion of the respective healthcare systems.

Healthcare in the United States

The American healthcare system has been more fragmented than most developed country counterparts. In particular, the United States has not had a universal healthcare system. Most Americans have been privately insured by their employer or as individuals. A good number of others are publicly insured via programmes such as Medicare and Medicaid. Yet, between the introduction of Medicare and Medicaid in 1965 and introduction of the Affordable Care Act in 2014, Americans without health insurance averaged well over 10%.[15] Disparities in access and quality of healthcare have also varied according to state and socio-economic background, among others.[16] While most American healthcare organisations are private, about a fifth are public. One of the poignant aspects of the corporate healthcare system in America has been its expense; healthcare expenditures accounted for 17.2% of GDP in 2016.[17]

Table 1. Comparison of institutional environments in the United States, Britain and Japan.

	United States	Britain	Japan
Education and skills	World leading universities with considerable public and private funding	Some leading universities with moderate levels of public funding	Some leading universities with moderate levels of public funding
Labour market	Liquid	Liquid	Illiquid
Financial system	Vibrant venture capital market with angel investors	Some venture capital with angel investors	Limited venture capital market or angel investors
Inter-firm relations	Arms-length, Alliance for Regenerative Medicine (industry association)	Arms-length, Alliance for Regenerative Medicine (industry association)	Relationship-based, Forum for Innovative Regenerative Medicine (industry association)
Health care system	Mix of public and private hospitals and insurers	Largely public hospitals with public universal health care	Mix of public and private hospitals; largely public insurance, supplemented by private insurance
State	Generous public funding of research; FDA; strong IP protection; robust development/approval process for therapies	Public funding of research; EMA; strong IP protection; NICE as health technology assessment agency	Public funding of research; PMDA; moderate IP protection; biennial price reductions

For decades, the American healthcare system has run on a fee-for-service basis.[18] Owing to the large variation in providers and insurers, patient payment levels have varied accordingly. Some have suggested that, because of its fragmentation, American insurers have not been able to negotiate the low prices of medicines in the way that countries with single-payer systems are able.[19] At the same time, within this private healthcare setting, America's university hospitals, assisted by vast public funding for R&D and world leading academics, have provided an unparalleled setting for entrepreneurial firms to pursue the development of innovative therapies.

Healthcare in Britain

The British National Health Service (NHS) is a publicly sponsored, universal healthcare system created in 1948. The NHS offers hospital services, primary care via general practitioners, and community services.[20] It has provided free healthcare to all permanent residents at the point of service, financed from general taxation. Britain spent around 9.7% of its GDP on healthcare in 2016.[21] While NHS inpatient and consultation services have been free at the point of service, most patients must pay a small fee for each prescription (currently £8.60 or approximately US$12.10).[22] Since 1999, the NHS has subjected all health care technologies to cost-effectiveness analysis by the National Institute for Health and Clinical Excellence (NICE), which determines whether a given therapy is worthy of public funding.[23] The creation of NICE has had significant implications for firms developing novel therapies in Britain, as firms could find it difficult to secure NHS coverage for therapies that were not considered cost-effective – such as those that were risky or likely to extend life at very high cost.[24]

Healthcare in Japan

The Japanese healthcare system has been situated between the more market-oriented healthcare system in the United States, and the largely state-run healthcare system in Britain.

Since 1961, Japan has provided universal healthcare, which has been delivered on a fee-for-service basis according to a national fee schedule, under which patients pay 10–30% of total healthcare costs.[25] Numerous private insurers have offered supplementary services to cover out-of-pocket costs not covered by public insurance, such as for co-payments or private hospital rooms.[26] Japanese healthcare expenditures stood at 10.9% of GDP in 2016.[27]

Unlike Britain, but as in the United States, Japanese patients may access any clinic and hospital, which are largely privately run. Under Japan's state-subsidised healthcare system, prescription medicines covered under health insurance are registered on an official reimbursement list. Public insurance has not covered partial treatment – mixed billing – when patients receive a combination of insured and uninsured treatments, which may include novel therapies yet to be approved.[28] While Japan does not have a health technology assessment body similar to NICE, all medicines in Japan face cost-containment pressures to rein in rising healthcare costs.[29] Combined with the prohibition on mixed billing, this feature of the Japanese healthcare system has made it difficult for firms with novel therapies to recoup their investment in Japan.

Literature review

Business historians have published studies on medicine that include industry level histories[30] as well as historical studies of individual firms such as GlaxoSmithKline, Genentech, and Centocor.[31] They have also documented the business of novel therapies, such as aspirin in the late nineteenth century;[32] penicillin after World War II;[33] and the beginnings of the biotechnology industry in the 1970s and 1980s.[34] Business historians of medicine have explored a range of themes, including the political dynamics of regulation;[35] R&D and innovation;[36] intellectual property;[37] as well as sales and marketing.[38] Geographically, the business history of medicine has spanned the globe, from Britain,[39] the United States,[40] Germany,[41] Russia[42] to Japan.[43]

A parallel body of work has explored the histories of national healthcare systems.[44] Among scholars who have studied the history of American health insurance,[45] Chapin recently examined the origins of the corporatist and fragmented US healthcare system in the first half of the twentieth century, emphasising the role of the American Medical Association and physicians in creating an insurance company managed system.[46] Scholars of the British system have also produced a wealth of work on the origins and evolution of the NHS over the decades.[47] Researchers on Japan – with the seminal works of Kawakami[48] – have further documented the changes to the country's healthcare system since 1945.[49] Many historical studies of Japan's healthcare system have focussed on the evolution of the insurance system.[50]

While the above-mentioned works have enhanced our understanding of health contexts across countries, few historians of health have examined the relationship between health contexts and the commercialisation of new therapies. A recent volume by Owen and Hopkins examined Britain's relative weakness in biotechnology by evaluating the broader 'ecosystem' of British universities, the country's financial system, government policy and healthcare system as compared with that of the United States.[51] This article builds upon such insights.

Sources and methodology

A qualitative approach is adopted in this contribution. The primary sources consulted include press coverage, academic journals such as *Nature*, firm-level documents and government publications from the three countries. The sources were interpreted using the business history methodology described by Kipping, Wadhwani and Bucheli, which included triangulation, source criticism and hermeneutics.[52] For several reasons, historical patent data is not used to compare levels of innovative activity in regenerative medicine. First, the rules governing the patentability of stem cells– as well as requirements for novelty – vary between countries, and make comparative assessments suspect.[53] Second, the lack of a consistent definition and use of terms such as regenerative medicine complicate the identification of relevant patents. Third, practitioners in the regenerative medicine industry have suggested that patent protection is potentially unnecessary in this sector, given the very complex nature of the technology.[54]

The regenerative medicine industry in the United States, Britain and Japan

The emergence of the regenerative medicine industry should be contextualised within the beginnings of the broader biopharmaceutical industry, which began with the revolutionary medical discoveries in the 1970s. These ranged from the discovery of recombinant DNA technology and monoclonal antibody production to the culture of human cells.[55] While – as in many new technology sectors – the definition of biopharmaceuticals varies, this article refers to biopharmaceuticals as therapeutics created by or from living organisms.[56] Unlike the prevailing pharmaceutical industry that had come into existence from the late nineteenth century, the technological base of biopharmaceuticals lay in biological sources rather than chemicals. This paradigm shift in technology involved much greater risk and higher cost in R&D for firms developing novel therapies.[57]

Over the decades, firms have commercialised biopharmaceuticals, from therapeutic monoclonal antibodies, gene therapies and tissue engineering to cell therapies. At the same time, the business of medicine has evolved, as university-based start-ups, for instance, act as seeds of knowledge to the large pharmaceutical firms that assist in the development, marketing and sometimes financing of new therapies. Since the passage of the US Orphan Drug Act in 1983, firms have also sought to develop therapies for orphan diseases, which tend to have lower development costs, shorter development processes and higher approval rates.[58]

Owing to their intense complexity, biopharmaceuticals have taken decades to be commercialised. For example, the first approved therapeutic monoclonal antibody was Ortho Pharmaceutical's Orthoclone OKT3 in 1986,[59] followed by Centocor's ReoPro (abciximab) in 1994.[60] Others are just coming of age. After decades of experimentation, the European Medical Agency (EMA) approved the first gene therapy in the developed world with the Dutch firm uniQure's Glybera in 2012, which was only to be withdrawn in 2017.[61] The United States approved its first gene therapy – Spark Therapeutics' blindness treatment, Luxturna – at the end of 2017.[62]

Regenerative medicines are situated at this technological frontier. By 2015, some regenerative medicines had been approved, although they varied across regions. For example, 10 therapies have been approved by the FDA in the United States; three by the EMA for the EU;

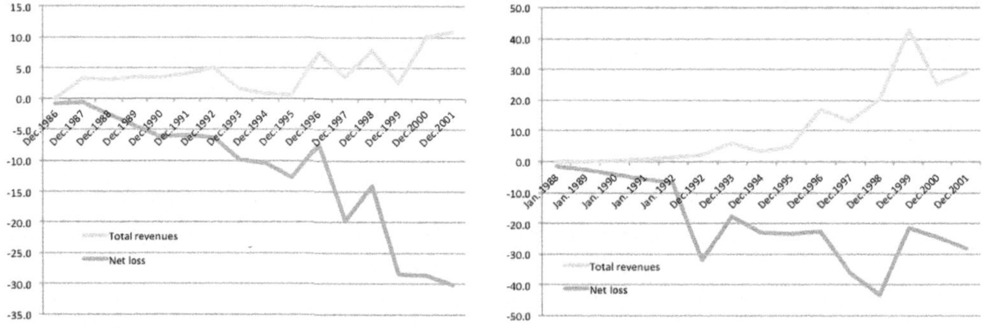

Figure 1. Revenues and Losses at Organogenesis and Advanced Tissue Sciences, in millions of US dollars. Source: Organogenesis, Advanced Tissue Sciences, *Annual Reports*.

and four by the Pharmaceutical and Medical Devices Agency (PMDA) in Japan.[63] Regenerative medicine had also become a global industry, although most (349) of the over 670 regenerative medicine firms still existed in North America, followed by Europe (185) and Asia (112).[64] While the metrics for evaluating the relative strength of an emerging industry are not singular and can be imperfect, this article considers the regulatory approvals and the number of active firms to provide some indication of a country's relative strength in the regenerative medicine industry.

The following section follows the paths taken by regenerative medicine firms across the three countries over two phases. The first phase refers to the 1970s to 2002, from scientific discovery to the rise and the collapse of the pioneering regenerative firms. The second phase refers to the rebuilding of this sector, from 2003 to 2015.

Building the regenerative medicine industry: the first phase, 1970s to 2002

The initial boom in regenerative medicine was primarily an American affair.[65] At a time when academic entrepreneurship began to flourish in the United States, scientists initially dreamed of growing 'organs' for therapeutic use. American firms benefitted, not only from the relative freedom in which academic scientists could engage in entrepreneurship, but also from a robust regulatory framework, and the availability of public investors ready to support risky initiatives – often without a viable business model – during the biotech boom of the 1980s. As shown in Figure 1, while the leading regenerative medicine companies of the 1980s generated mounting losses, share prices showed little relation to financial performance.

As firms encountered difficulties in pursuing their initial plans based on scientific ideals, the firms lowered and narrowed their therapeutic aims, and began to develop other revenue sources, such as providing cell-based products for drug testing. The pioneering American firms focused on the development of allogeneic, tissue-engineered products. By the turn of the millennium, the initial excitement in the sector waned as the pioneering firms faced delays in approval for drugs under development, or encountered difficulties in reimbursement for approved therapies. American investors were quick to respond to this downturn, and the pioneering firms filed for bankruptcy.

Near the end of the first phase of the regenerative medicines, a handful of start-ups in Britain were established, often with the help of British venture capital. The pioneering firms pursued the commercialisation of their therapies, which tended to be more targeted in their therapeutic focus compared with the ambitions of the early American firms. British firms had relatively more freedom to pursue stem-cell therapies in the early 2000s compared with the United States. Japanese firms also came into existence, often supported by large firms. Propelled by the opportunity to rejuvenate the Japanese economy, these firms imported American tissue-engineering technology for commercialisation in the Japanese market.

One of the pioneers of the regenerative medicine industry was Advanced Tissue Sciences, originally Marrow-Tech Inc.[66] Based on the academic work of New York-based Gail and Brian Naughton, the company gained $1 million in funding from the investor Herbert Moskowitz to establish the company,[67] and later raised $6 million through an initial public offering in 1986. At the time, the technology was so novel that the term, 'tissue engineering' or 'regenerative medicine' had yet to be developed,[68] and start-up firms had little access to local or federal funds. What the firms did benefit from was the rising tide of exuberance toward biomedical start-ups in the 1980s, including later household names such as Genentech and Amgen.

Marrow-Tech initially sought to develop a product that would replicate bone marrow for diseases such as cancer that destroyed bone marrow. However, the firm encountered considerable challenges in gaining scientific credibility for the product. The New York State Health Commissioner at the time, for instance, argued that the company should be closed down for a product that was 'untried and technically and medically deficient', while the Consumer Protection Board argued that their advertisements were 'deceptive and misleading'.[69]

Despites its early ambitions such as creating human organs over the long term,[70] Marrow-Tech struggled to develop a viable business model for its initial bone marrow product.[71] In 1991, the firm renamed itself as Advanced Tissue Sciences as it shifted its focus toward cultivating tissue to treat a wider range of ailments; first to treat burns patients, and later, to treat larger patient populations, such as those with diabetic or venous ulcers.[72] By the mid-1990s, Advanced Tissue Sciences had secured prominent executives and developed networks with a range of leading hospitals and universities, including the Massachusetts Institute of Technology (MIT). The company was also able to secure substantial funds. By 1996, Advanced Tissue had secured more than $42 million from public markets, $50 million from private investors, with the potential to receive another $60 million through a joint venture with the leading wound-healing company, Smith&Nephew.[73] The firm also began to enhance its pipeline beyond wound care, exploring therapies for orthopaedics, cardiovascular disease, as well as aesthetic and reconstructive surgery.

However, while the initial product for burns, TransCyte, was swiftly approved in 1998, the firm was unable to demonstrate efficacy for its diabetic foot ulcer product and secure FDA approval for Dermagraft until 2001.[74] An announcement in 1998 referring to delays in the FDA approval prompted a rapid decline in the firm's share prices (from $17 to $3.86 per share). Facing lawsuits from shareholders, the firm struggled financially.[75] In 2002, Advanced Tissue Sciences filed for bankruptcy, sold Dermagraft to its joint venture partner, Smith & Nephew, and ceased to exist the following year.[76]

Another American regenerative medicine company, Organogenesis, was established in 1986 by the MIT professor, Eugene Bell, whose research involved the cultivation of human skin for grafting onto wounds.[77] Similar to Advanced Tissue, Organogenesis sought to create living tissue for replacement in human patients, and the firm's initial plans were ambitious, from treating wounds arising from burns and diabetes to creating human organs.[78] The firm conducted an initial public offering soon after its establishment. As early as 1987, the company began to run clinical trials at hospitals with specialised burns units,[79] and formed alliances with pharmaceutical firms for additional financing and marketing. With Eli Lilly, for instance, Organogenesis formed an agreement in which the pharmaceutical firm would finance the research for an artificial artery in exchange for exclusive marketing rights.[80]

By the mid-1990s, the company developed an impressive network of research alliances with leading American universities and hospitals to develop its products, including Harvard Medical School and Massachusetts General Hospital. Around the same time, the firm began to adjust their business model by outsourcing research to universities. For instance, Organogenesis awarded a grant to the University of San Francisco to conduct research on Testskin, a living skin product used for drug testing.[81] In 1998, Organogenesis Apligraf became the first regenerative medicine product to receive FDA approval for a mass-produced therapy comprised of living cells.[82]

However, Organogenesis ran into problems following FDA approval, especially in marketing. In 1996, the company had formed an alliance with the pharmaceutical firm Novartis to market its products in exchange for financing. Novartis was unfamiliar with the distinct attributes of cell-based therapies, and Organogenesis struggled to achieve profits on Apligraf units sold by Novartis. Furthermore, Organogenesis was unable to contain manufacturing costs arising from product defects, recalls and delays, secure reimbursement or maintain a stable supple chain, and the alliance soured. Organogenesis filed for bankruptcy in 2002.[83] Organogenesis's experience and Novartis's difficulties in the handling of living, cell-based therapies show how a lack of 'fit' between regenerative medicines and the prevailing health context slowed the development of this industry.

In Britain, the first regenerative medicine firms were established around the turn of the century. Reneuron, for example, was founded in 1997 by three neuroscientists affiliated with the Institute of Psychiatry (later part of Kings College London): Jeffrey Grey, John Sinden and Helen Hodges. Based upon their research, Reneuron sought to deliver a cell therapy to treat brain diseases such as Alzheimer's or Parkinson's. Unlike the tissue-engineering pioneers in the United States, Reneuron planned to cultivate neural stem cells from embryonic tissue, and provide these to neurosurgeons for injection into patients with brain disease.

Established as a private firm, initial funds were secured from the venture capital firm Merlin Ventures (£5 million).[84] The firm benefitted from the founders' academic and hospital connections. Reneuron also secured a £4.2 million grant from the European Commission in 2000 and formed an alliance with Novo Nordsk to help develop a pain therapy.[85] During the biotech boom year of 2000 – which saw over 80 IPOs and over $30 billion of investment in the sector – Reneuron conducted an initial public offering and raised £18 million from the Alternative Investments Market (AIM) of the London Stock Exchange.[86] These funds helped the firm pursue clinical trials of its own pain therapy for diabetes and arthritis.[87] As development delays ensued, however, the firm's share prices dropped precipitously (from 221p to 39p) in 2001.[88]

Another British firm, Intercytex, was established in 1999 by Paul Kemp, a former executive of Organogenesis. The company initially harboured similar ambitions as Organogenesis, and offered living cell skin substitutes for both cosmetic and therapeutic use: from treating hair loss to burns victims.[89] In the longer term, the firm was also interested in growing kidneys for transplantation. To pursue its ambitions, the company secured venture capital funding from Johnson & Johnson Development Corporation, Avlar Bioventures, 3i, and Merlin Biosciences.[90] It is worth noting that British firms such as Reneuron benefitted from a less hostile environment toward research in stem-cell-based therapies compared with the United States. The British parliament had relaxed the 'Human Fertilisation and Embryology Act' to allow research on human embryos for specific purposes, just as the American President Bush had prohibited the use of federal funds for research on newly created embryonic stem-cell lines.[91]

Japanese firms' entry into regenerative medicine also occurred around the millennium. Unlike the American or British start-ups, Japanese entrants were often larger firms seeking to diversify into new business areas, as their established business was losing ground to global competition. They included Japan Tissue Engineering (J-TEC), Menicon, and Terumo.[92] These firms co-existed alongside a handful of academic start-ups, such as Cardio, an Osaka University-based start-up launched by the cardiologist Yoshiki Sawa in 2001, which was supported by the Japanese venture capital firms TransScience, NIF Ventures, along with the Development Bank of Japan.[93] As Goto has noted, the Japanese innovation system has been based on large firms, supported by close relations with government.[94] Historically, many of these firms imported technologies from abroad to develop existing industries in Japan. These strategies to develop innovative sectors were, to some extent, path dependent.

There were several other reasons for the relative dearth of Japanese start-ups in regenerative medicine in the 1990s. Much had to do with regulation. First, until 1998, academic scientists employed at Japanese universities were considered civil servants governed by the Civil Service Code, and were not permitted to engage in outside employment.[95] This restriction effectively suffocated the type of academic entrepreneurship that had occurred in the United States. Second, cell cultivation was only permissible under physician monitoring within a hospital setting until 2014.[96] This restriction limited any business from cultivating cells for tissue engineering or cell therapy products outside the hospital until 2014.

Third, Japanese regulators in the 1990s were notoriously slow to approve drugs, and Japan featured considerable drug lags compared with the United States or Europe.[97] These delays were caused, not only by the much smaller numbers or lower qualifications of regulators in the PMDA compared with the FDA, but also by a tainted blood scandal in which haemophiliacs succumbed to HIV following treatment from approved, unheated blood products. While this was a worldwide scandal, the regulator who approved the drug – along with executives at the Japanese firm that produced the product – later received a prison sentence for criminal negligence.[98] For Japanese bureaucrats who rotated posts every few years, there was strong incentive to delay approvals of risky therapies until the end of their designated term.

By the end of the first wave of industry development around 2002, it became clear that commercialising regenerative medicines was a much more complex process than that of existing therapies. Scientists and entrepreneurs had ambitious plans to develop regenerative medicines based on their scientific potential, and overestimated the ease of commercialisation and the therapeutic effectiveness of the new medicines.[99] Many had overinvested in facilities to develop therapies that were too scientifically complex or expensive to commercialise. In the United States, the development of cell-based therapies challenged the patience of investors who became frustrated with delays in approval (Advanced Tissue Sciences) or losses stemming from manufacture and marketing (Organogenesis). The bankruptcies of the two companies were reflective of the broader climate for regenerative medicine firms, particularly those with novel therapies that would take time to recoup their investments. By 2002, the share prices of many biotechnology firms had fallen and left firms unable to seek additional public funds. At the time, 35% of public biotechnology firms had less than a year's worth of cash, and many firms had been forced to downsize considerably.[100]

Rebuilding the regenerative medicine industry: the second phase, 2002–2015

The rebuilding of regenerative medicine from 2002 was also led by firms in the United States. In that year, more than half of the 89 regenerative medicine firms worldwide were within US borders. Yet few clinical trials were successful, and no firm had yet to become profitable.[101] During the second phase, the American firms tried to develop a viable business model, and narrowed the therapeutic applications of their technology. They also tried to lower the cost of manufacture, retain control over marketing and secure adequate reimbursement. Over time, firms restructured their operations further: reducing R&D activities and focussing on a single technology or product that would face fewer regulatory barriers, such as in orphan diseases or cosmetics.[102] Companies increasingly adopted more sophisticated strategies that often involved diminishing the initial ideals of their products in the short term; developing non-therapeutic applications – such as diagnostics or drug discovery tools – in the medium term; in the hopes of eventually attaining part of those initial ideals in the long term. Companies also began to leverage different health contexts around the world, expanding internationally to secure finances, access knowledge or seek regulatory approval. Yet even within the largely private healthcare system in the United States, firms were influenced significantly by public insurers' decisions over reimbursement.

In the United States, the fallen pioneers responded in different ways. Their collapse may have been sparked by delays in regulatory approval, but even after approval, firms had difficulty securing reimbursement and overestimated demand. For example, Advanced Tissue's Dermagraft replacement skin, priced at $4,000, could not encounter sufficient demand without reimbursement.[103] The companies also had problems with cost containment in large-scale manufacture, which also led to low margins. The logistics of distributing living cells added further to costs. Moreover, FDA approval did not result in any major health insurance company willing to cover the product. Furthermore, unlike other American therapeutics firms, regenerative medicine firms had yet to generate revenue from approvals in overseas markets. European approvals, for instance, were delayed owing to issues arising from dealing with human tissue.[104] These cumulative expenses limited the amount of funds that could be reinvested to R&D. These were the issues that firms faced during the second phase.

Following the folding of Advanced Tissue, the firm's founder Gail Naughton founded a new company, Histogen, in 2007. Aware of the challenges of reimbursement, Histogen adjusted its business model to develop products that would require fewer regulatory challenges. The company focussed its near-term efforts on developing cosmeticeuticals and hair growth products, as the former required no evidence for efficacy, faced robust market demand and would avoid problems regarding reimbursement. The company also sought to leverage regulatory regimes, forming licensing agreements in China and starting clinical trials in Japan and the United States.[105] The firm's strategy involved the utilisation of a base technology that would be applied to cosmetic products in the short term; hair growth products in the medium term; and cancer therapeutics in the long term. By using the same manufacturing process for multiple products, the company was able to reduce product development costs.

In comparison, Organogenesis managed to rebuild its operations after filing for Chapter 11 bankruptcy as a private company, narrowing its therapeutic offerings and focusing on a product that would generate revenue. Decades earlier, the firm had sought to apply its technology to a wide range of indications, from vascular grafts, a liver-assist device, to pancreatic cell-transplantation.[106] But the firm concentrated on Apligraf as its major revenue source, and dedicated substantial efforts to containing manufacturing costs. For instance, the firm invested in a manufacturing facility to lower the cost of mass-producing living tissue.[107] The company also withdrew from its alliance with Novartis and took control of both the manufacture and marketing of its products.[108] Within a few years of bankruptcy, Organogenesis had become the first profitable regenerative medicine company.[109] The company then began to develop Gintuit, a tissue-engineered product for gum disease. This was the first regenerative medicine product approved as a biologic through the Center for Biologics Evaluation and Research of the FDA.[110] Earlier products had been approved as medical devices. As observed in other jurisdictions, regulatory development succeeded the scientific advances made in regenerative medicine.

In the second phase of the industry's development, companies realised that while regulatory approval was important, reimbursement was essential. Even within the largely private American healthcare system, reimbursement from state-sponsored insurance was particularly important for tissue-engineering firms, as the majority of wound care patients were Medicare beneficiaries.[111] Organogenesis was not an exception. For instance, when Medicare expanded coverage of Apligraf in 2012, the firm was profitable and expanded facilities.[112] When Medicare reduced reimbursement levels in the following year, Organogenesis was forced to reorganise,[113] and to focus on its wound-healing business to secure revenue.[114] Coincidentally, in early 2014, Organogenesis inherited the rights to Dermagraft, which had been Advanced Tissue's flagship product. Following Dermagraft's sale to Smith & Nephew (2002), the product was sold to Advanced BioHealing (2006), then to Shire (2011). All of these firms had struggled to realise gains from a living cell product within the existing health context.[115]

While the European regenerative medicine industry led by British firms was smaller than its American counterpart, there appeared to be grounds for optimism in the sector during the second phase. After all, publicly funded researchers in Britain were able to work with embryonic stem cells, unlike researchers in the United States. Moreover, unlike in the 1990s, the British infrastructure was improving, from facilities, venture capital, and government grants to support science.[116]

Following its public listing in 2000, Reneuron delisted from the AIM in 2003 after development delays. In the meanwhile, the firm discovered their platform technology, and began to develop a more sophisticated business model. In 2002, Reneuron discovered a means to cost-effectively produce cell lines capable of treating thousands of people from a selected cell. The company also expanded its product offerings from the same technology base and developed a more global operation through networks of collaboration. For instance, through an alliance with Proteome Sciences, Reneuron launched a drug discovery tool using neural stem cells, ReNcell, in 2003. In addition, the firm broadened its therapeutic areas to include stroke and diabetes,[117] and widened its geographical focus to the United States, not only for clinical trials but also for technological alliances, such as with the cross-licensing agreement with the American firm, StemCells Inc.[118] Nevertheless, British investors and entrepreneurs at the time sensed that, while British academia offered more freedom to pursue stem-cell research, the environment for biotech entrepreneurship in the United States was superior, particularly in securing funds. To some extent, Reneuron's re-listing on the AIM in 2005 was considered a test as to whether the firm would remain in Britain or move to the United States.[119]

While the NHS offered a solid platform for conducting clinical trials, the challenge for British firms was not only to secure approval, but also to secure NHS reimbursement. The priority of the public healthcare system was to secure cost-effective, preferably low cost, therapies to deliver universal healthcare. To leverage this domestic risk, regenerative medicine firms, including Reneuron, formed overseas technical alliances and conducted clinical trials to develop their therapies overseas. The heightened concerns of the British life sciences industry were reflected in the publications of government reports in 2009 and 2010. These referred explicitly to the country's emerging regenerative medicine sector, and the challenging environment facing British firms, from financing, academic-industry collaboration, to the NHS.[120] The reports also reflected the growing commitment of the state to upgrade the health context in which firms operated.

In the mid-2000s, Intercytex pursued the development of its wound-healing products and hair loss product,[121] through financing with British-based venture capital firms such as Merlin Biosciences, Avlar BioVentures and 3i.[122] While the firm faced several delays, Intercytex listed on AIM in 2006, which allowed the firm to expand its R&D facility in Manchester. At the time, Intercytex's founder, Paul Kemp, claimed that 'regenerative medicine is about to 'come of age',[123] and expressed considerable optimism about the firm's prospects. He also noted renewed enthusiasm for the industry among American investors, showing an awareness of the varied industry dynamics across countries.[124] Given the firm's need to raise capital, such optimism was understandable yet premature, as Intercytex experienced an existential crisis shortly thereafter.[125] The firm had expanded its products, from wound care to aesthetic medicine, but investors reacted negatively to the failure of its lead therapy to pass clinical trials, and AIM delisted the firm in 2009.[126] Intercytex did not survive, and folded several years later after selling its technologies to other firms.

In Britain, leading regenerative medicine companies actively pursued the development of their therapies, and conducted initial public offerings in the mid-2000s. In addition to their key therapies, firms diversified their business areas to generate revenue. Much like their American counterparts, they too, developed collaborative networks in academia and industry, and expanded their overseas networks, primarily in the United States. As a smaller industry compared with their American counterpart, greater government support manifested over the years to support the growth of the sector, such as with the creation of the Cell Therapy Catapult in 2012. Yet cell-based therapies originating from Britain have yet to be approved by the EMA, and made widely available through the NHS.[127]

Industry dynamics also differed in Japan, where leading firms endeavoured to commercialise tested technologies for particular therapeutic uses. Japan's own pioneering tissue-engineering firm, Japan Tissue Engineering (J-TEC) was established in 1999 as a part of Nidec, a medical devices company that sought to diversify into new business areas. As in many large Japanese firms, J-TEC adopted a business strategy based on in-licensing.[128] The company imported tissue-engineering technology developed by Howard Green who was at MIT in the 1970s, which had already been commercialised overseas. Genzyme's autologous tissue-engineered product, Epicel, was launched in the United States in 1987 and was marketed in France, South Korea and Italy.

As noted earlier, Japan had a notoriously difficult regulatory environment that featured long delays in approval processes and no prior approvals of cell-based therapies.[129] After the scientist Shinya Yamanaka's discovery of iPS cells in 2007 – which was followed by a Nobel Prize Award in 2012 – Japanese academic scientists and entrepreneurs lobbied regulators to alter the regulatory environment to facilitate the commercialisation of cell-based therapies. iPS cells were stem cells – cells that can differentiate into any other type of cell – that could be created from adult cells. For Japanese researchers facing ethical constraints posed by handling embryonic stem cells, the discovery also seemed to offer the opportunity for Japanese firms to take advantage of a breakthrough in Japanese science and become global leaders in a frontier industry.

As enthusiasm for the regenerative medicine industry grew, the Japanese government made substantial steps to support the sector, from grants to regulatory reforms to facilitate the approval of novel therapies. In 2007, J-TEC received Japan's first regulatory approval for its autologous skin product. While the company managed to secure reimbursement in 2009, the firm faced considerable challenges, not only regarding the lengthy path to approval, but also after reimbursement.[130] For example, *JACE* was initially priced at 306,000 yen for each 80 cm^2 sheet, for up to 20 sheets, limited to patients with severe burns that covered more than 30% of the body.[131] In reality, however, patients with severe burns required more than the reimbursement amount. Furthermore, around a third of the patients passed away before the company could produce the product. As the company provided the remaining skin sheets free of charge, they generated little revenue.

In this context, Japanese firms benefitted from patient capital. Unlike shareholders in the United States, Japanese investors were not sensitive to share prices. Japanese investors, were in fact, more sensitive to Shinya Yamanaka's Nobel Prize award for the discovery of iPS cells rather than the firm's financial performance. Japanese firms could pursue the development of their therapies without the shareholder pressures felt by their British and American counterparts.

Over time, J-TEC, also began to seek foreign markets, through approval in other Asian jurisdictions, such as China and Thailand.[132] J-TEC also offered contract manufacturing and contract research services while seeking the approval of additional products. In 2012, J-TEC gained a second approval for *JACC*, an autologous cartilage product based on research at Hiroshima University, and secured reimbursement in 2013.[133] More than adjusting its technological ambitions, the latecomer firm's business model was to develop technologies already commercialised overseas; indulge in the patience of its investors; and appeal to regulators.

After lobbying from, and in collaboration with, academia and firms, Japanese regulators introduced the Act on the Safety of Regenerative Medicine and revised the existing Pharmaceutical Affairs Law to accommodate regenerative medicines in 2014. At last, organisations outside the hospital were permitted to cultivate cells, and cell-based therapies could be launched on the market for a designated period after two, rather than three, phases of clinical trials.[134] While similar expedited approval schemes such as the Breakthrough Therapy scheme or the Early Access to Medicines scheme were also introduced in the United States and Britain since 2010, the Japanese regulation was distinct in its explicit tailoring of regulation to regenerative medicines.[135]

Not all Japanese regenerative medicine firms were importing technologies. In fact, a growing number of firms aspired to commercialise novel, untested technologies. For example, ReproCELL, established in 2003, is an academic start-up utilising frontier research from Tokyo and Kyoto Universities. Headed by a former McKinsey consultant, Chikafumi Yokoyama, the firm has had a long-term aim of commercialising iPS cell therapies. The company's business model was to focus on the contract manufacturing of iPS cells and contract research services using iPS cells in the short term; and expand into global markets to build the capabilities and funds to offer iPS cell-based therapies in the long term. More recently, ReproCELL conducted an initial public offering in 2015, and expanded its global reach through acquisitions of biotechnology companies in the United States (Stemgent, Bioserve) and Britain (Reinnervate, Biopta).[136]

Another pioneering Japanese regenerative medicine firm, Healios, was established in 2011 by an ophthalmologist, Tadanao Kagimoto. This company partnered with a leading scientist in regenerative medicine, Masayo Takahashi at the government research institute Riken, to commercialise a therapy for macular degeneration.[137] The company's aim has been to be the first in the world to commercialise iPS cell therapies. In pursuit of this goal, the company secured government grants,[138] developed networks of collaboration with universities and with firms such as iPS Academia Japan.[139] The firm has also formed partnerships to expand into new product areas, from developing retinal cells with Dainippon Sumitomo Pharmaceuticals to developing a cell cultivation device with Nikon.

In recent years, Healios' business strategy has become more global. For instance, the company formed a collaboration with Athersys to help commercialise the American firm's stem-cell therapy in Japan under the new regulatory framework,[140] while it also planned to conduct clinical trials for its eye disease product in the United States.[141] As the firm improved its business model and progressed its pipeline, Healios conducted its initial public offering in 2015 on Mothers, the start-up section of the Tokyo Stock Exchange, and raised 3.3 billion yen.[142] Healios has been the first in the world to conduct clinical trials using iPS cells, which have been conducted in collaboration with partner universities and hospitals.[143]

In Japan, the experience of latecomer firms in regenerative medicine was slightly different to those of newcomer firms, as the former experimented with more narrow, tested scientific technologies. At J-TEC, for instance, the company tried to commercialise engineered tissue, based on a technology that was first identified in the 1970s and commercialised in the United States more than a decade earlier. Innovative firms using untested technologies such as ReproCELL and Healios developed different business models. These business models not only involved contract manufacturing and contract research services in the short- to medium term but also involved the adoption of a global strategy based on international partnerships that would extend their markets as well as facilitate the development of cell-based therapies in the long term. In a country where support for regenerative medicine became a national project to revitalise the country's frontier industries, regulatory reforms and the creation of an industrial association for regenerative medicine did much to inject dynamism in the sector in the 2010s.

Concluding discussion

As in the broader biopharmaceutical industry, advances in the regenerative medicine industry have been an arduous process across countries because of the nature of the technology and the challenge of 'fit' discussed in the introduction. Living, cell-based therapies were extraordinarily complex to understand, and costly to handle – whether in R&D, manufacture, distribution or administration. However, these challenges facing regenerative medicine firms pursuing commercialisation were not the same in the three countries. For instance, the timing of industry emergence had much to do with the support for academic entrepreneurship and the availability of capital. Firms' access to different types of finance also shaped their size and longevity. American firms could grow relatively quickly, but investors were not patient, and were quick to withdraw under poor business performance. The healthcare system – public or private, single or multiple payers – also informed the decisions of regulators decisions to approve, and insurers decisions to reimburse the product.

The obstacles to commercialisation appeared greatest in Britain and the least in the United States. Yet this article also tried to highlight how comparative institutional advantages were blurry at best in such a technologically complex industry with many stages in commercialisation. At a given time in history, a country could demonstrate comparative institutional advantages in one part of, but often not the entire value chain – whether in terms of financing, regulatory approval or reimbursement.

By the end of the historical period covered here, regenerative medicine firms had become keenly aware of the differences in health contexts and their varied advantages and disadvantages to commercialisation. Firms capitalised on this realisation by expanding their collaborative networks overseas, to take advantages of the opportunities for specific activities in a given country. For instance, British and Japanese firms such as Reneuron and Healios formed technical alliances with American firms and planned clinical trials in the United States. Not only did British and Japanese firms benefit from knowledge exchange with American firms, but also they sought to commercialise their therapies in the largely private American healthcare system. On the other hand, American firms such as Athersys sought to take advantage of the improved regulatory environment in Japan to commercialise their therapy with a Japanese partner. This expansion of international collaboration in the regenerative medicine industry was a marked phenomenon during the second phase.

This article has adopted a more holistic perspective to the business history of medicine, and has explored how the development of the regenerative medicines industry was shaped, not only by the nature of the technology, but also by the different contexts in which firms were embedded. The technological base of cells demanded adjustments from a broad constellation of actors within the broader health context– from producers (companies), users (patients and doctors), financial organisations, to the government. In the interim, the varied health contexts shaped the regenerative medicine industry in different ways; by factors such as the support for academic entrepreneurship; availability of venture capital; or the existence of universal healthcare. Over time, firms expanded globally, leveraging various health contexts for commercialisation; to enhance the institutional 'fit' across different stages of the value chain.

Commercialisation is the product of a complex process of engagement with a range of actors in the broader healthcare setting, and making various adjustments, from the narrowing of therapeutic indications, leveraging regulation, improving dosages, to securing reimbursement. As the business of health becomes more global, it is hoped that future research in business history will continue to adopt this broader and comparative perspective to better understand how frontier industries evolve over time – and place.

Notes

1. Andrew Pollack, 'Dendreon, Maker of Prostate Cancer Drug Provenge, Files for Bankruptcy,' *New York Times*, 10 November 2014; Ledford, 'Therapeutic Cancer Vaccine'.
2. David, 'Clio and QWERTY'; David, 'The Dynamo and the Computer'; Hughes, *Networks of Power*.
3. 'National Institute of Biomedical Imaging and Bioengineering, 'Tissue Engineering and Regenerative Medicine'.
4. Ibid.
5. American Society of Gene and Cell Therapy, 'Cell Therapy Defined'.
6. Fischbach, Bluestone, and Lim, 'Cell-Based Therapeutics'.
7. OECD, *OECD Health Statistics*.
8. See for example, Cohen, 'Macro Trends in Pharmaceutical Innovation'.
9. Malerba, 'Sectoral Systems of Innovation'; Carlsson and Stankiewicz. 'Technological Systems'; Edquist, *Systems of Innovation*; Lundvall, *National Systems of Innovation*.
10. Freeman, *Technology Policy and Economic Performance*; Hall and Soskice. *Varieties of Capitalism*; Allen, 'Institutional Embeddedness of Innovative Capabilities'.
11. Hall and Soskice, *Varieties of Capitalism*.
12. Goto, 'Japan's National Innovation System'.
13. Cockburn, Henderson, Orsenigo and Pisano, 'Pharmaceuticals and Biotechnology'.
14. Malerba and Orsenigo 'Innovation and Market Structure'.
15. Obama, 'United States Health Care Reform,' 526.
16. Centers for Disease Control and Prevention, *Health Disparities & Inequalities Report*.
17. OECD, *OECD Health Statistics*.
18. Chapin, *Ensuring America's Health*, p. 4.
19. Simon and Giovannetti, *Managing Biotechnology*, 152.
20. Grosios, Gahan, and Burbidge. 'Overview of Healthcare in the UK'.
21. OECD, *OECD Health Statistics*.
22. Department of Health and Dunne, 'NHS Prescription Charges'.
23. NICE, 'History of NICE'.
24. Timmins, Rawlins and Appleby, *A Terrible Beauty*.
25. Ministry of Health and Welfare, *Kosei Hakusho*.
26. Ministry of Health and Welfare, *Kosei Hakusho*, Yoshiwara and Wada, *Nihon Iryō Hoken Seidoshi* [History of the Japanese Health Insurance System].
27. OECD, *OECD Health Statistics*.
28. Ministry of Health, Labour and Welfare, 'Hoken Shinsatu to Hokengai Shinsatu' [Combining Insured and Uninsured Consultations].
29. Central Social Insurance Medical Council, 'Yakka Kaitei no Suii [Changes in Drug Price Revisions]'.
30. Chandler, *Shaping the Industrial Century*; Galambos and Sturchio, 'The Transition to Biotechnology'; Li, *Blockbuster Drugs*; Malerba and Orsenigo. 'Evolution of the Pharmaceutical Industry'.
31. Hughes, *Genentech*; Liebenau, 'Industrial R & D in Pharmaceutical Firms'; Marks, 'Collaboration – A Competitor's Tool'; Slinn, 'Glaxo and May & Baker'.
32. Mann and Plummer, *The Aspirin Wars*; Gootenberg, *Andean Cocaine*.
33. Liebenau, 'The British Success with Penicillin'.
34. Marks, *The Lock and Key of Medicine*; Rasmussen, *Gene Jockeys*.
35. Tobbell, *Pills, Power, and Policy*.
36. Quirke, *Collaboration in the Pharmaceutical Industry*.
37. Gabriel, *Medical Monopoly*.
38. Gaudillière and Thoms, eds., *Development of Scientific Marketing*.
39. Quirke and Slinn, *Twentieth-century Pharmaceuticals*.
40. Liebenau, *Medical Science and Medical Industry*.
41. Cramer, 'Building the 'World's Pharmacy'.
42. Conroy, *The Soviet Pharmaceutical Business*.
43. Umemura, 'Crisis and Change'.

44. Starr, *Social Transformation of American Medicine*; Burnham, *Healthcare in America*.
45. Murray, *Origins of American Health Insurance*; Blumenthal, 'Employer-Sponsored Health Insurance'.
46. Chapin, *Ensuring America's Health*.
47. Klein, *The New Politics of the NHS*. Rivett, *From Cradle to Grave*; Timmins, *The Five Giants*; Webster, *The National Health Service*.
48. Kawakami, *Gendai Nihon Iryōshi* [History of Contemporary Japanese Healthcare]; Kawakami, *Sengo no Iryō Mondai* [Healthcare Challenges since the Postwar Period]; Kawakami, *Gendai Nihon B yōninshi* [Contemporary Japanese Patient History].
49. Sugaya, *Nihon Iryō Seidoshi* [History of Japanese Healthcare]; Ikegami, *Nihon no Iryo to Kaigo* [Japanese Healthcare and Old-age Care]; Sakai, *Iryō Keieishi*; Ikai, *Byōin no Riron* [Theory of the Hospital]; Fukunaga, *Nihon Byōinshi* [History of Japanese Hospitals].
50. Yoshiwara and Wada, *Nihon Iryō Hoken Seidoshi* [History of Japanese Health Insurance System]; Maeda, *Kokumin Kaihon e no Michi* [Path to Universal Health Insurance].
51. Owen and Hopkins, *Science, the State and the City*.
52. Kipping, Wadhwani and Bucheli, 'Analyzing and Interpreting Historical Sources'.
53. Ordover, 'A Patent System'; Furman, 'Patents in Regenerative Medicine'.
54. Parliament, *Regenerative Medicine*.
55. Vacanti, 'History of Tissue Engineering'.
56. Rader, '(Re)defining Biopharmaceutical'.
57. Mason, Brindley, Culme-Seymour and Davie, 'Cell Therapy Industry'.
58. Fagnan, Gromatzky, Stein, Fernandez, and Lo. 'Financing Drug Discovery'.
59. John Newell, 'Futures: Blueprint of Mice and Men/The Second Generation Monoclonal Antibody' *The Guardian*, 18 July 1986.
60. 'Centocor Wins FDA Approval for Heart Drug,' *The New York Times*, 23 December 1994.
61. EMA, 'Glybera'.
62. FDA, 'FDA Approves Novel Gene Therapy'.
63. FDA, *Cellular and Gene Therapy Products*; European Commission, Report from the Commission. PMDA, 'Shōnin Jōhō no Ichiran [List of Approvals]'.
64. Alliance for Regenerative Medicine, *Annual Industry Report*.
65. Philip Hilts, 'Skin Grown in Lab Offers New Hope for Burns and Unhealable Wounds,' *The New York Times*, 28 June 1995, 10.
66. Edmund Andrews, 'Patents; a New Way to Grow Skin in Laboratory,' *New York Times*, 20 October 1990, 30.
67. Asuda, Gene, 'Firm Makes Strides in Growing Human Tissue,' *LA Times*, 22 March 1990.
68. Nerem, 'Regenerative Medicine'.
69. 'Officials Assail Offer to Store Bone Marrow,' *The New York Times*, 19 August 1986, 4.
70. 'Business People; Bone Marrow Company Names Chief Executive,' *The New York Times*, 22 June 1988, 5; Gene Asuda, 'Firm Makes Strides in Growing Human Tissue,' *Los Angeles Times*, 22 March 1990.
71. Advanced Tissue Sciences, *Annual Report*.
72. Ibid.
73. Ibid.
74. FDA, 'DERMAGRAFT® – P000036 Approval Order.' Washington, D.C., 28 September 2001; FDA, 'DERMAGRAFT® – P000036 Summary of Safety and Effectiveness Data.' Washington, D.C., 28 September 2001.
75. McKitty, et al. v. Advanced Tissue Sciences, Inc., et al. (No. 98-CV-1146) (1998) Complaint for Violation of the Federal Securities Laws, United States District Court, Southern District of California, 1998.
76. Cell Therapy News, 'Advanced Tissue Goes Bankrupt, ' October 2002, Vol 1, No. 2; Terry Brennan, 'Advanced Tissue Sale Ok'd,' *Daily Deal*, 20 March 2003.
77. Bell, Sher, Hull, Merrill, Rosen, Chamson, Asselineau et al. 'Reconstitution of Living Skin.'.
78. BJ Spalding, 'Human Organs Grow in the Lab,' *Chemical Week*, 11 November 1987, 28.
79. Sally Macmillan, 'Artificial Skin Grown for Grafts, *The Advertiser* 26 June 1987.

80. 'Organogenesis, Eli Lilly Set New-Product Venture,'. *Wall Street Journal*, 14 July 1987; Organogenesis, *Annual Report*.
81. Organogenesis, *Annual Report*.
82. FDA, 'P950,032. Apligraf' FDA, 'Aplifgraft® – 950032 Summary of Safety and Effectiveness Data'.
83. Bruce Hoffman, et al. v Philip Laughlin, et al. (No. 04-CV-10027) Class Action Complaint for Violations of Federal Securities Laws, United States District Court, District of Massachusetts, 2004; 'In Brief.' *Nature Biotechnology*; Bouchie, 'Tissue Engineering Firms Go Under'.
84. Reneuron, 'New Company to Treat Brain Damage.' Merlin Invests £10.5 m in Biotech Firms,' *Pharma Marketletter*, 24 March 1998.
85. Lisa Bushrod, 'Seeking a Listing: Reneuron Heads for AIM,' *European Venture Capital Journal*, 1 November 2000; Reneuron, 'Novo Nordisk Outlicenses Project'.
86. Mark Court, 'Stem Cell Firm Restores Investors' Hopes for Biotech Sector,' *The Times*, 10 November 2000.
87. Reneuron, 'Reneuron's Ren1869 Ready'.
88. 'New Technology: Brave New World,' *Investors Chronicle*, 23 November 2001.
89. Intercytex, Certificate of Incorporation 25 Feb 1999; Franklin and Kaftanzi, 'Industry in the Middle'.
90. Intercytex, 'Intercytex Raises £7 million'.
91. The Human Fertilisation and Embryology (Research Purposes) Regulations 2001; National Institutes of Health, 'Human Embryonic Stem Cell Lines'.
92. '"Saisei Iryō" no Yume, Chaku Chaku, Kowareta Zōki Kaifuku, Mirai No Gijutsu [the Dream of 'Regenerative Medicine' Moves Forward, Future Technology That Recovers Damaged Organs' *Asahi Shimbun*, 25 December 2000, 23; 'Saisei Iryō de Kyōdō Kaihatsu [Joint Development in Regenerative Medicine]' *Asahi Shimbun* 6 September 2002, 13.
93. Koji Tanaka, 'Shinkin Shūfuku suru Saibō Kenkyū' *Nikkei Sangyo Shimbun* 16 November 2002, 11; Miyake and Matsui, *Saisei Iryō Bijinesu Saizensen* [Frontlines in the Business of Regenerative Medicine].
94. Goto, 'Japan's National Innovation System'.
95. Collins and Wakoh, 'Universities and Technology Transfer'; Kushida, 'Japanese Entrepreneurship';.
96. Saisei Iryō nado no Anzensei no Kakuho nado ni Kansuru Hōritsu [Act on the Safety of Regnerative Medicine], 2014.
97. Yasuda, 'Shinyaku no Shōnin Shinsa Kikan'.
98. 'Sabakareta Kanryō Kojin, Matumura Motokachō ni Yūzai [Individual Bureaucrat on Trial: Matsumura Ex Section Chief found Guilty],' *Asahi Shimbun* 28 September 2001, 23.
99. Kemp, 'History of Regenerative Medicine'.
100. Andrew Pollack, 'Companies that Seek Cures Now Fight for Life,' *The New York Times*, 3 November 2002.
101. Lysaught and Hazlehurst, 'Tissue Engineering'.
102. BJ Spalding, 'Human Organs Grow in the Lab,' *Chemical Week*, 11 November 1987, 28; Craig D. Rose, 'Advanced Tissue Sciences to Fold,' *The San Diego Union Tribune*, 14 November 2002; Bruce Bigelow, 'Histogen Raises $10 M for Regenerative Hair Growth, Other Treatments,' *The San Diego Union-Tribune*, 1 December 2010.
103. Denise Gellene, 'Advanced Tissue Woes a Blow to Industry,' *Los Angeles Times*, 12 October 2002.
104. Craig D. Rose, 'Advanced Tissue Sciences to Fold,' *The San Diego Union Tribune*, 14 November 2002.
105. Terri Somers, 'Withdrawal of Investors, Lawsuit Hit Histogen Hard,' *The San Diego Union-Tribune*, 24 February 2009; Bigelow, Bruce. 'Histogen Raises $10 M for Regenerative Hair Growth, Other Treatments,' *The San Diego Union-Tribune*, 1 December 2010.
106. Organogenesis, *Annual Report*, various years.
107. Jon Chesto, 'Organogenesis Completes the First Stage of Its Canton Expansion.' *The Patriot Ledger*, 29 September 2010.
108. Terry Brennan, 'Organogenesis Set to Emerge,' *The Deal*, 14 August 2003.
109. Julie Jette, 'Healing its Wounds: A Year After Bankruptcy, Organogenesis Claims a Profit, *The Patriot Ledger*, 30 November 2004, 19.

110. 'FDA Clears Organogenesis Oral Soft Tissue Regeneration Product,' *Medical Industry Week*, 12 March 2012.
111. Fife, Carter, Walker and Thomson, 'Wound Care Outcomes'.
112. Steve Adams, '"Skin in the Game," *The Patriot Ledger*, 19 May 2012, 20.
113. John Carroll, 'Organogenesis Preps 'Heart Breaking' Cuts as Medicare Slashes Reimbursement,' *Fierce Biotech*, 4 December 2013.
114. Massachusetts Biotechnology Council, *Impact 2020*.
115. Andrew Pollack, 'Companies That Seek Cures Now Fight for Life,' *The New York Times*, 3 November 2002, 1. Andrew Pollack, 'Shire Buys Biotech Firm for $750 Million,' *New York Times*, 17 May 2011.
116. Richard Fletcher, 'The Brain Gain,' *The Sunday Telegraph*, 17 March 2002.
117. Sinden, 'Reneuron Group plc'.
118. Reneuron, 'Reneuron Enters Cross-License'.
119. Gross, 'Pushing Stem Cells to Market'.
120. Office for Life Sciences, *Life Sciences Blueprint*; Office for Life Sciences, *Life Sciences 2010*.
121. 'Intercytex' wound-healing drug enters Ph III,' *Pharma* Marketletter, 9 August 2005; Bilger Burkhard, 'The Power of Hair.' *New Yorker* 81, No. 43 (January 9, 2006): 43–48.
122. 'Intercytex raises £12 M in new venture round,' *Fierce Biotech*, 1 August 2005.
123. Kemp, Paul. 'History of Regenerative Medicine'.
124. Franklin and Kaftantzi, 'Industry in the Middle.'.
125. Intercytex, Full accounts made up to 31 December 2008.
126. *Financial Times*, 'Biotech Groups beset by Trials and Tribulations, 4 September 2009.
127. Holocar, an eye therapy from the Italian firm Chiesi was approved by the EMA in 2014. This treatment for rare eye disease was approved by NICE in 2017.
128. 'Hifu Baiyō Kokunai Hatsu no Jigyōka [First Commercialisation of Engineered Tissue in Japan] *Nihon Keizai Shimbun*, 1 January, 1999, 9.
129. 'Kokomade Kita Saisei Iryō [Advances in Regenerative Medicine] *Nihon Keizai Shimbun*, 22 October 2007, 19.
130. Japan Tissue Engineering, *Yūka Shōken Hōkokusho* [Company Securities Filings].
131. 'Baiyō Hifu, Yakedomuke Kakuhan [Expanding Sales of Engineered Tissue to Burns] *Nihon Sangyō Shinbun*, 28 November 2011, 9. Takayuki Inoue, 'JTEC: Jikobaiyō no Hyōhi o Hanbai [JTEC Sells Autologous Skin]' *Nihon Sangyō Shimbun* 27 February 2012, 22.
132. 'J-TEC ga Jigyō Keikaku, Saisei Kakumaku Jyōhi, Ajia Zen'iki ni [J-TEC Business Plan to Provide Autologous Corneal Epithelium throughout Asia],' *Nikkei Sangyō Shimbun*, 27 August 2008, 15; METI, 'Saisei Iryō Jitsuyōka Purojekuto [Project to Realise Regenerative Medicine]'.
133. Jihō, *Yakuji Handobukku*.
134. Saisei Iryōtō no Anzen Kakuho ni Kansuru Hōritsu [Act on the Safety of Regenerative Medicine]; Iryakuhin Iryōkikitōhō [Revised Pharmaceutical Affairs Act]. Drug approvals for existing therapies require three phases of clinical trials prior to regulatory approval.
135. FDA, 'Breakthrough Therapy'; Medicines and Healthcare Products Regulatory Agency, 'Early Access to Medicines Scheme.' In December 2016, the United States introduced the Regenerative Medicine Advanced Therapy designation with the twenty-first Century Cures Act.
136. ReproCELL, *Yūka Shōken Hōkokusho* [Company Securities Filings].
137. Takahashi, 'Mōmaku no Saisei Iryō'.
138. These include, for example, Japan Science and Technology Agency, *Saisei Iryō Jitsugenka Purojekuto* [The Project for the Realization of Regenerative Medicine]. 2003–2012; Japan Agency for Medical Research and Development (AMED), Project Focused on Developing Key Evaluation Technology: Evaluation for Industrialization in the Field of Regenerative Medicine, 2015.
139. 'iPS Saibō Chiken 17 Nen Ni Kaishi Keikaku, Mōmaku Ishoku [Ips Cell Cliinical Trials to Begin in 2014, Retinal Transplant],' *Asahi Shimbun* 2015, 7. Healios, *Yūka Shōken Hōkokusho* [Company Securities Filings].
140. Healios, *Yūka Shōken Hōkokusho* [Company Securities Filings].
141. Ibid.

142. Ibid.
143. 'iPS Matomete Chiken E Mōmaku No Byōki Fukusū O Taishō, Riken [Riken Aims to Develop Several iPS Cell Therapies Involving Retinal Cells].' *Asahi Shimbun*, 23 January 2014, 7.

Disclosure statement

No potential conflict of interest was reported by the author.

Bibliography

Advanced Tissue Sciences. *Annual Report*, various years.

Allen, Matthew. "Comparative Capitalisms and the Institutional Embeddedness of Innovative Capabilities." *Socio-Economic Review* 11, no. 4 (2013): 771–794.

Alliance for Regenerative Medicine. *Regenerative Medicine Annual Industry Report*. Washington, DC: Alliance for Regenerative Medicine, 2014.

American Society of Gene and Cell Therapy, "Gene Therapy and Cell Therapy Defined." Accessed November 1, 2016. http://www.asgct.org/general-public/educational-resources/gene-therapy–and-cell-therapy-defined

Bell, Eugene, Stephanie Sher, Barbara Hull, Charlotte Merrill, Seymour Rosen, Annette Chamson, Daniel Asselineau, et al. "The Reconstitution of Living Skin." *Journal of Investigative Dermatology* 81, no. 1 (1983): S2–S10.

Blumenthal, David. "Employer-Sponsored Health Insurance in the United States: Origins and Implications." *New England Journal of Medicine* 355, no. 1 (2006): 82–88.

Bouchie, Aaron. "Tissue Engineering Firms Go Under." *Nature Biotechnology* 20, no. 12 (2002): 1178–1179.

Burnham, John C. *Health Care in America: A History*. Baltimore, MD: Johns Hopkins University Press, 2015.

Carlsson, Benny, & Rikard Stankiewicz. "On the Nature, Function and Composition of Technological Systems." *Journal of Evolutionary Economics* 1, no. 2 (1991): 93–118.

Centers for Disease Control and Prevention (CDC). *CDC Health Disparities & Inequalities Report*. Washington, DC: CDC, 2013, 2016.

Central Social Insurance Medical Council, "Yakka Kaitei no Suii to Yakuzaihi oyobi Suitei Kairiritsu no Neji Suii [Changes in Drug Price Revisions and Annual Trends in Pharmaceutical Expenditure and Rate of Deviation from Estimates]." *Reference Material*, 31 July, 2013, 1.

Chandler, Alfred D. *Shaping the Industrial Century: The Remarkable Story of the Evolution of the Modern Chemical and Pharmaceutical Industries*. Cambridge, MA: Harvard University Press, 2005.

Chapin, Christy. *Ensuring America's Health: The Public Creation of the Corporate Health Care System*. Cambridge: Cambridge University Press, 2015.

Cockburn, Ian, Rebecca Henderson, Luigi Orsenigo, and Gary Pisano. "Pharmaceuticals and Biotechnology." In *U.S. Industry in 2000: Studies in Competitive Performance*, edited by David Mowery, 363–398.Washington, DC: National Academies Press, 1999.

Cohen, Fredric. "Macro Trends in Pharmaceutical Innovation." *Nature Reviews Drug Discovery* 4 (2005): 78–84.

Collins, Steven, and Hikoji Wakoh. "Universities and Technology Transfer in Japan: Recent Reforms in Historical Perspective." *The Journal of Technology Transfer* 25, no. 2 (2000): 213–222.

Conroy, Mary Schaeffer. *The Soviet Pharmaceutical Business during its First Two Decades*. Bern: Peter Lang, 2006.

Cramer, Tobias. "Building the 'World's Pharmacy': The Rise of the German Pharmaceutical Industry, 1871–1914." *Business History Review* 89, no. 1 (2015): 43–73.

David, Paul A. "Clio and the Economics of QWERTY." *The American Economic Review* 75, no. 2 (1985): 332–337.

David, Paul A. "The Dynamo and the Computer: An Historical Perspective on the Modern Productivity Paradox." *The American Economic Review* 80, no. 2 (1990): 355–361.

Department of Health and Philip Dunne MP. "NHS Prescription Charges from April 2017." March 16, 2017. Accessed November 24, 2017. https://www.gov.uk/government/speeches/nhs-prescription-charges-from-april-2017

Edquist, Charles, ed. *Systems of Innovation: Technologies, Institutions and Organizations*. London: Pinter, 1997.

EMA. "Glybera." Accessed April 13, 2018. www.ema.europa.eu/ema

European Commission. *Report from the Commission to the European Parliament and the Council in accordance with Article 225 or Regulation (EC) No 1394/2007 of the European Parliament and of the Council on advanced therapy medicinal products and amending Directive 2001/83/EC and Regulation (EC) No 726/2004*. Brussels: European Commission, 2014.

Fagnan, David E., Austin A. Gromatzky, Roger M. Stein, Jose-Maria Fernandez, and Andrew W. Lo. "Financing drug discovery for orphan diseases." *Drug Discovery Today* 19, no. 5 (2014): 533–538.

FDA. Letter to Michael Sabolinki Re: P950032, Apligraf, 10 November 1998. Accessed November 20, 2017. https://www.accessdata.fda.gov/cdrh_docs/pdf/p950032a.pdf

FDA. "Summary of Safety and Effectiveness Data." 20 June, 2000. Accessed November 20, 2017. https://www.accessdata.fda.gov/cdrh_docs/pdf/P950032S016b.pdf

FDA. "FDA Approves Novel Gene Therapy to Treat Patients with a Rare form of Inherited Vision Loss." *Press release*, December 19, 2017. Accessed April 13, 2018. https://www.fda.gov/NewsEvents/Newsroom/PressAnnouncements/ucm589467.htm

FDA. Vaccines, Blood and Biologics, Cellular and Gene Therapy Products Marketed Products [Online]. FDA. Accessed May 13, 2014. http://www.fda.gov/BiologicsBloodVaccines/CellularGeneTherapyProducts/ApprovedProducts/

FDA. "Fact Sheet: Breakthrough Therapies." Accessed November 24, 2017. https://www.fda.gov/RegulatoryInformation/LawsEnforcedbyFDA/SignificantAmendmentstotheFDCAct/FDASIA/ucm329491.htm

Fife, Caroline, Marissa Carter, David Walker, and Brett Thomson. "Wound Care Outcomes and Associated Cost Among Patients Treated in US outpatient Wound Centers: Data from the US Wound Registry." *Wounds* 24, no. 1 (2012): 10–17.

Fischbach, Michael, Jeffrey A. Bluestone, and Wendell A. Lim. "Cell-Based Therapeutics: The Next Pillar of Medicine." *Science Translational Medicine* 5, no. 179 (2013): 179ps7.

Franklin, Sarah, and Lamprini Kaftantzi. "Industry in the Middle: Interview with Intercytex Founder and CSO, Dr Paul Kemp." *Science as Culture* 17, no. 4 (December 2008): 449.

Freeman, Christopher. *Technology Policy and Economic Performance*. London: Pinter Publishers, 1989.

Fukunaga, Hajime. *Nihon Byōinshi* [The History of Japanese Hospitals]. Tokyo: Pilar Press, 2014.

Furman, Eric. "The Dynamic State of Patents in Regenerative Medicine." *Tissue Engineering and Regenerative Medicine* 10, no. 5 (2013): 230–233.

Gabriel, Joseph M., and Medical Monopoly. *Intellectual Property Rights and the Origins of the Modern Pharmaceutical Industry*. Chicago, IL: University of Chicago Press, 2014.

Galambos, Louis, and Jeffrey Sturchio. "Pharmaceutical Firms and the Transition to Biotechnology: A Study in Strategic Innovation." *Business History Review* 72 (1998): 250–278.

Gaudillière, Jean-Paul, and Ulrike Thoms, eds. *The Development of Scientific Marketing in the Twentieth Century: Research for Sales in the Pharmaceutical Industry*. Abingdon: Routledge, 2015.

Gootenberg, Paul. *Andean Cocaine: The Making of a Global Drug*. Chapel Hill, NC: University of North Carolina Press, 2009.

Goto, Akira. "Japan's National Innovation System: Current Status and Problems." *Oxford Review of Economic Policy* 16, no. 2 (2000): 103–113.

Grosios, Konstantina, Peter B. Gahan, and Jane Burbidge. "Overview of Healthcare in the UK." *The EPMA Journal* 1, no. 4 (2010): 529–534.

Gross, Michael. "Pushing Stem Cells to Market." *Current Biology* 15, no. 15 (2005): R576–R577.

Hall, Peter, and David Soskice. *Varieties of Capitalism: The Institutional Foundations of Comparative Advantage*. Oxford: Oxford University Press, 2001.
Healios. *Yūka Shōken Hōkokusho* [Company Securities Filings]. various years.
Hughes, Thomas. *Networks of Power: Electrification in Western Society, 1880–1930*. Baltimore, MD: Johns Hopkins University Press, 1983.
Hughes, Sally. *Genentech: The Beginnings of Biotech, Synthesis*. Chicago, IL: University of Chicago Press, 2011.
Ikai, Shuhei. *Byōin no Seiki no Riron* [Theory of the Hospital over a Century]. Tokyo: Yuhikaku, 2010.
Ikegami, Naoki. *Nihon no Iryō to Kaigo* [Japanese Healthcare and Old-age Care]. Tokyo: Nihon Keizai Shimbun Shuppansha, 2017.
Intercytex. "Intercytex Raises £7 Million for Pioneering Research Into Kidney Transplant and Human Tissue Replacement Technologies." *Press Release*, March 2, 2001.
Japan Tissue Engineering. *Yūka Shōken Hōkokusho* [Company Securities Filings]. various years.
Jihō, ed. *Yakuji Handobukku* [Pharmaceutical Affairs Handbook]. Tokyo: Jihō, various years.
Liebenau. Jonathan. "Industrial R & D in Pharmaceutical Firms in the Early Twentieth Century." *Business History* 26, no. 3 (1984): 329-346.
Kawakami, Takeshi. *Gendai Nihon Iryōshi: Kaigyōisei no Hensen* [The History of Contemporary Japanese Healthcare: Changes in the Physician-owned Clinic System]. Tokyo: Keisō Shobō, 1965.
Kawakami, Takeshi. *Sengo no Iryō Mondai* [Healthcare Challenges since the Postwar Period]. Tokyo: Keisō Shobō, 1980.
Kawakami, Takeshi. *Gendai Nihon Byōninshi* [Contemporary Japanese Patient History]. Tokyo: Keisō Shobō, 1982.
Kemp, Paul. "History of Regenerative Medicine: Looking Backwards to Move Forwards." *Regenerative Medicine* 1, no. 5 (September 2006): 653–669.
Kipping, Matthias, R. Daniel Wadhwani, and Marcelo Bucheli. "Analyzing and Interpreting Historical Sources: A Basic Methodology." In *Organizations in Time: History, Theory, Methods*, 305–329. Oxford: Oxford University Press, 2014.
Klein, Rudolf. *The New Politics of the NHS: From Creation to Reinvention*. Abingdon: Radcliffe Publishing, 2006.
Kushida, Kenji. "Japanese Entrepreneurship: Changing Incentives in the Context of Developing a New Economic Model." *Stanford Journal of East Asian Affairs* 1, no. 1 (2001): 86–95.
Ledford, Heidi. "Therapeutic Cancer Vaccine Survives Biotech Bust." *Nature* 519, no. 7541 (2015): 17–18.
Li, Jie Jack. *Blockbuster Drugs: The Rise and Decline of the Pharmaceutical Industry*. Oxford: Oxford University Press, 2014.
Liebenau, Jonathan. "The British Success with Penicillin." *Social Studies of Science* 17, no. 1 (1987): 69–86.
Liebenau, Jonathan. *Medical Science and Medical Industry: The Formation of the American Pharmaceutical Industry*. Baltimore, MD: Johns Hopkins University Press, 1987.
Lundvall, Bengt-Åke, ed. *National Systems of Innovation: Toward a Theory of Innovation and Interactive Learning*. London: Anthem Press, 2010.
Lysaght, Michael J., and Anne L. Hazlehurst. "Tissue Engineering: The End of the Beginning." *Tissue Engineering.* 10, no. 1–2 (2004): 309–320.
Maeda, Nobuo. *Kokumin Kaihon e no Michi: Sennin no Igyō Hyakunen* [Path to Universal Health Insurance: Efforts over a Hundred Years]. Tokyo: Keisō Shobō, 2016.
Malerba, Franco. "Sectoral Systems of Innovation and Production." *Research Policy* 31, no. 2 (2002): 247–264.
Malerba, Franco, and Luigi Orsenigo. "Innovation and Market Structure in the Dynamics of the Pharmaceutical Industry and Biotechnology: Towards a History-friendly Model." *Industrial and Corporate Change* 11, no. 4 (2002): 667–703.
Malerba, Franco, and Luigi Orsenigo. "The Evolution of the Pharmaceutical Industry." *Business History* 57, no. 5 (2015): 664–687.
Mann, Charles, and Mark L. Plummer. *The Aspirin Wars: Money, Medicine, and 100 Years of Rampant Competition*. New York: Knopf, 1991.
Marks, Lara Vivienne. "Collaboration – A Competitor's Tool: The Story of Centocor, an Entrepreneurial Biotechnology Company." *Business History* 51, no. 4 (2009): 529–546.

Marks, Lara. *The Lock and Key of Medicine: Monoclonal Antibodies and the Transformation of Healthcare*. New Haven, CT: Yale University Press, 2015.

Mason, Chris, David Brindley, Emily Culme-Seymour, and Natasha Davie. "Cell Therapy Industry: Billion Dollar Global Business with Unlimited Potential." *Regenerative Medicine* 6, no. 3 (May 2011): 265–272.

Massachusetts Biotechnology Council. *Impact 2020*. Cambridge MA: , 2014.

Medicines and Healthcare Products Regulatory Agency. "*Apply for the Early Access to Medicines Scheme*." 28 December, 2014. Accessed November 24, 2017. https://www.gov.uk/guidance/apply-for-the-early-access-to-medicines-scheme-eams

Mergent. Mergent Online Database. Accessed November 1, 2016. www.mergentonline.com

Ministry of Economy, Trade and Industry (METI) "Chūgoku, Tai Ōkoku ni okeru Saisei Iryō Jitsuyōka Purojekuto [Project to Realise Regenerative Medicine in China and Thailand]." METI, February 2014. Accessed May 5, 2015. http://www.meti.go.jp/policy/mono_info_service/healthcare/kokusaika/downloadfiles/fy25kobetsu/outbound_11.pdf

Ministry of Health, Labour and Welfare. "Hoken Shinsatu to Hokengai Shinsatu [Combining Insured and Uninsured Consultations]." Accessed November 15, 2017. http://www.mhlw.go.jp/topics/bukyoku/isei/sensiniryo/heiyou.html

Ministry of Health and Welfare. *Kōsei Hakusho* [White Paper on Health and Welfare]. 1961. Section 2, Chapter 1.

Miyake and Matsui. *Saisei Iryō Bijinesu Saizensen* [Frontlines in the Business of Regenerative Medicine]. Tokyo: Nikkan Kōgyō Shimbunsha, 2004.

Murray, John. *Origins of American Health Insurance: A History of Industrial Sickness Funds*. New Haven, CT: Yale University Press, 2007.

National Institute of Biomedical Imaging and Bioengineering, National Institutes of Health. "Tissue Engineering and Regenerative Medicine." Accessed November 1, 2016. https://www.nibib.nih.gov/sites/default/files/Tissue%20Engineering%20Fact%20Sheet%20508.pdf

National Institutes of Health. Human Embryonic Stem Cell Lines Available Under Former President Bush (Aug.9, 2001-Mar.9, 2009). Accessed November 22, 2017. https://stemcells.nih.gov/research/registry/eligibilityCriteria.htm

Nature Biotechnology. "In Brief." *Nature Biotechnology* 20, no. 11 (2002): 1071–1077.

Nerem, Robert M. "Regenerative Medicine: The Emergence of an Industry." *Journal of the Royal Society Interface* 7, no. Suppl 6 (2010): S771–S775.

NICE. "History of NICE." Accessed November 24, 2017. https://www.nice.org.uk/about/who-we-are/history-of-nice

Obama, Barack. "United States Health Care Reform: Progress to Date and Next Steps." *JAMA* 316, no. 5 (2016): 525–532.

OECD, *OECD Health Statistics*, various years.

Office for Life Sciences. *Life Sciences Blueprint*. HM Government, 2009.

Office for Life Sciences. *Life Sciences 2010*. HM Government, 2010.

Ordover, Janusz A. "A Patent System for Both Diffusion and Exclusion." *The Journal of Economic Perspectives* 5, no. 1 (1991): 43–60.

Organogenesis. *Annual Report*, various years.

Owen, Geoffrey, and Michael Hopkins. *Science, the State and the City: Britain's Struggle to Succeed in Biotechnology*. Oxford: Oxford University Press, 2016.

Parliament, House of Lords, Science and Technology Committee: First Report, Regenerative Medicine. London: The Stationery Office, 2013.

PMDA. "Shōnin Jōhō no Ichiran [List of Approvals]." Accessed May 30, 2017. http://www.pmda.go.jp/review-services/drug-reviews/review-information/ctp/0002.html

Quirke, Viviane. *Collaboration in the Pharmaceutical Industry: Changing Relationships in Britain and France, 1935–1965*. Abingdon: Routledge, 2008.

Quirke, Viviane, and Judy Slinn, eds. *Perspectives on Twentieth-century Pharmaceuticals*. Bern: Peter Lang, 2010.

Rader, Ronald. "(Re) defining Biopharmaceutical." *Nature Biotechnology* 26, no. 7 (2008): 743.

Rasmussen, Nicholas. *Gene Jockeys: Life Science and the Rise of Biotech Enterprise*. Baltimore, MD: Johns Hopkins University Press, 2014.

Reneuron. "New Company to Treat Brain Damage." *Press release*, November 11, 1999.
Reneuron. "Novo Nordisk Outlicenses Development Project to ReNeuron." *Press release*. May 30, 2000.
Reneuron. "Reneuron's Ren1869 Ready for Phase II Trials." *Press release*. December 20, 2000.
Reneuron. "Reneuron Enters Stem Cell Cross-License with StemCells, Inc." *Press release*. July 7, 2005.
ReproCELL. *Yūka Shōken Hōkokusho* [Company Securities Filings], various years.
Rivett, Geoffrey. *From Cradle to Grave: 50 Years of the NHS*. London: Kings Fund, 1998.
Sakai, Shizu, ed. *Iryō Keieishi* [History of Healthcare Management]. Tokyo: Nihon Iryō Kikaku, 2013.
Simon, Francoise, & Glen Giovannetti. *Managing Biotechnology: From Science to Market in the Digital Age*. Hoboken, NJ: John Wiley & Sons, 2017.
Sinden, John. "Reneuron Group plc." *Regenerative Medicine* 1, no. 1 (2005): 143–147.
Slinn, Judy. "Innovation at Glaxo and May & Baker, 1945–1965." *History and Technology* 13, no. 2 (1996): 133–147.
Starr, Paul. *The Social Transformation of American Medicine: The Rise of a Sovereign Profession And The Making of A Vast Industry*. New York: Basic Books, 1982.
Sugaya, Akira. *Nihon Iryō Seidoshi* [A History of the Japanese Healthcare System]. Tokyo: Hara Shobō, 1976.
Takahashi, Masayo. "iPS Saibō o Mochiita Mōmaku no Saisei Iryō." *Iyaku Jānaru* 47, no. 10 (2011): 87–91.
The Human Fertilisation and Embryology (Research Purposes) Regulations. 2001. Accessed November 22, 2017. http://www.legislation.gov.uk/uksi/2001/188/made
Timmins, Nicholas. *The Five Giants: A Biography of the Welfare State*. London: Harper Collins, 1995.
Timmins, Nicholas, Sir Michael Rawlins, and John Appleby. *Muang, Nonthaburi*. Thailand: Health Intervention and Technology Assessment Program, 2016.
Tobbell, Dominique. *Pills, Power, and Policy: The Struggle for Drug Reform in Cold War America and Its Consequences*. Berkeley: University of California Press, 2012.
Umemura, Maki. "Crisis and Change in the System of Innovation: The Japanese Pharmaceutical Industry During the Lost Decades, 1990–2010." *Business History* 56, no. 5 (2014): 816–844.
Vacanti, Charles A. "History of Tissue Engineering and A Glimpse Into Its Future." *Tissue Engineering* 12, no. 5 (2006): 1137–1142.
Webster, Charles. *The National Health Service: A Political History*. Oxford: Oxford University Press, 1998.
Yasuda, Kuniaki. "Nihon ni Okeru Shin-iyakuhin no Shōnin Shinsa Kikan [Approval Times for New Pharmaceutical Products in Japan]." *Research Paper Series, Office of Pharmaceutical Industry Research, Japan Pharmaceutical Manufacturers Association* 35 (December 2006).
Yoshiwara, Kenji, and Masaru Wada. *Nihon Iryō Hoken Seidoshi* [History of the Japanese Health Insurance System]. Tokyo: Tōyō Keizai Shimbunsha.

'Importance of Germany to Countries around and to World Economy makes it impossible to ignore' – The Rockefeller Foundation and Public Health in Germany after WWII

Sabine Schleiermacher

ABSTRACT
After WWII, the restoration of medical care and Public Health Service were the most important goals of the allied forces in Germany. They saw a connection between the population's health condition and its economic prosperity, which the Western Allies perceived as prerequisite for democracy. The allies participated in reforming the social security system. The Rockefeller Foundation provided grants for the modernisation of public health in Germany by initiating a transatlantic visitation program and a school of Public Health. This involvement stands in connection with the European Recovery Program and can be understood as an addition to US-American economic plan.

The Rockefeller Foundation's (RF) activities in medicine and related fields, such as biomedicine, neurology, genetics, and medical education as well as public health in Europe in the interwar years are topics of research. Up to now, the focus was not on the RF's activities in post-war Europe, especially in Germany. The question was rather if and to what extent the RF built on research content and structure it had already promoted during the Weimar Republic and National Socialism when it resumed activity in Germany after 1945.[1] In the context of examining medicine during National Socialism, the analysis of the RF started to focus on their former protégés projects' contents and objectives, whose medical experiments were scrutinised in the course of the Doctor's Trial 1946/47. Present examinations underscore that the purpose of investing in Germany was to construct a democratic society on their side of the Iron Curtain. Medicine and public health were not thoroughly examined and the RF's initiatives in the context of economically reorganising West Germany have been ignored.[2] From 1945 to 1951, the RF did spend $1,191,300 for various projects, including public health and Medical Sciences.[3] The question arises, in what kind of a situation did the occupation authorities' staff, such as the RF, arrive in Germany after WWII, what kind of structures for provision of healthcare they found, how they thought they could intervene and what kind of personnel they could resort to. The RF figured that its means would be best spent in the field of Public Health, ie training physicians and medical staff. In doing so, it hoped to influence medical thinking and future healthcare activity in a long-term perspective in the most efficient way possible. In the full knowledge of the importance of public health (in other words the mechanisms between health and social conditions) for smooth functioning of a society, which the RF described as 'Democratisation', the foundation had financed Schools of public health across the globe for many years, with which it tried to spread the focal idea of preventive medicine. Because the RF saw the requirements for an economically functioning society was the population's soundness, that was the goal it was committed to. Thus, the question is: How did explicit philanthropic legitimation of the RF reconcile with economic interests and Marshall-Plan and what significance did public health have in connection to the attempt to democratise West? What kind of dynamics underlay the explicit and implicit manipulation during global processes, in which the RF acted as transatlantic player? Finally, there is the question of whether the RF's involvement in the field of Public Health and their training in Germany can be described as 'democratisation'[4] and adequately encapsulated by the term 'Americanisation'.

The Situation in Germany after 1945

The Allies (USA, Soviet Union, GB, France) had split postwar Germany into four occupation zones and each army of occupation was politically responsible for the respective occupation zone it administered, up until the formation of Federal Republic of Germany (FRG) and the GDR in the year 1949. Although the allied forces formulated their political objectives as occupiers together, they used various methods to implement them. While American authorities followed the principles of 'indirect rule', rejected any dirigiste interference with functioning structures and hoped for the German's intellectual capability to reason, the French implemented a system of direct control, quite similar to the Soviets.[5]

At the beginning of the occupation of Germany US, representatives had no concrete understanding of the Public Health System in Germany. They also did not have a strategy to implement a new system of medical care. The situation in Germany after 1945 primarily required the securing of medical care for the general population, refugees, and displaced persons (DPs). This was mostly done for the protection of the occupation authority's staff. Therefore, the Allies maintained the structure of the German system and supported it in its function.

The restoration of medical care for the people and Public Health Service were the most important goals of the allied forces in all occupation zones of Germany. In the post-war years, concrete and practical issues were at the centre of attention. Among these problems were: preventing the spreading of transmittable diseases and plagues, medical assistance for the local population, DPs and refugees, as well as issues concerning food and water supply. The allied authorities tried hard with the German health administration to find solutions for these problems while not forgetting their own personnel's health and soundness. Consequently, on the instruction of the military authorities, large-scale vaccination programs were enforced and medical supplies were offered to German health authorities. The occupying authorities believed that a decline in health status would pose a security risk, which they aimed to minimise.[6]

Besides preventing specific impairments to health, able-bodied Germans were needed to reconstruct the country. The occupation authorities particularly assumed that nationalism and National Socialism could be countered with wealth and prosperity, which includes social stability and health security. Hence, a sound physical constitution of the population was not only a prerequisite for reconstruction but also for establishing a democratic state. The occupying forces' goal, next to the denazification of public administration, was to ensure that German health departments continue to function properly. The German health departments were a government responsibility and served as agencies for monitoring and ensuring the physical health of people living in Germany at the time. This institution 'purged of all active Nazis and ardent Nazi sympathisers, and of Nazi agencies and ideologies, was to be continued in full function as the official German health organisation'.[7]

In addition, the Anglo-American as well as the French occupation authorities did not have enough staff to fill all positions which is why they felt compelled to leave health administration in German hands or rather hand it back to the Germans. As a result, from summer 1945 on, Public Health Officers that had previously held positions in health administration returned to work autonomously in the American occupation zone and starting in the autumn of 1946, they gradually re-assumed the sole responsibility for the healthcare system.

As from December 1945, American authorities started to reduce their presence, especially on lower levels of government. They dissolved their agencies in rural and urban administrative districts and counties. At the Federal State level however, German state administration was still subordinate to the military government.[8] However, up until August 1949, ie before the establishment of the FRG, the American military government gave German authorities 'full legislative, executive and judicial power'. Nevertheless, the American High Commissioner was still obliged to 'do everything in his power to prevent the return of anti-democratic forces and to support and advise democratic forces in German society based on a positive program'.[9] The Germans distributed the responsibility over issues concerning healthcare, including healthcare legislation, among the federal government and federal states. At the same time, as of 1949 the federal states were responsible for implementing healthcare legislation that the federal government had passed. Yet, a central department for health on federal level was not created. Healthcare matters were minor divisions of the Department of the Interior.

Social Insurance and Public Health

One of the Allies' goals was to reform authoritarian and hierarchical structures extending back to the German Empire. German Empire social security system was part of that. According to public health officers, the structures of the healthcare system demonstrated 'backwardness' as well as disconnection from modern developments, caused by National Socialism and war.[10]

The general outline of the German healthcare system was created in the course of Bismarck's welfare policies during the 1880s. Medical-, accident- and disability insurance had been introduced over time and created a unit in social legislation. Its main function was to prevent poverty among people incapable of working. Central institutions in this system were insurance institutions that managed the funds. The whole project was equally financed by wage-dependent labourers and their employers. Freelancers and persons with other kinds of income did not contribute to funding this system. Payouts were only made to compensate for impairments. Private medical procedures were only financed in special cases.[11]

After WWII, the German social security system was basically bankrupt. In this light, the Allied Control Council, assisted by German experts, contemplated reforming German Social

Security. A national insurance (Einheitsversicherung) that combined all types of insurance was to be introduced in every occupation zone in Germany. Especially, this national insurance was supposed to be funded by all people with an income, no matter how high.[12] These reforms were designed to 'save costs' and 'remove defects in Bismarck's system' through standardisation.[13]

Not least because of economic considerations, US occupation authorities and the other Allies agreed on fundamentally changing the Social Insurance system by introducing a national insurance, which united all forms of insurance. They thought this system was more efficient when it came to generating means even though a system of this kind did not exist in the USA.

The French occupation authorities discontinued health insurance funds and transferred all the insured to a single general local insurance fund, creating a path towards a national insurance. British and American occupation authorities avoided that and took a different approach. Only Berlin succeeded in creating a national insurance in all zones; the VAB (Versicherungsanstalt Berlin). It provided insurance coverage not only for all gainfully employed persons, including their families and students but also the unemployed. The newly founded VAB was solely financed by contributions. Revenues rose rapidly and in 1947 amounted to about 624 million RM (Reichsmark) surplus so that reserve funds could be created. The contributions were set to 20% of one's gross income, equally paid by employees and their employers with a 600 RM limit per month. As a result, 96% of Berlin, that is over 3.1 million people, were unitarily insured against occupational disability and illness as well as secure pensions and other benefits.[14]

The approach in Berlin corresponded to the Allied Control Council's considerations to reform the German social security system. Following these observations, in 1947, the soviet occupation authorities began to introduce national insurance in their administrative area.[15] The Western Allies, who hoped that the implementation of their ideas would be met with the Germans' ability to reason, had to face 'massive' resistance by Germans in their occupation zone when it came to changing the insurance system.[16] There were wide-ranging discussions about national insurance in the western zones. Supporters as well as opponents were hoping to find legislative majorities for their respective position after the occupation. In the course of the increasing conflicts between East and West, the Western Allies completely abandoned their project in 1948 and cancelled the VAB in West Berlin in order to restore the old system.

However, American experts were familiar with the system based on Bismarck's social legislation, whose efficiency they honoured. They combined what they knew with their knowledge of the system's criminal degeneracy during National Socialism, which they wished to eliminate. The structures of medical care, public health and supervision were to remain untouched.

Even though British authorities were an occupying force, they were afraid to modify the existing social security system according to the changes the Allies had agreed upon. Yet, following the Beveridge-Plan, they completely reorganised their social security system and introduced government funded-healthcare in Great Britain between 1946 and 1948, thereby basically installing a national insurance.

By 1949, 72% of the German population had compulsory health insurance and by the end of the fifties, that number had increased to about 85% as a result of the economic miracle.[17]

To the ruling politicians of the FRG 'expanding and improving the repertoire of (the) welfare policy ... [was] not a primary objective'. The government wanted to realise the so-called 'social component' by a controlled market and not by sociopolitical intervention.[18] The claim was that the increasing economic wealth of dependent employees would automatically led to prosperity (by pay raises), since those who had the means to insure themselves, could. That way, the state was only responsible for maintaining and controlling the framework that enabled employees to attain wealth. This is how the government forced half of the responsibility for their insurance upon the citizens themselves. In addition to compulsory health insurance, the state governments had established the Public Health Service as a part of public assistance and welfare work in Germany. It was a state-run facility, financed by the federal states and under these states' and their respective municipalities' control. Since the days of the Weimar Republic, the Public Health Service became increasingly more important. During National Socialism, the central state re-organised and expanded the Public Health Service's field of activity by creating public health departments.

Following 1945, the Western Allies held on to the previously established structure and to their scope of tasks. At least they initiated the removal of racist terms from the respective legislative texts but without nullifying and removing these very laws. The entire field of racial hygiene, which the Nazis used in order to prosecute and murder minorities and which was a typical special field for public health officers and health departments, was not removed but replaced by the term 'Eugenics' without critically reviewing the associated mindset. The Public Health Services' duties were aimed to be preventative and considered an addition to compulsory health insurance by taking preventive measures and providing medical advice as well as offering treatment to uninsured persons. Beside verification activities and medical reviewing, its field of activity included: health consultation, welfare for mothers, children and adolescents, treating patients with tuberculosis or STDs as well as supporting the physically and mentally disabled. The Public Health Service even analyzed the relation between living habits, housing conditions and illnesses. In addition to that, it was also responsible for hygienic monitoring. That way, it united medicinal, societal and socio-political levels of action. Its focus of activity alternated between the Poles 'medizinische Polizey' ('medical police') and social hygiene, according to political context. After 1945 its structures remained unchanged. Once the German government assured the doctors the monopoly on ambulatory care with the 'Physicians compulsory law' of 1955 (Kassenarztgesetz), the Public Health Service became less and less important and physicians could progressively focus on their field of activity, such as preventative health care and consulting.[19]

The Rockefeller Foundation and Public Health in Germany

The RF was one of the biggest foundations in the USA. It operated internationally and had promoted projects in the fields of medicine, science and research since 1913. Under the Weimar Republic and during National Socialism the Foundation had backed individual scientists as well as research projects in the field of medicine.[20] Funding Public Health in the Weimar Republic did not come into question for the RF, seeing that with the appearance of social-hygienic issues and the establishment of one of the first Chairs for social hygiene, the preconditions for the advancement of Public Health in Germany seemed to have been met. During National Socialism the foundation only promoted basic research on neuroscience and bio-medicine in Germany.[21]

After 1945, the RF as well as the Allies sought to economically rebuild Germany, which they saw as the center of Europe. According to Carola Sachse: 'The objective of this discussion process was to define the RF's place in the new Cold-War world order and to investigate the ways in which it could continue to be active worldwide in this new situation, as called for by its ambitious purpose, 'to promote the wellbeing of mankind'.[22] In his letter to the chief of the US military government's economic department, William H. Draper junior, Under Secretary of the Army, Department National Defence, the president of the RF, Raimond B. Fosdick, described the flipside of this philanthropic maxim: 'It is hoped that the Foundation's opportunity to work in these areas may be of benefit not only to the people of these countries but also to our own'.[23] In the course of their ERP, they focused on counteracting the 'cultural isolation of Germany'. The president of the foundation held the view that Germany just as Austria could only be economically and politically integrated into a democracy-oriented Europe if they shared Europe's spiritual and moral values.[24]

From 1948 to 1952, the US Government pursued the same goals with their ERP. It was a 'key component of American policies aimed at containing communism in Western Europe. A united, economically sound Europe, which shares similar values to the US, would be immune to left-wing just like right-wing populism'.[25] The RF worked towards enforcing aid programs for the professionalisation and modernisation of theory and practice found in the field of Public Health in Germany with the intention to thereby contribute to political stability and order in Europe. During the process of conceptualising of grants-in-aid, the foundation staff used standards of US health policies, which according to them 'were promisingly used' worldwide and could 'solve the development issues of the massively crisis-prone modern Europe' without simply implementing an existing structure.[26]

Before the committees in the RF decided on their amount of participation, they let individual staff members observe the general situation in East and West Germany and fields they considered funding for many years. In the course of repeated evaluations, disillusionment set in among the rapporteurs regarding German insight and the success of the Allies' efforts to democratise Germany. There was the impression that there were not sufficient changes and that authoritarian thinking was still widespread. In 1937 Franz Goldman, who had been the officer of the Health Service in Berlin, had to flee Nazi-Germany due to racial persecution and then went on to become the Professor of the School of Public Health in Harvard University.[27] In the beginning of 1949, he was sent back to Germany by American military authorities as an independent observer to investigate the current developments in German healthcare.

During the formation of FRG, the military authorities planned to hand over managing Public Health Service to the Germans. In addition, the RF wished to assist the US military authorities in formulating proposals for the future design of the 'Public Health Service in Germany.

> 'The more important goal would be in line of the increasing self-government being devolved on the German authorities by OMGUS (Office of Military Government for Germany, US). The reorganization of public health in Germany consequently should as far as possible stem from the Germans themselves. Unfortunately, apart from their natural conservatism, they have been pretty much cut off from the world for the past 15 years. It would therefore seem essential that the first step would be to provide opportunity for selected Germans to visit countries where recent trends are most in evidence and upon their return to formulate recommendations to government of a public health program for Germany'.[28]

So Goldmann was not only supposed to conduct a survey on German healthcare (social insurance, the medical profession, public health) but also find eight German Public Health Officers that were worth considering for a trip through Western Europe and the US.

One had hoped that the impressions of foreign healthcare structures, which the Germans would gather on their journey, would encourage them to re-orientate themselves, enabling them to make proposals to restructure and modernise public health and medical services in West Germany.[29]

Subsequently, Goldman was expected to take part in drafting health legislation and administrative guidelines with German public health departments and German Public Health Leaders and thus acted as a link between German and Military authorities. The topics Goldman had to deal with were amongst others:

(1) Organising the medical profession and their relation to the government;
(2) The structure of healthcare provisions on federal state and municipal, but especially on national level, 'for which there is as yet no provision but which must be formulated immediately.'
(3) Revising health laws 'which largely date back to the first decade of this century';
(4) The National Health Insurance system, especially the question of optionality and payment;
(5) Merging the various forms of medical education on national level, which until then had been administered at federal state level.[30]

The responsible members of the RF hoped that Goldmann 'is not only able to advise the latter in a significant manner, but, more important, is helping the Germans to shape their own ideas in a manner which will prove in line with modern trends and acceptable to MG (Military Government)'.[31] The RF wanted to assist the OMGUS in formulating proposals for the future shape of Public Health Service. While forming the FRG, the military government advocated establishing their own Health Ministry. However, the military government had to face the fact that the German government did not show the same amount of appreciation for the subject of health. Just as the Weimar Republic and the GDR; the German government had not incorporated a right to healthcare into its constitution. In fact, it had merely set up a division at national level in the Ministry of the Interior that was supposed to focus on the issue of Public Health but had no influence in politics. Administering health concerns had been delegated to the federal states.

More information was not available to the OMGUS. Its Public Health branch had 'absolutely no information as to what, if any, provisions State are planning for Public Health'.[32] For instance George Strode, final director of the International Health Division (IHD) of the RF, who wrote in his diaries:

> 'The principal problem today … is medical care, a subject which the Army was not prepared to handle. As a substitute, a string of consultants was brought in, none of whom stayed long enough to be effective and the impression on the Germans was very bad. …, and FG (Goldmann) believes that the Bonn Government will throw out much that has been done. It has been said, …, that the military did a first-class job in disease control during the first year of occupation. After that they had to operate in fields that they were not particularly qualified in.'[33]

In his search for qualified local and state health officers worth considering for a voyage, Goldmann had to face that with a high average age, a large number of former NSDAP members and a lack of qualifications, only few officers even came under consideration.

> 'The relatively small number of experienced health officers are almost always in their sixties, if not older. Experienced men in their forties and fifties are conspicuous by their absence. A substantial number of the health officers under 60 and over 40 years of age have had little, if any, training or experience in public health administration, and many have come into public health administration by force of circumstances rather than by choice.'[34]

The personnel Goldmann could find after a political review included undersecretaries and executive Public Health officers from various federal states in the British and American occupation zones.[35] Although the visit program was thoroughly prepared and sufficiently funded, it still never took place. Several Executive Public Health officers were kept from participating in such a project by the ministry, which did not approve of trips for that purpose. Other Public Health Officers could not get a visa for the United States due to their former membership in the NSDAP although they had been classified as 'followers' in the process of denazification and were now in leading roles in Public Health. But there were also 'three German chiefs of public health for Lands Bavaria, Wuerttemberg-Baden, and Hesse', who withdrew their application for participating in the program, which the military authorities found 'extremely unfortunate and regrettable'.[36]

The reports which Goldmann had made about the impressions he got during his visitation of Germany remained unaffected by the termination of the visit program. His observations and assessments of compulsory health insurance, chambers of physicians, German Federal Public Health Office, and postgraduate education of German Health Officers were fundamental to the shift from Military Government to State Department control.

Since the Governmental Reorientation Funds were expected to get cut, the military government hoped that the RF would continue to remain active and make a special commitment to training German public health leaders, which they thought was urgently necessary. Even Goldmann put 'postgraduate education in public health' on the very top of the agenda in his extensive reports. He especially criticised that there was not an overall plan and the lack of resources, qualified teaching staff and scholarships.[37] Furthermore, he recommended, 'study trips to democratic countries and regular training at foreign schools of public health … (which) have the great advantage of exposing the German health officers to democratic principles and practices as well as of imparting technical information'. In addition, even if Goldman was perfectly aware of the fact that German public health administration was not comparable to the system in the USA in many respects, he still considered regular visits abroad for German Public Health Officers as well as additional support for fields specific to Germany necessary. So Goldmann did not want to just simply apply the American system to Germany; in addition to assistance in specific cases, he wanted to influence the thinking of German experts and disseminators in a democratic way, a view which the RF shared. The long-term plan's objective needed to be to successively create institutions for postgraduate education for all physicians and people of related professions who want to become active in the field of public health, and to continuously train existing staff. He did not want to follow the tradition of academies social hygiene from the era of the Weimar Republic since their syllabuses were outdated. Instead, he wanted modern schools of public health to be built in Germany, which would be an invaluable asset for the improvement of the curricula of medical training. These new institutions were supposed to be supported financially and technically, but also morally by both occupation authorities and foreign private agencies. In 1951, the RF proposed (1) looking for people and facilities that were of importance to regaining Germany's leadership position and therefore worth sponsoring, (2) find successful young scientists for research grants and (3) determine a location for public health education.[38]

Projects to democratise Public Health

Transatlantic Visits

In 1952, the RF once again tried to invite a number of German Public Health Officials to come on a trip to Canada and the USA in order to indirectly influence health policy developments in Germany. The Foundation assigned Hildegard Rothmund, Consultant of Public Health and Welfare Branch of the US High Commissioner for Germany (HICOG) in Frankfurt/Main to suggest suitable people. Rothmund then selected people with political responsibilities from different federal states.[39] The project was funded not only by the Division of Medicine and Public Health (DMPH) in the RF but also by the Exchange Program of HICOG.[40] Ernest L. Stebbins held the operation's scientific responsibility; he was a Professor at Johns Hopkins School of Public Health and a WHO-member, who had developed the visitation program.[41] The Germans should once again be given the opportunity to discover new prevention strategies in the field of medicine and public health, in order to use them fruitfully in their own work.[42] The purpose of the visit was to prepare 'suggestions to the Bonn Government for the establishment of a school of Public Health'.[43] The plan was to visit John Hopkins School of Public Health and Hygiene, Harvard School of Public Health and the School of Hygiene of the University of Toronto. The School of Hygiene in Toronto was founded 1925 with financial assistance from the RF and one of the first universities that offered postgraduate Public Health courses. By participating in creating this School in Toronto, the RF pursued their plan 'to circle the globe with schools' of Public Health, for which they provided '$357 million in current dollars'.[44] By doing so, the Foundation contributed to establishing Schools of Public Health in almost every European as well as some South-American and Asian metropolises, some of which were among the most important institutions. Since it was founded, the RF had devoted itself to public health education and in the 1920's, it financed 20 Schools of Public Health worldwide.[45] In doing so, RF's 'vision of a world-wide network of similar schools of medicine, public health, nursing and social work, staffed by personnel trained through the fellowship program' had been '… largely realised'. The not unintended effect was that 'fellows and others associated with the Foundation came to play key roles in ministries, schools, hospitals, and institutes in nearly every part of the world, as well as in the work of the League of Nations Health Organisation, the UN Relief and Reconstruction Agency, and the World Health Organisation. The understanding of 'health' and the model of scientific medicine that the Foundation did so much to plant world-wide remained largely unquestioned – at least until the 1970s, when economic, social, and health-related costs began to evoke interest in alternatives.'[46]

Several attempts to convince the German government to build a School of Public Health on the federal level failed. The representatives of the Federal Ministry of the Interior hoped for a reinstatement of centralist structures in a reunited Germany. A School for Public Health was supposed to then be built under the administration of the Federal Health Office (Bundesgesundheitsamt) in Berlin according to their expectations. In the early 1950s, the people in charge of the field of Public Health Education dismissed any need for action.[47] Later on, the staff members of the RF distanced themselves from the Federal Ministry of the

Interior, also concerning the anti-American attitudes they had met.[48] Since, according to JM Maier of the RF, 'public health services are run by the Länder (federal states), the Federal service at Bonn being responsible for nothing but communicable disease and drug control. All social hygiene is under the Länder. The legal regulation is by Bonn, but the executive regulation by the Länder'.[49]

School of Public Health in Hamburg

Negotiations between the RF and the Universities of Heidelberg and Frankfurt/Main to jointly create a School of Public Health in 1948 were unsuccessful. RF officers looked for a scope of influence since they held the view that 'public health in Germany has been dominated by the 19th century concept of the public health authority as a police function' and that 'the development of preventive services has been hindered by this authoritarian approach'. This situation manifested itself in the training as well as in the 'approach' of most teachers of public health and preventive medicine in Germany'. While they searched for a new organisational framework for the establishment of a training facility one year later, they found the Academy for Public Health (Akademie für Staatsmedizin) in Hamburg, which had been founded in 1946 where Public Health Officers from northern German federal states (Hamburg, Hanover, Schleswig-Holstein, Bremen) and Berlin were being trained and which the foundation could participate in.[50]

The academy's curriculum included: social medicine, social service, psychology and mental health; all subjects that the RF wished to find in a School of Public Health. The RF did not intend to just set up an American model of the School of Public Health. They much rather wanted to train physicians in a postgraduate education, inspired by the German structures, in close connection with the medical faculty. This was supposed to have a retroactive effect on the curriculum of medical education.[51] The academy was equally financed by tuition fees and the five northern German federal states involved.

After long contemplation, the RF decided to assist the Academy for Public Health with constructing a School of Public Health. Consequently, from 1954 to 1958 the academy annually received $35,000 which was transferred to the Health Authority of Hamburg. The sum matched the annual amount that the academy got from the federal states.

The objective of promoting this plan was to revise the academy's curriculums and get additional scientific and teaching assistants, annual local fellowships and equipment for investigative fieldwork by students. The number of enrolled students remained the same. The additional funds enabled guest lecturers who stood in contact with the WHO's European Office and worked for Public Health Schools in different European countries, to get invited to hold lectures.[52] British occupation authorities had handed over management of the academy to social-hygienist and demographer Hans Harmsen, who was simultaneously appointed Chair of General and Social Hygiene at the University of Hamburg. Harmsen was national-socially minded, but had not been a member of the NSDAP,[53] which made him seem trustworthy in the eyes of American and British occupation authorities. At the British occupation authorities' invitation, he became acquainted with Britain's National Health Service (NHS) and took part in a study trip organised by the RF.[54]

Foundation staff noticed that Harmsen had argued in favour of modernisation, a Public Health structure based on municipal needs and 'a more democratic spirit and tradition' in various discussions they had held in Western occupation zones and the FRG since 1949. They expected him to make 'a change in undergraduate and postgraduate public health teaching both in curriculum content and in method of instruction', whereas 'the development of preventive services' was of great importance to the planned modernisation.[55] Harmsen however, stuck to his belief in a social hygiene based on eugenics. He did not use the impressions he got abroad very constructively. He thought that German Public Health Officer education was 'not worse' and that American training concepts could not be applied to Germany, since classes in the Schools of Public Health were too specialised according to him. In order to meet the RF's expectation of a close linkage between theory and practice, Harmsen initiated two research projects. He let students conduct a field study on the 'health and hygiene condition of all camps of former DPs still in Germany' and arranged the ethnic registration of the DPs who were still in Germany by 1954.

At the end of 1958, the RF decided to discontinue funding the Academy for Public Health in Hamburg, because measured by their expectations of Harmsen they found no apparent signs of modernisation of Public Health in the academy. One of the staff members wrote: 'From Harmsen's annual reports, I do not quite see how this program will be able to introduce a modern public health approach in Germany.'[56]

Summary

The US-American occupation authorities knew of the importance of health policy as an economic factor and they greatly appreciated the German health insurance- and public health system. The problem, however, was that they had no expertise of their own and therefore had to hire experts from the private sector, in this case the RF, that had operated as a global protégé of public health in the past and had qualified staff at hand.[57] Through its involvement, the RF reached a position of influence (gained major influence) in terms of shaping this field.

In the post-war situation in Germany, solving urgent concrete problems had priority. In this situation, occupation authorities chose to fundamentally restructure the social insurance industry in the shape of a national insurance that did not follow the US-American example but was based on German experts planning. In its simplicity, which allowed it to function without a large number of agencies and had a simple financing structure, the system was efficient and functionally adequate and therefore to the liking of the USA. But national insurance did not fail due to occupation authorities, but rather due to the resistance from German elites, who were given certain decision-making powers by the Americans, following the idea of indirect rule, so we cannot speak of 'transatlantic transfer' at this point.[58] The RF, whose senior staff had access to the highest circles, the Rockefeller family even to the President of the USA, did not however want to be perceived as 'the military government's tool' or 'an appendage of the State department'.[59] It was important that RF's involvement, without which an immaterial dividend was not feasible, was visible, which is why the RF was active in the field of public health and wanted to add a German School of Public Health to its global network. Inderjet Pamar describes the foundation's policy, which had vast financial resources, operated in times of crisis and functioned as 'gatekeeper of ideas' as follows: 'The aim is, of course, to promote ideas and theories that, …, will either maintain the status quo, or successfully manage change, without seriously disrupting existing patterns of power.'[60]

After WWI, the RF had already been interested in the field of medicine in Europe. W. H. Schneider believes the RF's reason among others was that Europe 'possessed the best developed medical infrastructure in the world. Therefore, according to the business mentality of the Foundation directors, investment in restoring these resources would be likely to 'pay dividends in future. ... assistance to European medicine would have a world-wide impact.'[61] As a result, in 1948, the RF sent experts on public health to Germany, who were given the task of evaluating the situation and making suggestions for possible initiatives. However, these experts were expatriates from Germany, which on the one hand sharpened their senses for problematic areas, but on the other hand mostly created issues concerning possible transatlantic manipulation. If we define Americanisation as 'selected and adapted transfer ... from the US to ... other states', we cannot speak of Americanisation at his point. The RF officers explicitly rejected an 'Americanisation'. It is rather a circulating process in which experts from the USA and Europe participated.[62] The RF also had a clear objective: creating a global network of Schools of Public Health. So, in this respect, we cannot speak of Americanisation but rather globalisation, which from a German perspective, appeared to represent Americanisation. At the same time, the RF's attitude can be characterised by the will to impact things. If staff members came to the conclusion that their demands could not be met by their transatlantic partners and their goal could not be reached, funding was suspended, which allowed them to 'cash in' on the symbolic dividend of having shown philanthropic engagement in Germany nevertheless.

Since US occupation policy took the view that Germans should educate Germans and thereby democratise and denazify them, they were unwilling to make any changes against the will of the Germans. They counted on Germany's willingness and ability to reason. On this side however, scientists assumed that they were representatives of a model system that did not need any adjustments, which is why there was no reason to discuss other approaches. This attitude did not correlate with the scheduled procedures of the USA, which is why their offers were not fruitful and German structures could not be influenced. The German Federal government's economic policy operated under the catchword 'Social Market Economy'. Social security, however, was not seen as principle of solidarity and implemented accordingly, but rather as a part of the market on which everyone had to individually strive to acquire 'social capital'.[63]

The RF's failed efforts in Hamburg show that its influence was quite limited and therefore in this context one cannot speak of an 'Americanisation'. Intellectual, cultural, cognitive and political differences impeded constructive collaboration between the Foundation and the German representatives. In the 20 opinion of the Foundation perceptible modernisation of the medical training and Public Health had not occurred for which reason the Foundation ceased its support.

But even this involvement, which was unsuccessful in their own eyes, had made the RF an agent in US foreign policy, as Berghahn put it: 'Philanthropy and diplomacy became close partners in the cold culture wars of the post-1945 era.'[64]

In the case of the medical care system, it cannot be said that there was any form of 'Americanisation' until the mid-fifties. The perceivable 'Westernisation' of the system was not about health politics but rather an economic transfer, which did not remain without consequences.[65] The point of reference was in this case Europe itself.

Notes

1. See Weindling, Paul J. '"Out of the Ghetto": The Rockefeller Foundation and German medicine after the Second World War.' In *Rockefeller Philanthropy and modern Biomedicine. International Initiatives from World War I to the Cold War,* edited by Schneider, William H., 208–222.

Bloomington: Indiana University Press, 2002. Sachse, Carola. 'What research, to what end? The Rockefeller Foundation and the Max Planck Gesellschaft in the Early Cold War.' *Central European History* 42 (2009): 97–141.

2. With the exception of Ellerbrock, Dagmar, *'Healing Democracy' – Demokratie als Heilmittel. Gesundheit, Krankheit und Politik in der amerikanischen Besatzungszone 1945 – 1949*. Bonn: J. H. W. Dietz Nachf., 2004. Ellerbrock completely underrated the modernity of the Public Health Officers' approaches, which legislation prescribed as of 1934, as well as the technology including serial X-ray examinations and concepts with wide-ranging acquisition of date and statistics, which can be seen clearly during the battle against tuberculosis. Reinisch, Jessica. *The Perils of Peace. The Public Health Crisis in Occupied Germany*. Oxford: Oxford University Press, 2013. See also Schleiermacher, Sabine. 'Contested Spaces: Models of Public Health in Occupied Germany.' In *Shifting Boundaries of Public Health. Europe in the Twentieth Century*, edited by Susan Gross Solomon, Lion Murard and Patrick Zylberman, 175–204. Rochester: University of Rochester Press, 2008. Ellerbrock and Reinisch do not elaborate on the RF.
3. Projects in Germany during the period May 9, 1945 to June 12, 1951. Rockefeller Archive Center (RAC), RF RG 1.1 series 717 box 7 folder 37.
4. After the Potsdam agreement in the year 1945, Demilitarization, Denazification, Decentralization und Democratization were supposed to break to the 'negative traditions 'National Socialism had brought and thereby create the 'requirements for a permanent foundation for peace'. Jarausch, Konrad. *Die Umkehr. Deutsche Wandlungen 1945–1955*. Bonn: Bundeszentale für politische Bildung, 2004: 130. The Allies' understanding of Democratization was the transformation of German politics in all social realms, especially education and the press, as well as the admission of parties and unions.
5. Wengst, Udo. 'Rahmenbedingungen.' In *Geschichte der Sozialpolitik in Deutschland seit 1945. Zeit der Besatzungszonen. Sozialpolitik zwischen Kriegsende und der Gründung zweier deutscher Staaten*. Vol. 2/1, edited by Bundesministerium für Arbeit und Sozialpolitik und Bundesarchiv, 1–76, 11. Baden-Baden: Nomos, 2001.
6. Ellerbrock, *'Healing Democracy'*: 109, 112, 118f.
7. Ibid., 105, 107.
8. Ibid., 107, 115, 124f.
9. Rupieper, Hermann-Josef. *Die Wurzeln der westdeutschen Nachkriegsdemokratie. Der amerikanische Beitrag 1945 - 1952*. Darmstadt: Westdeutscher Verlag, 1993: 38.
10. The office for political affairs formulated 1949: 'A government need not to be totalitarian to be non-democratic. Neither the Empire nor the Weimarer Republic were totalitarian, but neither were they democratic.' NA RG 59, 862.00/12–849, cited in: Ibid., 39.
11. Tennstedt, Florian. 'Sozialgeschichte der Sozialversicherung". In *Handbuch für Sozialmedizin* edited by Blohmke, Maria, Christian v. Ferber, Karl Peter Kisker and Hans Schaefer, 385–492, 386. Stuttgart: Ferdinand-Enke-Verlag, 1976.
12. Hockerts, Hans Günter. *Sozialpolitische Entscheidungen im Nachkriegsdeutschland. Alliierte und deutsche Sozialversicherungspolitik 1945 bis 1957*. Stuttgart: Klett-Cotta, 1980: 26–28.
13. Abelshauser, Werner. 'Erhard oder Bismarck?' *Geschichte und Gesellschaft* 22 (1996): 376–392, 384.
14. Schellenberg, Ernst. *Versicherungsanstalt Berlin 1945–1947. Ein Arbeitsbericht*. Berlin: self published 1947: 29f. Hoffmann, Dierk. *Sozialpolitische Neuordnung in der SBZ/DDR. Der Umbau der Sozialversicherung*, München: R. Oldenbourg Verlag, 1996: 70.
15. See also Schagen, Udo, and Sabine Schleiermacher, 'Gesundheitswesen und Sicherung bei Krankheit und im Pflegefall.' In *Die Sowjetische Besatzungszone und Berlin. Geschichte und Sozialpolitik in Deutschland seit 1945* edited by Bundesministerium für Arbeit und Sozialpolitik und Bundesarchiv, 511–528, 524. Baden-Baden: Nomos 2001. Arndt, Melanie. *Gesundheitspolitik im geteilten Berlin 1948–1961*. Köln, Weimar and Wien : Böhlau, 2009: 68–72.
16. Hockerts. 'Entscheidungen': 51–85.
17. Tennstedt. 'Sozialgeschichte': 385–492, 422.
18. Abelshauser. 'Erhard': 378.

19. Lindner, Ulrike. *Gesundheitspolitik in der Nachkriegszeit. Großbritannien und die Bundesrepublik Deutschland im Vergleich*. München: De Gruyter, 2004: 36–38.
20. RAC, RF RG 6.1 series 2.1 box 66 folder 623.
21. Weindling. 'Ghetto'.
22. Sachse. 'Research': 136.
23. Raymond B. Fosdick to William H. Draper. January 14, 1948. RAC, RF RG 1.2 series 700 box 10 folder 84.
24. *The Annual Report - Rockefeller Foundation 1948* edited by Rockefeller Foundation. New York: self published, 1948: 46–47.
25. Kimmel, Elke. 'Gemeinsam gegen die 'Achsenmächte'. Bundeszentrale für politische Bildung 31.10.2005. Accessed November 19, 2016. http://www.bpb.de/geschichte/deutsche-geschichte/marshallplan/39982/gemeinsam-gegen-die-achsenmaechte. 'The ERP was designed not only to stimulate economic growth and foreign trade but at the same time to turn western Europe into a bulwark against communism'. Schröter, Harm G. *Americanization of the European Economy. A compact survey of American economic influence in Europe since the 1880s*. Dordrecht: Springer Verlag, 2005: 47.
26. Rausch, Helke. 'Professionalisierung als Diplomatische Strategie: Das us-amerikanische Carnegie Endowment in Europa vor 1945', 2. Themenportal Europäische Geschichte. Accessed November 7, 2016. www.europa.clio-online.de.
27. Antoni, Christine. *Sozialhygiene und Public Health: Franz Goldmann (1895–1970)*. Husum: Matthiesen Verlag 1997.
28. Grant to Strode. January 1, 1949. RAC, RF RG 1.2 series 717 box 4 folder 35.
29. International Health Division, special research projects, p. 3. RAC, RF RG 1.2 series 700 box 10 folder 89. Kubin (OMGUS) to Grant February 18, 1949. RAC, RF RG 1.2 series 717 box 4 folder 35.
30. Grant to Strode July 2, 1949. Ibid. See also Conference between John Grant and Franz Goldmann July 9, 1949. Ibid.
31. Grant to Strode July 2, 1949. Ibid.
32. Grant to Strode August 8, 1949. Ibid.
33. Strode Diary, November 17, 1949. RAC, RF RG 1.2 series 717 box 4 folder 36.
34. Goldmann, Franz. 'Report on Interviews of Candidates for the Study trip to foreign countries, 1949.' RAC, RF 1.2 RG 717 box 4 folder 35.
35. Goldmann, Franz. 'Final report'. August 11, 1949. Ibid.
36. Grant to Strode. August 21, 1949. Ibid.
37. Goldmann, Franz. 'Postgraduate Education of German Health Officers.' September 15, 1949. RAC, RF RG 1.2 series 717 box 4 folder 36. There will be citations in the following segment.
38. Excerpt from a memo from Struthers. November 30, 1951. RAC, RF RG 6.1. series 2.1 box 63 folder 581.
39. Interoffice Correspondence Struthers. September 25, 1952. Corresponds with John Maier, October 21, 1952. Floyd Lyle, November 13, 1952. RAC, RF RG 1.2 series 717 box 4 folder 33.
40. Struthers to Wilson, RF, Toronto, September 19, 1952. Ibid. Struthers to Russell. Ibid.
41. Cook, Joan and Ernest L. Stebbins. 'Expert on Public Health' (New York Times May 9, 1987).
42. Strode to the Rockefeller Foundation, September 10, 1948. RAC, RF RG 12.1. box 61, pp. 123.
43. Grant-in-Aid for Dr. Hildegard Rothmund. RAC, RF RG 1.2 series 717 box 4 folder 33.
44. Our History – The Rockefeller Foundation. Accessed November 7, 2016. https://www.rockefellerfoundation.org/about-us/our-history/
45. Weindling, Paul. 'Public Health and Political Stabilisation. The Rockefeller Foundation in Central and Eastern Europe between the Two World Wars.' *Minerva* 31 (1993): 253–267. Fee, Lizabeth, and Bu Liping. 'Models of Public Health education: Choices for the future?' *Bulletin of World Health Organization* 85 (2007): 977–979. Schleiermacher, Sabine. 'Die Rockefeller Foundation und ihr Engagement bei einer Neuorientierung von Medizin und Public Health in Deutschland in den 1950er Jahren'. *Medizinhistorisches Journal* 45 (2010): 43–65, 50.
46. Page, Benjamin B. 'The Rockefeller Foundation and Central Europe: A Reconsideration.' *Minerva* 40 (2002): 265–287, 285.
47. Diary John Maier March 25, 1952. RAC, RF RG 6.1. series 2.1. box 31 folder 343, p.74.

48. Akademie für Staatsmedizin March 7, 1952. Staatsarchiv Hamburg 364–12,16.
49. Diary John Maier March 25, 1952. RAC, RF RG 6.1. series 2.1. box 31 folder 343, p.74.
50. See also Münchow, Siegfried. 'Über die Gründung der Akademie für Staatsmedizin in Hamburg.' *Hamburger Ärzteblatt* 21 (1967): 302–305.
51. Grant for the Akademie für Staatsmedizin, RAC, RF RG 1.2 series 717 box 2 folder 12.1.
52. Harmsen, Annual report for 1955, December 16, 1955. RAC, RF RG 1.2 series 717 box 2 folder 12.1.
53. See also to Harmsens healthcare policy during the National Socialist period and before: Schleiermacher, Sabine. *Sozialethik im Spannungsfeld von Sozial- und Rassenhygiene. Der Mediziner Hans Harmsen im Centralausschuß für die Innere Mission.* Abhandlungen zur Geschichte der Medizin und der Naturwissenschaften, Heft 85. Husum: Matthiesen Verlag, 1998.
54. Harmsens journey describe in: RAC, RF 1.2 series 717 box 2 folder 12.1.
55. Grant for the Akademie für Staatsmedizin October 23, 1953. RAC, RF RG 1.2, series 717 box 2 folder 12.1.
56. Maier August 22, 1957. RAC, RF RG 1.2. series 700 box 4, folder 31.
57. Barona, Josep L., *The Rockefeller Foundation, Public Health and International Diplomacy, 1920–1945*. London: Pickering and Chatto, 2015.
58. See also Berghahn, Volker R. 'The debate on ‚Americanization' among economic and cultural historians.' *Cold War History* 10 (2010): 107–130, 110.
59. Sachse. 'Research': 136f.
60. Parmar, Inderjeet. 'To relate knowledge in action': The impact of the Rockefeller Foundation of foreign policy thinking during America's rise to globalism 1939–1945.' *Minerva* 40 (2002), 235–263, 238.
61. Schneider, William H. 'The Model American Foundation Officer: Alan Gregg and the Rockefeller Foundation Medical Division.' *Minerva* 41 (2003): 155–166, 157.
62. Schröter, Harm. 'Economic culture and its transfer: an overview of the Americanisation of European economy, 1900–2005.' *European Review on History: Revue européenne d'histoire* 15 (2008): 331–344, 333.
63. Abelshauser. 'Erhard.'.
64. Berghahn, Volker R. 'Philanthropy and Diplomacy in the 'American Century'. *Diplomatic history*, 3, 23 (1999): 393–419, 396; see also 402.
65. Doering-Manteuffel, Anselm. *Wie westlich sind die Deutschen? Amerikanisierung und Westernisierung im 20. Jahrhundert*. Göttingen: Vandenhoek & Ruprecht, 1999.

Disclosure statement

No potential conflict of interest was reported by the author.

Bibliography

Abelshauser, Werner. "Erhard oder Bismarck?" *Geschichte und Gesellschaft* 22 (1996): 376–392.

Antoni, Christine. *Sozialhygiene und Public Health: Franz Goldmann (1895–1970)*. Husum: Matthiesen Verlag, 1997.

Arndt, Melanie. *Gesundheitspolitik im geteilten Berlin 1948-1961*. Köln, Weimar and Wien: Böhlau, 2009.

Barona, Josep L. *The Rockefeller Foundation, Public Health and International Diplomacy, 1920–1945*. London: Pickering and Chatto, 2015.

Berghahn, Volker R. "Philanthropy and Diplomacy in the 'American Century'." *Diplomatic History* 23, no. 3 (1999): 393–419.

Berghahn, Volker R. "The Debate on ‚Americanization' among Economic and Cultural Historians." *Cold War History* 10 (2010): 107–130.

Doering-Manteuffel, Anselm. *Wie westlich sind die Deutschen? Amerikanisierung und Westernisierung im 20. Jahrhundert*. Göttingen: Vandenhoek & Ruprecht, 1999.

Ellerbrock, Dagmar. *"Healing Democracy" – Demokratie als Heilmittel. Gesundheit, Krankheit und Politik in der amerikanischen Besatzungszone 1945 – 1949*. Bonn: J. H. W. Dietz Nachf., 2004.

Fee, Lizabeth, and Bu Liping. "Models of Public Health Education: Choices for the Future?" *Bulletin of the World Health Organization* 85 (2007): 977–979.

Hockerts, Hans Günter. *Sozialpolitische Entscheidungen im Nachkriegsdeutschland. Alliierte und deutsche Sozialversicherungspolitik 1945 bis 1957*. Stuttgart: Klett-Cotta, 1945.

Hoffmann, Dierk. *Sozialpolitische Neuordnung in der SBZ/DDR. Der Umbau der Sozialversicherung*. München: R. Oldenbourg Verlag, 1996.

Jarausch, Konrad. *Die Umkehr. Deutsche Wandlungen 1945-1955*. Bonn: Bundeszentale für politische Bildung, 2004.

Kimmel, Elke. "Gemeinsam gegen die ‚Achsenmächte'." (Bundeszentrale für politische Bildung, 31.10.2005). Accessed November 19, 2016. http://www.bpb.de/geschichte/deutsche-geschichte/marshallplan/39982/gemeinsam-gegen-die-achsenmaechte

Lindner, Ulrike. *Gesundheitspolitik in der Nachkriegszeit. Großbritannien und die Bundesrepublik Deutschland im Vergleich*. München: De Gruyter, 2004.

Münchow, Siegfried. "Über die Gründung der Akademie für Staatsmedizin in Hamburg." *Hamburger Ärzteblatt* 21 (1967): 302–305.

Page, Benjamin B. "The Rockefeller Foundation and Central Europe: A Reconsideration." *Minerva* 40 (2002): 265–287.

Parmar, Inderjeet., "To Relate Knowledge in Action': The Impact of the Rockefeller Foundation of Foreign Policy Thinking During America's Rise to Globalism 1939-1945." *Minerva* 40 (2002): 235–263.

Rausch, Helke. "Professionalisierung als Diplomatische Strategie: Das us-amerikanische Carnegie Endowment in Europa vor 1945," 2. Themenportal Europäische Geschichte. Accessed November 7, 2016. www.europa.clio-online.de

Reinisch, Jessica. *The Perils of Peace. The Public Health Crisis in Occupied Germany*. Oxford: Oxford University Press, 2013.

The Annual Report - Rockefeller Foundation 1948. Edited by Rockefeller Foundation. New York: self published, 1948.

Rupieper, Hermann-Josef. *Die Wurzeln der westdeutschen Nachkriegsdemokratie. Der amerikanische Beitrag 1945 - 1952*. Darmstadt: Westdeutscher Verlag, 1993.

Sachse, Carola. "What Research, to What End? The Rockefeller Foundation and the Max Planck Gesellschaft in the Early Cold War." *Central European History* 42 (2009): 97–141.

Schagen, Udo, and Sabine Schleiermacher. "Gesundheitswesen und Sicherung bei Krankheit und im Pflegefall." In *Die Sowjetische Besatzungszone und Berlin. Geschichte und Sozialpolitik in Deutschland seit 1945*, edited by Bundesministerium für Arbeit und Sozialpolitik und Bundesarchiv, 511–528. Baden-Baden: Nomos, 2001.

Schellenberg, Ernst. *Versicherungsanstalt Berlin 1945-1947. Ein Arbeitsbericht*. Berlin: self published, 1947.

Schleiermacher, Sabine. *Sozialethik im Spannungsfeld von Sozial- und Rassenhygiene. Der Mediziner Hans Harmsen im Centralausschuß für die Innere Mission*. Abhandlungen zur Geschichte der Medizin und der Naturwissenschaften, Heft 85. Husum: Matthiesen Verlag, 1998.

Schleiermacher, Sabine. "Die Rockefeller Foundation und ihr Engagement bei einer Neuorientierung von Medizin und Public Health in Deutschland in den 1950er Jahren." *Medizinhistorisches Journal* 45 (2010): 43–65.

Schleiermacher, Sabine. "Contested Spaces: Models of Public Health in Occupied Germany." In *Shifting Boundaries of Public Health. Europe in the Twentieth Century*, edited by Susan Gross Solomon, Lion Murard, and Patrick Zylberman, 175–204. Rochester, MN: University of Rochester Press, 2008.

Schneider, William H. "The Model American Foundation Officer: Alan Gregg and the Rockefeller Foundation Medical Division." *Minerva* 41 (2003): 155–166.

Schröter, Harm G. *Americanization of the European Economy. A compact survey of American economic influence in Europe since the 1880s*. Dordrecht: Springer Verlag, 2005.

Schröter, Harm. "Economic Culture and Its Transfer: An Overview of the Americanisation of European Economy, 1900-2005." *European Review of History: Revue europeenne d'histoire* 15 (2008): 331–344.

Tennstedt, Florian. "Sozialgeschichte der Sozialversicherung." In *Handbuch für Sozialmedizin*, edited by Maria Blohmke, Christian V. Ferber, Karl Peter Kisker, and Hans Schaefer, 385–492. Stuttgart: Ferdinand-Enke-Verlag, 1976.

Weindling, Paul. "Public Health and Political Stabilization. The Rockefeller Foundation in Central and Eastern Europe between the Two World Wars." *Minerva* 31 (1993): 253–267.

Weindling, Paul J. "'Out of the Ghetto': The Rockefeller Foundation and German medicine after the Second World War." In *Rockefeller Philanthropy and modern Biomedicine. International Initiatives from World War I to the Cold War*, edited by Schneider, William H., 208–222. Bloomington: Indiana University Press, 2002.

Wengst, Udo. "Rahmenbedingungen." In *Geschichte der Sozialpolitik in Deutschland seit 1945. Zeit der Besatzungszonen. Sozialpolitik zwischen Kriegsende und der Gründung zweier deutscher Staaten*. 2/1 vols., edited by Bundesministerium für Arbeit und Sozialpolitik und Bundesarchiv, 1–76. Baden-Baden: Nomos, 2001.

Socialisation of healthcare demand and development of the French health system (1890–1938)

Jean-Paul Domin

ABSTRACT
This work assesses, by relying on methods of business history, the transformations of health policy from the end of the nineteenth century till the eve of the Second World War. The objective of this policy is to favour the access to health care of an increasing share of the population. The transformation went through two distinct stages. During the first period (1890–1914), the presence in the circles of power of supporters of social reform favoured the emergence of welfare and insurance laws. But at the end of World War One, the system showed its limitations. The public authorities then engaged in a debate on the vote on social insurance. The bill, submitted to the House of Commons, was finally passed in 1930. The Act was carried by a relatively large political majority and a small number of civil servants. This law would have undoubtedly beneficial effects on the medicalisation of French society.

1. Introduction

Comparative studies highlight that France was lagging behind with welfare protection in the late nineteenth century.[1] There were several explanations for this: government instability, the slow growth rate of welfare spending, and the belated legislation on mandatory welfare insurance. Even so, the Third Republic saw a renewal of policies promoting assistance and facilitating the institutionalisation of primary forms of welfare protection. The unregulated provident fund model vaunted by early nineteenth-century economists gradually gave way to collective welfare schemes and soon to socialised medicine.

The state progressively put together administrative apparatus capable of institutionalising primary mechanisms of collective support. The decree of 4 November 1886 set up a department for public assistance within the Interior Ministry as an advisory body on welfare legislation but also to oversee its enforcement. There were two reasons for setting up the department. Administrative streamlining had become essential because of the change of political regime; and the Third Republic needed to introduce a programme for secularising welfare directed against the Catholic Church.[2]

The reorganisation also entailed the formation by the decree of 14 April 1888 of the Senior Public Assistance Board (*Conseil supérieur de l'assistance publique*). This consultative body adopted positions on matters referred to it by the ministry and was to overhaul thinking on assistance by asserting the state's right of intervention in place of private benevolence. Much of the Third Republic's legislation on assistance was nourished by the board's ideas.[3] The surge in welfare issues reflected primarily a shift in the balance of power. Although the liberals lost ground, the turnaround can be explained essentially by Catholic economists rallying around the positions of the supporters of state interventionism.[4]

Institutionalisation took two main forms: assistance (statute of 15 July 1893 on free medical assistance, statute of 14 July 1905 on the elderly, invalids, and incurably ill, statute of 17 June 1913 on women in labour) and insurance (statute of 1 April known as the Mutual Insurance System Charter – *Charte de la mutualité*). But the non-mandatory character of this legislation considerably limited its scope and effectiveness. The vote on the 1928 and 1930 social insurance statutes crowned this long process of so-called extensive medicalisation. The socialisation of healthcare spending was the vehicle for this change. At each stage, a growing share of such spending was paid for collectively.[5]

This research sets out to analyse the successive evolutions of the French health system from 1890 to 1938. It looks at the action and role of the different players. It is based on a compilation of data from the French statistics office (*Statistique Générale de la France*) and evaluates the health policies implemented. It is argued that the socialisation of healthcare spending is a form of social regulation, promoting collective payment, through either assistance or insurance, for what had previously been individual spending. Although the aim of the policy was to promote access to care for a growing proportion of the population, it was directly to promote the creation of a market for healthcare and in particular hospitals.

It will be shown that this change occurred in two separate stages. A first period (1890–1914) saw the combined development of assistance and insurance and the slow socialisation of healthcare (part 1). But by the end of the Great War, the system was reaching its limits. The authorities then headed down the road towards insurance. This choice had unquestionable effects in terms of the medicalisation of society and promoted the opening up of the hospital market (part 2).

2. Socialisation of health issues and generalisation of access to care (1890–1914)

The late nineteenth century saw the beginnings of a demographic crisis characterised by a negative natural population balance. From 1872 to 1914, France's population grew only slightly from 36.1 million to 39.6 million inhabitants. Births averaged merely 90,000 per year. The death rate dipped from 22‰ to 18.5‰, but remained high overall, particularly compared with Germany and Great Britain. The high death rate was caused by the combined effects of a succession of wars and the persistence of certain diseases (smallpox, tuberculosis, cholera, etc.). The child mortality rate went up during the second half of the nineteenth century. Unfettered industrialisation and urban overcrowding favoured the spreading of epidemics. The appearance of a new disease (cholera) caused the deaths of many children. From the end of the nineteenth century, thanks to increasing use of aseptic practices and public monitoring of children and nurses, child mortality resumed its downward trend – dropping from 180 per thousand in 1872 to 111 per thousand in 1914.[6] While the birth rate was downward trending, slipping from 26.7 per thousand in 1872 to 18.1‰ in 1914, mortality remained high. Some years (1890, 1891, 1892, 1895, 1900, 1907, 1911) even saw a deficit in births.[7]

The authorities sought to respond to the demographic crisis by introducing new forms of collective support (section 1.1). This was reflected, before World War One, by a first form of socialisation of healthcare spending (section 1.2).

2.1. *Institutional changes: assistance and insurance*

The period which began in the early 1890s is marked by the stabilisation of political life. The parliamentary elections of 1889 gave a majority to the moderate republicans and their Radical Party allies.[8] The social issues which so far had been sidelined came to the fore once more in the political debate. Reform takes shape in the field of social policy, as in other sectors of French society, around people whose politics are quite different and even opposed. According to convention, those called reformers are to be found in institutions, organisations and circles associated with reform.

On the subject, Christian Topalov uses the metaphor of the nebula which – according to him – indicates the task to perform.[9] The *Conseil supérieur de l'Assistance publique* represents a characteristic example of such an institution. The Préfet, Henri Monod (1843–1911), enjoyed a certain political stability. He had been at the helm of this administrative organisation since 1887, which explains why he knew his business. The composition of the *Conseil supérieur de l'assistance publique* combined a scientific approach and a political criterion: its members' professional competence guaranteed their objectivity while some of them had been elected to positions of importance such as deputies and senators. This reforming nebula favoured the emergence of a common sense approach to reform. Its goals were clear. On behalf of the general interest skills had to be brought together and solutions found. Some examples point to this evolution. The afore-mentioned *Conseil supérieur de l'assistance publique* was to serve as an advisory body for social change.[10] The Musée social (Social Museum) created in 1894 became the locus of a whole movement towards social reform.[11] These institutions would contribute to the setting up of a debate over welfare policy.

From the late nineteenth century onwards, the authorities were to opt for institutional changes in social protection. Two paths were chosen. The first gave precedence to assistance for the least well-off (subsection 1.1.1). The second provided new possibilities in social insurance for wage-earners (subsection 1.1.2).

2.1.1. *The expansion of assistance*

The statute of 15 July 1893 on free medical assistance was a first significant moment of change. Designed within the Senior Public Assistance Board, the legislation was in line with the outlook taken by numerous welfare laws in Europe. The board discussed a first draft in 1889. After various modifications, the bill was tabled for a first reading on 5 June 1890 and finally enacted more than three years later. Article 1 of the statute of 15 July 1893 states that 'all French citizens without means of subsistence shall receive free-of-charge, from local or central government, depending on their address for receiving care, medical assistance at home, or if they cannot be properly cared for at home, in hospital'.[12]

The legislation was based on a new factor challenging the nineteenth-century liberal logic: a duty to provide assistance now embodied in French law and opening entitlement to anyone who was temporarily or permanently without means of subsistence and unable to pay their medical expenses. This obligation was part of a political strategy designed to medically assist able-bodied but momentarily debilitated individuals to recover their health and by the same token get back into work.[13] The statute also asserted an interventionist republican policy on social issues that ran counter to the experimentation of the Catholic Church.[14] This republican turn in the policy of assistance was primarily part of a state strategy to wrestle power from the Catholic Church.[15]

The statute was not designed to provide means of subsistence to the poor based on income criteria. It concerned only people who could not cover their healthcare expenses. It is in this sense that it must be seen as a new policy.[16] The change was a significant one. In 1897, nearly 1.9 million people were registered on the rolls for free medical assistance according to the French statistics office. Their number varied very little until the Great War. In 1912, 2.1 million people were covered, that is, 287,000 more than in 1897. Between the two dates, the population benefitting from free medical assistance rose on average by 17,000 per year. Over the same period, spending attributed to the free medical assistance was multiplied by 1.8 rising from 14.5 million to 27 million 1905–1913 inflation-adjusted francs (i.e. from an average of 7.67 to 64.32 francs per beneficiary).

2.1.2. The expansion of insurance

The second path was a marked change with respect to assistance and involved entrusting to an intermediary the protection of wage-earners against certain welfare risks. This approach, related to nineteenth-century industrialisation, implied collective cover. The surge in industrialisation in the 1820s–1840s largely re-shaped French society. Economic change sped the growth of mutual benefits societies. These performed the traditional missions of assistance and solidarity and came to coordinate collective working-class actions.[17]

The statute of 15 July 1850 meant mutual benefits societies could become state-approved. They came under the responsibility of local authorities and could receive donations.[18] These advantages did not come without something in exchange for the authorities. The mayor was the mandatory chair of the mutual benefits societies in his municipality, and provision for unemployment was prohibited as were retirement pensions. The decree of 28 March 1852 crowned this development by introducing a new category of approved society enjoying tax privileges and closely supervised by the prefect. The decree was of capital importance insofar as it directed the mutualist movement in two specific directions: the mutual benefits societies were organised on the basis of municipal geography and controlled by the ruling classes.

Things gradually loosened up with the Third Republic. On 19 November 1881, member of parliament Hippolyte Maze tabled a bill to deregulate the way mutual benefits societies were run. The government thought the bill too liberal and threw it out, but the ideas in it largely inspired the statute of 1 April 1898 known as the Mutual Insurance System Charter (*Charte de la Mutualité*). This considerably overhauled the legal framework for mutual benefits societies. It recognised three types of society (unregulated, approved, and state-accredited), abolished the prefects' political control over them, no longer required them to be based on their local area, and extended their scope to healthcare, retirement, unemployment, and life insurance. Last, the legislation more generally recognised they had an active role in the emergence of a primary form of social protection.[19] This was a major victory for mutual benefits societies in that the legislation conferred new responsibilities on the movement.

A second law passed on 9 April 1898 after 18 years of debate compelled the employer to meet all the health costs related to accidents at work.[20] This law was extremely important inasmuch as it contributed to the medicalisation[21] of the workforce. The development was not a minor one inasmuch as the legislation replaced passive apportionment based on recognition of risks by active apportionment based on redistribution and transfer. This was therefore the birth of a paradigm of collective support superseding the old model of individual responsibility.[22] This should be seen as the initial shift in the mode of regulation.

The implementation of social protection resulted from a triple evolution: the introduction of welfare policies, the rise of mutual insurance societies and, to a lesser extent, the development of new managerial practices. In some firms, employers developed social insurance funds (for pensions, child benefit, against tuberculosis of the bones) akin to mutual insurance societies[23] In other cases, employers appealed to existing mutual insurance societies which were already developing at the time.[24]

2.2. The progressive socialisation of the healthcare system

The late nineteenth-century welfare laws were to have major repercussions on the operation of the healthcare system (subsection 1.2.1). They also contributed to the development of the mode of regulation (subsection 1.2.2).

2.2.1. The impact on the health system

An attempt has been made to quantitatively measure the effects of the early welfare legislation on the healthcare system by aggregating several scattered series from the French statistics office (see box 1). The enactment of the 1893–1898 legislation was probably a first turning point for the health system. It was a first step towards socialisation.

In 1890, only 3% of the population was actually covered by a socialised system; this corresponded to the 1.2 million mutual benefits society members. Beneficiaries of free medical insurance were counted as from 1897. There were 1.8 million of them, or 4.8% of the total population. Free medical insurance beneficiaries outnumbered mutual benefits society members until 1901. From that date on, their number was to surge to 2 million in 1902 and 3.7 million in 1912. At that date, mutual benefits society members made up 57% of those covered while the number of beneficiaries of free medical insurance stagnated at around 2.1 million or 33% of those covered. The enactment of the Mutual Insurance System Charter probably boosted this growth.

On the eve of the First World War, the rate of cover (assistance and insurance) rose to 17% of the total population. A small share of health and social needs was therefore covered collectively either by mutual benefits societies or by a primary form of national collective support. But the optional character of insurance still restricted its effects. From 1890 to 1912, socialised healthcare spending rose from 0.02% to 0.30% of gross domestic product (GDP). But analysis as a percentage of GDP is not wholly satisfactory in that variations in national wealth and inflation interfere with it. It has been supplemented by a study using inflation-adjusted francs for 1905–1913 (see Graph 1).[25] From 1890 to 1912, socialised health spending rose from 8 million (6.5 francs per person covered) to 140 million inflation-adjusted francs for 1905–1913 (21 francs per person covered).

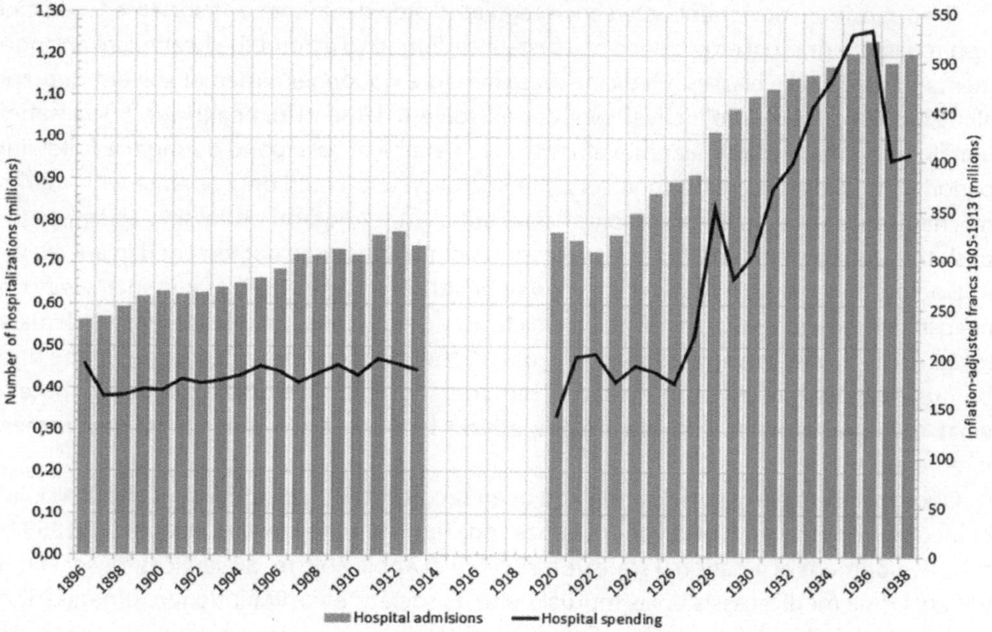

Graph 1. Comparative changes in socialised healthcare spending and population covered between 1890 and 1912.

Box 1: Methodology and statistical sources

Methodology

The series were formed by aggregating scattered data from the French statistics office (*Statistique générale de la France*).

The total number of beneficiaries includes mutual benefits society members (unregulated and approved); plus beneficiaries under the statute of 15 July 1893 (free medical assistance) as from 1897; beneficiaries under the statute of 14 July 1905 (invalids, elderly, and the incurable) as from 1908, and the beneficiaries of social insurance legislation (statute of 30 April 1930) counted from 1931 onwards.

The rate of cover corresponds to the ratio of the total number of beneficiaries to the total population. It is calculated with the *SGF* population series. Total provision corresponds to the sum of repayments by mutual benefits societies, expenses paid under the legislation of 15 July 1893 and 14 July 1905, and social insurance reimbursements. These amounts were converted to inflation-adjusted francs of 1905–1913 by the method devised by Jean-Claude Toutain Le produit intérieur brut de la France de 1789 à 1982, Le produit intérieur brut de la France de 1789 à 1990, .

Statistical sources

Statistique Générale de la France, *Annuaire Statistique de la France*, Paris, Imprimerie nationale, 1878-1938.

Statistique Générale de la France, *Statistique annuelle des institutions d'assistance*, Paris, Imprimerie nationale, 1871 à 1899.

Statistique Générale de la France, *Statistique annuelle des institutions d'assistance*, Paris, Imprimerie nationale, 1900 à 1913.

Statistique Générale de la France, *Statistique annuelle des institutions d'assistance, années 1914 à 1919*, Paris, Imprimerie nationale, 1922.

Statistique Générale de la France, *Statistique annuelle des institutions d'assistance, années 1934, 1935, 1936*, Paris, Imprimerie nationale, 1941.

The opposition movement between unregulated provident funds and socialised medicine resulted in the gradual emergence of a system designed to extend the healthcare arrangements to new social classes. Medicine was therefore no longer aimed at solvent demand alone but also, through collective cover, at non-solvent demand for healthcare. Socialisation remained partial and a similar movement was to enable it to expand during the following period. For its most radical supporters, the liberal system could only operate with market mechanisms and reduced provision of care. Initially the medical profession attempted to push through its demands, but the profession's difficulties were not lessened in any way.

Doctors disregarded social recognition of healthcare needs. Their arguments were confined initially to a refusal of socialisation which, they claimed, was unable to meet the demand for care. The profession argued that doctors had therefore no interest in caring for the poor because they only received in exchange remuneration that was quite disproportionate to what they would have received if competition had not been skewed by government intervention.[26]

Once the principle of socialisation had been secured, the trade unions set about a policy of income consolidation and patient allocation. The first of these was reflected in 1897 by the development of a national scale (*le tarif Jeanne*) applicable for all services for socialised patients (free medical assistance, mutual benefits society, etc.). Practitioners' organisations also participated in defining rules of medical ethics, the main purpose of which was to prevent doctors from fighting over patients, especially by cutting fees. Paradoxically, the socialisation of healthcare needs reinforced fee-for-service payment whereas liberal doctors had previously thought the welfare legislation would undermine this form of remuneration.

2.2.2. From regulated competition to regulated contracting

This slow transformation of society was characteristic of the transition from regulation based on competition to regulation based on primary contracting. The opposition between unregulated provident funds and socialised medicine was the vector of this change. Initially, in the face of demographic stagnation, that called into question the productive capacities of the workforce, the authorities explored new approaches (assistance and insurance) and translated them into welfare legislation. The economic crisis that began in 1872–1873 negatively impacted the healthcare system. Stagnation of solvent demand hampered the development of the health professions. Medical incomes fell, Brouardel argues, by half from 1885 to 1900 and practitioners' purchasing power reportedly slumped by 50% from 1850 to 1900.[27]

Some of the medical profession took charge of the debate and refused socialisation arguing that it challenged the fee-for-service arrangement and resulted in lower incomes for them. Rejecting this suicidal logic, most of the profession came progressively to organise itself setting out deontological rules in the form of special rates for socialised patients. In this way, the crisis of regulated competition promoted the socialisation of medicine, which itself shaped new forms of behaviour among practitioners. It is possible to speak of regulated primary contracting insofar as no rules governed relations between the medical corps and welfare protection. This was no longer to be the case under the legislation on social insurance of 1928–1930.

This, then, was a fleeting moment in the development of the form of regulation. While regulated competition was dead, simple regulated contracting was not yet born. The socialisation of healthcare needs was still inadequate inasmuch as nearly 83% of the total population had no cover. But the situation did seem amenable to the implementation of new arrangements on a grander scale. The establishment of the Ministry of Labour and Social Providence was an important juncture. Its attributions in terms of welfare protection enabled it to prepare the debate on social insurance that began after the war.[28]

3. Socialisation of healthcare and development of the healthcare market (1914–1938)

The socialisation of the health system was to assert itself progressively after the Great War. The continuing demographic difficulties were of concern to the authorities (section 2.1) and hastened the implementation of welfare insurance in 1928–1930 (section 2.2). These contributed to raising the rate of cover of the population and helped a healthcare market to emerge (section 2.3).

3.1. The demographic crisis and its consequences

The First World War was a major turning point in French demographic history. Nearly 1.3 million men died in combat and more than 250,000 civilians perished from the consequences of war. The deficit of births was put at more than 1.4 million children. In all, the war caused the loss of 3 million people, or 7.2% of the total population.[29] The 1921 census put the population at 39,210,000, which was barely more than that for 1876 despite the country winning back three *départements* (Haut-Rhin, Bas-Rhin, Moselle). To the war dead one should add the victims of the great Spanish flu epidemic which impacted France from September 1918 to April 1919. The total number of influenza-related deaths totalled around 210,900. The flu was thus seven times less lethal than the war.[30]

The consequences were very significant in that they concerned comparatively young adult males. The war removed 10.5% of the male population and entailed a premature ageing of the population. This was a serious blow that had lasting effects on French society in the interwar years.[31] The war also upset the balance between the sexes. In 1921, the mean proportion was 1,103 women for 1,000 men. This figure conceals sizeable disparities for some age ranges: 1,323 women for 1,000 men for the 25–29 year-old bracket.[32]

After the war, the downward trend of the death rate resumed, falling from 18.2‰ in 1911–1913 to 17.2‰ in 1921–1925, and 16.8‰ in 1926–1930. But this fall was slower than in other European countries and remained somewhat selective. Between 1914 and 1930, the death rate fell from 18.5‰ to 15.6‰ in France, and from 19‰ to 11‰ in Germany. Child and female mortality declined while male mortality tended to rise. The excess male death rate already observed during the war tended to worsen after. The death rate of young people was also worrying. For the 25–44 year-old bracket, the death rate was three times that in Denmark or the Netherlands.[33] In 1930, more than half of deaths occurred before the age of 65. The main causes were inadequate public hygiene, increased alcoholism, and harsh working conditions. The demographic difficulties also affected the active population which declined in number from the late nineteenth century onwards.

The demographic argument was at the heart of debates on the enactment of social insurance. Demography-related difficulties also impacted the working population whose numbers fell after the turn of the nineteenth century and into the post-war period. The demographic argument lay at the heart of the debate around the vote on social insurance. The degradation of demographic conditions was the government's main concern. The chairman of the Senate's

Finance Committee, Charles Debierre, summed up as follows this worrying trend: 'Our falling birth rate, the heavy losses we have just sustained, the rise of the great social illnesses, notably tuberculosis and syphilis as a result of the war, make it a priority for France to focus on the conservation of the race'.[34] The rapporteur for the law on social insutance, Édouard Grinda, said so most clearly: 'It is important for the future of the la race to provide as soon as possible the army of producers with legislation on insurance and social hygiene'.[35]

3.2. *The slow implementation of social insurance (1920–1930)*

The debate over social insurance signalled a moment of change in the health system. The major stages in its development highlight the big oppositions between old and new forms of welfare. While doctors initially opposed the 1928 legislation (subsection 2.2.1), they perceived it was in their interest to work with the social insurance funds once the 1930 legislation was passed (subsection 2.2.2).

3.2.1. *Opposition from doctors to the first statute on social insurance*

In the aftermath of the war, the government was clearly looking to phase in a social insurance scheme. The necessity of aligning French social regulations with those in the three departements annexed by the Germans in 1870 (Bas-Rhin, Haut-Rhin and Moselle) accelerated the debate over social insurance. On 3 February 1920, Édouard Grinda put in a bill aiming to reorganise the hospital system around a social insurance scheme in order to guarantee their permanent funding. But the bill was rejected by a good number of parliamentarians who found it too close to the German model. A new impetus came from the executive branch. Alexandre Millerand, President of the Council since January 1920, asked Minister for Labour Paul Jourdain to prepare an extension of social insurance to cover the whole country. On 30 June, he set up an extra-parliamentary committee headed by Georges Cahen-Salvador and tasked with the drafting of a bill on social insurance. The minister insisted on the necessarily compulsory nature of the scheme without which the law would come to nothing.[36] After due scrutiny, the committee approved the bill prepared by Jules Laurent and Jacques Ferdinand-Dreyfus.[37]

The social insurance bill that Charles Daniel-Vincent tabled before the Chamber of Deputies (the Chamber had a right-wing majority at the time) on 22 March 1921 was variously received in medical circles.[38,39] Most of the profession was wary of this so-called social medicine bill. For the Seine *département* doctors' organisation (Paris), the bill was primarily a way of alienating the profession. They argued that by imposing a social insurance fund between doctor and patient, the statute would break the bond of friendship and trust between the two. It was not a new argument and had already been made when the statue of 15 July 1893 on free medical assistance was under debate. For Paul Boudin,[40] the bill risked transforming professional mores. The Alsace federation of medical organisations took a different approach, considering the bill advantageous for doctors who would see their incomes rise automatically.

In March 1921, the bill was brought before the Chamber's social insurance and providence commission chaired by Édouard Grinda.[41] He was moderately favourable to mutual benefits and social arguments and intended to have the bill involve less state control: 'the management of social insurance is conferred entirely on the interested parties with no state intervention'.[42] The bill revolved around three principles. First was the free choice of practitioner.

Alongside this, the funds had to contract with medical and pharmaceutical consortia. Finally, the bill provided that patients should pay a part of the total cost of the consultation (user fee principle). For Édouard Grinda, 'free choice, the collective contract, the user fee are the only requirements placed on the management bodies'.[43] This version was therefore more flexible than the bill tabled by the minister.

A first text was passed on 8 April 1924 in the Chamber of Deputies. It provided (article 23) for the establishment of lists of doctors by *département* from which the insured could choose their practitioner. This version of the text also proposed that collective agreements be signed between the funds and medical and pharmaceutical consortia. Lastly, the text introduced (article 25) a comprehensive remuneration procedure (capitation) copied from the German legislation, associated with a user fee (article 26). This challenged three of the medical profession's founding principles: the free choice of practitioner, direct agreement, and fee-for-service. The question of doctors' agreement came up incessantly during the parliamentary debate. For Édouard Grinda: 'the medical profession has always been in favour of all scientific progress, and social or political advances; it is in no manner opposed to enacting a major law for the general interest' and even cited one of the wishes of the general assembly of doctors of the Seine *département* for whom 'the organized medical profession is ready to provide its full and loyal support for any social insurance legislation'.[44]

On 9 April 1924, the bill was passed on to the Senate's commission for social hygiene, assistance, insurance, and providence. The rapporteur, Claude Chauveau,[45] was more favourable to the arguments of the more radical of the liberal practitioners. The bill was passed a couple of days before the victory of the left-wing Cartel des gauches and only came up for public discussion on 9 June 1927. Between the two dates, the Senate commission radically overhauled the text passed by the Chamber of Deputies. As Étienne Antonelli shows, whereas the first bill was based on the fundamental role of mutual benefits societies, the second was based primarily on individual provision.[46]

The return of Raymond Poincaré and his national unity government in 1926 accelerated the passing of the law. The text passed by the Senate on 7 July 1927 evolved in a way that was more favourable to the doctors' demands. The free choice of practitioner was guaranteed insofar as the local area list was defined jointly by the funds and the doctors' organisations. The senators also abandoned the principle of comprehensive remuneration on a capitation basis as they did the user fee. However, the text did still include the principle of the third-party payer authorising the funds to bear the fees. The profession rejected this decision en bloc and militated for direct payment by the insured on the basis of syndicate rates.

The text went back to the Chamber of Deputies and was initially examined by Édouard Grinda and Étienne Antonelli.[47] Public discussion began on 8 March 1928. Édouard Grinda began by underscoring how close the two texts were. Étienne Antonelli observed that the two rapporteurs were practitioners, as were several members of the commissions of the two houses, and hoped the new legislation would be brought in rapidly with the profession's full cooperation. Lastly, Édouard Grinda in the session of 9 March came back to the stumbling block: the third-party payer. He understood that doctors preferred direct payment but thought that poor wage-earners could not always pay the fees up front.[48] On 14 March, despite an alternative proposal from the communist group, the bill was passed unanimously and without any change from the Senate's version. It was promulgated on 5 April 1928.

Despite the many changes in the political majority of the Chamber of Deputies, a first version of the Act was thus passed in 1928. The latter was pretty much the same except for a couple of changes imposed by doctors'unions. This persistence is probably due to the reform-oriented galaxy within the higher ranks of French administration. A few individuals, some of whom belonged to the Council of State (*Conseil d'État*), would play a key role in the elaboration of social insurance. Georges Cahen-Salvador is but one characteristic example. A member of the *Conseil d'État*, this senior civil servant would become a specialist in social insurance until 1939.[49] He enlisted in this matter some young auditors such as Pierre Laroque and Alexandre Parodi.[50] They were to draft the decrees implementing the two acts of 1928 and 1930[51]. The National Economic Council (*Conseil national économique*), created in 1925, is one of the bodies where the reformers'galaxy worked out its positions on social issues, as well as a number of networks: Georges Cahen-Salvador, Pierre Laroque, Alexandre Parodi would become members, but also Arthur Fontaine and Charles Picquemard.[52]

3.2.2. The compromise in the statute of 30 April 1930

By 1927, practitioners were attempting to redefine their area of representation. On 30 November 1927, the congress of medical organisations (*Congrès des syndicats médicaux de France*) voted for the medical charter. It reasserted some of the profession's fundamental principles: free choice, medical confidentiality, the right to charge fees, direct payment, freedom of therapeutic choice and prescription. The unification of the organisation was concluded on 6 December 1928 by the creation of the Confederation of French Medical Syndicates (*Confédération des syndicats médicaux français* (CSMF)) which from that date on, engaged in guerrilla warfare with the cost-cutting medicine of the social insurances.

The 1928 elections changed the face of politics. The Radical Party joined the opposition and the Chamber of Deputies now had a right-wing majority. However, political changes did not hinder the intent to push specific policies. Under pressure from the CSMF, the authorities set about reforming the law progressively. On 31 July 1928, the minister for labour, Louis Loucheur, set up an extra-parliamentary commission to give an opinion on the enforcement of the law and any amendments required. The CSMF was radically opposed to the legislation on social insurance and its lobbying bore fruit. On 19 March 1929, the government tabled a first bill which was abandoned because of the CSMF practitioners' sharp protests. A second bill of 11 July 1929 merely made slight amendments to the legislation that was taken up in the statute of 5 August 1929. Lastly, a third bill (26 July 1929) provided that in the absence of any contract, the funds' responsibility to the insured was limited to a rate set by a tripartite commission.

This was a far-reaching change in the philosophy to the 1928 legislation because the principle of a binding price was dropped and replaced by a liability rate. The contracts were maintained but they were only binding on the funds and no longer on the medical profession. After lengthy debate, a new version of the legislation was passed on 30 April 1930. It sought to appease the confederation's anger by taking up some of the themes in the medical charter. The legislature had abolished the binding character of prices, so practitioners were entirely free to set their own fees. The text maintained the arrangement for collective bargaining designed to set a liability rate. The main point of the statute now rested on a new principle of agreement.

The new provisions were supported by practitioners who saw them as enforcing some of the charter's principles. The medical profession wished to protect most of its members' incomes. But patients were not properly protected in that, if the liability rate was too low, the insured would not be properly reimbursed. Under the circumstances, the medical

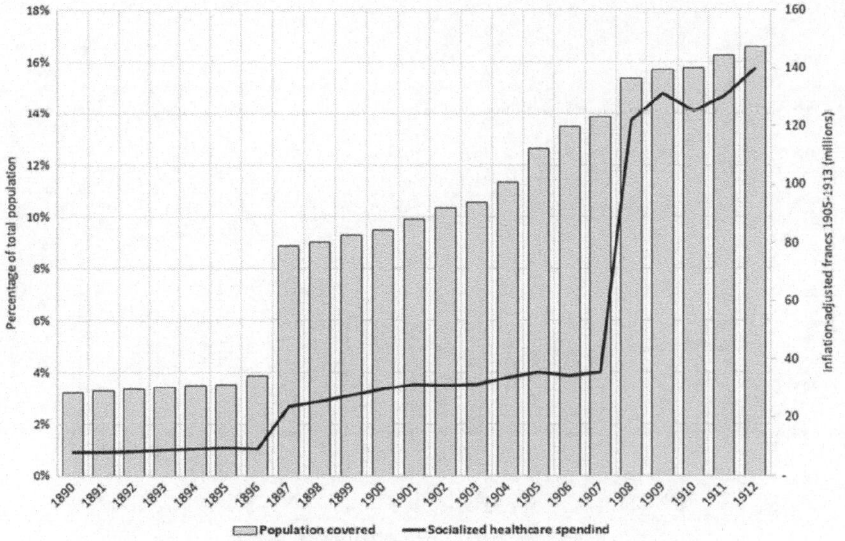

Graph 2. Comparative changes in socialised healthcare spending and population covered between 1920 and 1934.

profession was satisfied and had no further reason to oppose the statute. On 30 July 1930, the general meeting of the CSMF voted massively for working with social insurance but specified 'its determination for there to be no departure from the charter's principles'.[53]

The legislative reform and abandoning of certain points speeded the practitioners' participation. On 7 May 1931, an agreement was signed between the Federation of Medical Syndicates of the Seine (*Fédération des syndicats médicaux de la Seine*) and the Seine and Seine-et-Oise Interdepartmental Social Insurance Fund (*Caisse interdépartementale des Assurances sociales de la Seine et Seine-et-Oise*). At the end of the same year, agreements were signed in seventeen *départements*.[54] How the law was applied varied from one *département* to the next. In Charente-Inférieure, some of the medical profession applied the CSMF rates which were higher than the prices applied in other *départements* before the law came in. In Millau, the mutual benefits society fund of the Aveyron failed to sign an agreement with dentists. This meant the insured had to pay the price asked and had to pay for medication. The fund reimbursed the expenses at the liability rate.

The enactment and implementation of the two statutes on social insurance were a major break in the history of the French health system. In the late nineteenth century, less than 5% of the population was covered by a collective system (beneficiaries of free medical assistance, mutual benefits society members). But the authorities' acceptance of the idea of the right to relief was to accelerate the generalisation of welfare protection. After enactment of the 1928–1930 legislation, more than 46% of the population enjoyed welfare cover. In 1936 the number of people registered directly with social insurance funds exceeded 11 million. The period was therefore one of expanding medicalisation.

It was indeed a compromise insofar as the emergence of socialisation of healthcare was accepted against adherence to the principles of liberal medicine. The legislation ushered in a new period in which socialisation ensured the triumph of fee-for-service. The solution chosen also appears to be a compromise between unregulated provident funds and the

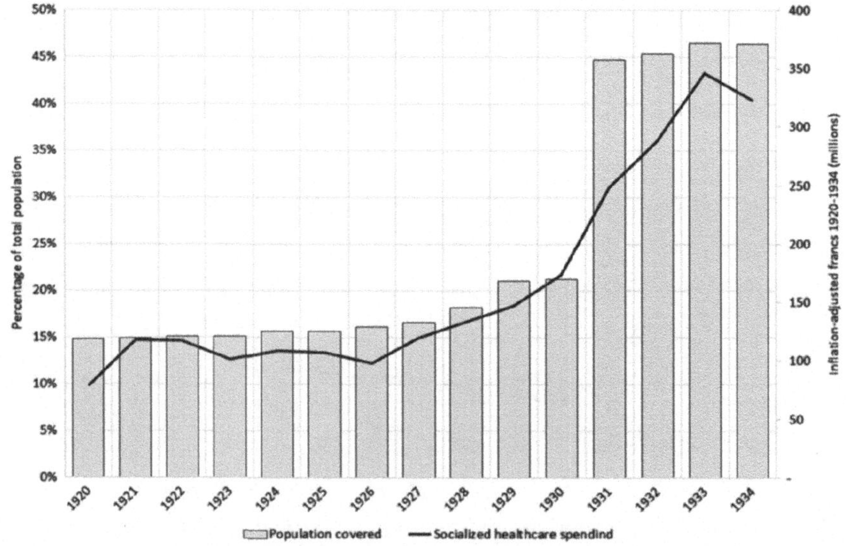

Graph 3. Comparative changes in hospital spending and admissions between 1920 and 1934.

national social insurance scheme. The system was no longer one of private initiative (Mutual Insurance System Charter), but of entitlement to social protection.[55]

3.3. Socialisation of healthcare and development of a hospital market

The change in society was not just a legislative change. The two statutes of 1928 and 1930 accelerated the transformation of society. The first visible feature involved the expansion of socialisation (subsection 3.3.1). The system now rested on simple contractual regulation (subsection 3.3.2).

3.3.1. The expansion of the socialisation of healthcare

In 1920, 5.7 million people (15% of the total population) were covered by a socialised scheme (see Graph 2). They were mostly mutual benefits society members (58%). The remainder of the covered population benefitted from free medical assistance (31%), or the 1905 statute on the elderly and incurable (11%). Mutual benefits society membership increased constantly from 3.3 to 6 million between 1920 and 1934. In 1931, 9.3 million beneficiaries of social insurance were included. Insurance stole a march on assistance. This trend intensified after the statute on social insurance was passed inasmuch as it provided for free medical assistance beneficiaries to be reintegrated. Their numbers levelled off at 1.8 million. Conversely, free medical assistance spending rose quite swiftly from 18 million to 143 million inflation-adjusted francs. This was because free medical assistance consultation rates were aligned on those of the social insurance.[56]

In 1934, nearly 20 million people, i.e. 46% of the population, had collective cover whether public (1893 and 1905 statutes) or insurance-based (mutual benefits societies and social insurance). The change in society was therefore far-reaching. Between 1920 and 1935, the weight of socialised healthcare in national wealth grew steadily from 0.18 to 0.65 of GDP. The increase in healthcare spending was even greater in money terms since socialised medical expenses rose from 78 million francs to 326 million francs (inflation-adjusted 1905–1913) (see Graph 2), or a mean annual growth rate of 19.8%. The effects of the policy for socialisation of healthcare spending were therefore unquestionable. This evolution of health spending must be considered in the more general context of the improvement in social funding. Thus, from 1920 to 1938, public expenditure on social protection (health, pensions, ...) rose from 1.7 to 6% of Gross Domestic Product.[57]

The progressive socialisation of medicine was also manifest in a transformation in the hospital sector.[58] This was reflected by a surge in admissions. The number of hospitalisations rose from 630,000 in 1898 to 850,000 in 1912. After the First World War admissions rose continually. In 1920, 773,365 patients were admitted and in 1930 the figure exceeded one million (see Graph 3). The authorities attempted to counter this logic. The circular of 31 March 1926 stated that 'Hospitals were created for the needy and to admit as a matter of course paying patients was to divert them from their purpose'.[59]

But the process of socialisation of healthcare accelerated the transformation of hospitals. Reimbursements for care rose. In 1939, they came to 53.9% of funding as against 20.3% in 1900 and 42.4% in 1930.[60] Revenue from charity, which still made up 7% of hospital funding in 1890, was down to 1.2% just before World War Two. The structure of funding of the hospital system in France underwent evolution earlier than in Britain.[61]

Pressure from social insurance hastened the transformation of hospitals that lost their negative image of the poor house infirmary and became the centre of the healthcare system.[62] In practice, the patients' hospital stay was charged on a per day price and the way it was calculated changed over time. In 1938, the health minister tasked two general inspectors with modernising hospital articles. When war broke out their work was sufficiently advanced to serve as a basis for drafting the legislation of 21 December 1941 known as the hospital charter.[63]

3.3.2. The implementation of a contractual system

The movement of the early 1920s crowned the transformation in the form of regulation insofar as from then on relations between the medical profession and the social insurance funds were governed contractually. The contractual arrangement was based on coherent administration. Its organisation was totally de-concentrated and the funds fuelling it were managed by multiple organisations: mutual benefits societies, area social insurance funds set up by the authorities. The law promoted negotiations between actors. The CSMF signed agreements with social insurance funds and participated in the new system. Employers entered into agreements with the mutual insurance system to set up funds within firms.[64]

Contractual arrangements probably accelerated the institutionalisation of collective healthcare. But government was preponderant in organising social insurance. The labour minister was ubiquitous, deciding on the level of wage-earners' contributions, arbitrarily setting liability rates, regulating the internal workings of area funds. These drew in a far greater number of members than the mutual benefits society funds.

This juncture should be seen as a succession of de-structuring and reconstruction by a specific process, closely related to economic transformations. The crisis accelerated the destruction of the old health organisation and promoted the emergence of an alternative structure to meet social needs. This transformational movement imposed itself and contributed to the birth of a new form of regulation. The core of this development was still dialectical opposition. On one side, a conservative pressure group refused the emergence of new social forms which, in its view, were the cause of the difficulties. On the other side, a progressive group called for the necessary transformation of a system that no longer met the new conditions imposed by the crisis. The emergence of a new healthcare arrangement was the outcome of this dialectical construction. It had to introduce a new form of regulation compatible with the economic system and ensuring its development.

4. Conclusion

This research analyses the different changes which affected the French health system from 1890 to 1938. The evolution was carried by a reforming nebula that can be found at different times and in different guises. First, within the *Conseil supérieur de l'assistance publique* which was instrumental in the elaboration of the two Acts of 1893 and 1898. Then, the evolution of the laws on social insurance was favoured by the emergence of an elite specialised in social issues, notably councillors of state like Georges Cahen-Salvador and Pierre Laroque. The many political changes of this protracted period would in no way hinder the progress of change.

The period 1890–1930 can be understood as a time of radical change in several ways. Whereas, in the early 1890s, the two paths of assistance and insurance seemed to lie open, this trend was to inflect in favour of insurance alone. In 1930, assistance seemed to have been completely abandoned. The order of 4 October 1945 creating the Social Security confirmed this development. The path chosen in 1930 relied on wage-earners to generate social rights, but also marked the complexity of the French Bismarkian system. In 1934, while the social insurance system prevailed (16 million people covered), a small part of the population (1.8 million) still benefitted from free medical assistance. So the transfer of free medical assistance to social insurance, although provided for by the 1930 law, became a dead letter, as the authorities had planned to abandon the non-combination of the two.

The radical break also promoted the emergence of two new categories of players in the institutional game: the mutual insurance system and the medical profession. For the former, the passing of the legislation on social insurance was a windfall, since it made the mutual insurance system, through the weight of its members among parliamentarians, the principal manager of the social insurance funds. Just before the First World War, mutual benefits society members covered by a healthcare system made up less than one tenth of the population. While the *Mutual Insurance System Charter* contributed to the medicalisation of French society,[65] the enactment of the social insurance legislation enabled the system to expand its scope.

The medical profession was also the great beneficiary of the 1930 compromise. While firmly opposed to the principle of the 1921 statute, practitioners managed to defend their interests, especially by developing their professional lobbying. This change was no small thing inasmuch as the medical profession participated in the expansion of medicalisation whereas just a few years earlier many practitioners had refused the very principles of socialisation of healthcare on financial grounds.

The period from the early 1890s up until the *Libération* should therefore be seen as a whole, marked by early experiments with mandatory assistance up until the creation of the social security. Over this period, the enactment of social insurance legislation meant the end of a world, that is, of a honeycomb society, a hierarchised arrangement of separate social classes.[66] From then on, those who became wage-earners were no longer prisoners of a social class, they also benefited from new healthcare and welfare rights.

Notes

1. Dutton, Origins of the French welfare state. The struggle for social reform in France (1914–1947); Elwitt, The third Republic defended. Bourgeois reform in France (1880–1914); Mitchell, The divided path: the German influence on social reform in France after 1870; Stone, The search for social peace. Reform legislation in France (1890–1914).
2. Renard, Logiques politiques et logiques de programme d'action : la création des administrations sociales sous la IIIe République.
3. Bec, Politique sociale et initiative administrative: l'exemple du conseil supérieur de l'assistance publique (1886–1906).
4. Renard, Assistance publique et bienfaisance privée, 1885–1914.
5. Socialisation must be understood as the meeting of part of the health costs by the community. Before 1890 health spending was essentially private. After 1890, an increasing share of the spending was paid for by mutual insurance societies, local councils, the departements or the State, or by social insurance (after 1928).
6. Vallin, La population française.
7. Bideau, Biraben, & Dupâquier, La mortalité de 1800 à 1914.
8. Mayeur, Les débuts de la IIIe République (1871–1898).
9. Topalov, Laboratoires du nouveau siècle. La nébuleuse réformatrice et ses réseaux en France, 1880–1914.
10. Bec, Politique sociale et initiative administrative : l'exemple du conseil supérieur de l'assistance publique (1886–1906).
11. Horne, Le Musée social : aux origines de l'État providence.
12. '*[T]out Français, privé de ressources, reçoit gratuitement de la commune, du département ou de l'État, suivant son domicile de secours, l'assistance médicale à domicile ou s'il y a impossibilité de le soigner utilement à domicile, dans un établissement hospitalier*', 'Loi du 15 juillet 1893 sur l'assistance médicale gratuite', *Bulletin des lois*, n° 1583, Paris, Imprimerie nationale, 1893, p. 841.
13. Bec, Les politiques d'assistance : de l'intégration à la relégation.
14. Renard, Les rapports entre assistance et assurance dans la constitution du système de protection sociale français.
15. Théret, Les dépenses d'enseignement et d'assistance en France au XIXe siècle : une réévaluation de la rupture républicaine.
16. Renard, Assistance publique et bienfaisance privée, 1885–1914.
17. Dreyfus, Histoire de la Mutualité.
18. Gueslin, L'invention de l'économie sociale. Idées, pratiques et imaginaires coopératifs et mutualistes dans la France du XIXe siècle.
19. Dreyfus, Histoire de la Mutualité.
20. Hesse and Le Gall, L'assurance accident du travail.
21. A society's degree of medicalisation is usually assessed according to the place taken by the doctor. From the eighteenth century, doctors, as well as the different medical institutions, extended their scope of intervention to the whole social field. Thus the constitution, classification and normalisation of medical knowledge bestowed it with an authority which made it possible to impose hygiene rules on the population Foucault, Il faut défendre la société. Cours au Collège de France (1976), , with the hospital as the adequate locus for the discipline of medicine. The transformation which began in the eighteenth century concerns the preservation, maintenance and conservation of the workforce Foucault, La politique de santé au XVIIIe siècle. This evolution primarily relies on a technology of population.
22. Ewald, L'État Providence.
23. Fraboulet, L'Union des industries métallurgiques et minières. Organisation, stratégies et pratiques du patronat métallurgique (1901–1940).

24. Martin, Deux siècles d'assurance mutuelle. Le groupe Azur.
25. For details of how the index is constructed, see Toutain, Comparaisons entre les différentes évaluations du Produit intérieur brut de la France de 1815 à 1938 ou l'histoire économique quantitative à-t-elle un sens, .
26. Guillaume, Le rôle social du médecin depuis deux siècles (1800–1945).
27. Darmon, Le médecin parisien en 1900.
28. Renard, Un train peut en cacher un autre. La création du ministère du travail et de la prévoyance sociale en 1906.
29. Sauvy, Histoire économique de la France entre les deux guerres.
30. Darmon, Une tragédie dans la tragédie: la grippe espagnole en France (avril 1918-avril 1919).
31. Garden and Le Bras, La population française entre les deux guerres.
32. Becker and Bernstein, Victoire et frustations (1914–1929).
33. Garden, Le lent recul de la mort.
34. *'[La] faiblesse de notre natalité, la lourde saignée que nous venons de subir, le redoublement des grandes maladies sociales, notamment la tuberculose et la syphilis – comme conséquences de la guerre – font* à la *France un impérieux devoir de soigner la conservation de la race'* Archives nationales, AD XVIII^{c} 1884.
35. *'[Il] est important pour l'avenir de la race de doter au plus tôt l'armée des producteurs d'une législation d'assurance et hygiène sociale'.* Édouard Grinda, *Rapport au nom de la Commission d'assurance et de prévoyance sociales de la Chambre*, 31 janvier 1923, p. 2, Archives nationales, F^{22}2060.
36. Archives nationales, F^{22}2056.
37. Dreyfus, Ruffat, Viet, Voldman, & Valat, Se protéger, être protégé. Une histoire des assurances sociales en France.
38. Charles Daniel-Vincent (1874–1946) was member of parliament for the Nord *département* since 1910. He held several ministerial positions. He was minister of work and social provision from January 1921 to January 1922.
39. The passing of the different versions of the Act by the Chamber of Deputies and the Senate undoubtedly point to a measure of political consensus. The different changes in the complexion of the House majority - from the Horizon Blue Chamber (1919–1924) dominated by the Right, to the Left Cartel (1924–1926) and the victory of the moderates in 1928, did not make any difference to the process initiated in 1920. There was a real convergence between the Socialists, who claimed to be motivated by social justice, the moderates, concerned about philanthropy and public order, and the Social Christians, influenced by the encyclical *Rerum Novarum*.
40. Boudin, Le projet de loi assurance-maladie-invalidité-vieillesse.
41. Édouard Grinda (1866–1959), surgeon, was minister of work and social provision in 1930–1931.
42. *'[L]a gestion toute entière des assurances sociales est confiée aux intéressés sans aucune intervention de l'État',* Édouard Grinda, *Rapport au nom de la Commission d'assurance et de prévoyance sociales de la Chambre*, 31 janvier 1923, p. 16, Archives nationales, F^{22}2060.
43. *'[L]e libre choix, le contrat collectif, le ticket modérateur sont les seules obligations imposées aux organes de gestion',* Édouard Grinda, *op. cit.*, p. 18, Archives nationales, F^{22}2060.
44. *'[L]e corps médical a toujours été favorable à tous les progrès d'ordre scientifique, comme d'ordre social ou politique ; il ne s'oppose nullement au vote d'une grande loi d'intérêt général'.* '[L]*e corps médical organisé est disposé à apporter son concours entier et loyal à toute loi d'assurances sociales',* Journal Officiel, Chambre des députés, avril 1924, p. 1889.
45. Claude Chauveau (1861–1940), doctor, senator of Côte d'or, 10 June 1910, president of the commission for social hygiene, assistance, insurance, and provision.
46. Antonelli, Guide pratique des assurances sociales.
47. Étienne Antonelli (1879–1971) was an economist, elected member of parliament for Haute-Savoie in May 1924 Le Van Lemesle, Étienne Antonelli (1879–1971), un économiste moderniste aux origines de la Sécurité sociale, .
48. Journal officiel (DP 5727).
49. Chatriot, Georges Cahen-Salvador, un réformateur social dans la haute administration française (1875–1963).
50. Jabbari, Pierre Laroque and the welfare state in post war.

51. Chatriot, Réformer le social sous la troisième République.
52. Chatriot, Les hauts fonctionnaires du Conseil d'État au Conseil national économique. La construction d'une institution d'État.
53. *'[S]a ferme volonté de ne pas laisser déroger aux principes de la Charte'*, cited *in* Guillaume, Le rôle social du médecin depuis deux siècles (1800–1945), p. 197.
54. Guillaume, L'assurance maladie-maternité-invalidité-décès dans les années trente.
55. Catrice-Lorey, L'État social en France : genèse et évolutions d'un modèle institutionnel (1920–1996).
56. Renard, Assistance et assurance dans la constitution du système de protection sociale à la française.
57. Delorme and André, L'État et l'économie, un essai d'explication de l'évolution des dépenses publiques en France, 1870–1980.
58. Domin, Les assurances sociales et l'ouverture des hôpitaux à l'ensemble de la population : les prémices d'une politique globale de santé publique (1914–1941).
59. *'[L]'hôpital a été créé pour les indigents et c'est le détourner de sa destination que d'y recevoir normalement des malades payants'.*
60. Domin, Une histoire économique de l'hôpital (XIXe-XXe siècles). Une analyse rétrospective du développement hospitalier. Tome I (1803–1945).
61. Gorsky, Mohan, & Powell, The financial health of voluntary hospitals in interwar Britain.
62. Imbert, Les hôpitaux en France.
63. Domin, Une histoire économique de l'hôpital (XIXe-XXe siècles). Une analyse rétrospective du développement hospitalier. Tome I (1803–1945).
64. Renard, Initiative des politiques et contrôle des dispositifs décentralisés. La protection sociale et l'État sous la IIIe République.
65. Dessertine and Faure, La mutualité et la médicalisation de la société française (1880–1980).
66. Dreyfus, et al., Se protéger, être protégé. Une histoire des assurances sociales en France.

Disclosure statement

No potential conflict of interest was reported by the author.

References

Antonelli, É. *Guide pratique des assurances sociales*. Paris: Payot, 1928.

Bec, C. "Politique sociale et initiative administrative : L'exemple du conseil supérieur de l'assistance publique (1886–1906)." *Le Mouvement social*, no. 163 (1993): 67–84.

Bec, C. "Les politiques d'assistance : De l'intégration à la relégation." *La revue de l'IRES*, no. 30 (1999): 72–92.

Becker, J.-J., and S. Bernstein. *Victoire et frustations (1914–1929)*. Paris: Éditions du Seuil, 1990.

Bideau, A., J.-N. Biraben, and J. Dupâquier. "La mortalité de 1800 à 1914." In *Histoire de la population française (tome III)*, edited by J Dupâquier, 279–298. Paris: Puf, 1988.

Boudin, P. "Le projet de loi assurance-maladie-invalidité-vieillesse." *Le concours médical*, no. 15 (1921): 2045–2051.

Catrice-Lorey, A. « L'État social en France : Genèse et évolutions d'un modèle institutionnel (1920–1996). » In *Un siècle de protection sociale en Europe*, 59–90. Paris: CHSS, La Documentation française, 2001.

Chatriot, A. "Réformer le social sous la Troisième République". *Revue d'histoire moderne et contemporaine*, no 5bis (2009): 40–53.

Chatriot, A. "Georges Cahen-Salvador, un réformateur social dans la haute administration française (1875–1963).» *Revue d'histoire de la protection sociale*, no 7 (2014): 104–128.

Chatriot, A. «Les hauts fonctionnaires du Conseil d'État au Conseil national économique. La construction d'une institution d'État.» In *Serviteur de l'État. Une histoire politique de l'administration française (1875–1945)*, edited by M.-O. Baruch and V. Duclert, 379–391. Paris: Éditions de la Découverte, 2000.

Darmon, P. "Une tragédie dans la tragédie : La grippe espagnole en France (avril 1918–avril 1919)." *Annales de démographie historique* 2000, no. 2 (2001): 153–175.

Darmon, P. *Le médecin parisien en 1900*. Paris: Hachette littératures, 2003.

Delorme, R., and C. André. *L'État et l'économie, un essai d'explication de l'évolution des dépenses publiques en France, 1870–1980*. Paris: Éditions du Seuil, 1983.

Dessertine, D., and O. Faure «La mutualité et la médicalisation de la société française (1880–1980).» In *Démocratie, solidarité et mutualité. Autour de la loi de 1898*, edited by M. Dreyfus, B. Gibaud, and A. Gueslin, 138–149. Paris: Économica, 1999.

Domin, J.-P. "Les assurances sociales et l'ouverture des hôpitaux à l'ensemble de la population: Les prémices d'une politique globale de santé publique (1914–1941)." *Revue française des affaires sociales* 56, no. 1 (2002): 133–154.

Domin, J.-P. *Une histoire économique de l'hôpital (XIXe-XXe siècles). Une analyse rétrospective du développement hospitalier. Tome I (1803–1945)*. Paris: CHSS/La Documentation française, 2008.

Dreyfus, M. "Histoire de la Mutualité." In *Traité de Sécurité sociale*, edited by Y Saint-Jours, 9–51. Paris: LGDJ, 1990.

Dreyfus, M., M. Ruffat, V. Viet, D. Voldman, and B. Valat. *Se protéger, être protégé. Une histoire des assurances sociales en France Rennes*. Rennes: Presses universitaires de Rennes, 2006.

Dutton, P. *Origins of the French Welfare State*. Cambridge: Cambridge University Press, 2002.

Elwitt, S. *The Third Republic Defended. Bourgeois Reform in France (1880–1914)*. Baton Rouge, LA: Louisiana State University Press, 1986.

Ewald, F. *L'État Providence*. Paris: Éditions Grasset, 1986.

Foucault, M. La. *politique de santé au XVIIIe siècle Dits et écrits, tome III*, 13–27. Paris: Gallimard, 1994.

Foucault, M. *Il faut défendre la société. Cours au Collège de France (1976)*. Paris: Gallimard et Éditions du Seuil, 1997.

Fraboulet, D. "L'Union des industries métallurgiques et minières. Organisation, stratégies et pratiques du patronat métallurgique (1901–1940)". *Vingtième siècle* n 114 (2012): 117–135.

Garden, M. «Le lent recul de la mort.» In *Histoire des français XIXe-XXe*, edited by Y. Lequin. Paris: Éditions Armand Colin, 1984: 289–305.

Garden, M., and H. La Le Bras. "population française entre les deux guerres." In *Histoire de la population française*, edited by J. Dupâquier, 83–146. Paris: Puf, 1988.

Gorsky, M., J. Mohan, and M. Powell. "The Financial Health of Voluntary Hospitals in Interwar Britain." *The Economic History Review* 55, no. 3 (2002): 533–557.

Gueslin, A. *L'invention de l'économie sociale. Idées, pratiques et imaginaires coopératifs et mutualistes dans la France du XIXe siècle*. Paris: Économica, 1999.

Guillaume, P. *Le rôle social du médecin depuis deux siècles (1800–1945)*. Paris: CHSS, 1996.

Guillaume, P. "L'assurance maladie-maternité-invalidité-décès dans les années trente." In *Contribution à l'histoire financière de la Sécurité sociale*, edited by M Laroque, 243–271. Paris: La Documentation française, 1999.

Hesse, P.-J., and Y. Le Gall. "L'assurance accident du travail." In *Contribution à l'histoire financière de la Sécurité sociale*, edited by M Laroque, 181–207. Paris: La Documentation française, 1999.

Horne, J. Le. *Musée social: Aux origines de l'État providence*. Paris: Belin, 2004.

Imbert, J. *Les hôpitaux en France*. Paris: Puf, 1988.

Jabbari, E. *Pierre Laroque and the Welfare State in Post-war France*. Oxford: Oxford University Press, 2012.

Le Van Lemesle, L. "Étienne Antonelli (1879–1971), un économiste moderniste aux origines de la Sécurité sociale." In *De la charité médiévale à la sécurité sociale*, edited by A. Gueslin and P. Guillaume, 287–298. Paris: Les Éditions ouvrières, 1992.

Martin, P. *Deux siècles d'assurance mutuelle. Le groupe Azur*. Paris: Édition du CTHS, 2009.

Mayeur, J.-M. *Les débuts de la IIIe République (1871–1898)*. Paris: Éditions du Seuil, 1973.

Mitchell, A. *The divided path: The german influence on social reform in France after 1870*. Chapel Hill: University of North Carolina Press, 1991.

Renard, D. "Assistance publique et bienfaisance privée, 1885–1914." *Politiques et management public* 5, no. 2 (1987): 107–128.

Renard, D. «Les rapports entre assistance et assurance dans la constitution du système de protection sociale français.» In *Comparer les systèmes de protection sociale en Europe (Rencontre d'Oxford)*, 105–125. Paris: MIRE, 1994.

Renard, D. "Assistance et assurance dans la constitution du système de protection sociale à la française." *Genéses* 18 (1995): 30–46.

Renard, D. *Initiative des politiques et contrôle des dispositifs décentralisés. La protection sociale et l'État sous la IIIe République*. Paris: Mire, 2000.

Renard, D. "Logiques politiques et logiques de programme d'action : La création des administrations sociales sous la IIIe République." *Revue française des affaires sociales* 55, no. 4 (2001): 33–39.

Renard, D. "Un train peut en cacher un autre. La création du ministère du travail et de la prévoyance sociale en 1906." *Revue française des affaires sociales* 55, no. 2 (2001): 81–103.

Sauvy, A. *Histoire économique de la France entre les deux guerres*. Paris: Économica, 1984.

Stone, J. *The Search for Social Peace. Reform Legislation in France (1890–1914)* New York: University of New York Press, 1985.

Théret, B. "Les dépenses d'enseignement et d'assistance en France au XIXe siècle : Une réévaluation de la rupture républicaine." *Annales Économie, Sociétés, Civilisations* 46, no. 6 (1991): 1335–1374.

Topalov, C., ed. *Laboratoires du nouveau siècle. La nébuleuse réformatrice et ses réseaux en France, 1880–1914*. Paris: Éditions de l'EHESS, 1999.

Toutain, J.-C. "Le produit intérieur brut de la France de 1789 à 1982." *Économies et sociétés, série AF n* 15 (1987): 49–237.

Toutain, J.-C. "Comparaisons entre les différentes évaluations du Produit intérieur brut de la France de 1815 à 1938 ou l'histoire économique quantitative à-t-elle un sens." *Revue économique* 47, no. 3 (1996): 893–919.

Toutain, J.-C. "Le produit intérieur brut de la France de 1789 à 1990." *Économies et Sociétés, série HEQ* n 1 (1997): 5–236.

Vallin, J. *La population française* Paris: Éditions de La Découverte, 2004.

China: The development of the health system during the Maoist period (1949–76)

Roser Alvarez-Klee

ABSTRACT

The Maoist period (1949–76) is considered an outstanding stage in Chinese history for its improvements in public health and welfare. In particular, the decrease in infectious diseases led to reduced mortality rates and increased life expectancy. This success can be attributed to the policies implemented in the health-care system during this period. However, different stages defined this process. The aim of this article is to determine whether health inequality in China was evident and consistent during the whole period. To determine this, provincial data were drawn on to undertake a comparative study in the allocation of health resources in different regions. In order to understand the dynamics of the health system during this period, the article focuses on one province in particular, that of Henan. The findings indicate that there were variations in the distribution of health resources among provinces during the Maoist era. The available figures indicate that there was a general increase in health resources in China. However, this did not prevent Henan province from experiencing a great decline in its health system during the Cultural Revolution (1966–76). Future research must be carried out to determine whether the inequality of health inputs in China during the Maoist period was positively correlated with the inequality of the health outputs nationwide.

1. Introduction

Since the 1980s, the health of the Chinese population has improved and entered a new nutritional and health transition linked to the spread of obesity, diabetes, and cardiovascular diseases.[1] Some scholars suggest that the decline of infectious diseases among the Chinese population in recent decades might be associated with the increase in incomes, rather than the efficiency of the health system.[2]

The transition towards a market economy after the late 1970s opened the way to the emergence of economic and social inequalities in China.[3] In the health sector these inequalities are also evident between urban and rural areas,[4] as well as between different provinces.[5] This reflects the fact that health-care reforms have sometimes been deferred in order to concentrate on economic reforms.[6]

While health inequalities have been studied intensively for the years following the economic reforms, there is less literature on inequalities in the health-care system during the

Maoist period (1949–76). Already in the 1980s, international health agencies claimed that China had taken the path of an epidemiological transition during this period, by reducing mortality and birth rates by 50 per cent and 40 per cent, respectively, and increasing life expectancy from 44 years to 68 years.[7] This success was attributed to the great improvements in the health system in a country with lower incomes than in any industrialised country in the past, achievements that were described as unique in the developing world.[8]

During the Maoist period the clear objective was to spread an egalitarian health-care system to the whole country and reduce existing health inequalities, which had increased during the Republican era (1912–49).[9] However, the evidence indicates that, while there were health improvements at the national level, there were also great inequalities in health between the rural and urban populations.[10]

A range of publications has concentrated on health outputs during this period,[11] yet to my knowledge, few have studied the specifics of the distribution of health resources in China.[12] Previous studies claim theoretically, that the geographical distribution of health resources contributes to health improvements in a society.[13] Therefore, the supply side of inputs (health resources) has an impact on the demand side of outcomes (access to health care).[14] The aim of this article is to investigate the distribution of health resources in China during the Maoist period.

Yip claims that the focus on economic reforms contributed to the deterioration of the quality of the health system and dismantled the near-universal health system of the previous decades.[15] The aim of this article is to investigate whether the inequalities that exist in the health sector today were already present prior to the economic reforms. To this end, I will analyze the distribution of health-care resources among the different provinces in China,[16] using the allocation of health resources to understand and evaluate the impact of the Maoist period health reforms.

A second aim of this article is to investigate the particular case of Henan Province, an agricultural region located in the Central Plain and characterised as one of the most populated provinces in the country (see Map 1). The great demographic density of this region, nearly 95 per cent of whose population was rural throughout the Maoist period, adds particular interest to Henan as a case study. Therefore, the second question I aim to answer in this article is whether the distribution of health resources in Henan Province was constant at the different stages of the Maoist period.

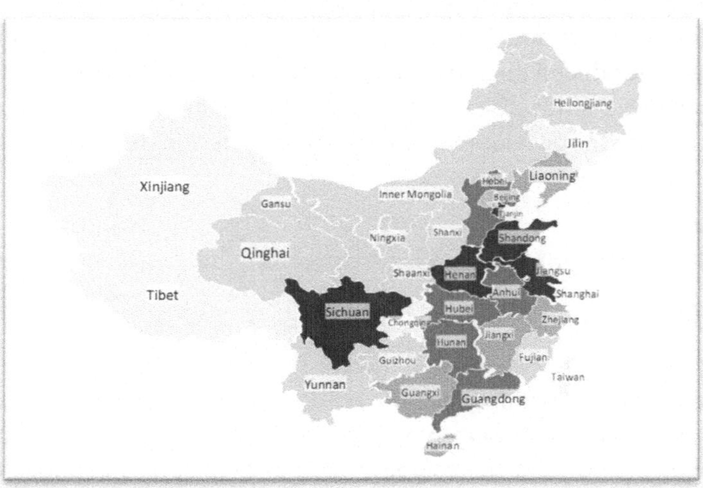

	0	10,000,000
	10,000,000	20,000,000
	20,000,000	30,000,000
	30,000,000	40,000,000
	40,000,000	60,000,000

Map 1. Mean population in China by province during the Maoist period (1949–76). Source: Author's elaboration based on the Comprehensive Statistical Data and Materials on 50 Years of New China (1950–1998).

During the 27 years of the Maoist period, the health system assumed different forms in response to demand and social structure, but more importantly, to the prevailing political circumstances as well. Four different phases can be identified: (1) the Initial Stage (1949–57); (2) the Great Leap Forward (1958–61); (3) the Adjustment Stage (1962–65); and (4) the Cultural Revolution (1966–76). At that time, health policies were focused on preventive medicine linked to national political campaigns and investments in medical institutions and medical personnel. In this article, I examine the distribution of health resources at each of these stages. While a general increase in the supply of health inputs can be identified, the distribution of these resources reveals inequality gaps between the different provinces.

In this article, the overview of the health system in China during the Maoist period is based on institutional health indicators compiled from four Chinese statistical sources: Comprehensive Statistical Data and Materials on 50 years of New China (1950–1998) (*Xin Zhongguo Wushi Nian Tongji Ziliao Xupian*); and a new data-set including different health indicators from the Provincial Archive of Public Health Records (*Weishengzi*), the China Statistical Data Compilation (1949–2003), and the 1988 National Survey of Fertility and Contraception.[17] For Henan, I have used the Henan Provincial Gazetteers – 1985 Yearbook.[18]

The use of aggregate data published by the government implies certain limitations for this study. First, the reliability of official statistical data in China cannot be assured, especially for the Maoist period. I address this issue in Section 3, where in certain provinces some figures appear to have been exaggerated, particularly during the GLF stage. Secondly, the aggregated data cannot be used to assess the development and availability of health resources at the micro-level. Recent studies concerning the state of the health system following the economic reforms use household data such as the China Health and Nutrition Survey (CHNS), China Health and Retirement Longitudinal Study (CHARLS), China Institute for Income Distribution data-set (CHIP), and China Family Panel Studies (CFPS). The data in these datasets lack information on the allocation of health resources during the Maoist period, but previous studies have used the CHNS data on heights, as an indicator of health. They show a similar trend to the final conclusions of this study, that is, of improvements in health and health resources nationwide, but with great inequality between provinces and at different political stages during the period under study.[19] Finally, the provincial gazetteers provide valuable information on developments in the supply of health resources, described in Section 4.

This article is divided into five sections. Section 2 describes the different policies and health institutions that were introduced in China during the Maoist period, based on the four different stages listed above. Section 3 analyzes the data at both the national and provincial levels. Section 4 focuses on the development of the health system in Henan Province specifically. Section 5 offers some final conclusions.

2. Health system: policies, campaigns, and institutions

2.1. The Initial Stage (1949–57)

When Mao Zedong came to power in 1949, China's health situation was in a precarious situation. The scarcity of health institutions and the unequal distribution of health resources between rural and urban areas left a great percentage of the Chinese population with no access to health-care.[20] Immediately after the establishment of the People's Republic of China (PRC), the Chinese Communist Party (CCP) focused on the development of a state-run health-care system based on the communist ideals developed during the revolutionary era (1927–49), in defence of a public health system governed by policies concerned with the control of epidemics. In November of that year, the Ministry of Health (MOH) was established as the organisation responsible for health, with subnational local branches. Labour insurance and government health insurance were introduced in the early 1950s, with free health care being provided to industrial workers and families, government employees, teachers, and students. However, because of financial constraints, the central government allocated only 1.2 per cent of the national budget to the health-care sector, rapidly creating congested health services demand and limitations on state finance. Ironically, this situation widened the gap between the urban and rural areas, leaving the peasants behind.

The central government was aware of the precarious situation in the rural areas and its own financial constraints. As a result, it became important to concentrate on the *prevention first policy*, which insisted on averting the spread of infectious diseases, thus allowing the state to 'gain political capital by reducing human suffering'.[21] The means to accomplish this objective relied on the state's control of society, especially in the countryside, by launching patriotic health and mass mobilisation campaigns to increase health awareness. While at the beginning of the 1950s private health facilities still existed, by the mid 1950s the health-care system had become mostly an activity of the state. The MOH identified 20 communicable diseases, but due to the financial and institutional constrains, only cholera, smallpox, and the plague were targeted as priorities.[22] In addition, by 1957 the fight against schistosomiasis and venereal diseases had become a central goal. At the end of this stage, two thirds of all the counties in China had an epidemic prevention station (EPS) applying communicable disease control (CDC) programs, vaccination, and environmental sanitation and hygiene.[23] While the *prevention first policy* was successful in the long run (eg, the last outbreak of small-pox was in 1960, 20 years before its global eradication),[24] the health-care system had a long way to go in providing the rural population, with curative treatments and tackling infectious diseases not targeted by the CDC programs, which remained a latent problem. Nevertheless, by the end of the initial stage of implementing the health-care system, Mao had won popularity among peasants and local officials, to the extent that he felt powerful enough to weaken the intervention of the MOH bureaucracy, as he understood it, thus acquiring complete authority to supervise health activities in the years that followed. [25]

2.2. The Great Leap Forward (GLF) (1958–61)

Policies during the GLF were basically concentrated on collectivizing China's socioeconomic structure. The establishment of a commune system in rural areas, controlled politically, clearly changed the social and economic structure of the system and also had an impact on health-care. Already in the mid 1950s some communes in Central China, including Henan, adopted the so-called Cooperative Medical Schemes (CMS), which provided free health-care for the whole of the rural population. By the end of 1958, all cooperatives had adopted the CMS. Mostly decentralised, free medical services, financed by county and commune budgets, provided peasants with an incentive to adopt the system of collectivisation in its entirety. The rural public health-care system was supported by two main sources of funding: the commune members' annual fees, and the revenues collected from agricultural production. The former provided only very low revenues and ultimately became practically non-existent, while the later was only likely to be effective if the primary sector of the economy at the provincial level was successful; this proved not to be the case, and three years after the GLF's policies had been implemented, the system had reached a state of collapse.

The *prevention first policy* nonetheless remained the focal domain in the public health system during the GLF. One of the most emblematic hygiene campaigns was the so-called *Four Pests,* which made the wiping out of mosquitoes, flies, rats, and sparrows a top state priority in order to eliminate schistosomiasis. Avoiding most of the technical and professional leaders of the MOH, Mao proclaimed the mobilisation of rural labour to catch and kill the *four pests.*[26] By the end of 1959, 50 per cent of patients suffering from schistosomiasis disease had been cured.[27] However, the Hundred Flowers Campaign in 1956 and the Anti-Rightist Campaign in 1957 'set in motion a bandwagon effect with localities competing for rapid elimination of schistosomiasis'.[28] The same pattern was evident in the setbacks to agricultural production during this period, one of the main reasons for the famine in the GLF.[29] Low nutritional intake and the unprecedented consumption of non-edible goods during the subsistence crisis increased disease levels, especially in the rural areas. By 1961, the decrease in the amount of revenue allocated to health resources could not support the increased demand for medical provision, leading to greater fiscal constrains with clear negative effects for maintaining an efficient health-care system. The national budget also fell during the period due to the increased investment in the secondary sector in urban areas, meaning that the communes and counties could not turn to the central government for financial assistance. To confront the problems of welfare funding, local cadres considered increasing peasants' fees for access to health, but levels of poverty at the commune level had reached their peak. In addition, contrary to Mao's initial objectives, the health gap between the urban and rural areas widened due to intensification of the industrial sector.

2.3. The Adjustment Stage (1962–65)

After the GLF Famine, the state and local governments worked to improve the agricultural system in order to increase food production based on more bureaucratically oriented policies. This was the beginning of the modernisation of the primary sector, which would be pursued with greater force in the mid 1960s. Collectivisation was relaxed; but the setbacks during the GLF met their response in Mao's silence on healthcare issues from July 1960 to August 1964.[30] The subsistence crisis at the previous stage weakened the rural population's ability to engage in mass mobilisation on preventive health issues, and patriotic hygiene campaigns were discouraged until 1964. During this new stage, commune health centers declined in all respects, and the gap between rural and urban areas increased. By 1964, 30 per cent of government health-care funding was being allocated to urban areas, and only 16 per cent to rural areas. In addition, 90 per cent of senior health workers were appointed at or above the county level, leaving behind residents in the communes, which constituted the greater part of the Chinese population.[31]

2.4. The Cultural Revolution (1966–76)

By the mid 1960s, Chairman Mao felt he was losing political control after leaders such as Liu Shaoqi and Deng Xiaoping had gained political influence with revisionist policies during the adjustment period to overcome the failures of the GLF. In 1964, the coup against Nikita Khrushchev in the USSR alerted Mao that a similar outcome could take place in China. At this point, loyalty towards party personnel became more important than its policies, and Mao concentrated all his power on preserving its leadership.[32] This political environment produced a new stage in China that lasted for 10 years: the Cultural Revolution (CR). During this decade, major changes took place in the country that involved political repression, which also affected the health-care system. By the mid 1960s the confrontation between Mao's revolutionary views and the MOH's bureaucratic practices returned to the situation of the mid 1950s. At this point, Mao's major concern regarding health issues was the existing inequalities, between the rural and urban areas, and he referred to the MOH as the 'Ministry of Urban Lords'.[33]

Mao's political agenda had two main policies for the health system. The first was to transfer a large number of professional doctors from urban to rural areas. The second was to restructure the education of medical technical personnel by reducing the number of years of training from six- and eight-year programs to three-year programs.[34] These measures faced great opposition from the MOH. However, between 1968 and 1973, after the fall of Liu Shaoqi and Deng Xiaoping in 1967, the MHO lost all its influence in the policy-making process. Mao's most engaging health program at the time was the *barefoot doctor* (BFD) program, established as national policy in 1968 and regarded as an effective measure solving the problem of the scarcity of doctors in rural areas and minimizing costs.[35]

The typical BFD was actually a peasant who provided basic health care, sanitation, health education, and preventive medicine at the brigade and working team levels. Many BFDs, who received credits for work points in health and agriculture, were urban medical personnel transferred to rural areas. In 1965, fewer than 19,000 medical personnel were sent to the countryside; at the end of the period, the figure peaked at 1.8 million.[36] The package, mainly founded by brigades, provided a more continuous service and achieved a higher population reach than the preventive campaigns of the 1950s.[37] Together with midwives and physicians, the new system adopted a bottom-up rather than top-down approach and responded to the failures of the GLF, using fees and other market mechanisms to prevent overuse and unnecessary use of health services.[38] The BFD program remained in existence until the 1980s.

3. Analysis of the data

3.1. National statistics

During the Maoist period, great achievements in health were related to the improvement of health institutions dating from the previous Republican era and the construction of new ones. From the establishment of the PRC in 1949 to 1976, the number of health institutions increased by 23.2 per cent (see Graph 1). These institutions included major investment in hospitals and clinics, and to a lesser extent also in sanitary and epidemic stations, sanatoriums, specialized prevention and treatment centers and stations, and maternity and child-care centers.

Maternity and child-care centers represented a low proportion of total health bodies, but they experienced the greatest increase during the period, reaching at 36 per cent. The introduction of health institutions was one of the main factors in reducing infant mortality in China. Based on public health records, from 1950 to 1976, the infant mortality rate and the mortality rate of children under five years old decreased by 62 per cent and 90 per cent, respectively. Map 2 illustrates the great decrease in infant mortality in the different regions

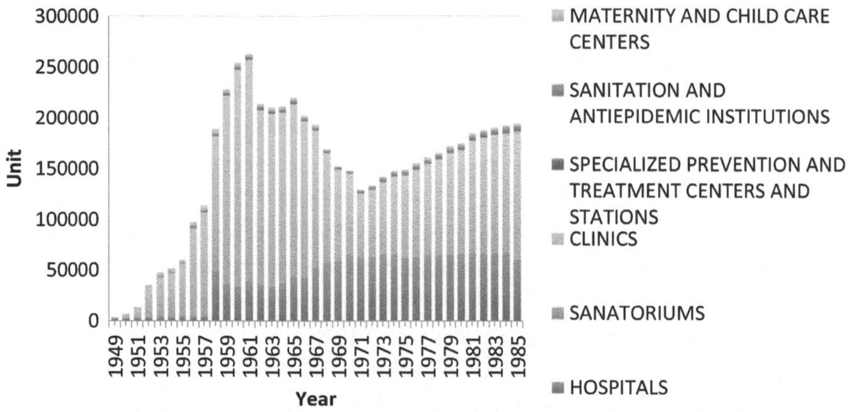

Graph 1. Health institutions in China (1949–85). *Source: Author's elaboration from the Comprehensive statistical data and materials on 50 years of new China (1950–1998).*

and at the different stages between 1950 and 1985. Most provinces reached infant mortality rates higher than 55 per thousand in the initial stage (1949–57). The excessive deaths of infants under a year old in China during the GLF are attributed to the critical effects of the Great Famine. During the Cultural Revolution, over 50 per cent of the provinces indicated on the map decreased their infant mortality to rates to between 15 per thousand and 35 per thousand. By the initial years of the reform stage, only Guizhou Province still had rates of infant mortality higher than 35 per thousand.

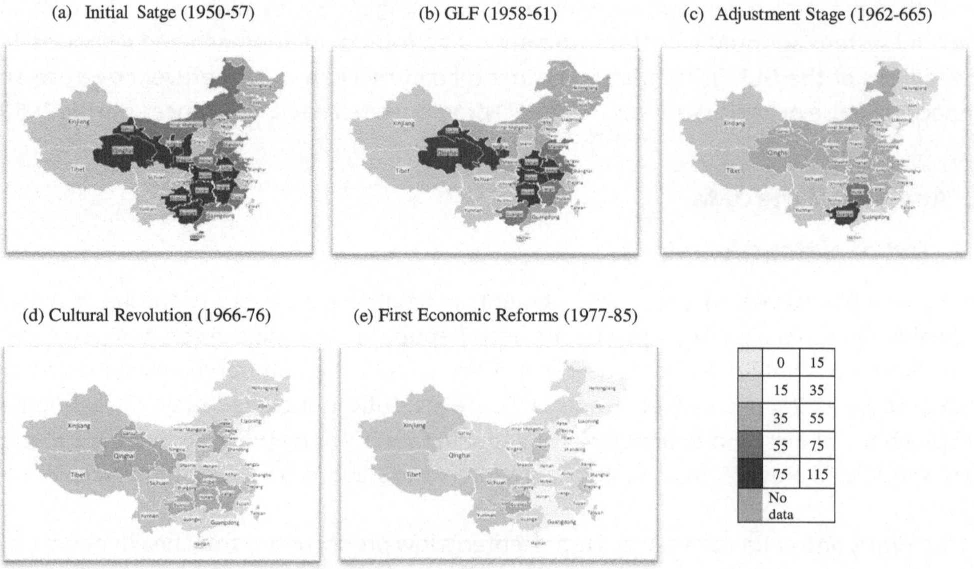

Map 2. China's Infant mortality rate per mil (1950–85). *Source: Author's elaboration from the Provincial Archive of Public Health Records.*

Nearly one million midwives were re-trained, reducing newborn and puerperal infection rates, including the rate of neonatal tetanus.[39] The increase in women's enrolment in education was also positive for the reducing infant mortality, as it not only contributed to the provision of health information, but also increased the age at marriage for females from 17.5 years in 1952 to 22.3 years in 1980.[40] Sanitation and anti-epidemic stations and specialized prevention and treatment centers also experienced representative increases, reaching 26.3 per cent and 25.7 per cent, respectively. As previously mentioned in Section 2, the *prevention first policy* played a major role in reducing infectious diseases.

Medicine and chemical test laboratories and medical science research institutes, not shown in Graph 1 due to their low representation in the total figures for health institutions, also increased by 38.6 and 34.8 per cent respectively. These figures are not representative in the whole picture for two main reasons. First, even though Western medicine started to play a greater role in the health system during the Maoist period, Chinese traditional practices still had greater representation. Statistical records show that until 1970 more doctors were practicing traditional Chinese medicine than Western medicine.[41] This situation was reversed in 1971, when there were 206,000 doctors of traditional Chinese medicines and 241,000 doctors of Western medicine. By 1976, the figures had reached 236,000 and 308,000 respectively. The second explanation is related to the intellectual and scientific setbacks experienced during the Cultural Revolution. The limits placed on the MOH in the process of policy-making had a great negative impact on the developments in this particular area. It was not until 1978, with the new economic reforms of Deng Xiaoping, that medical research would win a representative share of the health system.

Despite the remarkable increase in the number of health institutions during the Maoist period, the pace of growth at each stage of the health system differed greatly. The most outstanding increase came at the initial stage, with a 55 per cent growth rate; no other stage was to reach such a representative rate. In fact, after 1958, the growth in health institutions not only slowed to 8 per cent during the GLF, but also suffered stagnation and a decline in growth after 1962 (0.7 per cent growth during the adjustment stage and 2.4 per cent decline during the Cultural Revolution). Such percentages show the fiscal defaults since the beginning of the 1960s, previously explained. However, in Graph 1 we can see that that in any case the figures were lower than in the achievements of 1957. Even in 1971, with fewer health institutions being registered since 1959, the figures are higher than in 1957. It should also be noted that the decrease in the number of health institutions after the mid 1960s is to be explained by a decline in the number of clinics, despite which the number of hospitals almost doubled, from 35,500 in 1959 to 65,000 in 1970.

The number of beds in health institutions is another indicator of improvements to the health system. From 1949 to 1976, the number of beds available increased by 18.7 per cent. Graph 2 shows that, despite the increase in the number of beds in health facilities in the initial stage, the figures are not representative when taking the total population into account. In addition, in light of the clear inequalities between rural and urban areas, we should stress that figures did not exist for the countryside. Even during the Cultural

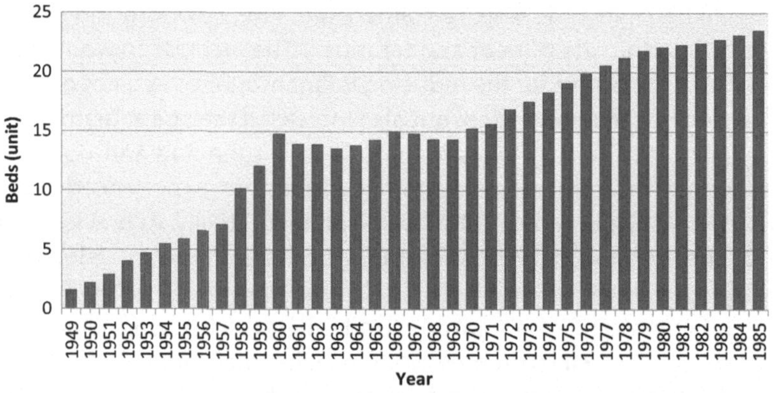

Graph 2. Number of beds in health institutions (per ten thousand persons) (1949–85). Source: Author's elaboration from the Comprehensive statistical data and materials on 50 years of new China (1950–1998).

Revolution, when a great effort was made to reduce the gap between rural and urban areas, two thirds of these resources were allocated to the latter. During the GLF there was a clear increase in the number of beds per ten thousand persons, which can be attributed to the change in the population structure, given that this particular period is characterized by high mortality rates (the levels of mortality and infant mortality in China increased to 15 per thousand and 66 per thousand respectively). The situation remained one of stagnation until the early 1970s, when there was a constant increase in the number of beds. By the end of the Maoist period, records give a figure of twenty beds per ten thousand persons.

3.2. Provincial differences in health endowments

Health policies were implemented nationwide during the Maoist period. Yet, the decentralized system translated into provincial differences in fiscal revenues and, therefore, investment in local health-care systems.[42] Records show that the adoption and construction of health institutions remained very low in Western China (especially Qinghai, Ningxia, Xinjiang) (see Table 1). Qinghai and Ningxia provinces did not reach 1 per cent share of the total health-care facilities in the country for the whole period. A similar pattern is shown for Xinjiang and the southern region of Hainan until the decade of the 1960s. Even then, the share remained lower than 2 per cent. Table 2 shows a similar picture when the share of total hospitals in China is examined. Several features may explain this pattern. First, the western regions were, as they still are today, low-income provinces with high levels of poverty. Secondly, although these provinces constitute a great proportion of China's total geographical area, most of its land is infertile and cannot be used for agriculture. Given that, at some stages in the Maoist period the communes based partially on agricultural production funded the health system in rural areas, it is understandable that the budget for health-care would be lower in these regions. Thirdly, the western provinces are not only less populated, but a greater proportion of minority populations are settled in these regions. Unbiased political mechanisms might be used in these cases.

Table 1. Percentage of hospitals per province during the Maoist period (1949–76).

	Initial stage	Great Leap Forward	Adjustment stage	Cultural Revolution	Reform stage
Provinces	1949–57	1958–61	1962–65	1966–76	1977–85
Beijing	1.6	0.3	0.3	0.6	0.6
Henan	4.5	42.[b]	3.0	3.3	3.9
Tianjin	1.1	0.1	0.1	0.1	0.5
Hebei	5.9	3.5	4.6	6.8	6.6
Shanxi	3.6		1.0	3.6	3.6
Jilin	2.4	1.9	0.8	1.9	1.9
Heilongjiang	3.5	2.0	2.7	2.5	2.7
Shanghai	5.9	1.1	1.2	0.7	0.7
Jiangsu	3.3	5.1	1.3	3.7	3.8
Zhejiang	3.6	8.7	0.8	5.5	5.4
Anhui	2.8	24.8[b]	1.0	3.4	4.8
Fujian	3.2	3.9	1.0	1.6	1.7
Jiangxi	3.2	20.9	0.8	2.8	3.3
Shandong	5.9	19.2	1.2	3.6	3.9
Hubei					
Hunan	4.3	12.1	1.2	6.8	6.7
Guangdong	5.2		3.5	2.9	3.0
Guangxi	3.3	0.5	0.7	1.9	1.9
Yunnan	4.0	3.5	0.6	2.7	2.8
Shaanxi	3.8	20.1[b]	0.7	4.2	4.7
Gansu	2.5	3.1	1.9	2.5	2.5
Qinghai	0.7	0.2	0.1	0.2	0.8
Ningxia	0.5	0.1	0.1	0.5	0.5
Xinjiang	2.5	1.4	1.9	1.2	1.4
Hainan	0.7	0.9	0.5	0.7	0.7
Inner Mongolia	2.1		1.0	2.5	2.7
Remaining provinces [a]	27.3	−88.7[c]	69.4	41.3	25.9
Total hospitals in China	3.580	37.073	35.562	62.766	65.450

Notes: (a) This group includes 9 additional provinces, where not data is available. We have estimated the percentage share of this group from the figures of the other provinces. (b) and (c) Our estimations give evidence that some figures were exaggerated during the GLF. Source: Author's calculation based on the Comprehensive Statistical Data and Materials on 50 Years of New China.

In Section 2, I mentioned how during the GLF requiring the different localities to compete in the areas of health and agriculture allegedly led to actual socioeconomic achievements being exaggerated. Figures for the total number of health institutions and hospitals recorded during the GLF prove to be misleading when the share by province is computed. Such estimations suggest that provinces such as Henan, Anhui, Shandong, Hunan and Shaanxi may indeed have exaggerated their statistics regarding the number of hospitals each had (see Table 1). Many of the figures in these regions are exaggerated by as much as a factor of ten, going back to the same records as at the initial stage during the adjustment period.

A similar pattern is observed in Table 2, which focuses on all health institutions. While the increases in these figures are not as evident as when the figures for hospitals alone are examined, there is a general and representative increase in the proportions of institutions in almost all regions. The absolute figures indicate that the total number of hospitals during the GLF increased to 247,000 units from 52,000 in the previous stage. It has proved difficult to determine the reasons why these figures increased at such great rates during the GLF and with such variations across provinces. In any case, the alleged over-reporting during the GLF shown in Tables 1 and 2 suggests that the number of health institutions had had a representative increase since the beginning of the 1960s and that the number of hospitals reached its peak during the Cultural Revolution. All through this 27 years period, Hunan and Hebei Provinces seem to have had the greatest shares of the total of health institutions and of hospitals respectively. Yet both regions had high infant mortality rates during this period.

Table 2. Percentage of health institutions per province during the Maoist period (1949–76).

Provinces	Initial stage 1949–57	Great Leap Forward 1958–61	Adjustment stage 1962–65	Cultural Revolution 1966–76	Reform stage 1977–85
Beijing	1.0	0.8	1.2	1.5	2.1
Henan	5.4	11.6	7.9	4.3	4.4
Tianjin	1.0	0.6	1.0	1.7	1.8
Hebei	4.5	2.6	3.5	5.1	5.3
Shanxi	7.2		1.6	3.0	2.9
Jilin	3.2	4.5	2.9	2.3	2.3
Heilongjiang	3.7	2.0	2.6	3.8	4.7
Shanghai	2.3	1.3	1.3	1.4	3.3
Jiangsu	6.1	6.6	5.4	4.9	5.5
Zhejiang	3.6	3.7	2.8	4.1	4.1
Anhui	4.8	9.3	3.9	4.0	3.7
Fujian	1.6	3.2	3.2	2.8	2.3
Jiangxi	3.8	5.5	2.7	3.1	2.9
Shandong	7.0	8.9	8.0	4.7	5.0
Hubei	6.0	4.9	4.9	5.3	3.5
Hunan	6.5	7.6	5.3	5.4	5.4
Guangdong	3.9		6.0	3.9	4.2
Guangxi	5.4	5.7	2.7	2.7	3.0
Yunnan	1.2	4.0	2.7	3.1	3.2
Shaanxi	2.0	5.0	2.3	3.3	3.2
Gansu	1.0	5.5	2.0	1.9	2.0
Qinghai	0.2	0.9	0.4	0.6	0.6
Ningxia	0.4	0.2	0.2	0.4	0.5
Xinjiang	0.6	1.0	0.9	1.4	1.6
Hainan	0.4	0.9	1.0	2.1	1.9
Inner Mongolia	2.7		1.7	2.8	2.4
Remaining provinces [(a)]	19.3	−0.6[(b)]	28.0	28.5	17.6
Total health institutions in China	52.038	246.577	216.738	151.733	190.126

Notes: (a) This group includes 9 additional provinces, where not data is available. We have estimated the percentage share of this group from the figures of the other provinces. (b) Our estimations give evidence that some figures were exaggerated during the GLF. Source: Author's calculation based on the Comprehensive Statistical Data and Materials on 50 Years of New China.

From 1949 to 1976, the number of medical technical personnel and doctors increased by 8.5 per cent and 5.4 per cent, respectively. Even though the highest figures are recorded after the 1960s, the growth rate is higher in the initial stage (4.7 per cent) and the GLF (4.6 per cent), when compared to the remaining two stages (2.6 per cent). While the increase was representative, the allocation of doctors was not equally distributed nationwide.

Map 3 illustrates the development of the allocation of doctors in China from 1949 to 1985. It is notable that during the initial stage (Map 3(a)) there is a low share of doctors per ten thousand inhabitants in most regions, with the exception of Shaanxi, Hubei, Shanghai, and Beijing. During the GLF Shanxi and Shaanxi increased the rate to 27 and 20 doctors per ten thousand inhabitants respectively. While there was a general increase in the allocation of doctors nationwide, Liaoning and Guangdong reduced their share of doctors, while Tibet and Gansu Provinces remained with the same proportion (see Map 3(b)).

Map 3(c) and (d) show a clear decline in the allocation of doctors during the Cultural Revolution. While the share of doctors is greater during this period than at the initial stage and during the GLF, the adjustment stage seems to have had a greater allocation of this type of medical resources. However, while we notice an increase in the share of doctors at the recovery stage, previous publications indicate that the allocation was distributed mainly in urban areas, thus widening the gap between them and the rural areas.

During the Cultural Revolution 20 out of 28 provinces decreased the share of doctors, by between 2 per cent in Zhejiang Province and 41 per cent in Henan Province. During the initial years of the reform stage, the allocation of doctors per ten thousand persons increased to as high as 18 per cent in Ningxia and 154 per cent in Tibet. Note that only Anhui (2 per cent increase), Fujian (1 per cent increase), and Gansu (no increase) remained stagnant in terms of health allocation. Indeed, Gansu Province had very low share of doctors (0,1 doctors per ten thousand inhabitants) and a high infant mortality rate (70 per thousand) throughout the Maoist period.

Annual figures show that the number of medical personnel and doctors per ten thousand persons declined during the initial stage of the Cultural Revolution, but recovered again at the beginning of the 1970s to the end of the Maoist period (see Graph 3). There are no specific notes in the official statistics showing whether the BFDs were included in the category of doctors or in some other category of medical personnel. In any case, while a great emphasis was placed on the BFD program covering rural areas, there was also a strong campaign to reduce the number of years of training, leading to the shutting down of a great number of medical universities nationwide. Indeed, the number of medical personnel per ten thousand persons, including doctors, in the early 1970s dropped to rates very close to those of 1957. This decline, which started in 1966, was reversed after 1972, and by 1976 the number of medical personnel per ten thousand persons exceeded all figures registered in any previous year.

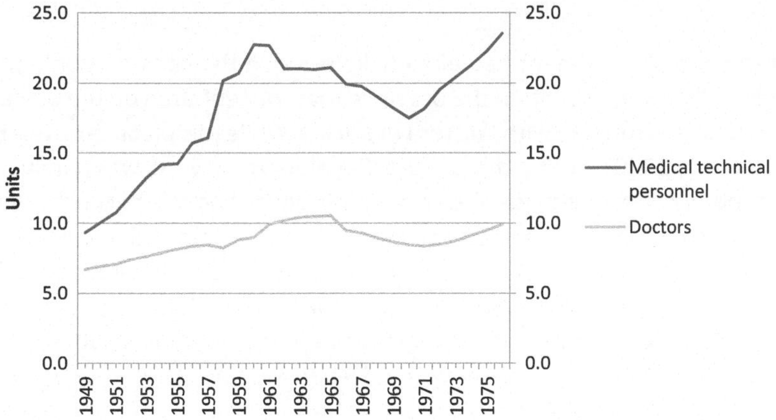

Graph 3. Number of medical technical personnel and doctors per ten thousand persons (1949–76). Source: Author's calculation based on the Comprehensive Statistical Data and Materials on 50 Years of New China.

4. Henan province

During the Republican era, most practitioners of traditional Chinese medicine (TCM) were working in the private sector, either in self-owned offices or in private hospitals that combined TCM with Western medicine. Based on Henan Province's gazetteers, nearly 2,700 private practitioners were located in the province, though only 154 had been approved and registered by the Provincial Health Department. With the establishment of the People's Republic of China, one of the main focuses of the new government was to promote the practice of TCM once again. Henan Province concentrated on the production of medical herbs and established a state-owned pharmaceutical industry open to the local and national market.

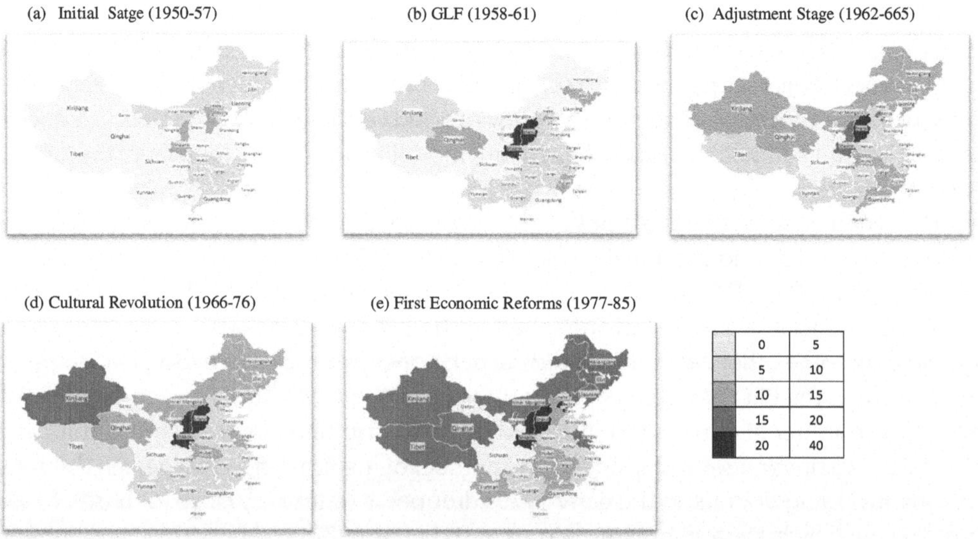

Map 3. Allocation of doctors (per 10,000 inhabitants) in China (1949–85). *Source: Author's elaboration from the Comprehensive statistical data and materials on 50 years of new China (1950–1998).*

By 1954 the local government had already invested in the construction and spread of different hospitals and clinics within the province that concentrated on the practice of TCM, many of which were combined with Western medicine. While this practice developed during the 1950s and early 1960s, during the Cultural Revolution the work was paralyzed. Indeed, one third of the TCM hospitals closed down, many clinics had their licenses revoked, and about 150,000 practitioners in the sector were relocated. TCM policies were implemented again in 1978, in circumstances of their rapid development, which spread to different prefectures in the region and acquired greater importance in the 1980s.

While several studies define the BFD program as a positive system established during the Cultural Revolution, statistical data show that Henan Province lagged behind during this period in health levels. Graph 4 shows a representative decrease of the number of doctors per 10,000 inhabitants. The decline started at the beginning of the Cultural Revolution and did not recover to the levels of the mid 1960s until the early 1980s. During this period the share of doctors declined from 9.5 doctors per 10,000 inhabitants in 1965 to 5.8 per 10,000 inhabitants in 1976, reaching its lowest point in 1971 with 4.8 doctors for every 10,000 inhabitants. Indeed, during this time many hospitals in the province closed down, and all the progress made in preventive medicine in previous years was wiped out. The provincial gazetteers show that during the Cultural Revolution, thirteen hospitals were either merged or closed down.[43] Also, the development of medical technology stagnated until the beginning of the 1970s.

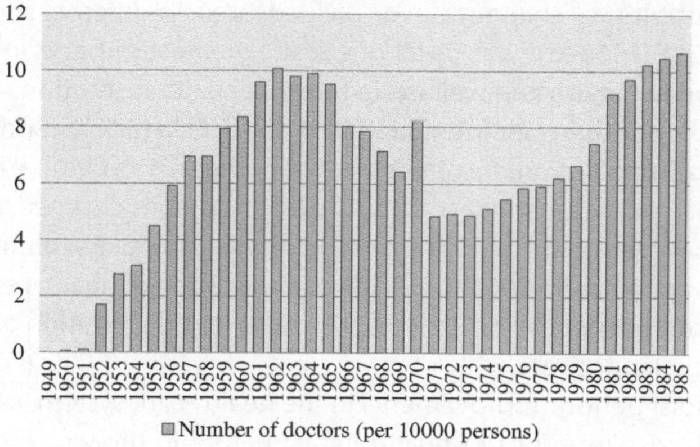

Graph 4. Number of doctors per ten thousand inhabitants in Henan province (1949–85). Source: Comprehensive Statistical Data and Materials on 50 years of New China.

The provincial health and epidemic stations were reduced from 153 units in 1965 to 62 units in 1969. Therefore, prevention of tuberculosis and other parasitic diseases ended until the beginning of the 1970s. Between 1956 and 1962 a "seven year plan to eliminate malaria' was implemented, but it failed in Henan due to the GLF. However, by 1964 the province had become one of the greatest successes nationwide in malaria eradication, reducing the cases to 1.3 per cent. Nonetheless, the interruption of malaria treatments during the Cultural Revolution increased the rate of malaria cases and gastrointestinal diseases increased by more than 40 per cent in some prefectures. At this point, Henan Province became one of the worst provinces in China.

While during the initial stage of the Maoist period great stress was placed on maternal health care, during the Cultural Revolution maternal and child health-care institutions also suffered a substantial decline, with nearly 70 per cent of stations closing down between 1965 and 1969. Most women lost their labour protection, which had been introduced at the beginning of the Maoist period by the local Health Department and the Provincial Women's Federation: pre-natal and post-natal leave was abolished, and female health rooms and nursing rooms in factories and mines were closed down. These developments contributed to an increase in the incidence of common disease among women and a greater deterioration in child health-care. By 1975, child mortality and maternal morbidity had increased to figures higher than the national average. Between 1976 and 1978, Henan Pediatric Medical College conducted a survey of 100,000 children between 0 and 14 years old in eighteen brigade teams and three cities. The results showed increased death rate among children between 0 and 12 months of 25.7 per cent. The death rates for cohorts aged 1 to 3 years old, 4 to 7 years old, and 8 to 14 years old were 2.9 per cent, 1.3 per cent, and 0.6 per cent respectively. The recovery begun in 1978, when provincial health bureaus developed new standards for women's and children's health-care, with a greater focus on the rural areas.

5. Conclusions

The Maoist period is characterized by improvements in health indicators nationally, leading to the demographic transition in China and increased life expectancy. However, between

1949 and 1976, institutional changes can be divided into four different stages in the health-care system. The GLF (1958–61) was by far one of the greatest setbacks in China from every perspective, including health and welfare. In terms of health institutions there were representative increases, but there are irregularities in the data, a problem noted in subsection 3.2. Also, while health institutions increased nationally during the Cultural Revolution (1966–76), the number of medical personnel per ten thousand persons declined from 1966 to 1972, reaching the same levels as in 1957. The decade of the Cultural Revolution is divided into two stages: a first period, from 1966 to 1971, when allocation of health resources suffered a decline; and a second period, from 1972 to 1976, when the distribution of health resources increased at an accelerated rate.

During the Maoist period, improvements in the health-care system were not positive in all provinces. Indeed, allocations of health infrastructure in the western regions, such as hospitals and clinics, were not representative nationwide. This is a problem, given that the population of the western regions is sparser than in other Chinese regions and therefore a greater number of hospitals and beds per person in such regions should reduce inequality nationally, a setback that still has to be solved in China.[44] Still, the allocation of doctors per ten thousand inhabitants was representative in comparison to other provinces located in the southeast of the country, especially after the adjustment stage (1962–65).

In order to acquire a better understanding of existing health inequalities and the development of the health system in China, the case of Henan Province has been analyzed in this article, based on provincial gazetteers and statistical yearbooks. This province was chosen due to its middle position in China regarding well-being and its high population density. Official sources show that the Cultural Revolution represented a great leap backwards in terms of health, as denoted by the representative increase in infectious diseases and infant mortality. This was mainly due to the restrictions on the development of the sector. Therefore, in the case of Henan Province, this particular decade was a backward stage not only for education, as previous studies have invariably indicated, but also for the structure and efficiency of the health system. Yet other regions such as Gansu Province had a lower share of health resources and higher rates of infant mortality. Such conclusions prompt a new question, namely whether the BFD system implemented in the mid 1960s was indeed a well-functioning system in all-Chinese provinces, as past studies have indicated.

There are some limitations to this article that must be mentioned. First, the data it uses give no information about exactly where the health resources were allocated within each province, making impossible to determine whether the health inputs were equally distributed between the urban and rural areas, nor which counties and/or districts were better provisioned. Therefore, it cannot be determined whether access to health resources was equal throughout the local population. Secondly, there are no specific figures about the number of barefoot doctors during the Cultural Revolution. While this might prevent the figures during this period being clearly interpreted, it must be remembered that not only did the number of doctors and medical personnel per ten thousand inhabitants decline at this stage, so did the quality of the health inputs because of the fewer years spent in medical education and research. Finally, so far, it has not been possible to make a clear correlation between the inequalities of health inputs and the health outputs; further study is needed in this regard. In any case, we have found a relationship between the increase in allocations of health resources and the decline in the rate of infant mortality nationwide.

Despite these limitations, it has proved possible to answer the questions set out in the introduction to this article. First, contrary to Mao's aim, to reduce health inequalities in China, variation was indeed found in the distribution of health resources among the provinces before the spread of the economic reforms at the end of the 1970s. Secondly, using Henan Province as a case study, it can be concluded that, while health inputs increased from 1950 to 1976, the health policies implemented during the GLF and, especially, the Cultural Revolution simply produced a deterioration of the health system in the region. Future research must be carried out to determine whether the inequality of health inputs in China during the Maoist period had a positive correlation with the inequality of the health outputs nationwide.

Notes

1. Deaton, *El Gran Escape. Salud*; Li et al. 'Exposure to the Chinese'; FAO, *Nutrition and Consumer Protection*; Popkin, 'The nutrition transition' and 'Will China's nutrition transition'; Popkin and Du, 'Dynamics of the nutrition transition'. Some of these studies are based on health surveys conducted in China in recent decades such as the China Health and Nutrition Survey (CHNS), which has rich information about individual and household health since the late 1980s.
2. Whyte and Sun, 'The impact of China's market'; Kwon and Schafer, 'Improving but unequal'; Li and Wei, 'Multidimensional inequality in health'.
3. Zhu, 'Current approaches to social'; Keidel, 'Chinese regional inequalities'.
4. Evadrou et al. 'Individual and province inequalities'; Biao, 'How far are the left-behind'; Feng et al. 'An exploratory multilevel analysis'; Yin and Lu, 'Individual and community factors'; Zhao, 'Income inequality, unequal health'; Chou and Wang, 'Regional Inequality in China's Health'.
5. Li and Wei, 'Multidimensional inequality in health'; Pan and Shallcross, 'Geographic distribution of hospital beds'; Zhang, et al. 'Study on equity and efficiency'; Qin and Hsien, 'Economic growth and the geographic maldistribution'.
6. Zhu, 'Current approaches to social protection'.
7. White, 'From "Barefoot Doctor" to'; Brown et al. 'Reforming Health Care in China'.
8. White, 'From "Barefoot Doctor" to'; Hipgrave, 'Commutable disease control in China'.
9. Huang, *Governing Health in Contemporary China*.
10. Ibid.
11. Slaff, 'Mortality decline in People's Republic'; Mason et al. 'The decline of infant mortality'; Campbell, 'Mortality Change and the Epidemiological'; Banister and Zhang, 'China, Economic Development and Mortality'; Chen and Zhou, 'The long-term health and economic'; Hipgrave, "Commutable disease control in China'; Song and Burgard, 'Dynamics of inequality'.
12. Jamison et al., *China: the health sector*; Babiarz et al. 'An exploration of China's mortality'.
13. Andersen et al. *Changing the US health care system*; Horev et al. 'Trends in geographic disparities'; World Health Organisation, *World health report*.
14. Pan and Shallcross, 'Geographic distribution of hospital'.
15. Yip, 'Disparities in health care'.
16. Notice that even though the health resources have increased since the economic reforms, the privatisation of the health system has led to unequal access of these resources (Hu et al. 'Reform of how healthcare is paid'; Wagstaff and Lindelow, 'Health Reform in Rural China'; Yip and Hsiao, 'China's Health Care Reform'; Li and Wei, 'Multidimensional inequality in health'). On the other hand, for most of the Maoist period, the health system was state-owned, and therefore, the allocation of the health inputs had greater relevance to understand health output and inequality, than the income of households.
17. This new data-set developed by the Stanford University and Central University of Finance and Economics has recently been available to the public. The data-set includes health records at a provincial level from 1950 to 1988. Find additional information at (Babiarz et al. 'An exploration

of China's mortality'). I kindly thank the authors for giving me direct access to the data-set Mao Mortality Analysis.

18. *Henan Xian Difang Zhi – 1985 Nianjian*.
19. Alvarez-Klee 'The Nutritional Status'.
20. Seventy-five per cent of hospital beds and 62 per cent of the senior Western-style physicians were located in urban areas (Huang, 2013: pp. 41). Notice that at this point in history over 90 per cent of the population was located in the rural areas.
21. Perkins and Yusuf, *Rural Development in China*, 135.
22. Huang, *Governing Health in Contemporary China*, 44.
23. Hipgrave, 'Commutable disease control in China' 225.
24. Xu, 'Control of communicable diseases'.
25. Huang, *Governing Health in Contemporary China*, 45; Li Rui, *Li Rui 'zuo' wenxuan*, 276; Perkins and Yusuf, *Rural Development in China*, 137.
26. Xu Yunbei, *Kaizhan weida de renmin weisheng gongzuo*, 10).
27. Huang, *Governing Health in Contemporary China*, 48.
28. Ibid. 50.
29. Other reasons attributed to the famine are natural disasters and the elimination of all sparrows in rural areas, which contributed to locust pest. However, main reasons are contributed to political and institutional setbacks in the GLF.
30. Huang, *Governing Health in Contemporary China*, 54; Hipgrave, 'Commutable disease control in China, 226.
31. Ministry of Health, *Research of National Health Services*.
32. MacFarquhar and Schoenhais, *Mao's Last Revolution*, 26.
33. Yu, *Counterattack the right-est rehabilitation wind;* Li, *The private life of Chairman Mao*, 419–20.
34. Dobson, 'Health care in China after Mao', 43; Huang, *Governing Health in Contemporary China*, 57.
35. Hu The-wei, 'The financing and the economic efficiency'.
36. Wu Chieh-ping, Medicine and Health: For Workers, Peasants, 10; Hipgrave, 'Commutable disease control in China', 227.
37. Lee, 'Medicine and Public Health'.
38. Cook, 'Changing Health in China'; Huang, *Governing Health in Contemporary China*.
39. Banister, *China's Changing Population*; Bien, 'The Barefoot Doctors'; Hipgrave, 'Commutable disease control in China'.
40. Song and Burgard, 'Dynamics of inequality'; Wang and Yang, 'Age at marriage', 303; Babiarz et al. 'An exploration of China's mortality', 5.
41. Department of Comprehensive Statistics of National Bureau of Statistics, *Comprehensive Statistical Data and Materials*.
42. Huang, *Governing Health in Contemporary China*.
43. *Henan Sheng Zhi*.
44. Pan and Shallcross, 'Geographic distribution of hospital'.

Disclosure statement

No potential conflict of interest was reported by the author.

Funding

This work was supported by the University of Barcelona [grant number Ajut per Docència i Recerca (Financial Aid for Te].

References

Alvarez-Klee, R. "Nutritional Status in China during the Maoist Period (1949-76)." PhD diss., University of Barcelona, submission date Summer 2018.

Andersen, R., T. Rice, and G. Kominski. *Changing the US Health Care System: Key Issues in Health Services Policy and Management*. San Francisco: Wiley, 2011.

Babiarz, K., K. Eggleston, G. Miller, and Q. Zhang. "An Exploration of China's Mortality Decline under Mao: A Provincial Analysis, 1950-80." *Population Studies: A Journal of Demography, Popul Stud (Camb)* 69, no. 1 (2015): 39–56.

Banister, J. *China's Changing Population*. Satandford, CA: Standford University Press, 1987.

Banister, J., and X. Zhang. "China, Economic Development and Mortality Decline." *World Development* 33, no. 1 (2005): 21–41.

Biao, X. "How Far Are the Left-behind Left behind? A Preliminary Study in Rural China." *Pop. Sp. Place* 13 (2006): 179–191.

Bien, Ch. "The Barefoot Doctors: China's Rural Health Care Revolution, 1968-1991." PhD diss. [Honors Thesis], Wesleyan University, 2008

Brown, R., D. Garcia, Y. Liu, and J. Moore. "Reforming Health Care in China. Historical, Economic and Comparative Perspectives." *Pubpol* (2012): 716.

Campbell, C. "Mortality Change and the Epidemological Transition in Beijing, 1644-1990." En *Asian Population History*, editado por de T. et al. Liu and Y. et al. Liu, 221–247. Oxford: Oxford University Press, 2001.

Chen, Y., and L. Zhou. "The Long-Term Health and Economic Consequences of the 1959-61 Famine in China." *Journal of Health Economics* 26 (2007): 659–681.

Chou, W. L., and Z. J. Wang. "Regional Inequality in China's Health Care Expenditures." *Health Economics* 18 (2009): S137–S146.

Cook, D. "Changing Health in China: Re-Evaluating the Epidemological Transition Model." *Health Policy* 67 (2004): 329–343.

Deaton, A. *El Gran Escape. Salud, Riqueza Y Los Orígines De La Desigualdad*. Madrid: Fondo de Cultura de España, 2015.

Department of Comprehensive Statistics of National Bureau of Statistics. *Xin Zhongguo Wushi Nian Tongji Ziliao Xupian* [Comprehensive Statistical Data and Material on 50 Yeards of New China]. Beijing: China Statistics Press, 1999.

Devereux, S. *Famine in the Twentieth Century*. Working Paper. Brighton: IDS, 2000.

Dobson, A. "Health Care in China after Mao." *Health Care Financing Review* 2 (1981): 41–53.

Evandrou, M., J. Falkingham, Z. Feng, and A. Vlachantoni. "Individual and Province Inequalities in Health among Older People in China: Evidence and Policy Implications." *Health and Place* 30 (2014): 134–144.

Feng, Z., W. Wang, K. Jones, and Y. Li. "An Exploratory Multilevel Analysis of Income, Income Inequality and Self-Rated Health of the Elderly in China." *Social Science and Medicine* 75, no. 12 (2012): 2481–2492.

Food and Agriculture Organization. "Nutrition and Consumer Protection. China Summary." *Agriculture and Consumer Protection Depatment* (2010). Accessed 3 de November de 2012. http://www.fao.org/ag/agn/nutrition/chn_en.stm

Hipgrave, D. "Commutable Disease Control in China: From Mao to Now." *Journal of Global Health* 1, no. 2 (2011): 224–238.

Horev, T., and I. Pesis_Katz. "Trends in Greographic Disparities in Allocation of Health Care Resources in the U.S." *Health Policy* 68 (2004): 223–232.

Hu, T. "The Financing and the Economic Efficiency of Rural Heath Services in the People's Republic of China." *International Journal of Health Services* 6, no. 2 (1976): 239–249.

Hu, S. L., Y. L. Tang, Y. X. Liu, Zhao, M. L. Escobar, and D. D. Farranti. "Reform of How Healthcare is Paid for in China: Challenges and Opportunities." *Lancet* 372 (2008): 1846–1853.

Huang, Y. *Governing Health in Contemporary China*. New York: Routledge, 2013.

Jamison, D., J. Evans, T. King, I. Porter, N. Prescott, and A. Prost. *China: The Health Sector*. Washington, DC: World Bank.

Keidel, A. "Chinese Regional Inequalities in Income and Well-Being." *Review of Income and Wealth* 55, no. 1 (2009): 538–561.

Kwon, S., and M. Schafer. "Improving but Unequal: Temporal Trends in Chinese Self-Rated Health, 1990-2012." *SSM - Population Health* 2 (2016): 77–83.

Lee, P. R. "Medicine and Public Health in the People's Republic of China." *The West Journal of Medicine* 120 (1974): 430–437.

Li, Zh. *The Private Life of Chairmal Mao*. New York: Random House, 1994.

Li, R. *Li Rui "zuo" wenxuan* [Selected Anti-leftist Works of Li Rui]. Beijing: Zhongyang bianyi chubanshe, 1995.

Li, Y., and otros. "Exposure to the Chinese Famine in Early Life and the Risk of Metabolic Syndrome in Adulthood." *Diabetes Care* 34, no 4 (2011): 1014–1018.

Li, Y., and D. Wei. "A Spatial-Temporal Analysis of Health Care and Mortality Inequalities in China." *Eurasian Geography and Economics* 51, no. 6 (2010): 767–787.

Li, Y., and D. Wei. "Multidimensional Inequality in Health Care Distribution in Provincial China: A Case Study of Henan Province." *Royal Dutch Geographical Society* 105, no. 1 (2014): 91–106.

MacFarquhar, R., and M. Schoenhals. *Mao's Last Revolution*. Cambridge and London: Harvard University Press, 2006.

Mason, W., W. Lavely, H. Ono, and A. Chan. "The Decline of Infant Mortality in China: Sichuan, 1949-1988." En *Social Differenciation and Social Inequality: Essays in Honor of John Pock*, editado por J. N. Baron, J. Baron, D. Grusky, D. Treiman, 153–207. Boulder, Colorado: Westwiew Press, 1996.

Ministry of Health. *Guojia weisheng fuwu yanjiu* [Research of National Health Services]. Beijing: Ministry of Health, 1999.

Pan, J., and D. Shallcross. "Geographic Distribution of Hospital Beds throughout China: A County-Level Econometric Analysis." *International Journal for Equity in Health* 15, no. 15 (2016): 981.

Perkins, D., and S. Yusuf. *Rural Development in China*. Baltimore, MD: Johns Hopkins University Press, 1984.

Popkin, B. "The Nutrition Transition and Its Health Implications in Lower Income Countries." *Public Health Nutrition* I, no. I (1997): 5–21.

Popkin, B. "Will China's Nutrition Trnasition Overwhelm Its Health Care System and Slow Economic Growth?" *Health Affairs* 27, no 4 (2008): 1064–1076.

Popkin, B., and S. Du. "Dynamics of the Nutrition toward the Animal Food Sector in China and Its Implications: A Worried Perspective." *The Journal of Nutrition* 113, no 11 (2003): 3898S–3906S.

Qin, X., and C. R. Hsien. "Economic Growth and the Geographic Maldistribution of Health Care Resources: Evidence from China, 1949-2010." *China Economic Review* 31 (2014): 288–288.

Salaff, J. "Mortality Decline in People's Republic of China and the United States." *Population Studies* 27 (1976): 551–576.

Song, S., and S. Burgard. "Dynamics of Inequality: Mother's Education and Infant Mortality in China 1970-2001." *Journal of Health and Social Behavior* 53, no. 3 (2011): 349–364.

Wagstaff, A., and M. Lindelow. "Health Reform in Rural China: Challenges and Options." En *Public Finance in China: Reform and Growth for a Harmonious Society*, editado por J. Wang and S. Lou, 265–286. Washington, DC: World Bank, 2008.

Wang, F. "The Future of a Demographic Overachiever: Long-Term Implications of the Demographic Transition in China." *Population and Development Review* 37 (2011): 173–190.

Wang, F., and Q. Yang. "Age at Marriage and the First Birth Interval: The Emerging Change in Sexual Behaviour among Young Couples in China." *Population and Development Review* 22, no. 2 (1996): 299–320.

White, S. "From 'Barefoot Doctor' to 'Village Doctor' in Tiger Springs Village: A Case Study of Rural Health Care Transformations in Social China." *Human Organization* 57, no. 4 (1998): 480–490.

Whyte, M. K., and Z. Sun. "The Impact of China's Market Reforms on the Health of Chinese Citizens: Examining Two Puzzles." *China: An International Journal* 8 (2010): 1–32.

World Health Organization. *World Health Report*. Report. Geneva: World Health Organization, 2000.

Wu, Chieh-ping. "Medicine and Health: For Workers, Peasants, and Soldiers." *Peking Review* 8 (February 1975): 9–11.

Xu, Y. "Kaizhan weida de renmin weisheng gongzuo [Launch A Movement for Great People's Health Work]." *Hongqi* 6 (1960).

Xu, X. "Control of Communicable Diseases in the People's Republic of China." *Asia Pacific Journal of Public Health* 7 (1994): 123–131.

Yin, D., and J. Lu. "Individual and Community Factors Associated with Activities of Daily Living among the Oldest-Old, an Application of the HLM Method." *Popul. Res. Policy Review* (2007): 60–70.

Yip, W., and W. Hsiao. "China's Health Care Reform: A Tentaive Assessment." *China Economic Review* 20 (2009): 613–619.

Yip, W. "Disparities in Health Care and Health Status: The Rural-Urban Gap and beyond." En *One Country, Two Societies: Rural-Urban Inequality in Contemporary China*, editado por M. Whyte, 147–165. Cambridge, MA: Harvard University Press, 2009.

Yu, M. "Fanji weisheng zhanxian de youqing fanan feng [Counterattack the Right-Est Rehabilitation Wing in the Health Sector]." *Hongqi* 4 (1976): 5–11.

Zhang, X., L. Zhao, Z. Cui, and Y. Wang. "Study on Equity and Efficiency of Health Resources and Services Based on Key Indicators in China." *PLoS One* 12 (2015): 1–15.

Zhao, Z. "Income Inequality, Unequal Health Care Access, and Mortality in China." *Population and Development Review* 32 (2006): 461–483.

Zhu, Y. "Current Approaches to Social Protection in China." En *Social Protection, Economic Growth and Social Change, Goals, Issues and Trajectories in China, India, Brazil, and South Africa*, editado por J. Piachuad and D. Midgley, 44–58. Cheltenham: Edward Elgar, 2013.

Archives

Provincial Archive of Public Health Records (*Weishengzi*).

China Statistical Data Compilation (1949-2003).

1988 National Survey of Fertility and Contraception.

Websites

http://www.fao.org/ag/agn/nutrition/chn_en.stm , accesses November 2012 and November 2016.

http://aparc.fsi.stanford.edu/asiahealthpolicy/publication/exploration-chinas-mortality-decline-under-mao-provincial-analysis-1950-1980, accessed August 2016.

http://www.hnsqw.com.cn/sqsjk/dfzsj/ , accessed November 2016 and September 2017.

Architects and knowledge transfer in hospital systems: The introduction of Western hospital designs in Japan (1918–1970)

Pierre-Yves Donzé

ABSTRACT
This article addresses hospitals as medical technology in itself and discusses the evolution of hospital design. As a case study, it focuses on Japan from 1918 to 1970. Hospital systems in this country experienced a major shift between the prewar and postwar periods. While the prewar period was characterised by the domination of numerous private small hospitals in urban areas, the postwar reconstruction was based on the extension of large public hospitals. This article demonstrates the major roles that architects played in introducing hospital designs in Japan and adapting the Western functional model for use in the country.

1. Introduction

The relationships between factory management systems and workshops layout are a classic theme in business history and the history of technology.[1] In particular, numerous works have demonstrated that the organisation of shop floors in the automobile industry was intimately linked to the implementation of new management practices inspired by Taylorism.[2] The objective of this article is to apply this approach to the service sector, using the case of hospitals for investigation. It focuses particularly on the key roles of architects, both as organisers of the hospital system through planning and as the designers of specific buildings. Throughout the world, architects contributed – especially during the first part of the twentieth century – toward improvements in the efficiency of hospital work, modelled after the manufacturing industry.

This article builds on a broad range of literature in the history of medicine, business history and the history of technology. Most of the works on hospitals adopt a monographic approach in a long-term perspective and explain the development of particulars hospitals as the consequences of the progresses of medicine and the will of local elites to provide modern care to the population. Under the influence of Foucault, a major issue was to analyse how hospitals contributed to the so-called 'medicalisation' of societies and social disciplinarisation.[3]

Yet, when one considers the development of hospitals, a still under-addressed issue is that of organising the hospital system itself. Based on an approach inspired by Thomas

Hughes,[4] a 'hospital system' can be defined as an ensemble of institutional (public hospitals, private hospitals, medical clinics, faculty of medicine, medical schools) and social (doctors, patients, architects, politicians) actors in interaction depending on a common political, economic and social environment.[5] A major concern is to understand how these systems were constructed and evolved. Basically, there are two main ways to organise them: competition and free market principles; and regulation, mostly by the central government. A second important question is the form taken by individual hospitals, particularly their internal organisation, within the system. The structure of the hospital system and the nature of individual health care institutions are indeed related. They have an influence on the way modern societies can provide medical care to the population, especially in a situation of fast-growing demand. However, in the literature, there is a divide between works on hospital systems and on the design of specific institutions.

First, scholars focusing on national hospital systems have emphasised that the transformation and the growth of health care institutions have taken the form of a bottom-up process. It resulted essentially from the action of local activists (doctors, municipalities, traditional elites), such as Charles E. Rosenberg and Rosemary Stevens showed for the United States,[6] Jean-Paul Domin and Olivier Faure for France,[7] and Alfons Labisch and Reinhardt Spree for Germany.[8] The action of the central government is usually limited to the regulation of health insurance, except in a few cases like the United Kingdom, where hospitals were nationalised with the introduction of the National Health Service in 1948.[9] In this perspective, the hospital system itself has a function to cure a growing number of patients, but the internal organisation of specific institutions is not considered as a significant factor.

Second, the internal organisation of hospitals has been addressed by historians who maintained that their ability to treat a growing number of patients relied on the adoption of management principles and of a functional division of space. Their research was influenced by the works of Alfred D. Chandler, some of them mentioning explicitly this inspiration.[10] In his seminal work on New York Hospital and Pennsylvania Hospital, Joel D. Howell demonstrated that growth relied on a bureaucracy based on scientific management and the efficiency movement.[11] As for Morris J. Vogel, he emphasised the action of the administrators of hospitals, who introduced this new management.[12] In Europe also, some studies showed that hospitals became managed like private enterprises to support their development.[13] Finally, some rare contributions in the history of architecture make the link between the rationalisation of the spatial organisation of hospitals and their transformation into fast-growing institutions.[14]

Yet, it is necessary to overcome this literature divide and to offer an explanation that includes both the level of the hospital system and the level of the single institution. This article argues that the internal organisation of hospitals was a consequence of the structure of hospital systems, and not only the result from the actions of individual medical doctors and architects. The need to treat a growing number of patients efficiently, given the demographic development and the will of the population to access new medical technology installations at hospitals (X-ray devices, operating rooms and laboratories, for instance), fostered a new hospital model during the interwar years in Western countries. Developed primarily by German and American architects and doctors, the so-called 'functional hospital' was characterised by a vertical (medical specialty-based) and horizontal (ward and technical service-based) division of work, inspired by the organisation of work in the manufacturing industry. Although there was a broad variety of hospitals throughout Western Europe and the United States until the early twentieth century, in terms of design and internal organisation, the pressures toward standardisation for coping with the huge increases in the volume and scope of patients led to the emergence of a new model. That model made its way to non-Western countries through the activities of doctors, private companies, international organisations and, particularly, architects. Yet, scholars in business history and management have emphasised that, in the case of technology and knowledge, the success of an international transfer depends on the adaptation of the original models to local conditions.[15] Hospital design is not an exception; the case of Japan, where the new functional model was gradually introduced and diffused throughout the national hospital system between 1918 and the early 1970s, illustrates that fact.

Japan is a particularly relevant example because of its specificity with regard to Western cases, which have caught the attention of scholars until now. Hospitals were introduced in Japan after the Meiji Restoration (1868) as a modern institution and technology, like other industries. Unlike Western countries, such institutions did not exist before that time, and Christian philanthropy had no influence on their development. Hence, hospitals were mostly considered as an infrastructure for the private practice of medicine and, in some cases, for medical education. Individual doctors were, hence, the driving force of the growth of hospital systems in Japan, which were organised on free-market principles and on a weak state of intervention. Consequently, the main research question addressed in this contribution is: how were hospitals designed to cure a growing number of patients in a system based on competition? Secondary issues include the way the Western functional model was introduced to Japan, the role of public hospitals in this process and the action of architects. Academic literature on the history of Japanese hospitals is rather limited. It consists mostly of descriptive studies that focus on the general development of hospitals in a chronological perspective.[16] One must, however, mention the seminal work of Shuhei Ikai on the growth of the Japanese hospital system during the twentieth century.[17] He emphasised, in particular, the distinction between private and public hospital in this development, but he did not focus on hospitals as a technology and, hence, did not approach the issue of hospital design. This later issue was addressed by Yuji Katsuki in a perspective of history of architecture for the period of 1880–1930.[18]

This article is divided into four sections. Section 1 gives a macroeconomic view of the development of the Japanese hospital system in a long-term perspective, to offer a general understanding of its main phases and to clarify the major changes. Next, Section 2 analyses hospital design and construction during the interwar years, precisely when the functional model emerged in Western countries. Then, Section 3 discusses the postwar reforms of hospital policy and the attempts of state intervention. Finally, Section 4 shows how the new public hospitals constructed in the postwar era became a universal model in Japan.

2. Development of the Japanese hospital system: A macroeconomic view

Before discussing hospital design, it is necessary to have a macroeconomic overview of the development of the hospital system in Japan in a long-term perspective. By 'hospital system' or 'hospital network', the author refers to hospitals throughout Japan considered as a whole. Looking beyond single hospitals makes it possible to highlight some specificity in terms of average size and ownership that express hospital policy and enables scholars to choose representative cases. Hence, I start here with a discussion of the structure of this hospital system.

Figures 1 and 2 show, respectively, the number of hospitals and of hospital beds in Japan between 1880 (1913 for beds) and 1980 according to the legal ownership (public vs. private). They are based on numbers published in the volumes of the *Historical Statistics of Japan.*[19] These numbers do not include 'clinics' (*shinryojo*), which are basically extensions of private surgeries by doctors, not 'hospitals' (*byoin*) owing to their tiny size. The official distinction between the two kinds of institutions (clinics and hospitals) first took form in 1933, with the number of beds determining institutional status: hospitals were establishments with at least 10 beds, and clinics were those with fewer than 10. This definition was in force until 1948, when policymakers raised the cutoff to 20 beds.[20] Figures 1 and 2 show that the prewar and the postwar years have highly varying hospital systems.

First, the six decades from 1880 to 1940 show a development based on the high growth of small private hospitals during the interwar years. In 1880, the system still relied very much on few public institutions. The 242 public hospitals represented 61.3% of hospitals at that time. They were especially teaching institutions dispatched throughout the country to train a new generation of doctors in Western medicine and to diffuse this knowledge into Japan.[21] Yet, in the early 1880s, in the context of the new financial policy implemented by the minister Matsukata, the central government and local authorities started to withdraw from the hospital business and to sell their establishments to private doctors and organisations, like the Red Cross. Institutions that were not privatised were mostly transformed into hospitals destined for poor people, with private doctors keeping profitable patients for their own practices. Moreover, these public hospitals were integrated to schools of medicine to which they provided patients to train medical students (*gakuyo kanja*).[22] They belonged to municipalities, prefectures, public bodies and to the central government, and were the largest and most modern medical institutions in Japan.[23]

Hence, until World War I, the steady increase in hospital numbers (from 395 in 1880 to 1015 in 1914) went together with the dramatic growth in the shares of private hospitals

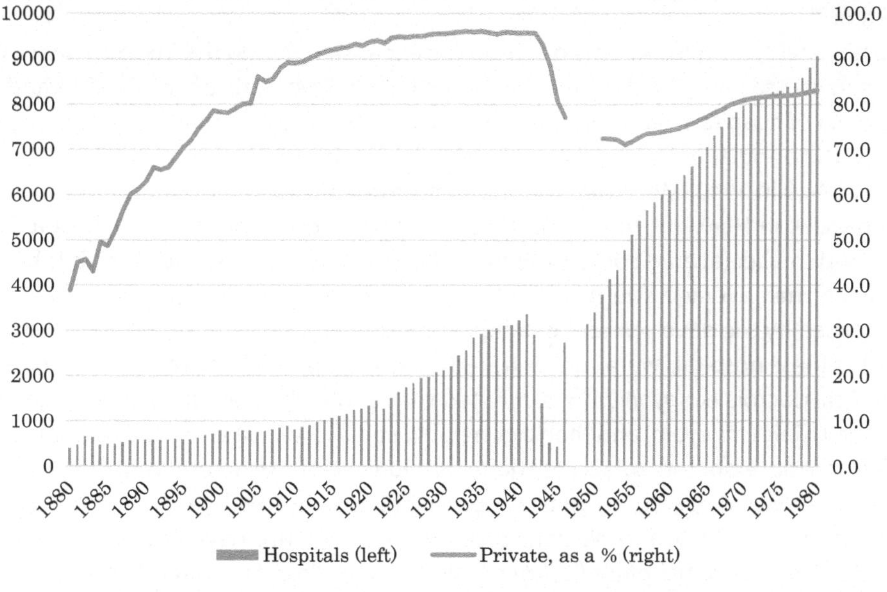

Figure 1. Total number of hospitals in Japan, and percentage of private hospitals, 1880–1980. Source: Nihon tokei kyokai. *Historical Statistics of Japan,* volume 5. Tokyo: Nihon tokei kyokai, 1988, 170–173.

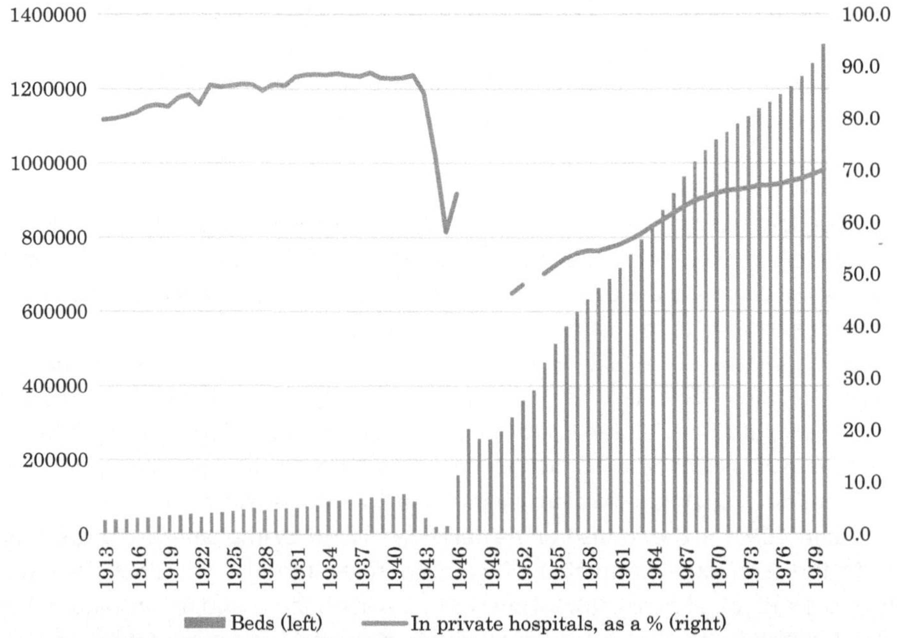

Figure 2. Total number of hospital beds in Japan, and percentage of beds in private hospitals, 1913–1980. Source: Nihon tokei kyokai. *Historical Statistics of Japan,* volume 5. Note: data unknown before 1913.

(91.5% in 1914). This development went beyond the increase in population. Indeed, the index of hospitals per one million people grew only slightly, from 10.8 in 1880 to 19.5 in 1914. However, public hospitals were larger, with an average of 89.7 beds in 1914 (representing 20% of all hospital beds in Japan that year) against 33.2 beds in private hospitals. This period was characterised as the 'golden age of private medicine' by medical historian Kawakami.[24]

The hospital system experienced a dramatic expansion during the interwar years, which main characteristic was the densification of the hospital network. Between 1914 and 1940, the number of hospitals was multiplied by 3 (from 1015 to 3226); that was a higher growth rate than the population's one. Hence, the number of hospitals per one million population peaked at 44.9 in 1940. Moreover, the share of private hospitals continued to expand and reached 95.6% in 1940, but was at only 87.8% for beds. Indeed, these private hospitals were smaller and smaller (average of 29 beds in 1940 against 33.2 in 1914), while public hospitals maintained their average size (88.4 beds in 1940). Consequently, the prewar period was characterised by the development of a hospital system based on small private hospitals.

Most of these hospitals were concentrated in urban areas and were opened by independent medical doctors (*kaigyoi*) who reinvested their profits in extending their surgery units into a small clinic (*shinryojo*) and then a general hospital (*byoin*). Ikai argued that this process enabled Japanese doctors to access the technological infrastructure of hospitals, such as X-ray equipment and operating rooms.[25] Opening his own hospital was the original Japanese way, while medical doctors in Western countries accessed this new infrastructure through contracts with opened hospitals (US) or employment in closed hospitals (UK).[26] In the West, the percentage of private and profit-oriented hospitals was low, and they were usually specialised clinics rather than general hospitals. Consequently, Japan was characterised in an international perspective as a country with a high density of establishments. Based on a census published by the League of Nations, Table 1 provides a comparison of various hospital systems throughout the world. This document clearly shows that Japan had the smallest hospitals in the world in 1929, with an average of 30.3 beds, compared to 73.3 in the US, 97.4 in Germany and 116.5 in France.[27]

Second, after World War II, the situation changed dramatically. The reconstruction of the hospital system was based, the first time, on the development of large public institutions. In 1951, the first year for which there are complete data, they represented 27.5% of all hospitals and more than half of beds (53.6%). Then, the hospital system experienced a fast growth for three decades, driven by the densification of the network until the mid-1960s and then by population growth. The number of hospitals per one million population went from 41 in 1950 to 65.2 in 1960, 76.2 in 1970 and 77.4 in 1980. As for the number of beds per one million people, it shows also a densification (3315 in 1950; 7351 in 1960; 10,152 in 1970), followed by a stagnation (11,271 in 1980).

Hence, the years 1950–1980 can be divided in two periods. First, a period of reconstruction and growth until 1965, during which public hospitals played a crucial role, which they had not played since the 1880s. They were leading institutions and embedded the postwar modern hospital imported from the US, a new kind of medical institution. During these 15 years, the importance of public hospitals declined slightly, from 27.5% of hospitals and 53.6% of beds in 1951 to 22.7% of hospitals and 40% of beds in 1965. These figures were however far above the numbers of the interwar years, so that it is not an exaggeration to consider it as a possible new situation. Second, private hospitals started to grow faster after 1965 and, in 1980, they gained a new position of domination. That year, they represented 83.1% of hospitals and 70.1% of beds. However, these hospitals were very different from the private hospitals of the interwar years. They were larger (83.8 beds on average in 1960 and 123 beds in 1980) and modelled after public hospitals in terms of organisation and management.

Table 1. International comparison of hospital systems, 1927–1929.

	General hospitals	Hospitals/million people	Beds	Beds/hospital	Beds/10,000 people	Year
Norway	182	64.9	10,986	60.4	39.2	1928
Germany	3842	60.6	374,260	97.4	59	1929
New Zealand	87	59.4	6661	76.6	45.5	1929
Denmark	177	50.6	17,462	98.7	49.9	1928
Finland	176	49	5606	31.9	15.6	1928
Switzerland	192	48	18,590	96.8	46.5	1928
United States	4925	40.4	361,079	73.3	29.7	1929
Latvia	65	33	4988	76.7	25.3	1929
Japan	2059	32.9	62,451	30.3	10	1929
France	1301	31.6	151,514	116.5	36.7	1929
Netherlands	230	29.6	34,902	151.7	44.8	1929
Poland	707	24.3	61,028	86.3	21	1929
Hungary	176	20.5	15,324	87.1	17.9	1929
Lithuania	41	17.8	1889	46.1	8.2	1929
Czechoslovakia	250	17.1	35,451	141.8	24.3	1929
Mexico	258	15.8	15,724	60.9	9.6	1927
Greece	67	10.7	4948	73.9	7.9	1929
Egypt	28	2	3848	137.4	2.7	1929
Turkey	5	0.3	450	90	0.3	1929

Source: League of Nations, *International Health Year-book 1930: Reports on the Public Health Progress of Thirty-Four Countries and colonies in 1929*, Geneva, 1932.

Consequently, what can we learn from this general macroeconomic view? The main outcome is to show that the long-term development of the Japanese hospital system results from various successive phases dominated by different kinds of health care institutions: small private hospitals (1914–1940); large public hospitals (1945–1965); and medium-sized private hospitals (since 1965). Each of these phases was characterised by different models of institution in terms of organisation. They are explored in the next three sections.

3. Building hospitals during the interwar years

In Western countries, the interwar years were a turning point in the construction and organisation of hospitals. Under the strong influence of Taylorism, the efficiency movement and rationalisation, these institutions were reorganised in order to be able to welcome and treat a growing number of patients. Hospitals were transformed from a *place* to cure sick patients into a *tool* to cure a mass of patients. They became a technology in themselves. Historians have demonstrated, particularly for cases in the United States, in Canada and in Switzerland, that the management of flows (patients, nurses, material, food, etc.) within the hospital led to a spatial reorganisation inspired by assembly-lines of the manufacturing industry.[28] The main characteristics of such functional hospitals were the clear separation between patients' rooms, medicotechnical equipment (particularly the operating room and X-ray equipment, which became the core of medical technology in hospitals) and technical services (laundry, kitchen, etc.). These divisions were spatially separated and linked by elevators and hallways.

Consequently, the design of hospitals became a specialty, and some architects focused on this new business. One of the most famous was undoubtedly the German architect Hermann Distel (1875–1945).[29] He was a promoter of rationally planned hospitals, in order to save construction and operating costs, first in Germany during the late 1920s, then internationally in the 1930s. He had been president of the Hospital Building Committee of the International Hospital Association (IHA) before World War II and cooperated with architects from different Western countries to discuss the best ways to build hospitals. The major outcome of these discussions was a book written in 1932, in which Distel emphasised that, although hospital equipment can be – and must be – standardised, it is not possible to offer a standardised plan for hospital construction, which must be adapted to local natural, legal and financial conditions. However, the idea to rationally and scientifically organise the hospital remains the main message of Distel.[30] At the instigation of German and American doctors and architects, the IHA organised congresses and published a newsletter to diffuse their conceptions of hospital organisation and construction.[31]

The activities of the IHA were introduced in Japan by architect Masao Takamatsu.[32] Born in 1885 in Yokohama, he graduated from the Department of Architecture of the University of Tokyo in 1910 and entered one of the most famous bureaus of architects of the country, Sone & Chujo, in Tokyo. In 1920–1921, he did a study tour in the US, and in 1922 he founded the Research Center in Hospital Building (*Byoin kensetsu kenkyujo*). In 1928, he was appointed lecturer in hospital building at Waseda University.[33] Takamatsu was one of the most famous designers of hospitals in Japan during the interwar years. Until his death in 1934, he built large hospitals based on the principles of the Western functional model throughout the country, particularly Surugadai Inoue Hospital (1929), Jikei University Hospital (1930) and Keio University Hospital (1932).

Moreover, Takamatsu had a major impact on the introduction of the Western model in Japan during the interwar years, notably through numerous articles he published in journals of architecture. For example, in 1932, he published a long paper in the *Journal of Architecture* on new designs of hospitals presented by architects from the United States and Europe during the 1931 congress of the IHA. His aim was to show his Japanese colleagues what innovations were being introduced in Western countries at that time.[34] Finally, he was also the author of the volume dedicated to hospitals in the encyclopedia *High Architecture* (*Koto kenchikugaku*), published in 1933.[35]

The Keio University Hospital, founded in 1932, is undoubtedly the best illustration of the new large hospital developed by Takamatsu (see Figure 3). Opened in 1917, the Faculty of Medicine in Keio was one of the most renowned places in Japan to train doctors and to carry out research in medicine. Funded by the imperial household and the Mitsui zaibatsu, this faculty was directed by the world-famous bacteriologist Shibasaburo Kitasato. Keio recruited excellent doctors in all disciplines, with the ambition to fully compete against the University of Tokyo.[36] Hence, Keio University wanted the most modern hospital equipment in the early 1930s and asked Takamatsu to design a building. He devised a four-floor construction, made in concrete and steel, with 219 beds, characterised by both a horizontal (e.g. doctor's offices, administration, operation rooms, etc. in the North building; patients' rooms in other aisles) and a vertical division of functions.[37] In a book published in 1933, he explicitly demonstrated the direct influence from American and French hospitals on this building.[38]

Figure 3. Keio University Hospital, 1932. Source: Takamatsu Masao-kun kinnen jigyokai (ed.), *Takamatsu Masao-kun no seisaku to chosaku*, Tokyo: Takamatsu Masao-kun kinnen jigyokai, 1935, p. 18.

Takamatsu was not the only architect to develop a new generation of large hospitals based on the Western model during the interwar years. Another significant designer was Mamoru Yamada (1894–1966), who graduated from the same department as Takamatsu eight years later (1918).[39] He entered the Ministry of Telecommunication after graduation and spent the first part of his career building post offices and local workshops throughout the country. In 1929, he went to Europe and to the US on a study tour. He was especially interested by hospitals in Berlin, Frankfort and New York.[40] Then, in the mid-1930s, he engaged in the construction of hospitals for his ministry, in Hiroshima (1935), Tokyo (1936–1937) and Osaka (1938), all characterised by their functional organisation (with centralisation of services) and the implementation of the operation room at the core of the building.[41] After WWII, he founded his own architecture company and enjoyed a successful career as a developer of hospitals.

The activities of this new generation of architects were supported by a new hospital policy adopted by Japanese health authorities after the Great Kanto Earthquake (1923). The need to reconstruct hospitals in Tokyo, provide access to health care to the entire population on a broader scale, and strengthen the nation in preparation for war amid the context of a militarist regime led the government to shift its attention from isolation hospitals to large general hospitals dedicated to the working classes.[42] Hence, while the number of public hospitals had been constantly declining since 1890, it started to grow steadily again, even if public hospitals' share of the total hospital count kept falling. Having bottomed out to 81 in 1923, it reached 95 in 1930 and 141 in 1940. This political change was a major incentive to introduce the new hospitals.

Yet, despite the activities of architects like Takamatsu and Yamada, the driving force of the hospital system's development was the free market and the action of independent doctors who built numerous small hospitals for their own needs in order to have access to the new medical technology. The reconstruction of Tokyo after the Great Kanto Earthquake was, of course, an opportunity to redesign small hospitals, but the development of these institutions goes further than this single event. It must be fitted in line with the growing number of medical doctors, particularly graduates from the imperial universities of Tokyo and Kyoto.[43] Between 1920 and 1940, the number of doctors grew from 45,488 (81 for 100,000 population) to 65,332 (89).[44]

The architectural model chosen by these doctors for their private hospitals was completely different from the new large hospitals introduced in Japan at that time. The functional division of space and the organisation of flow were not an issue. The only basic thing was to separate the private habitation (usually on the first floor) and the hospital itself (second floor). These doctors just needed a basic medicotechnical infrastructure and few beds. The average number of beds in private hospitals dropped from 34 in 1920 to 29 in 1940. In fact, the most widespread model for these buildings was the integration of a small hospital within the private house of the doctor.

Several books published by architects during the interwar years gave advice to doctors about some of the possible ways to rebuild their practice. One of the most popular publications was the book released by Seiichiro Yamazaki in 1927, which had six editions until 1935.[45] He gives many technical recommendations about the house itself and the different equipment of the rooms, but nothing about spatial organisation. The issue was that they had modern equipment, but not modern organisation. Then, Yamazaki provides more than 40 examples of small hospitals, with plans and description of materials (glass, wood, concrete) and equipment used, as shown in Figure 4.

Medical doctors organised themselves to support the development of these new small private hospitals. Seven of them founded the Union of Doctors of Tokyo for the Credit, the Purchase and the Use of Architecture (*Tokyo ishi kenchiku shinyo kobai riyo kumiai*) in 1924.[46] The number of members amounted to 114 doctors at the foundation, and it had increased to 607 by 1929.[47]

Therefore, the fast development of the Japanese system expressed by statistical data in Section 1 relied on two very different kinds of hospitals: public and non-profit private large hospitals, based on the Western functional model; and small private hospitals designed within doctor's houses. Hence, the new functional model was only partially adopted in Japan and limited to large health care institutions. The management of health care in the Japanese hospital system was, hence, not a matter of having few perfectly organised large hospitals, but rather a dense network of small clinics which foundation and development resulted from market mechanisms. In this perspective, hospital planning was not an issue, and the Japanese government was largely absent in the hospital system during the interwar years, while American and European authorities intensively discussed their intervention to plan hospital development during the same period.

4. Postwar reforms

Like many other sectors of economy and society, health was the target of reforms during the postwar years, particularly under the occupation by the US army (1945–1952). Although

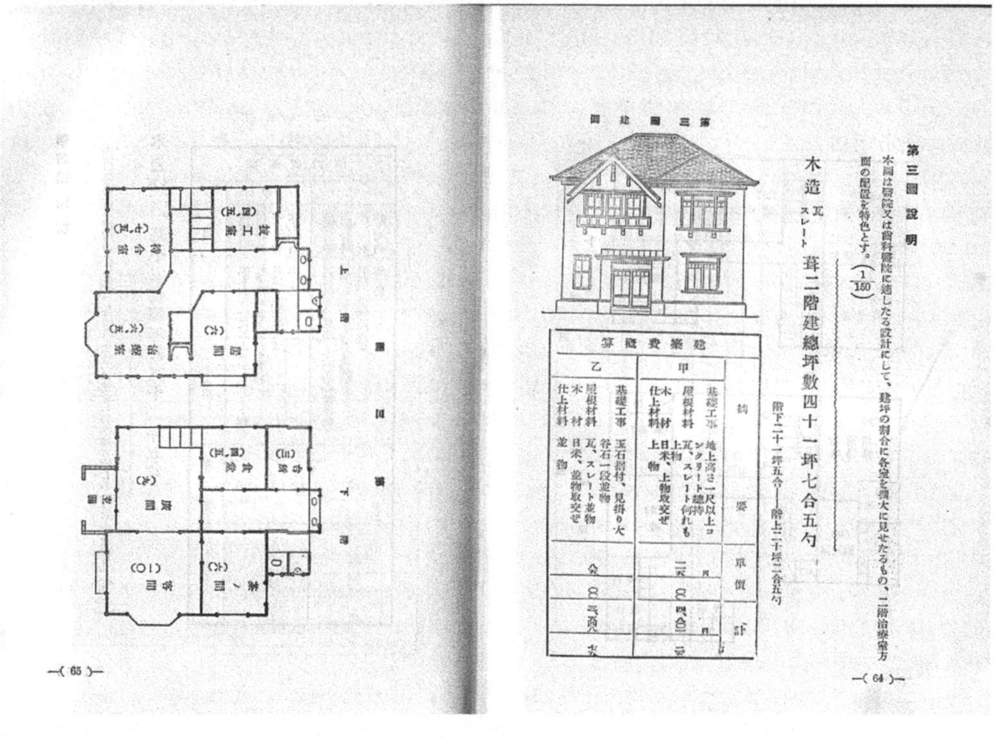

Figure 4. Example of a small hospital. Source: Seiichiro Yamazaki, *Saishin i-byoin kenchiku to sekkei*, Tokyo: Kanehara shoten, 1927, pp. 64–65.

the traditional historiography used to celebrate the advances made in Japan during this period in the field of epidemic disease control and prevention,[48] Christopher Aldous and Akihito Suzuki have recently demonstrated that these reforms followed health policies implemented during the interwar years.[49] Rather than a rupture, the postwar policy was in continuity with former measures. These authors did not address hospital policy, but the same conclusion can be made. The Japanese postwar government, together with the Supreme Commander for the Allied Powers, adopted new measures to transform the hospital system and the management of hospitals. Yet, the intervention of the State in the hospital business goes back to the late 1930s.

Soon after the creation of a Ministry of Health, in 1938, the new sanitary authorities attempted to reorganise the hospital system in the context of the struggle against tuberculosis and the building of a strong nation. The government decided to establish and finance divisions to cure patients from tuberculosis in public hospitals and adopted a plan for its intervention at various levels. The idea was to open two central general hospitals in Tokyo and Osaka (500 beds), 47 prefecture hospitals (250 beds), 588 regional hospitals (50 beds) and various small practices (number unplanned) in the countryside. Bureaucrats wanted to organise a hospital system relying on various levels of institutions, the spatial hierarchy between cities, towns and villages being discussed in the 1930s by geographers and economists such as Walter Christaller and August Lösch.[50] However, in Japan, owing to war and the strong opposition of medical doctors, this plan was only partially realised and stopped by the new authorities in 1947.[51]

During the occupation, in cooperation with US military authorities, the Japanese government reformed its public health policy and tried to intervene again in the hospital system. The planning of public institutions necessary for population needs adopted in 1950 and 1951 was based on a hierarchical system, similar to that adopted in 1942. In 1951, the Ministry of Health adopted the principle of three classes of national hospitals: central hospitals (more than 200 beds; one per prefecture); regional hospitals (90 or 120 beds according to the population of cities); local hospitals (30 to 120 beds).[52] The following year, it adopted a decree to support the funding of new hospitals and of modernisation of equipment. This plan was only partially implemented and abandoned during the early 1950s owing to a lack of political support.

The only successful reform in hospital policy was related to the improvement in the management of these institutions by the Ministry of Health through the foundation of a School of Hospital Administration (*byoin kanri kenshujo*) in 1949.[53] This institution was aimed at training hospital directors, who were usually medical doctors in Japan, in the basic rules of administration. It used a translation of the textbook *Hospital Organization and Management* published in 1935 by the American physician Malcom T. MacEachern.[54]

Consequently, during the postwar and high-growth eras, the development of the Japanese hospital system was driven by a market mechanism and characterised by a high degree of competition between institutions. Moreover, the State did not regulate the functions and equipment of hospitals, so that hospital construction occurred in a legally free environment. Yet, despite this lack of state regulation, trade associations were formed by important activists in order to self-regulate the business.

The most important organisation was the Japan Hospital Association (JHA, *Nihon byoin kai*), founded in June 1951 by directors of hospitals in the Tokyo region, with the aim to contribute to the modernisation of all aspects of hospital organisation and management (accountability, construction, medical equipment, human resources, etc.).[55] It diffused this knowledge through a journal entitled *Hospital.* Moreover, in 1956, the JHA joined the IHA and then introduced major global issues to Japan.[56] One of the objectives of the JHA was to participate in the establishment of global standards and to promote them in Japan. In particular, the JHA has organised visits to hospitals in Japan since 1961 and annual study tours to the United States and Europe since 1967.[57]

The JHA did not engage in hospital planning but rather engaged in the modernisation of hospitals as individual institutions. They promoted the adoption of a spatial organisation that enables rational flows and then a growing number of patients, as did the architect Takamatsu during the 1930s. The objective was to diffuse this functional model at a large scale. Hence, the JHA set up in 1966 a research group about hospital facilities.[58] The JHA has cooperated with hospital architects since 1966, especially with Yasumi Yoshitake, a professor at the University of Tokyo. In November 1966, the first workshop about hospital design and construction was organised in Tokyo. This gathered 120 members from all over the country and 10 architects.[59] Yoshitake, Tota Nomura (assistant professor at Yokohama University), Makoto Ito (assistant professor at Chiba University) and Ryoichi Ura (professor at Meiji University) gave presentations about their ideas for a modern hospital, which were then published in an edited volume.[60] This cooperation between administrators of large hospitals, mostly public, and architects was the basis of the development of the hospital system between 1950 and 1965 (see next section).

One must emphasise here the institutional support of the Japanese government to public hospitals up to the early 1960s. For example, in 1950, the government introduced the legal status of 'health care corporation' (*iryo hojin*) for both public and non-profit private hospitals, which gives some financial and tax incentives to enlarge and modernise their equipment.[61] Moreover, the adoption of the law on universal health insurance system (1961), which covers all the population, based on the British example, was also an important support for hospital development.

5. New public hospitals as models (1950–1965)

Based on the postwar new hospital policy and the action of the JHA, a new generation of public hospitals was built throughout Japan until the mid-1960s. The leader of this movement was a young professor of architecture at the University of Tokyo, Yasumi Yoshitake.[62] Born in 1916, he graduated from the Department of Architecture of the University of Tokyo in 1939, where he was appointed assistant professor in 1942, then full professor in 1959. After 1974, he pursued his career in local and private universities. Yoshitake was a representative of the theory planning school (*keikaku gaku*) which promoted the development of standardised and rational architecture, rather than attending a school based on artistic designs, to provide cost effective infrastructure to society (e.g. houses, schools and hospitals). Yoshitake was personally involved in numerous projects of hospital design and trained several architects in this specialty.

The second architect who promoted the diffusion of the functional model for hospitals was, however, not a disciple of Yoshitake. Kisaburo Ito (1914–1998) graduated from the Department of Architecture of Nihon University, a private institution, in 1938. He founded his own enterprise in 1952 in Tokyo, after military service and various employments.[63] Ito's first order was the design of a new large building (350 beds) for the Central Hospital of Social

Insurance (*Shakai hoken chuo byoin*). He specialised afterwards in hospital design and built a total of 52 hospitals in Japan by 1970, mostly large public institutions.[64]

An important inspiration of this generation of architects came from the United States, where the Truman administration adopted the Hospital Survey and Construction Act (Hill–Burton Act) in 1946, to support hospital development throughout the country. It provided funding for hospital construction for more than two decades (a total of 3.7 billion dollars between 1947 and 1971).[65] It also included the introduction of planning by states to coordinate hospital development. Even if this later point was not realised, it particularly attracted the attention of Japanese architects who wanted to move away from prewar market principles and organise the development of hospitals in their country. In 1956, Yoshimura and two of his disciples, Gentaro Watanabe and Makoto Ito, published the Japanese translation of a book originally entitled *Design and Construction of General Hospitals,* published three years later by the US government.[66] In a testimony published the following year, Masao Taguchi, a young architect who studied under the supervision of Yoshitake, explained that he was fascinated by the idea to adopt planning for developing a network of hospitals, from small clinics of eight beds to general hospitals of 200 beds, with all the various functions and equipment necessary for each kind of institution. The will to build '*hospitals for patients*',[67] i.e. not for doctors, was an important motivation in his work. He wanted to contribute to the establishment of a health care system driven by social policy rather than by pure market-based principles.

The model of hospitals introduced by Yoshitake and Ito was fundamentally similar to hospitals designed by Takamatsu during the interwar years. They were large buildings characterised by a functional division of space between aisles (horizontal division) and floors (vertical division), a rational management of flows to ensure the treatment of a growing number of patients, as well as the use of concrete rather than wood. In a paper published in 1957, Yoshitake exposed the principles of new hospital construction:

> In 1951, a hospital of 180 beds, although made of wood, was designed on the principles of the new hospital management introduced after the war. The major elements which express the new hospital architecture are visible: (1) an independent aisle for nurses, with a unit of 30 beds per nurse; (2) common use of health care equipment by outpatients; (3) a service division, particularly for food preparation; (4) positioning of an operating room, pharmacy, supply center, etc. between patient ward and outpatient ward.[68]

The plan for an operating room for a general hospital designed by Ito in 1962 embodies this objective to organise flows in order to make mass production of health care possible, as could already be observed in Western hospitals at the beginning of the twentieth century.[69] Figure 5 shows the new organisation of work introduced in departments of surgery and based on the US model. The operating area consists of a total of eight operating rooms, making it possible to treat several patients at the same time, while its organisation enables patients to move without disturbing work in other rooms. This embodies the new team work that appeared in surgery in the US and resulted mostly from a specialisation of medicine.[70] Finally, the introduction of air conditioning as well as the strict separation between the operating area and the outside (front room, dressing rooms, office) keeps a stable and aseptic environment for surgery.

Such an organisation of work within hospitals was not limited to the departments of surgery. Ito drew similar plans for X-ray divisions and for hospitals as a whole. This will to organise and standardise hospital design led a group of architects and engineers to create

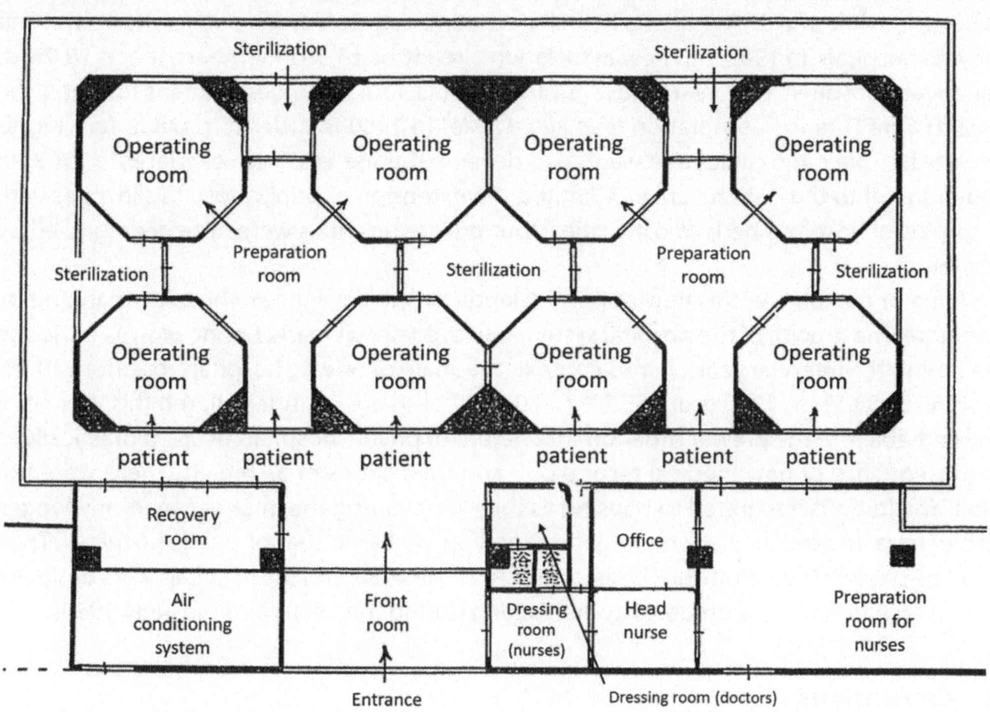

Figure 5. Operating room for a general hospital, 1962. Source: Kisaburo Ito, *Kenchiku sekkei seizu*, Tokyo: Rikozusho, 1962, p. 224.

an association in 1953, the Japanese Association of Hospital Architecture (JAHA, *Nihon byoin kenchiku kyokai*), with Yoshitake as a president. This association published a journal in 1959 to promote the diffusion of modern hospitals. Moreover, in 1965, the organisation released a book to introduce new hospitals built in the beginning of the decade.[71] Arguing that 'we are moving from the era of the hospital boom based on quantity to a new era based on quality',[72] the JAHA explained that improving the quality of the overall equipment of hospitals, including patients rooms and food, was necessary to catch up with Western countries. Hence, the objective of the book, published in 1965, was to offer an overview of the best hospitals in the country as models to follow, particularly by provincial and private hospitals.

Kisaburo Ito wrote the general introduction of the book. He insisted on the importance to focus on the 'functional structure of the hospital'.[73] He explained that health care institutions should include six main divisions: patient rooms, an outpatient ward, medicotechnical equipment (laboratories, X-ray device, operating area, pharmacy, etc.), administration, services (cafeteria, laundry, etc.) and others (such as nursing school). The issue was to give enough space for each of these divisions and to organise them in order to facilitate flows of persons and material. Afterwards, the plans and details of more than 30 hospitals are exposed.

The publication of this book by the JAPA occurred in the context of a major change in the government's hospital policy. In the early 1960s, the attention of the Ministry of Health shifted towards private and profit-oriented hospitals and clinics, notably under pressure by medical doctors and private hospitals. These private hospitals gathered in 1960 in a specific organisation, the All Japan Hospital Association (*Zennippon byoin kyokai*), to carry out lobbying, while the JHA essentially included administrators from public and non-profit private hospitals. In 1963, this new association already had 1,501 members, that is 29.9% of all private hospitals that year, and 2134 in 1970 (33.1%).[74] The government founded the Health Care Finance Corporation (*iryo kinyu koko*) in 1960 in order to provide funding to private hospitals and clinics that wanted to develop themselves. Two years later, in 1962, an amendment to the Health Care Law limited the extension of public hospitals in areas with a surplus of hospitals beds (mostly cities), but private hospitals were not encompassed by the law.[75]

A major outcome of this new political agenda was the absence of hospital planning by the state. The growth of the hospital system relied, again, on market principles, as it used to be during the interwar years. In this context, the share of private hospitals rose from 74.2% in 1960 to 83.1% in 1980 (from 55.2% to 70.1% if beds are considered). Yet, this was not a full comeback to the prewar situation. The nature of private hospitals evolved drastically as a consequence of new medical technology and the actions of architects. There were not small institutions integrated to housing as they were during the interwar years any longer, but general hospitals where the organisation was similar to that of public hospitals. Their average size increased from 83.8 beds in 1960 to 123 in 1980, and the hospitals were designed by the architects who promoted modernisation during the 1950s and the early 1960s.

6. Conclusions

The dynamics of the Japanese hospital system considered in a long-term perspective in this article are characterised by two major driving forces for its development. First, the state – including regional and local public authorities – played an important role during various phases. It opened public hospitals during the 1870s as tools to diffuse Western medical technology and to train the new generations of doctors to Western medicine. Then, although the development of the hospital systems relied on private organisations, the state attempted to implement a new hospital policy during the 1930s and the 1940s to promote the introduction of the functional model. The Ministry of Health, founded in 1938, was an important activist for this political turn. However, the intervention of the state was supported by the US occupation authorities after 1945 and peaked during the 1950s. Second, the action of individual doctors was the engine of growth of the Japanese hospital system during the interwar years and since the early 1960s. The market mechanism of a highly competitive environment led to the foundation and the development of numerous private small hospitals throughout Japan. This twofold growth of hospital infrastructure was discussed by Ikai, but this article has shown that this specific structure had a deep impact on the introduction of the functional model in Japan.

The transformation of hospitals from a mere place to practice medicine to technology itself – a 'machine to cure', to paraphrase Foucault – that enables the mass production of health care has been analysed by scholars at the level of single establishments. Yet, this article emphasised the links between the organisation of the hospital system and the adoption of a functional organisation of hospitals. It also stressed the key roles that architects played in this process. During the interwar years, this functional model was introduced by architects who had connections with Western colleagues, hospital planners and the IHA, particularly Takamatsu. They designed new kinds of public and non-profit private hospitals based on these new principles. However, most of the hospitals before 1945 were private small organisations that did not follow these functional principles. One can consider that the hospital system itself was functional, as market mechanisms led to a very dense network of small institutions that offered treatment for the population. After World War II, public hospitals continued to develop following the functional model, with the support of the new state policy and the action of a new generation of architects, such as Yoshitake. Finally, private hospitals also adopted this model in the 1960s, when the small institutions founded before the war started to grow and needed a new internal organisation to make the treatment of an endless increasing number of patients possible.

Beyond the specific case of Japan, this article gives two major implications for a better understanding of the development of health industries during the twentieth century. First, it showed that the structure (number and size of institutions) and the organisation (competition or regulation) of the hospital system have an important impact on the way institutions developed. Hence, although historians tend to focus on single institutions for their research, it is necessary to have a proper view of the system itself to properly understand the development of single institutions within it. Second, the nature of hospital systems (structure and organisation) strongly influences the diffusion and use of medical technology – and consequently the rising costs of medicine. In a competitive and atomised system like Japan, all institutions have incentives to adopt the newest technology in order to attract more patients. This explains why Japan is still, today, the country with the largest density of equipment, such as CT scanners and MRI.[76]

Notes

1. Biggs, *The Rational Factory,* Johnson, 'Early cost accounting for internal management control', Nelson, 'Scientific management, systematic management, and labor, 1880–1915', Lazonick, *Competitive advantage on the shop floor,* Geels, 'Major system change through stepwise reconfiguration'.
2. Udagawa, 'The development of production management at the Toyota Motor Corporation', Williams, Haslam, Williams, Adcroft & Johal, 'The myth of the line', Lewis, 'Redesigning the workplace', Hounshell, *From the American system to mass production.*
3. Foucault, *Naissance de la Clinique,* Foucault, "L'incorporation de l'hôpital", Jones and Porter, *Reassessing Foucault.*
4. Hughes, *Networks of Power.*
5. Donzé, *L'ombre de César,* 9.
6. Rosenberg, *The care of strangers,* Stevens, *In Sickness and in Wealth.*
7. Domin, *Une histoire économique de l'hôpital,* Faure, *Les cliniques privées.*
8. Labisch and Spree, *Krankenhaus-Report.*
9. Mohan, *Planning.*
10. Bridgman Perkins, 'Shaping Institution-Based Specialism', Goebel, 'American Medicine and the "Organisational Synthesis"'.
11. Howell, *Technology in the Hospital.*
12. Vogel, 'Managing medicine'.
13. Donzé, *L'ombre de César.*
14. Adams and Schlich, 'Design for Control', Adams, *Medicine by Design,* Lüthi, *Le compas et le bistouri.*
15. Rosenberg, *Perspectives on Technology,* Davidson and McFetridge. "Key characteristics", Kipping and Bjarnar, *The Americanisation of European Business,* Donzé and Nishimura, *Organizing Global Technology Flows.*
16. Sugaya, *Nihon no byoin,* Fukunaga, *Nihon byoin shi.*
17. Ikai, *Byoin no seiki.*
18. See, for example, Katsuki. 'Meiji 30 nen zengo'.

19. Nihon tokei kyokai. *Historical Statistics of Japan.*
20. Sugaya, *Nihon no byoin.* 9–10.
21. Sugaya, *Nihon no byoin.*
22. Shinmura, *Kindai nihon no iryo.*
23. Sugaya, *Nihon no byoin,* 104–105.
24. Kawakami, *Gendai Nihon Iryo Shi,* 329.
25. Ikai, *Byoin no seiki.*
26. Ibidem.
27. League of Nations. *International Health Year-book 1930.*
28. Howell, *Technology in the Hospital,* Adams and Schlich, 'Design for Control', Donzé, *L'ombre de César.*
29. Pawlik, *Von Bergedorf nach Germania.*
30. Distel, *Rationeller Krankenhaus-Bau.*
31. International Hospital Federation (IHF), Geneva, archives of the International Association of Hospitals.
32. Gakushikai, *Kaiin shimei roku,* 283.
33. Takamatsu, *Takamatsu Masao-kun,* 3.
34. Takamatsu, 'Nosokomeion wo toshite'.
35. Takamatsu, *Koto kenchikugaku.*
36. Bartholomew, *The Formation of Science in Japan,* 243–244 and *Keio gijuku.*
37. *Keio gijuku,* 44–45.
38. Takamatsu, *Koto kenchikugaku,* 33–60.
39. Mukai, *Kenchikuka Yamada Mamoru.*
40. Ibidem, 178.
41. Ibidem, 174–175 and 180.
42. Katsuki, 'Meiji taisho showa shoki'.
43. Ikai, *Byoin no seiki.*
44. Historical Statistics of Japan, 24–30 Medical Care Personnel (1874–2004), http://www.stat.go.jp/english/data/chouki/24.htm (accessed 26 October 2016).
45. Yamazaki, *Saishin i-byoin kenchiku to sekkei.*
46. Ogawa, *Ishi to keizai,* 44.
47. Ibidem, 52.
48. Sugiyama, *Senryoki no iryo kaikaku.*
49. Aldous and Suzuki, *Reforming Public Health.*
50. Christaller, *Die zentralen Orte,* Lösch, *Die räumliche Ordnung.* On the influence of these models on hospital planning in Europe, see Donzé, *L'ombre de César,* 260–263.
51. Sugaya, *Nihon no byoin,* 127–131, Sugiyama, *Senryoki no iryo kaikaku,* 191–192.
52. Sugaya, *Nihon no byoin,* 149–150.
53. Koseisho, *Soritsu 30 shunen.*
54. Mentioned by Sugiyama, *Senryoki no iryo kaikaku,* 198–200 and Fukunaga, *Nihon byoin shi,* 360, MacEachern, *Hospital Organization.*
55. *Nihon byoin kai.*
56. Ibidem.
57. Ibidem, 639.
58. Ibidem, 453–454.
59. Ibidem, 126.
60. *Byoin kenchiku.*
61. Shimazaki, *Nihon no iryo,* 76–77.
62. *Yoshitake Yasumi sensei.*
63. *Ito saburo kenchiku.*
64. Ibidem, 152–153.
65. Starr, *The Social Transformation,* 349–351.
66. *Design and Construction,* Yoshimura e.a., *Sogo byoin.*
67. Taguchi, 'Byoin kensetsu', 38.

68. Yoshitake, 'Byoin kenchiku', 36.
69. Adams and Schlich, 'Design for Control', Donzé, *L'ombre de César*.
70. Weisz, *Divide and Conquer*.
71. *Nihon no byoin kenchiku*.
72. Ibidem, 1.
73. Ibidem, 3.
74. *50 nen shi*, 327.
75. Shimazaki, *Nihon no iryo*, 78.
76. Health statistics of OECD, https://data.oecd.org/healtheqt/computed-tomography-ct-scanners.htm (accessed 7 March 2016).

Disclosure statement

No potential conflict of interest was reported by the author.

Funding

This work was supported by Japan Society for the Promotion of Science [grant number Grant-in-Aid for Scientific Research, (C) 25380424].

References

Adams, A. *Medicine by Design: The Architect and the Modern Hospital, 1893–1943*. Minneapolis, MN: University of Minnesota Press, 2008.

Adams, A., and T. Schlich. "Design for Control: Surgery, Science, and Space at the Royal Victoria Hospital, Montreal, 1893–1956." *Medical History* 50 (2006): 303–324.

Aldous, C., and A. Suzuki. *Reforming Public Health in Occupied Japan, 1945–52*. New York and London: Routledge, 2012.

Bartholomew, J. R. *The Formation of Science in Japan: Building a Research Tradition*. New Haven and London: Yale University Press, 1989.

Biggs, L. *The Rational Factory: Architecture, Technology, and Work in America's Age of Mass Production*. Baltimore, MD: Johns Hopkins University Press, 1996.

Bridgman Perkins, B. "Shaping Institution-Based Specialism: Early Twentieth-Century Economic Organization of Medicine." *Social History of Medicine* 10, no. 3 (1997): 419–435.

Byoin kenchiku nyumon. Tokyo: Nihon byoin kyokai, 1967.

Christaller, W. *Die zentralen Orte in Süddeutschland*. Jena: Gustav Fischer, 1933.

Davidson, W. H., and D. G. McFetridge. "Key Characteristics in the Choice of International Technology Transfer Mode." *Journal of International Business Studies* 16, no. 2 (1985): 5–21.

Design and Construction of General Hospitals. New York: Public Health Service, 1953.

Distel, H., ed. *Rationeller Krankenhaus-Bau*. Stuttgart: W. Kohlhammer, 1932.

Domin, J.-P. *Une histoire économique de l'hôpital (XIXe-XXe siècles)*, 2 volumes. Paris: Association pour l'étude de l'histoire de la sécurité sociale, (2008) 2013.

Donzé, P.-Y. "Les systèmes hospitaliers contemporains, entre histoire sociale des techniques et *business history*." *Gesnerus: Swiss Journal of the History of Medicine and Sciences* 62 (2005): 273–287.

Donzé, P.-Y. *L'ombre de César: Les chirurgiens et la construction du système hospitalier vaudois (1840–1960)*. Lausanne: BHMS, 2007.

Donzé, P.-Y., and S. Nishimura, eds. *Organizing Global Technology Flows: Institutions, Actors, and Processes*. New York: Routledge, 2014.

Faure, O. *Les cliniques privées: Deux siècles de succès*. Rennes: Presses universitaires de Rennes, 2012.

Foucault, M. *Naissance de la Clinique*. Paris: PUF, 1963.

Foucault, M. "L'incorporation de l'hôpital dans la technologie modern." In M. Foucault (ed.), *Dits et écrits*, vol. 3, 508–521. Paris: Gallimard, 1998.

Fukunaga, H. *Nihon byoin shi*. Tokyo: Pilar Press, 2014.

Gakushikai. *Kaiin shimei roku*. Tokyo: Gakushikai, 1930.

Geels, F. W. "Major System Change Through Stepwise Reconfiguration: A Multi-Level Analysis of the Transformation of American Factory Production (1850–1930)." *Technology in Society* 28, no. 4 (2006): 445–476.

Goebel, T. "American Medicine and the 'Organisational Synthesis': Chicago Physicians and the Business of Medicine, 1900-1920." *Bulletin of the History of Medicine* 68, no. 4 (1994): 639–663.

Hounshell, D. *From the American System to Mass Production, 1800–1932: The Development of Manufacturing Technology in the United States*. Baltimore, MD: Johns Hopkins University Press, 1985.

Howell, J. D. *Technology in the Hospital: Transforming Patient Care in the early Twentieth Century*. Baltimore, MD: Johns Hopkins University Press, 1995.

Hughes, T. P. *Networks of Power: Electrification in Western Society, 1880–1930*. Baltimore, MD: Johns Hopkins University, 1983.

Ikai, S. *Byoin no seiki no riron*. Tokyo: Yuhikaku, 2010.

Ito saburo kenchiku kenkyujo 60 nen no ayumi. Tokyo: Ito saburo kenchiku kenkyujo, 2013.

Johnson, H. T. "Early Cost Accounting For Internal Management Control: Lyman Mills in the 1850's." *Business History Review*, 46(4), 466–474.

Jones, C., and Roy Porter, eds. *Reassessing Foucault: Power, Medicine and the Body*. London and New York: Routledge, 1994.

Katsuki, Y. E. A. "Meiji taisho showa shoki ni okeru tokyofu oyobi tokyoshi ni yoru iryo jigyo no enkaku." *Nihon kenchiku gakkai kanto shibu kenkyu hokokushu II* 72 (2002): 641–644.

Katsuki, Y. "Meiji 30 nen zengo kenchiku zasshi keisai no byoin keikakuron to sono sanko shiryo." *Nihon kenchiku gakkai kanto shibu kenkyu hokokushu* 2, no. 77 (2007): 437–440.

Kawakami, T. *Gendai Nihon Iryo Shi: Kaigyo Isei No Hensen*. Tokyo: Keiso shobo, 1965.

Keio gijuku daigaku igakubu 60 nen-shi. Tokyo: Keio University, 1983.

Kipping, M., and O. Bjarnar, eds. *The Americanisation of European Business: The Marshall Plan and the Transfer of US Management Models*. Oxon: Routledge, 1998.

Koseisho byoin kanri kenkyujo. *Soritsu 30 shunen kinenshi*. Tokyo: Koseisho, 1980.

Labisch, A., and R. Spree, eds. *Krankenhaus-Report 19. Jahrhundert. Krankenhausträger, Krankenhausfinanzierung, Krankenhauspatienten*. Francfort: Campus Verlag, 2001.

Lazonick, W. *Competitive Advantage on the Shop Floor*. Cambridge: Harvard University Press, 1990.

League of Nations. *International Health Year-book 1930: Reports on the Public Health Progress of Thirty-Four Countries and colonies in 1929*. Geneva: League of Nations, 1932.

Lewis, R. "Redesigning the Workplace: The North American Factory in the Interwar Period." *Technology and culture* 42, no. 4 (2001): 665–684.

Lösch, A. *Die räumliche Ordnung der Wirtschaft*. Jena: Gustav Fischer, 1940.

Lüthi, D. *Le compas et le bistouri: Architectures de la médecine et du tourisme curatif: L'exemple Vaudois (1760–1940)*. Lausanne: BHMS, 2012.

MacEachern, M. T. *Hospital Organization and Management*. Chicago, IL: Physicians' record Co., 1935.

Mohan, J. *Planning, Markets and Hospitals*. London: Routledge, 2002.

Mukai, H. *Kenchikuka Yamada Mamoru*. Tokyo: Tokai University Press, 1992.

Nelson, D. "Scientific Management, Systematic Management, and Labor, 1880–1915." *Business History Review* 48, no. 4 (1974): 479–500.

50 nen shi. Tokyo: Zennihon byoin kyokai, 2011.

Nihon tokei kyokai. *Historical Statistics of Japan*, 5 volumes. Tokyo: Nihon tokei kyokai, 1987-1988.
Nihon byoin kai 30 nen shi. Tokyo: Nihon byoin kai, 1981.
Nihon no byoin kenchiku zushu, Tokyo: Nihon byoin kenchiku kyokai, 1965.
Ogawa, K. *Ishi to keizai*. Tokyo: Kokuseido shoten, 1929.
Pawlik, P. R. *Von Bergedorf nach Germania : Hermann Distel 1875–1945: Ein Architektenleben in bewegter Zeit*. Murken Altrogge: Verl, 2009.
Rosenberg, N. *Perspectives on Technology*. Cambridge: Cambridge University Press, 1976.
Rosenberg, C. *The Care of Strangers. The Rise of America's Hospital System*. New York: Basic Books, 1987.
Shimazaki, K. *Nihon no iryo: Seido to seisaku*. Tokyo: Tokyo University Press, 2011.
Shinmura, T. *Kindai nihon no iryo to kanja: Gakuyo kanja no tanjo*. Tokyo: Hosei University Press, 2016.
Starr, P. *The Social Transformation of American Medicine: The Rise of a Sovereign Profession and the Making of a Vast Industry*. New York: Basic Books, 1982.
Stevens, R. *In Sickness and in Wealth: American Hospitals in the Twentieth Century*. New York: Basic Books, 1989.
Sugaya, A. *Nihon no byoin: Sono ayumi to mondaiten*. Tokyo: Chuko shinsho, 1981.
Sugiyama, A. *Senryoki no iryo kaikaku*. Tokyo: Keisoshobo, 1995.
Taguchi, M. "Byoin kensetsu no kisoteki deta." *Shin-kenchiku* 242 (1957): 38.
Takamatsu, M. "Nosokomeion wo toshite mitaru gendai obei no byoin kenchikukai." *Kenchiku zasshi* 46, no. 565 (1932): 1601–1622.
Takamatsu, Masao E. A. *Koto kenchikugaku: Hoteru, byoin, sanatoria*. Tokyo: Tokiwa shobo, 1933.
Takamatsu Masao-kun kinnen jigyokai, ed. *Takamatsu Masao-kun no seisaku to chosaku*. Tokyo: Takamatsu Masao-kun kinnen jigyokai, 1935.
Udagawa, M. "The Development of Production Management at the Toyota Motor Corporation." *Business History* 37, no. 2 (1995): 107–120.
Vogel, M. J. "Managing Medicine: Creating a Profession of Hospital Administration in the United States, 1895–1915." In *Hospitals in History*, edited by Lindsay Granshaw and Roy Porter, 243–260. London: Routledge, 1989.
Weisz, G. *Divide and Conquer: A Comparative History of Medical Specialization*. Oxford: Oxford University Press, 2006.
Williams, K., C. Haslam, J. Williams, A. Adcroft, and S. Johal. "The Myth of the Line: Ford's Production of the Model T at Highland Park, 1909–16." *Business History* 35, no. 3 (1993): 66–87.
Yamazaki, S. *Saishin i-byoin kenchiku to sekkei*. Tokyo: Kanehara shoten, 1927.
Yoshitake Yasumi sensei wo shinobu. Tokyo: Yoshitake yasumi sensei wo shinobu kai, 2004.
Yoshimura, Y., G. Watanabe, and M. Ito. *Sogo byoin no sekkei to kozo*. Tokyo: Sagamishobo, 1956.
Yoshitake, Y. "Byoin kenchiku kenkyusha no shougen." *Shin-kenchiku* 242 (1957): 36–37.

The genesis, growth and organisational changes of private health insurance companies in Spain (1915–2015)

Jerònia Pons-Pons and Margarita Vilar-Rodríguez

ABSTRACT

The crisis of welfare states in Europe has offered a growing market share to private health insurance companies. Health insurance is currently one of the fastest growing branches of private insurance business in developed countries. However, much remains to investigate about the origin and evolution of the companies in this sector. This article analyses the genesis, growth and organisational changes of health insurance companies in Spain from the creation of the first medical associations in the 1930s to the modern health insurance companies of today. Spain represents an interesting case study to investigate how changes in the public health model for the long period under study allowed private companies to maintain a changing relationship competitive and partnership with the state.

1. Introduction

By the end of the twentieth century most European Union countries were already providing a universal compulsory health insurance scheme as part of a broader social protection system.[1] However, private health insurance has become increasingly important within this system in recent decades, in a context of cutbacks, waves of privatisations and a crisis of the welfare state.[2] As a result of this process, some member states have a private health insurance market that supplements public coverage (e.g. Sweden, Spain, Ireland and the United Kingdom). This means that the private sector offers services already provided by the compulsory system, but with extra advantages such as shorter waiting lists, and other benefits and comforts. In other countries, private health insurance plays a more important supplementary role by covering services or specialities excluded from the basic state package (e.g. Denmark, Hungary and the Netherlands). Finally, in some member states private insurance provides substitute cover for people excluded from some aspects of the statutory health insurance scheme due to various factors, such as level of income or type of work (e.g. Germany). Overall, the causes behind private health insurance are very heterogeneous and a result of historical evolution, the power of different interest groups and the public policies implemented. Its increasing importance, however, is a common trend in all European countries.[3]

Bearing in mind this typology, the population covered by PHI (private health insurance) in 2000 varied notably in OECD (Organization for Economic Co-operation and Development) countries. Among the highest percentages, we find the case of the United States, where PHI covered 71.9% of the population (primary and supplementary); while in Europe, the case of Holland stands out with 92% (28 as primary, that is principal, and 64 as supplementary). The lowest percentages correspond to Spain with 13% (2.7 primary and 10.3 duplicate or supplementary) and the UK with 10% (essentially duplicate or supplementary).[4]

With regard to the case of Spain, between 1908 and 1940 the premiums obtained in sickness insurance were never in excess of 6% of the total annual premiums obtained in private insurance business. Later, in 1950, 1960 and 1970, this branch accounted for 10.4%, 6.25% and 8.2% respectively. Overall, these are very low figures, especially if one takes into account the very high number of companies operating in sickness insurance. In 1950, they comprised 24% of the total number of insurers operating in the market; in 1960 it was 30.7% and by 1970 it had reached 52.1%.[5] From 1987 to 1997, health insurance premiums grew by an average of 16% annually, driven by middle class demand and also boosted, among other factors, by: (a) the deterioration of social security services within a context of cutbacks; (b) the growth of group insurance in companies; and (c) the mutual insurance funds for civil servants and other public employees which allowed 2 million people to choose insurance.[6] All in all, private health insurance accounted for 3.9% of total health expenditure in 2000.[7] In recent years, the growing interest of insurers and the banking sector in acquiring this segment of insurance business has led to them increasing their participation in the insurance industry. The proportion of total premiums accounted for by PHI rose from 7.2% in 2001 to 10.8% in 2011, at a time of serious economic crisis.

Despite this trend, the development of health insurance companies has hardly been studied from a historical perspective.[8] Little is known about the origin, management and organisation of these companies; there is also a lack of studies from a business history point of view on their progressive increase in scale, their internationalisation process and the important mergers that have taken place in the sector over recent decades.[9] Thus, the main aim of this article is to study, from a business history perspective, private health insurance companies in Spain before and after the belated introduction of state compulsory health insurance at the beginning of the Franco dictatorship in 1942. This analysis takes into account the fact that their evolution has been different from the development of other insurance companies. These discrepancies are based on three aspects: (1) in most cases, their foundation was not linked to entrepreneurs in the insurance sector, but rather to members of the medical profession; (2) their dual regulation imposed joint control of health insurance companies by a health care supervisory body and an insurance sector supervisory body, and (3) their marginal development within the insurance business until increasing demand attracted the interest of general insurers and the banking sector in recent decades.

Bearing in mind these key aspects, and with the proposed objectives, this article is divided into four main sections. In the first, the foundation, typology, location and financial resources of the first insurers that covered health insurance from 1915 to the Spanish Civil War (1936–1939) are analysed. Here, their minimal weight in the insurance market can be seen and the first entrepreneurs from the world of medicine are studied. The difficulties of growing in a market with little demand, which started to be transformed due to the increasing interest of large companies in providing the benefits of health care coverage for some of their employees, are also examined. In the second section, the collaboration between insurers providing health insurance and the Franco dictatorship in the management of compulsory health insurance, from its passage in 1942 until its withdrawal with the Basic Law of Social Security in 1963, is studied. The obligatory abandonment of this important part of their business led insurers to initiate processes of conversion into stock companies and to increase their mutual collaboration and associationism in order to increase the scale of their coverage from local or regional to national level. The third section focuses on the Spanish transition to democracy, when health insurance companies obtained a market share in the coverage of public servants. This prompted different growth strategies ranging from cooperativism and mergers to the creation of pools to increase the geographical scope of health care services. The fourth section analyses the growing interest of general insurance companies in the health branch, the concentration of business and the arrival of international and bank capital. All in all, this historical evolution makes it clear how private health insurance companies went from being marginal to being much coveted in the Spanish insurance market.

2. The marginal market: local and provincial initiatives (1915–1941)

The state was incapable of implementing compulsory health insurance in Spain in the first decades of the twentieth century. Industrial accident insurance, retirement pensions, maternity and unemployment were all legislated for, to a greater or lesser extent, but not health care coverage. During this first stage, the private insurance sector was very weak and showed little interest in this branch.[10] Consequently, and as had happened in other European countries, private companies did not compensate for the shortcomings of the state and friendly societies.[11] As regards demand, the low standard of living of the population, the high percentage of rural population and the low employment rate explain, among other factors, the slow development of the sector. As for supply, the private insurance law of 1908, which regulated the sector during this period, made minimal demands on companies in this branch with respect to share capital or deposits, which effectively determined their small size and high geographical concentration.[12] Both factors were the result of a fragmented market, made up of companies with scant capital and premiums, which operated at a local level in the large cities (above all Barcelona and Madrid) and, in most cases, covered the risk of sickness in return for a monetary fee (*iguala*). Altogether, the premiums collected in the branches of health and burials (combined in the statistics of the time) accounted for 5.18% of the premiums collected by the entire insurance sector in 1915; 4.97% in 1925; and only 2.87% in 1935.[13] The health branch, therefore, had a small and decreasing relative weight in the private sector as a whole during this period. However, while there were 45 companies registered in the branch of health and burials in 1915 (31 in Catalonia, 11 in Madrid, 2 in Zaragoza and 1 in Vigo), the number had risen to 70 by 1925. In 1915, the top 10 companies concentrated 71.83% of premiums, while in 1925 they only accounted for 57.56% (Table 1). It was, therefore, a fragmented branch with few companies of a significant scale in terms of premiums, managed in most cases by the doctors and specialists themselves, who were funded by the monthly fees or *igualas* paid by families.

Little is known of the founders of these companies started up by doctors' associations (known as *igualatorios médicos*), which were the first initiatives in the private health sector.

Table 1. Ranking of companies in the branch of health and burials in 1915 and 1925 (current pesetas).

1915				1925			
No.	Business name	Registered office	Premiums collected	No.	Business name	Registered office	Premiums collected
1	La Esperanza	Madrid	694,182	1	Seguro Médico	Madrid	1,148,680
2	Instituto Español de Seguros	Barcelona	601,987	2	La Equitativa de Madrid	Madrid	1,010,867
3	La Verdadera Unión Española	Barcelona	592,943	3	La VerdaderaUnión Española	Barcelona	933,212
4	La Equitativa de Madrid	Madrid	360,189	4	La Patria Hispana	Madrid	738,908
5	Patria	Barcelona	267,532	5	El FomentoNacional	Barcelona	512,820
6	Benéfica Catalana	Barcelona	260,416	6	Instituto Español de Seguro	Barcelona	499,705
7	El Fomento Nacional	Barcelona	182,078	7	España	Barcelona	319,455
8	La Independencia	Madrid	118,801	8	Cataluña	Barcelona	301,457
9	La Protección de las Familias	Zaragoza	116,737	9	Asociación Médico-Quirúrgica Española	Madrid	275,838
10	La Previsora Catalana	Barcelona	108,094	10	La Independencia	Madrid	273,948
Total top10 companies			3,302,959		Total top 10 companies		6,014,889
Total (45 companies)			4,598,135		Total (77 companies)		10,449,267

Source: Boletín Oficial de Seguros (1916 and 1926).

We assume that the initial capital for these associations was provided by the doctors themselves, who saw a business opportunity in view of the backwardness of public health care coverage and the lack of interest of private insurance companies in the sickness branch. In fact, large companies did not start operating in the branch of health insurance until after the civil war. If they did so earlier, they did not intervene directly but instead promoted specialised companies.[14] Overall, the typical corporate forms were professional associations and general partnerships, although they were progressively obliged to become joint-stock companies. The increase in the number of companies and the growing complaints received for breaches of contract drove the government to control their health care activity, through the creation of a Health Office (*Comisaría Sanitaria*) dependent on the Directorate General of Health (*Dirección General de Sanidad*), by the Royal Order of 31 March 1925. From this point on a certain bipolarity was created, as private health insurance companies were audited by the Directorate General of Insurance (*Dirección General de Seguros*), but controlled in terms of health provisions by the Directorate General of Health, something which was to have important consequences in the future.

Some of these companies had been founded in the late nineteenth century and gradually offered medical specialities to the upper middle classes in the main Spanish cities. This was the case of La Equitativa in Madrid, founded in 1896 by José García de la Serrana and which, in 1929, covered around 30,000 families who paid the monthly fee. The company had a team of medical practitioners and two clinics, one in the north of the capital and one in the south, where they offered routine consultations, general medicine, general surgery, and covered the ear, nose and throat, digestive system, ophthalmology, gynaecology and dermatology specialities. The two clinics had X-ray equipment, diathermy, phototherapy, an analysis laboratory and other modern facilities. In this year, 1929, it opened a clinic for surgical operations, equipped with a surgery and 30 rooms, run by Dr Mariano Cardona.[15]

Generally speaking, private health insurance made little progress in terms of premiums and relative weight within the sector, although this trend was similar to that of other European countries. This performance was due to the inability of the sector to offer premiums and services that were affordable for most of society and also because of certain misgivings among the population about taking out health insurance with companies whose main goal was to make a profit.[16] These factors can be added to those already mentioned above for the Spanish case. But who promoted the first private health insurance companies? Health care provisions introduced by companies and employers started in the late nineteenth century in those branches with the highest accident rates and nearly always linked to industrial accidents (mining and railway companies) and, in many cases, obliged by the law on industrial accidents of 1900.[17]

Later, during the aftermath of the First World War, with the spread of corporate capitalism linked to large companies, employers showed an increasing interest in providing other types of coverage apart from compulsory insurance, a process that was accelerated due to the increase in industrial disputes.[18] However, there was no homogeneous stance among employers in favour of voluntary insurance and, as it was not obligatory, the results were very inconsistent, in terms of both the insurance offered by employers and the coverage of workers.[19] In the case of Spain, the notable pioneers in providing complex programmes of health care coverage were electricity companies, banks and railway companies of a certain size.[20]

3. Health insurance companies and the start of strategies to increase scale in private business (1940–1975)

The post-Spanish Civil War period was marked by a profound economic crisis, characterised by shortages and scarcity, and accompanied by a climate of repression and harassment. Being fully aware of the dreadful health care situation and the population's desire to have health care coverage, the Franco dictatorship used the introduction of compulsory health insurance for propaganda purposes.[21] Compulsory health insurance was passed by the law of 14 December 1942 and established the provision of general medical and pharmaceutical care in the event of sickness or maternity, but with clear limits: it was not universal, the coverage available was temporary and economically precarious, and benefits were very low. Compulsory health insurance was first introduced without a basic health care infrastructure and without any plan for state funding; both of these factors were serious obstacles to implementing a complex and expensive insurance.

What was the role of private companies in this new context? Their role was crucial for a state with the serious limitations commented on above. The companies, for their part, encountered an opportunity to collaborate with the state, which desperately needed doctors and health care infrastructure, and thereby increase the scale of their operations.[22] The Decree of 2 March 1944 established the implementing rules for the special agreement between the National Welfare Institute (Instituto Nacional de Previsión), the body given the responsibility for introducing, managing and administrating state insurance, and the private entities. The private entities that collaborated in managing compulsory health insurance were the leaders in terms of the percentage of companies covered, and the number of members and beneficiaries, until 1966, the year in which they abandoned their collaboration with the state definitively.[23]

In spite of their participation in the management of public insurance, the private companies continued to operate in a market that was fragmented during the 1940s and 1950s, divided into a multitude of medical *igualatorios* of registered medical practitioners and health care associations, providing specialities at local or provincial level, and clinics, whose partners or associates were doctors and other medical staff. The insurance law of 16 December 1954 determined that insurance policies and health care provisions were to be subject to this law and obliged all insurers (of any branch) to operate under the legal form of mutual society or stock company.[24] Meanwhile, a joint order from the Ministries of Finance and the Interior obliged all insurers in the branch of health and burial insurance to enrol in a special Ministry of Finance register of insurers. However, the law maintained very low demands with respect to deposits, although the deposit required was increased: rising from between 5000 and 50,000 pesetas in 1927 to between 200,000 and 600,000 pesetas in 1954, depending on the type of benefits offered. Furthermore, the required capital (a million pesetas) remained lower than in other branches (fire, transport, theft, etc.). Consequently, the market continued to be fragmented due to the presence of a multitude of local firms, even though 75% of business was concentrated in the hands of around 20 companies, and the majority of these firms did not even operate at the national level. Nevertheless, the new regulations entailed a radical change in the branch of health insurance, since a number of insurers came to light due to the register (121 registered in 1950, and 475 in 1960), while at the same time there was a wave of insurers that became stock companies (Table 2). Overall, we find that during this period there were diffuse and indistinct boundaries between the provision of health

Table 2. Branch of health and burial insurance (1915–1965).

Year	Total entities	A Total premiums	B Total claims	B/A	C Commissions and production expenses	C/A
1915	45	62,203,557	35,409,396	56.92	6,885,906	11.06
1920	61	52,405,649	29,189,797	55.69	7,141,785	13.62
1925	74	85,912,950	40,591,619	47.24	21,322,925	24.81
1930	76	110,211,363	52,558,528	47.68	27,767,559	25.19
1935	73	133,753,899	70,812,348	52.94	33.403.737	24.97
1945	90	177,595,209	98,192,240	55.28	56.234.568	31.66
1950	121	283,675,278	164,686,403	58.05	63,406,074	22.35
1955	–	530,584,303	283,681,691	53.46	149,637,016	28.20
1960	475	1,027,626,918	643,901,176	62.65	242,592,941	23.60
1965	–	1,736,989,746	1,173,261,050	67.54	358,570,043	20.64

Source: Memoria Estadística Seguros Privados del Ejercicio 1951, 1960 and 1970. From 1966 the statistics appear separately by sickness, health care and burials. In order to calculate the constant pesetas the deflator of Maluquer has been used, see 'Del caos al cosmos'.

insurance by social welfare mutuals, state insurance companies, *mutualidades laborales* (workers' friendly societies created during the Franco regime) and private insurance companies and mutuals, which contributed to the opacity of the sector. On the other hand, the state needed these insurers in order to implement its health insurance project, yet even so it acted very warily in the signing of special agreements and maintained a posture of seemingly applying a temporary solution. Finally, collaboration with the state in managing public insurance came to an end with the Basic Law of Social Security of 1963, which terminated all collaboration with private insurers.

Apart from the termination of the agreements as collaborating bodies of compulsory health insurance, the private insurance companies in the branches related to health, sickness (benefits and health care provision) and burials were faced with two main problems that required reforms at the end of the dictatorship: the small scale of business and its dependence on two ministries (Finance and Interior), which put a brake on legislative changes and reforms. Meanwhile, two changes were underway within the sector, with a growing focus on health care insurance rather than cash benefits, and also a growing weight of health care provision compared to burials in the branch as a whole.

Generally speaking, insurance companies operating in the health branch were not run as genuine insurance companies during the 1960s and 1970s. The dual control (dependent on two ministries) and the lack of business organisation, insurance techniques and financial means justify this assertion. These factors explain why the evolution of health insurance companies in Spain was so slow and the market remained static, in spite of the transformations taking place in the socio-economic sphere and in medicine.[25] In the 1950s, the creation of stock companies by the doctors and specialists participating in the *igualatorios* and speciality centres proliferated. Thus, for example, Sanitas was formed in Madrid and Asistencia Sanitaria Colegial in Barcelona, and associations such as Igualatorio Médico Quirúrgico in Bilbao were transformed. However, the sector was largely comprised of a plethora of small-scale insurers, and there was an excessive number of companies with very limited share capital and practically no reserves or deposits, even though these were now obligatory in other branches, and in most cases they only operated on a local or provincial scale.

In 1970, the branch of health insurance had by far the largest number of companies (347), followed at some distance by the fire branch. Very few of these insurers were general insurance companies; almost all of them operated exclusively in the health branch, and only exceptionally extended the insurance provided to include burial insurance. Comparing the rankings from 1960 to 1970 shows a curious return to an extremely fragmented business as the Federación de Mutualidades de Cataluña, which had accounted for 43% of premiums in 1960, had disappeared from the statistics by 1970 due to a change in classification.

In the 1960s and 1970s, however, there was a change in demand as a result of the progressive implementation of state health insurance and increases in the cost of health care coverage due to medical advances, especially in surgery and medical specialties. Insurers had a growing clientele among the upper classes, who had previously used private medicine by means of direct payment and who started to take out policies with private insurance companies or mutuals. The friendly societies lost part of the working and middle classes as these registered for state health insurance. This situation was further aggravated in the 1970s with the economic crisis, when inflation affected premiums due to the increased costs of services, benefits and health care provisions.

One of the most noteworthy transitions was related to the strategy of territorial expansion of companies in the sector. The increase in scale, from local or provincial to national, was accompanied by an increase in their financial capacity through the growth of their share capital. This process has been accredited in the two leading companies in the ranking: Igualatorio Médico Quirúrgico in the province of Biscay and Sanitas. In the first case, the Basque *igualatorio*, founded by a doctors' association in 1934, became a *montepío* (similar to a friendly society) in 1952 and then became a stock company in 1959. Starting from the 1940s, it grew in the province of Biscay and then expanded to the rest of the Basque country, thanks to taking on the collective insurance of large companies. This growth was sufficient to make it the branch leader.

Sanitas provides another example of territorial growth, in this case due to successfully managing to sell premiums to the middle classes and its participation in organisations such as UNEAS (Unión Nacional de Entidades Sanitarias), a national union of health care organisations. This association, led by Sanitas (a company presided over by Marcial Gómez Gil), was created to reach agreements with medical *igualatorios* and health care associations operating at local or provincial level in order to conclude reciprocal agreements for providing the services of collective policies that covered the patients of the association's members. UNEAS was founded in 1959 and was composed of 41 provincial and local insurers, mainly medical *igualatorios*. Their participation in this association enabled them to contract collective policies with important companies. Sanitas' expansion strategy was complemented by the full payment of its capital in 1967 and with the increase of this capital to 10 million pesetas in 1968.[26] Thanks to this process, by 1973 it occupied first place in the ranking of a branch with 366 operators and 42nd position in the general branch of the entire private sector (Table 3).

In Barcelona, a doctor called Espriu founded the company Asistencia Sanitaria Colegial, SA in 1954. Originally, each associated doctor had three shares. The company was run by 15 directors chosen by a meeting of shareholders, all of them doctors. The company consolidated in the 1960s, while the number of shareholding doctors increased and an administrative and accounting infrastructure was created.[27]

In the 1960s the sector urgently needed legislative changes and a new form of management that would lead to its modernisation. During the second half of the Franco period, the progressive visibility of the insurance companies that had been operating clandestinely and without control in the branches of health and burials was achieved, although pressure from

Table 3. Ranking of insurers operating in the health branch in 1970 (voluntary insurance, in current pesetas).

	Insurers	Registered office	Type	No. policies	Premiums collected	% total branch
1	Igualatorio médico quirúrgico, SA	Vizcaya	NC	76,665	251,080,000	7.76
2	Sanitas SA	Madrid	NC	26,636	209,580,000	6.48
3	Asistencia Sanitaria Colegial	Barcelona	NC	39,176	177,020,000	5.47
4	Unión Previsora SA Cia. de seguros	Madrid	NC	88,562	173,280,000	5.36
5	Equitativa de Madrid, La	Madrid	NC	22,503	108,440,000	3.35
6	Honradez, La	Madrid	M	15,660	55,620,000	1.72
7	Previsión Médico Social, SA	Sevilla	NC	28,103	51,800,000	1.60
8	Interprovincial Esp. Seg. Intesa	Barcelona	NC	20,737	51,160,000	1.58
9	Crédito Español, SA	Valencia	NC	20,489	50,220,000	1.55
10	Poles	Madrid	NC	12,100	40,780,000	1.26
	Total top10 entities			350,631	1,168,980,000	36.13

Source: Revista del Sindicato Nacional del Seguro, número extraordinario de estadística, Madrid, 1971, 75–81.
Note: NC, National Company; M, Mutual.

doctors prevented these from becoming exclusively dependent on the supervisory institutions of the insurance sector. This made it more difficult to enforce the increased demands regarding solvency, actuarial techniques, guarantees and deposits that were required of companies operating in other branches. The weight of health insurance in the form of benefits and health care had recovered somewhat during the last decade of the Franco regime from 6.25% of private insurance premiums to 8.2% in 1970.[28] Nevertheless, insurance companies were faced with the considerable challenge of how to technically modernise the sector and concentrate business, and in fact very few companies were able to achieve this.

4. The demand generated by mutual insurance funds for public servants and the growth in the scale of health insurance companies (1975–1986)

From 1975 to 1986 Spanish politicians were incapable of reaching an agreement to establish the country's health care model in the new democratic era. The new General Health Law was not passed until 1986. However, Spain's public health care expenditure quadrupled between 1976 and 1986 in circumstances where health care coverage was democratised with measures that brought about its universalisation, the standardisation of medical staff and their salaries, and initiatives aimed at modernising infrastructures and incorporating new technologies.[29] Private insurance companies, for their part, were also awaiting the reform of the sector during Spain's political transition. In the mid-1970s private insurance was still regulated by the insurance law of 1954. The preliminary draft laws promoted by the Directorate General of Insurance aimed at introducing reforms did not come to anything until the private insurance law passed in 1984.[30]

Private health insurance companies took advantage of the delay in reforming public health insurance to obtain a share of a market with great potential: the mutual insurance funds for public servants. Law 29/1975, of 27 June, on the social security scheme applicable to public servants (*Seguridad Social de los Funcionarios Civiles*) led to the creation of a mutual fund for state public servants, the *Mutualidad General de Funcionarios Civiles del Estado*

(MUFACE). Meanwhile, Law 28/1975 of 27 June created a mutual fund for the armed forces, the *Mutualidad de las Fuerzas Armadas*. These were joined by similar funds for civil servants in the judiciary, the *Mutualidades de Funcionarios de la Administración de Justicia* (MUGEJU), and in local administration, the *Mutualidad de los Funcionarios de la Administración Local* (MUNPAL). These mutual funds were able to provide health care provisions either by direct coverage or by establishing agreements with public and private entities.

The majority of public servants chose private insurance companies. At one stage during this period (1976–1985) private companies covered 94% of all public servants.[31] Thanks to the above-mentioned agreements with mutual funds, health insurance companies expanded and increased in scale. Moreover, the growth in the number of insured and premiums gave rise to significant changes in how they were managed, which in turn led to providing improved and more complete services while reducing costs. Not all the effects were positive, however. The contract with the mutual funds established fixed payments that limited profit margins. This meant that few companies decided to maintain the annual agreements on a regular basis. On the other hand, insufficient premiums led some companies to decapitalisation and degradation of their services, and even to annual deficits.[32]

Within this context, one of the main problems of the health insurance market was still its fragmentation and the small scale of coverage of companies managed, in the majority of cases, by doctors and medical specialists. A total of 297 companies were operating in the branch in 1979 and 279 in 1980; figures that accounted for almost half of the 640 private insurance companies in Spain.[33] However, during the 1970s, the groups, *igualatorios* and local companies initiated projects of integration via associations and cooperatives with the aim of meeting the demand at national level resulting from the agreements with the public servant mutual funds. ADESLAS is the most noteworthy case.

ADESLAS (Agrupación de Entidades de Seguro Libre de Asistencia Sanitaria), a grouping of private health insurers, was not constituted in the 1970s as a commercial company, but rather organised as an association made up of companies of a local and regional scope. They shared the objective of providing health care provisions at national scale in order to be able to participate in the agreements with the different public servant mutual funds. ADESLAS collected a total of 5370 million pesetas in premiums in 1981 and was comprised of around 30 companies that were included in the official statistics on an individual basis. The continuance of the regulation of 1954 had enabled the survival of these groups thanks to an ambiguous legal situation. After a complaint of irregularities by one of the associates, Previsión Médico Quirúrgica, in 1981, ADESLAS carried out a legal restructuring that led to it becoming a stock company in 1983.

Another example of collaboration between local and provincial companies was the stock company ASISA, created in Barcelona in 1973, with similar objectives of mutual cooperation. This insurer, promoted by the company Asistencia Sanitaria Interprovincial, was constituted as a medical *igualatorio* although all its shares were the property of Lavinia, a cooperative of registered doctors. In 1984, 18,000 doctors were members of the cooperative and shareholders of ASISA, each of them holding one share. This company had a delegated committee in each province, comprising doctors elected by assemblies of cooperative members. There were sometimes offers to buy the company, but it continued as a doctors' cooperative with a 15% market share of health insurance from 2006 to 2010.[34] With this format, it provided care for public servants affiliated to their particular mutual funds throughout Spain.[35]

Few companies used mergers as a way to expand before the private insurance law was passed in 1984. One exception was the Sociedad Interprovincial Española de Seguros, SA (INTESA). This company took over at least 10 small local firms in the region of Catalonia between 1972 and 1983. This cycle of concentration ended with a change of business name as it became Aresa, SA a year later.[36]

In a second phase of expansion, health insurance companies attempted the internationalisation of their operations, with varying degrees of success, and established a strategy of either creating their own clinics or signing preferential agreements with hospitals for the care and treatment of their insured. An example of the former strategy was Sanitas, which, always under the leadership of the doctor Marcial Gómez Gil, created Sanitas Internacional (1980). As an example of the second strategy, since its constitution Sanitas, SA had maintained preferential agreements with Organización Ceyde, SA, belonging to the same Gómez family, and with Instituto de Cirugías Especiales, SA. Meanwhile, the Igualatorio Médico Quirúrgico of Bilbao had acquired the Clínica Vicente in San Sebastián, and Asistencia Sanitaria Colegial, SA converted a recently acquired hotel in the Avenida Diagonal in Barcelona into the Hospital de Barcelona which was opened in 1989.[37] These are just a few examples of a process that was really quite complex.

5. Private versus public health insurance (1986–2015)

The General Heath Law was finally passed in 1986, but it was a piece of legislation that satisfied virtually no one, as its contents were more a set of principles and long-term objectives than a plan for health care reform that could be implemented immediately.[38] The legislative status quo established with regard to private health insurance in the previous stage barely changed in general terms. In Spain, in 2001, of all the public servants who belonged to three of the state's mutual funds (MUFACE, ISFAS and MUGEJU), the vast majority, 84%, chose to insure themselves with private insurance companies, compared with the 16% who chose social security or the health services managed by the autonomous regions.[39] Meanwhile, along with these groups, consumers of health insurance turned increasingly to private health care for a different reason, and with a complementary function. This demand was aimed at avoiding the waiting lists of the public system, receiving specialised care without first having to go through the primary health care services and obtaining dental health care services for adults, which were not included in the public health insurance.[40]

The increase in individual clients contributed to the introduction of tax reforms in the 1990s that allowed a 15% tax allowance for medical expenses, including insurance company premiums.[41] This tax measure, despite the opposition of the insurance employers' organisation UNESPA, was repealed in 1999 although, in exchange, tax deductions for company insurance were incorporated.[42] This double health coverage, compulsory public and complementary private, was defended by employers within the sector and studies were published supporting this option, most of them based on the savings in health care expenditure that would ensue.[43] In 2012, health insurance premiums (covering sickness and health care) rose to €6720 million, 11.5% of total premiums in the insurance sector (life and non-life); €1400 million came from the agreements with the mutuals MUFACE, ISFAS and MUGEJU, 21% of the total income of private health insurance.[44]

Along with this growth in demand, the adaptation of the sector to Spain's incorporation into the EEC led to numerous mergers and takeovers that reduced the number of companies

Table 4. Comparison of the ranking of companies by premiums in the health branch (1993 and 2013).

1993				2013			
No.	Company	Premiums in millions of current pesetas	% Total	No.	Company	Premiums in millions of current pesetas	% Total
1	ASISA	53,834.81	23.8	1	Segurcaixa Adeslas	313,323.79	30.3
2	Sanitas	33,475.43	14.8	2	Sanitas	196,633.90	19.0
3	Adeslas	31,622.82	14.0	3	ASISA	161,223.32	15.6
4	Asistencia Sanitaria Colegial, SA	14,853.00	6.6	4	DKV	70,687.29	6.8
5	Previasa	11,338.78	5.0	5	Mapfre Familiar	42,246.18	4.1
6	Igualatorio Med. Quirúrgico	11,184.74	4.9	6	Igualatorio Méd. Quirúrgico	36,597.78	3.5
7	Aresa	6,919.38	3.1	7	Asistencia Sanitaria Colegial	30,519.05	2.9
8	FIATC	4,822.97	2.1	8	FIATC, Mutua de Seguros	23,198.02	2.2
9	Caja Salud	3,932.14	1.7	9	Caja de Seguros Reunidos	16,281.50	1.6
10	Aegon	3,244.29	1.4	10	Mutua General de Cataluña	12,505.14	1.2
	Total	175,228.36	75.6		Total	903,215.96	87.3

Source: *Estadística del seguro Privado 1984–1993*, 1994, UNESPA, Servicio Actuarial, Madrid, 253. Accessed August 24, 2015. https://www.dgsfp.mineco.es/sector/documentos/Informes%202014/Memoria%20Estad%C3%ADstica%20Anual%20de%20Entidades%20Aseguradoras%202013.pdf

Table 5. Evolution of the health branch (1982–1993) (in current pesetas).

Year	No. of insurers	Number of policies	Insured	Premiums in millions	Annual growth rate	Claims (millions of pesetas)
1982	–	1,808,216	4,563,219	39,629.01	–	–
1983	–	1,826,364	5,177,408	47,000.68	18.60	–
1984	243	1,740,586	4,817,388	52,040.35	10.72	44,448.41
1985	221	1,660,438	4,538,430	58,450.47	12.32	49,743.30
1986	199	1,747,500	4,210,847	71,544.88	22.40	58,313.30
1987	174	1,786,885	4,543,381	81,749.49	14.26	66,600.19
1988	171	1,990,955	4,833,283	93,049.29	13.82	75,106.92
1989	150	1,972,602	5,278,984	10,057.47	17.20	92,201.56
1990	132	1,827,274	5,419,516	12,281.11	17.63	97,754.20
1991	135	1,858,367	5,488,638	170,075.01	32.58	139,771.62
1992	129	2,102,435	5,709,080	201,760.90	18.63	164,754.43
1993	128	2,174,532	5,644,041	226,571.19	12.30	-

Source: Estadística del seguro Privado 1984–1993, UNESPA, Servicio Actuarial, Madrid, 1994, 251.

in the health insurance sector. Between 1985 and 2013, there were other important changes that modified this branch. Health insurance companies went from being operators in a marginal branch, with little weight in the sector, to occupying the leading positions of non-life branches of the insurance business by 2013. The health branch grew between 2000 and 2012, initially with an annual growth rate of 9–10% until it slowed down in 2008 due to the effects of the economic crisis and competition over prices. In 2012 the growth rate was 3.08%. The factors influencing this growth included the introduction of new types of coverage, tax incentives established in the reform of 2002, the development of group insurance in companies and the marketing of products for certain segments of the population.[45]

In 1973, the leading company operating in the health branch, Sanitas, SA, was in the 42nd position in the general ranking of the sector, comprising 687 entities. By 2013, we find several health insurance companies in the top 20 places of the ranking by volume of business in the non-life branch, comprising 200 companies.[46] As regards the ranking of companies by premiums in the health care branch, we find the same companies in the first three places both in 1993 and in 2013. However, by 2013 ASISA had fallen from first to third place, while ADESLAS (now in the hands of SegurCaixa) had risen from third place to lead the sector with 30.3% of premiums. Together, ASISA, Sanitas and ADESLAS (under the name Segur Caixa-Adeslas in 2013) accounted for 52% of total premiums in 1993 and 65% in 2013 (Table 4).

This new situation for the sector was due to important changes in the previous 30 years: (a) waves of mergers and takeovers that increased business concentration in the health branch, driven by the new solvency requirements after the 1984 law and incorporation into the EEC; (b) the increased demand that stimulated the interest of general insurance companies and the banking sector in this business; and (c) the entry of multinationals into health insurance.[47]

With respect to business concentration, the number of insurers operating in the health branch fell from 243 to 128 between 1984 and 1993 (Table 5). In this period the companies were still financed by national capital, and were mainly stock companies, which now controlled 97.5% of business (only five mutuals remained). The top 20 companies collected 85% of premiums in 1993, which shows the greater concentration. ASISA led this branch with 23.76% of premiums, followed by Sanitas with 14.77% and ADESLAS with 13.96%. The top three together accounted for almost 52.5% of business. If we add Asistencia Sanitaria Colegial (6.56%) and Previasa, SA (5%), this percentage rises to 64.05%. It must be remembered that in 1970, the top five in the ranking only accounted for 28.42% of premiums. The level of concentration increased between 2000 and 2012. In the former year the top 10 companies accounted for 77.86% of premiums while in 2012 this figure had reached 82.15%.[48]

Two phases can be detected in the merger process of health insurance companies. In the first, small provincial insurers were absorbed, whereas in the second, foreign capital and the banking sector now participated. The first waves of concentration processes were initiated in the second half of the 1980s, when the larger companies (ADESLAS, Aresa and Aegon) took over others that only operated on a local or provincial scale. This phenomenon accelerated in the insurance sector between 1990 and 1996, when 143 entities were involved in mergers or takeovers. Three important conclusions can be drawn regarding this trend:[49] (a) most of these operations were undertaken by stock companies (92% of total insurers); (b) 51 companies acted as the absorbing company for another 88 firms; (c) the waves followed this pattern: the largest number of agreements were concluded in 1991 and then there was another wave in 1994 and 1995. In this second phase, the entry of foreign capital, linked to incorporation into Europe, and the recent acquisition of health insurance companies by general insurance companies, were crucial factors. General insurers became very interested in the expansion of a branch which they had largely ignored during the entire twentieth century.[50]

With these two phases, the large health insurers consolidated their position. This was the case of ADESLAS and Aresa. The former acquired Madrid Salud, SA and Previsión Médico Social de Huelva, SA (1989). Later on, starting in 1991, it initiated the merger of almost 20 insurers that operated at a local level throughout Spain. In 1991, the French group Médéric acquired 45% of its capital, while the remaining 55% was in the hands of Aguas de Barcelona.

By 2006, thanks to this process, ADESLAS had become the leader in the health branch with 23.69% of premiums. This distribution of shares changed in October 2009 when one of the largest Spanish financial institutions, La Caixa, acquired ADESLAS through its own company SegurosSegurCaixa. For its part, Aresa (Interprovincial Española de Seguros, SA before 1984) absorbed dozens of small provincial and regional insurers between 1991 and 1999 until it was taken over by Mutua Madrileña in 2005. By 2014 this company enjoyed a market share of 27.4% with 3.2 million customers.[51]

The interest of foreign capital in the health branch led to other shares changing hands. The Dutch Aegon was one of the first multinationals interested in Spanish health insurance. It acquired Seguros Galicia in 1988 and, later, Labor Médica de Seguros and La Sanitaria, SA in 1996 and 1997. Also in 1988, 40% of the capital of Sanitas was acquired by COFIR (Corporación Financiera Reunida), linked to Carlos Benedetti. Differences of opinion between the new shareholders and the Gómez family led to the sale of the shares of the founder's heirs to the British mutual company BUPA (British United Provident Association).[52] By 1989 BUPA had acquired almost all the shares of Sanitas.[53] Meanwhile, the entry of the German multinational DKV into the Spanish insurance market was via the acquisition of Previasa, SA, a company founded in Zaragoza by Publio Cordón. In 1990, the British company Scottish Widows acquired 10% of its capital. In 1997, after the kidnapping of its founder by the terrorist organisation GRAPO, its sale to DKV, the leading European health insurance company, was agreed. This insurer currently belongs to Munich Health of the Munich Regroup. It is the fourth insurer in the health branch with 6.8% of premiums. The sale of Clínicas Quirón, which formed part of the Previasa Group and had played a very active role in the provision of health care in Spain in recent years, was not included in the acquisition agreement.

The crisis of the public health care model over the last few decades, mutilated by budgetary adjustments and cuts, fuelled the trend towards the privatisation of health care services managed by central and regional governments within the framework of neoliberal ideology. This change in trend opened the way to the participation of health insurance companies in the management of hospitals and medical services or publicly owned foundations. The development of this process coincided with the expansion of the private hospital network. Since 1990, almost all insurance companies have increased their medical centres, dental clinics, hospital groups and health care staff with the aim of giving preferential treatment to their policyholders and beneficiaries (Table 5). This is the case of ADESLAS, ASISA, DKV and Sanitas, companies which already had hospitals and clinics and took advantage of these resources to offer their services to insurers or to sign agreements with the public health service with the intention of reducing waiting lists for certain provisions.

The latest step in this process is the policy of privatising hospital management, which has accelerated over the last decade. This model is based on a system of public–private partnerships through which the public ownership of hospitals is maintained, and these also remain under public control and funding, but their management is privatised. This formula was introduced in 1999 at Alzira Hospital (Valencia). Insurance companies soon opted to participate in this system. Sanitas (BUPA) was one of the first companies to collaborate. Its first intervention was specifically in running the Manises Health Department, comprising two hospitals and 14 primary health care centres in the Autonomous Region of Valencia. Sanitas purchased all Ribera Salud[54] shares in Manises Hospital and took over its management in 2012. In the same year it acquired the Ribera Salud shares for the management of Torrejón Hospital in the Autonomous Region of Madrid.[55]

Sanitas was joined by other insurance companies attracted by the private management of public hospitals. The partner of the insurance companies in most cases was Ribera Salud. ASISA acquired 35% of the shares of the management company running Torrevieja Hospital, which opened in 2006, while Ribera Salud was the holder of the other 65% of the shares. DKV, always in partnership with Ribera Salud, collaborated in the management of Denia Hospital from 2009 with 65% of shares. ASISA also shares the management of Elche Hospital. This model has been the subject of debate in the last three years and, currently, private insurance companies are still conducting a strategic review of their participation.[56]

6. Conclusions

In recent decades, private health insurance has experienced an increase in activity in Europe, especially in its supplementary role to public health care coverage. The reduction in public expenditure, the privatisation of public health services and tax incentives to private insurance, along with changes in the population's consumption patterns and diversification of the offer, have fostered this process. Health insurance companies, founded by doctors themselves in their infancy, operated in a marginal market for years in Europe, until becoming an object of desire for banks and general insurance companies in recent decades, thanks to their attractive growth.

This process is evident in the case of Spain. Before the Spanish Civil War, private companies in the health branch had very little weight in the insurance sector. Although they multiplied in number throughout Spain, promoted by doctors, they were small, with very little capitalisation and concentrated in Madrid and Barcelona. We would highlight, among other obstacles to their growth, the minimal demands of legislation governing the sector (the laws of 1908 and 1954) and the dual control (Directorates General of Insurance and Health), factors that certainly did not favour modernisation.

The dictatorship managed to overcome the obstacles that hindered the introduction of state health insurance, which required the collaboration of the private sector in its management through special agreements, a key manoeuvre to address the lack of adequate funding and public infrastructures. The first agreements concluded with the private sector (1944–1954) enabled the progressive implementation of coverage of an increasing number of beneficiaries. Basically, the state offered business to the private health care sector, and this responded by facilitating its reorganisation. In 1954, many of the agreements with mutuals and private insurance companies were not renewed in the light of new and more stringent demands. Consequently, private companies tried to increase their existing market niche (upper and middle classes) in a context of limited coverage by state insurance and the rising costs of surgical and pharmaceutical provisions. The basic law of 1963 put an end to the private management of state health insurance and insurance companies focused their strategy on the growth of the private market. Between 1960 and 1975, territorial growth processes were initiated through the organisation of associations, doctors' cooperatives and collaborative mechanisms that enabled the treatment of those insured with small local and provincial companies via networks of broader geographic scope. This process led to the creation of health insurance companies at national and regional level (for example Sanitas and Igualatorio Médico Quirúrgico). In fact, insurance played a major role in the formation of health business systems in many countries (particularly in continental Europe, including Spain) because they contributed to regulating competition through the adoption of fixed fees and prices (so that hospitals, doctors, producers of drugs and equipment, etc., could benefit from minimal prices). This was important to ensure the long-term growth of the system.

There was an Impasse from 1975 to 1984/1986 while awaiting the passage of a law to modernise public and private insurance and it was necessary to define a public health care model within the new democratic framework. Additionally, there was also the need to meet the demands of integration into the EEC and the transfer of health care competencies to the autonomous communities. In this situation, health insurance companies progressed, aided considerably by providing coverage for the mutual insurance funds for public servants, to whom the state gave the right to choose between public or private health care.

The market for health care coverage has undergone a profound transformation in Spain since 1986, characterised by business concentration and increasing demand. Under these circumstances, the interest in providing private health insurance in Spain has grown significantly among general insurance companies, bancassurance companies and the multinationals of the sector. Meanwhile, the mutilation of the public health care system, with budgetary adjustments and the approval of formulas for the private management of public hospitals, increased the business opportunities for a growth sector in all European Union countries, and Spain is no exception.

Notes

1. In Europe, from a historical point of view, and although with significant variations in each case, public systems of health insurance coverage generally prevailed. These models contrast with the one that consolidated in the United States, where the population's health care has mainly been covered by private insurance companies; a system considered to be more expensive in the long term. Chapin, in *Ensuring America's Health*, examines from an institutional standpoint the management and consolidation of the model based on insurance companies, which determined the characteristics of the health system in the United States: its high cost, fragmentation and an anti-democratic corporate structure. The private interest groups involved in this process gained ascendency over the medical professionals and the politicians in government consolidating a system of private coverage. In a similar fashion, Thomasson, *From Sickness to Health*, analyses the creation of the model, although in this case he highlights the role of tax incentives and the fact that private insurance favoured hospitals.
2. More details on these aspects in Thomson and Mossialos, *Private Health Insurance*. Since the 1980s, public health insurance has suffered cuts and privatisations and has been opened up to management by private insurance companies in most developed countries. See Hassenteufel and Palier, "Towards Neo-Bismarkian"; Cabriedes and Guillén, "Adopting and Adapting Managed Competition"; Mossialos and Allin, "Interest Group"; Palier, *A Long Goodbye to Bismark?* Aguilar, Waitzkin, and Landwehr, *Multinational Corporations*.
3. Different forms of health care coverage took precedence in these countries depending on the period and the model adopted. The so-called mixed economy of welfare (coexistence of forms of solidarity, state action and private companies) was a preliminary step towards the creation of two basic models of health insurance by the mid-twentieth century; see Harris, *The Origins*. After the Second World War, state insurance prevailed in Western Europe, whilst private insurance companies took precedence in the United States. For more on these aspects, see Van der Linden, *Social Security Mutualism*; Beito, *From Mutual Aid*; Glenn, "Understanding Mutual"; Gorsky, "The Growth and Distribution"; Murray, *Origins of American*; and Dreyfus, *Les assurances socials,* among others.

4. Information taken from Table 2.7 of the OECD Health Project 2004, *Private Health Insurance* (https://www.oecd.org/health/privatehealthinsuranceinoecdcountries-theoecdhealthproject.htm), 51. Definition of functions of private health insurance in Box 2.2, 29.
5. The data from 1908 to 1940 in Pons, *Las estrategias de crecimiento*, and for 1950 to 1970 in Pons, *The Difficulties of Spanish*.
6. Tortella, *Historia del Seguro*, 344–7.
7. Public expenditure on health accounted for 71.7%, out-of-pocket payments 23.5% and all other private funds 0.9%. In Table 2.4 taken from OECD, *Private Health Insurance* (https://www.oecd.org/health/privatehealthinsuranceinoecdcountries-theoecdhealthproject.htm), 41.
8. There are a few exceptions, although outside the field of business history. These are works such as Murray, *Origins of American*, and Vonk, "In it for the Money?," that analyse the behaviour of private health insurance companies in the United States and the Netherlands, respectively, but tangentially within their broader research that focuses on friendly societies. For his part, Chapin, "The American Medical Association," studies the role of insurance companies in the creation of a health insurance system with a high-cost model in the United States. As for the impact of health insurance on private insurance business, the works on the 20 most important insurance markets in the world compiled in Borcheid and Hauter, *World Insurance*, highlight its emergence since the 1990s in countries such as Germany, France, Italy, and Japan, and also in emerging countries such as China and Brazil.
9. The interest of economists has certainly increased, and in some cases they include a brief history of the sector in their introductions, such as in Hurley and Guidon, *Private Health*, for the case of Canada, and in Buchmueller and Couffinhal, *Private Health*, for the case of France.
10. We find cases of some advanced projects in health coverage for women coming from the world of friendly societies, such as the Montepío de Santa Madrona founded in 1900 for health care provision for women, mainly maternity care. From 1920, the foundation of the Caixa de Pensiones integrated the Montepío into the Institut de la Dona que Treballa, which, as well as this friendly society, also encompassed dispensaries and clinics, a maternity service, a nursing school and housing for poor families: https://www.memoriaesquerra.cat/publicacions/3/52_1934317/IGUALADI_19340317_11.pdf. This example may be seen as indicative of Spain's participation in a trend of European specialisation in social maternity (Nash, *Maternidad y Construcción*).
11. The local and fragmented offer of sickness coverage provided by mutuals and friendly societies may, from the point of view of supply, be seen as an obstacle to the rationalisation of the sector; nevertheless, some studies have also demonstrated the advantages that these societies offered to the population in general and to the working class in particular by introducing a culture of insured people which provided health care coverage, security and citizen identity (Harris, *Welfare and Old Age*). Other works such as Cordery, "Friendly Societies," and Gorsky, *Mutual Aid*, reinforce the idea that the friendly societies offering sickness coverage, founded on the basis of worker solidarity, also created a sense of identity and respectability in the fight against social exclusion and division.
12. During much of the twentieth century there were different legal demands for private insurance companies in terms of minimum and subscribed capital, deposits and reserves depending on the branch of insurance. The demands for the health branch were lower (Pons and Vilar, *El seguro de salud*, 68). In particular, the 1908 law established a paid-up capital of 25%, but with no minimum capital; the Royal Decree-Law of 18 February 1927 introduced minimum capital, but set very low (50,000 pesetas with an exiguous outlay of 15,000 pesetas or payment of 15% when the subscribed capital was 60,000 pesetas or more). In 1920, only three of the 22 insurance entities in the branch of health and death insurance that appear in the yearbook *Anuario Financiero y de Sociedades Anónimas* (1921) had a share capital of more than 60,000 pesetas. Pons and Vilar, *El seguro de salud*, 67 (Table 1.11); Frax and Matilla, "Centenario de la Ley."
13. Pons and Vilar, "Friendly Societies," 81.
14. This was the case of Fomento Nacional. This health insurance company was founded on 3 April 1912 with a share capital of 50,000 pesetas, of which 12,500 were paid up. One of its first executives was Antonio Cabrer Sagauas, manager, a position he combined with the vice-presidency of La Unión y El Fénix Español in Barcelona until his death on 21 October 1918 (*La*

Vanguardia newspaper, November 13, 1918). This situation seems to be a clear indication of the connection between Fomento Nacional and the leading company in the sector at this time. Anuario Financiero y de Sociedades Anónimas, 1921, 311.

15. *ABC* newspaper, June 4, 1929, 12.
16. This is Vonk's argument in "In it for the Money?" to explain the limited development of private health insurance before the Second World War.
17. Some mining companies created hospitals that also treated sick workers (Martínez Soto and Pérez de Perceval, "Asistencia sanitaria," 99; Pérez Castroviejo, "La asistencia sanitaria," 139; Menéndez Navarro, "Hospitales de empresa," 334–5). For more on the medical infrastructure of the employers' industrial accident mutuals, see Pons, "El seguro de accidentes."
18. For the case of the large German companies, see Hilger, "Welfare Policy in German."
19. In 1924, the Board of Directors of Mutua General de Seguros, created in 1907 as an employers' industrial accident mutual, decided to offer associated employers health insurance coverage for their workers, which would allow them to cash in on their considerable health care infrastructure of clinics and hospitals. This branch of insurance, however, did not generate very high profits, see Pons, "El Seguro Obligatorio de Enfermedad," 230–1.
20. Aubanell, "La elite de la clase trabajadora."
21. Pons and Vilar, "Labor Repression"; Vilar and Pons, "The Introduction of Sickness Insurance."
22. To this end, many commercial insurance companies created mutuals in order to collaborate in the provision of compulsory health insurance. The company Hispania created the Mutualidad de Previsión Hispania (MUTUANIA) on 2 June 1944. By 1945 this mutual covered the health insurance of 8090 companies, 60,979 workers and 174,338 beneficiaries (Pons, *130 años de promesas*, 99).
23. They were also leaders in terms of premiums collected, see Pons and Vilar, *El seguro de salud*, Table 2.4, 131. On 31 December 1954, the Minister of Labour terminated all the agreements signed with the collaborating bodies since 1944, and most of them were not renewed. Greater demands made by the Ministry in terms of deposits and reserve funds, and the reduction of profit margins, did not favour the continuation of this collaboration.
24. Pons and Vilar, *El seguro de salud*, 170.
25. In line with the arguments of Guerrero, "Salud. Situación del ramo," 217.
26. Pons, "Biografía de Marcial Gómez Gil," 430.
27. Rodríguez, "Sanidad, Farmacia," 32–5.
28. Pons, "El Seguro Obligatorio de Enfermedad," 71.
29. For more on the health care reform during the transition to democracy, see the works of Ortega and Lamata, *La década de la reforma sanitaria*; Elola and Navarro, "Análisis de las políticas sanitarias"; and Pons and Vilar, *El seguro de salud*, 293–313.
30. Pons and Vilar, *El seguro de salud*, 325–7.
31. Guerrero, "Salud. Situación del ramo"; Sáez, "Las prestaciones y servicios."
32. Guerrero, "Salud. Situación del ramo," 226.
33. Pons, "Spain: International Influence," 204.
34. Pons and Vilar, *El seguro de salud*, 413.
35. Carreño, "La intercooperación," 167.
36. For a complete list of the firms absorbed, see Pons and Vilar, *El seguro de salud*, 338.
37. Pons and Vilar, *El seguro de salud*, 335; Rodríguez, "Sanidad, Farmacia," 35.
38. Muñoz, Delgado, and Seara, *Las estructuras del bienestar*, 224.
39. Guerrero, "Salud. Situación del ramo," 15.
40. Uri, "Seguros de salud en España," 2.
41. This tax deduction was maintained until the passage of Law 40/1998 which abolished the 15% deduction related to medical services and private health care insurance. Freire, *La nueva fiscalidad*, defends doing away with the deduction as it was detrimental to the national health service. In the United States, tax subsidies led to an increase in the purchase of insurance, not only reducing its relative price but also stimulating the growth of group insurance (Tomasson, *From Sickness to Health*).

42. Thanks to this tax change the premiums for this product increased by 30%. Companies extended this social benefit to their workforces. "Un buen momento para el negocio colectivo de salud," *Aseguranza: revista de los profesionales del seguro*, 73 (2003): 16–27.
43. See, for example, López Nicolás, "Seguros sanitarios," 28; Guerrero, "Salud. Situación del ramo," 16.
44. Herce et al., *Rol de las aseguradoras*, 53.
45. Tortella, *Historia del seguro*, 424–6.
46. For 1973, Anuario Español de Seguros, 1973–1974, 24–5. The data for 2013 from the Directorate General of Insurance. Accessed September 20, 2015. https://www.dgsfp.mineco.es/sector/documentos/Informes%202014/Memoria%20Estad%C3%ADstica%20Anual%20de%20Entidades%20Aseguradoras%202013.pdf
47. The concentration of the sector through mergers and acquisitions may introduce positive aspects in terms of the scale of companies, but the result may be different if the process is analysed from the consumer's point of view. Ethnographers such as Narotzky, "El lado oscuro," have evaluated the learning costs for families when it came to facing the disappearance of mutuals or small local and regional firms as they were replaced by large companies, with complex information and marketing systems.
48. Tortella, *Historia del seguro*, 426.
49. In line with Serra, Gómez, and Landete, "Resultados de las fusiones," 1001.
50. In the 1980s the era of strictly regulated and isolated national insurance markets came to an end, with the liberalisation of markets, especially in the European Economic Community: Borscheid, "Europe Review," 59–60. Spain's incorporation into the EEC obliged an opening up and liberalisation and encouraged the entry of foreign capital.
51. Herce et al., *Rol de las aseguradoras*, 7.
52. For the role of this mutual in British health insurance, see Doyle and Bull, "Role of Private Sector," 563–5.
53. For an exhaustive list of the mergers, see Pons and Vilar, *El seguro de salud*, Table 4.41, 419–20.
54. According to the information it provides itself, Ribera Saludis is the leading health care management company in the sector of health care administration licences in Spain. It was founded in 1997 to develop initiatives in public–private partnerships. Accessed September 27, 2015. https://www.riberasalud.com/
55. For more on the health care networks of the main insurance companies, including the administration of public hospitals in 2008, see Pons and Vilar, *El seguro de salud*, 423, Table 4.42.
56. Accessed September 27, 2015. https://www.elconfidencial.com/espana/comunidad-valenciana/2015-05-29/asisa-y-adeslas-venden-a-ribera-salud-su-participacion-en-los-hospitales-modelo-alzira_863642

Acknowledgements

Both authors gratefully acknowledge financial support from European Union, European Regional Development Fund (ERDF) & Spain's Ministerio de Economía y Competitividad, project entitled Management and Construction of the Spanish hospital system from the perspective of economic history: between public and private sectors Ref. HAR2015-66063-R.

Disclosure statement

No potential conflict of interest was reported by the authors.

ORCID

Jerònia Pons-Pons http://orcid.org/0000-0003-0491-7038
Margarita Vilar-Rodríguez http://orcid.org/0000-0001-9082-2734

References

Aguilar, R. J., H. Waitzin and A. Landwehr. "*Multinational Corporations* and Health Care in the United States and Latin America: Strategies, Actions, and Effects." *Journal of Health and Social Behavior* 45 (2004): 136–157.

Aubanell Jubany A. M. "La elite de la clase trabajadora. Las condiciones laborales de los trabajadores de las eléctricas madrileñas en el periodo de entreguerras." *Scripta Nova* VI 119, no. 17 (2002). Accessed December 11, 2016. http://www.ub.es/geocrit/sn/sn119-17.htm

Beito, D. T. *From Mutual Aid to the Welfare State. Fraternal Societies and Social Services, 1890–1967*. Carolina del Norte: The University of North Carolina Press, 2000.

Borscheid, P., and N. V. Haueter, eds. *World Insurance. The Evolution of a Global Risk Network*. Oxford: Oxford University Press, 2012.

Borscheid, P. "Europe Review". *World Insurance*, edited by P. Borscheid and N. V. Hauter, 37–66. Oxford: Oxford University Press, 2012.

Buchmueller, T. and A. Couffinhal. *Private Health Insurance in France*. OECD Health Working Papers, No. 12. Paris: OECD Publishing, 2012. https://doi.org/10.1787/555485381821

Cabriedes, L., and A. M. Guillén. "Adopting and Adapting Managed Competition: Health Care Reform in Southern Europe." *Social Science & Medicine* 52 (2001): 1205–1217.

Carreño, F. "La intercooperación en la asistencia sanitaria: el largo camino hacia el cooperativismo sanitario integral." *REVESCO: Revista de estudios cooperativos* 62 (1996): 157–162.

Chapin, C. F. "The American Medical Association, Health Insurance Association of America, and Creation of the Corporate Health Care System." *Studies in American Political Development* 24, no. 02 (2010): 143–167.

Chapin, C. F. *Ensuring America's Health*. New York: Cambridge University Press, 2015.

Cordery, S. "Friendly Societies and the Discourse of Respectability in Britain, 1825–1875." *The Journal of British Studies* 34, no. 1 (1995): 35–58.

Doyle, Y., and A. Bull. "Role of Private Sector in United Kingdom Health Care System." *British Medical Journal* 321, no. 7260 (2000): 563–565.

Dreyfus, M. *Les assurances socials en Europe*. Rennes: Presses Universitaires de Rennes, 2009.

Elola Somoza, J. and V. Navarro López. "Análisis de las políticas sanitarias españolas 1975–1992." *Revista de Ciencias Sociales* 126 (1995): 19–39.

Frax, E. and M. J. Matilla. "Centenario de la Ley de Seguros de 1908 (I): la legislación sobre el sector asegurador en España, 1908–1935." *Revista Española de seguros. Publicación doctrinal de Derecho y Economía de los seguros privados* 133-134 (2008): 85–114.

Freire, J. M. "La nueva fiscalidad de los seguros sanitarios privados y el Sistema Nacional de Salud." *Gaceta Sanitaria* 13, no. 3 (1999): 233–236.

Glenn, Brian J. "Understanding Mutual Benefit Societies, 1860–1960." *Journal of Health Politics, Policy and Law* 26 (2001): 638–651.

Gorsky, M. "The Growth and Distribution of English Friendly Societies in the Early Nineteenth Century." *The Economic History Review* 51, no. 3 (1998): 489–511.

Gorsky, M. "Mutual aid and civil society: friendly societies in nineteenth-century Bristol." Urban History 25, Issue 3 (Special Issue: Civil Society in Britain) (1998): 302–322.

Guerrero Castro, M. "El seguro de Asistencia Sanitaria y sus principales problemas." *Hacienda Pública Española* I (1996): 207–232.

Guerrero Gilabert, J. I. "Salud. Situación del ramo." *Mercado Previsor* 358 (2002): 14–23.

Harris, B. *The Origins of the British Welfare State*. Basingstoke, Hampshire: Palgrave Macmillan, 2004.

Harris, B. (ed.). *Welfare and old age in Europe and North America : The Development of Social Insurance*. London: Pickering & Chatto Publishers, 2012.

Harris, B., and P. Bridge, eds. *Charity and Mutual Aid in Europe and North America since 1800*. New York: Routledge, 2007.

Hassenteufel, P. and B. Palier, "Towards Neo-Bismarckian Health Care States? Comparing Health Insurance Reforms in Bismarckian Welfare Systems." In *Reforming the Bismarckian Welfare Systems*, edited by B. Palier and C. Martin, 40–61. Malden: Willey-Blackwell, 2008.

Herce, J. A., F. Azpeita, E. Martín, and A. Ramos. *Rol de las aseguradoras privadas en la sostenibilidad del Sistema Sanitario Público*. Barcelona: SegurCaixaAdeslas, 2014.

Hilger, S. "Welfare Policy in German Big Business after the First World War: VereinigteStahlwerke AG, 1926–33." *Business History* 40, no. 1 (1998): 50–76.

Hurley, J., and G. E. Guidon. *Private Health Insurance in Canada*, CHEPA Working Paper series, paper 08-04 (2008). Accessed November 21, 2016. http://hdl.handle.net/11375/16729

López Nicolás, A. "Seguros sanitarios y gasto público en España. Un modelo de micro-simulación para las políticas de gastos fiscales en sanidad." *Papeles de Trabajo del Instituto de Estudios Fiscales*. Serie Economía 12, no. 36 (2001). Accessed November 21, 2016. http://www.ief.es/documentos/recursos/publicaciones/papeles_trabajo/2001_12.pdf

Maluquer de Motes, J. "Del caos al cosmos: una nueva serie enlazada del Producto Interior bruto de España entre 1850 y 2000." *Revista de Economía Aplicada* 49, no. XVII (2009): 5–45.

Martínez Soto, A. P. and M. A. Pérez de Perceval. "Asistencia sanitaria en la minería de la Sierra de Cartagena-La Unión (1850-1914)." *Revista de la Historia de la Economía y de la Empresa* IV (2010): 93–124.

Menéndez Navarro, A. "Hospitales de empresa: los primeros pasos de la medicina del trabajo." In *Trabajo y salud: desde la protección a la prevención. Instituto Nacional de Seguridad e Higiene en el Trabajo*, edited by Instituto Nacional de Seguridad e Higiene en el Trabajo, 328–345. Madrid: Fundación Francisco Largo Caballero y Mutua Fraternidad-Muprespa, 2010.

Mossialos, E., and S. Allin. "Interest Group and Health System Reform in Greece." *West European Politics* 28, no. 2 (2005): 420–444.

Muñoz Machado, S., J. L. García Delgado, and L. González Seara, dir. *Las estructuras del bienestar. Derecho, economía y sociedad en España*. Madrid: Civitas, 1997.

Murray, J. E. *Origins of American Health Insurance. A History of Industrial Sickness Funds*. New Haven-London: Yale University Press, 2007.

Narotzky, S. "El lado oscuro del consumo." *Cuadernos de Antropología Social* 26 (2007): 21–39.

Nash, M. "Maternidad y construcción identitaria: debates del siglo XX." In *Debates sobre la maternidad desde una perspectiva histórica (siglos XVI-XX)*, edited by G. A. Franco Rubio, 23–49. Barcelona: Icaria, 2010.

Ortega, F., and F. Lamata. *La década de la reforma sanitaria*. Madrid: Exlibris, 1998.

Palier, B. *A Long Goodbye to Bismarck? : The Politics of Welfare Reform in Continental Europe*. Amsterdam: Amsterdam University Press, 2010.

Pérez Castroviejo, P. M. "La asistencia sanitaria de los trabajadores, mutualismo y previsión en Vizcaya, 1876–1936." *Revista de la Historia de la Economía y de la Empresa* 4 (2010): 127–152.

Pons Pons, J. "The Difficulties of Spanish Insurance Companies to Modernize During the Franco Years: The Mechanization of Administrative Tasks and the Introduction of the First Computers, 1950–79." In *The Development of International Insurances*, edited by R Pearson, 63–84. London: Pickering and Chatto, 2010.

Pons Pons, J. "El seguro de accidentes de trabajo en España: de la obligación al negocio (1900–1940)." *Investigaciones de Historia Económica* 2 (2006): 77–100.

Pons Pons, J. "El Seguro Obligatorio de Enfermedad y la gestión de las entidades colaboradoras (1942–1963)." *In Revista de la Economía y de la Empresa* 4 (2010): 227–248.

Pons Pons, J. *130 años de promesas cumplidas. Grupo Zurich en España*. Barcelona: Planeta, 2015.

Pons Pons, J. "Biografía de Marcial Gómez Gil." In *Los 100 empresarios Españoles del siglo XX*, edited by E. Torres, 428–431. Madrid: Ed. Lid Empresarial, 2000.

Pons Pons, J. "Las estrategias de crecimiento de las compañías de seguros en España 1900–1940." FUNEP. Programa de Historia Económica (WP 2002/1). Accessed June 10, 2016. ftp://ftp.fundacionsepi.es/phe/hdt2002_1.pdf

Pons Pons, J., and M. Vilar Rodríguez. *El seguro de salud privado y público en España. Su análisis en perspectiva histórica*. Zaragoza: Prensas Universitarias de Zaragoza, 2014.

Pons Pons, J., and M. Vilar-Rodríguez. "Friendly Societies, Commercial Insurance, and the State in Sickness Risk Coverage: The Case of Spain (1880–1944)." *International Review of Social History* 56 (2011): 71–101.

Pons Pons, J., and M. Vilar-Rodríguez. "Labor Repression and Social Justice in Franco's Spain: The Political Logic of Compulsory Sickness Insurance (1942–1957)." *Labor History* 53, no. 2 (2012): 245–267.

Pons Pons, J. "Spain: International Influence on the Domestic Insurance Market. World Insurance." In *The Evolution of a Global Risk Network*, edited by P. Borscheid, and N. V. Haueter, 189–212. Oxford: Oxford University Press, 2012.

Rodríguez Nozal, R. "Sanidad, Farmacia y Medicamento Industrial durante la II República (1931–1936)." *Revista ILUIL* 30 (2007): 123–150.

Sáez, C. "Las prestaciones y servicios de la Mutualidad de Funcionarios Civiles del Estado (MUFACE)." *Revista de estadística y sociedad* 25 (2007): 9–11.

Serra, V. M., M. A. Gómez, and M. Landete. "Resultados de las fusiones empresariales: una aproximación empírica en el sector asegurador." *In Revista Española de Financiación y Contabilidad* XX, no. 110 (2001): 1001–1036.

Thomasson, M. A. "From Sickness to Health: The Twentieth-Century Development of the Demand for Health Insurance." *The Journal of Economic History* 60, no. 2 (Jun 2000): 504–508.

Thomson, S. and E. Mossialos. *Private health insurance in the European Union. Final report prepared for the European Commission, Directorate General for Employment, Social Affairs and Equal Opportunities*. London: LSE Health and Social Care, London School of Economics and Political Science, 2009.

Tortella Casares, G., dir. *Historia del seguro en España*. Madrid: Marcial Pons, 2014.

Uri, A. "Seguros de salud en España." *Revista Trébol. Publicación de Mapfre Re* 11, no. abril (1999): 2–4.

Van der Linden, M., ed. *Social Security Mutualism: The Comparative History of Mutual Benefit Societies*. Berna: Peter Lang, 1996.

Vilar-Rodríguez, M., and J. Pons Pons. "The Introduction of Sickness Insurance in Spain in the First Decades of the Franco Dictatorship (1939–1962)." *Social History of Medicine* 26, no. 2 (2013): 267–287.

Vonk, R. "In it for Money? Insurers, Sickness Funds and the Dominance of Not for Profit Health Insurance in the Netherlands." In *Welfare and old age in Europe and North America: the development of social insurance*, edited by B Harris, 167–188. Londres: Pickering and Chatto, 2012.

Index

Note: Figures are indicated by *italics*. Tables are indicated by **bold**. Endnotes are indicated by the page number followed by 'n' and the endnote number e.g., 20n1 refers to endnote 1 on page 20.

Abbott Laboratories 12
academic entrepreneurship 81
Academy for Public Health in Hamburg 107
acquisitions 32
Advanced BioHealing 83
advanced markets 36; Barcelona 25–6
Advanced Tissue Sciences *78*, 79–82
Aegon 186
Affordable Care Act, 2014 74
Agrupación de Entidades de Seguro Libre de Asistencia Sanitaria (ADESLAS) 183, 186, 187
Aguas de Barcelona 186
Akademie für Staatsmedizin (Academy for Public Health) 106
Akira Sakai 47
Aldous, Christopher 164
Alexandre Parodi 124
Alexza 35
Alfresa Holdings Corporation 57
Allied Control Council 100
Allies 98, 100
All Japan Hospital Association 167–8
Alpha Therapeutic Corporation 34
Alternative Investments Market (AIM) 80
Álvarez, Roser 15
Alzheimer diseases 80
Alzira Hospital (Valencia) 187
American Civil War 10
American firms 74, 78, 79, 82, 83–4, 86, 87
American Hospital Supply Corporation (AHS Corp.) 12, 27, 29, 30–1
Americanisation 98, 108
American Sterilizer Company 12
American Surgical Trade Association 12
Anderson, Julie 8
Anglo-Saxon countries 10–11
Anhui Province 143
annealing process 54
anti-epidemic stations 141
Antonelli, Étienne 123
Apligraf units 80, 83
architecture 16, 155, 156, 160–3, 165–7
Aresa 186
Argentina 58
ASISA **185**, 186, 187
Asistencia Sanitaria Colegial 181
Athersys 87
Atomic Energy Research Institute 14, 61
Australia 58
Avlar BioVentures 80–1, 84

backwardness 99
Banco Santander Central Hispano 35
Barcelona 31, 35; advanced markets 25–6
Bard-Parker Company Inc. 12
barefoot doctor (BFD) program 139
Barinova 46
Basic Law of Social Security, 1963 176, 180
Basque *igualatorio* 181
Beckton, Dickinson and Company 12
Berg, Marc 10
Beveridge-Plan 100
BFD program 145, 146
bibliometric analysis history of health, hospitals and medicine, 2000–2016 **3**
Bijker, Wiebe 8
Bioengineering Institute of Catalonia (*Instituto de Bioingenieria de Catalunya*) 35
biological study 5
bio-medicine 101
biopharmaceutical industry 74, 77, 86–7
biotechnology 1, 15, 72, 76, 82
Bismarck's system 100
Blume, Stuart 8
Braun, B. 45
Brazil 58
Breakthrough Therapy 85
Britain 72–87
British firms 79, 80, 83, 84, 87
British United Provident Association (BUPA) 187
broader biopharmaceutical industry 77, 86–7
Bucheli 77
Bukov 46
business history 2, 4, 5, 8, 10, 21, 46, 76, 77, 87, 154, 156, 175; health 13–16

Caisse interdépartementale des Assurances sociales de la Seine et Seine-et-Oise (Seine and Seine-et-Oise Interdepartmental Social Insurance Fund) 125
Caixa Manresa 35
Canada 160
Cardio 81
Catholic Church 117
Cell Therapy Catapult, 2012 84
Centocor 76
Centocor's ReoPro (abciximab) 77
Central Hospital of Social Insurance *(Shakai hoken chuo byoin)* 165–6
Centro Nacional de Investigaciones Cardiovasculares (CNIC) 35
Chamber of Deputies 122, 123
Chandler, Alfred D. Jr. 10, 20–2, 155
Chandlerian' stages 22–5, 36
Charte de la Mutualité (Mutual Insurance System Charter) 115, 117
Cherry, Steven 11
Chief of the Public Health 52
child-care centers 139
child mortality 115
China 1, 9, 31, 35, 82, 85, 134–49; adjustment stage (1962–1965) 138; cultural revolution (1966–1976) 138–9, 148; economic and social inequalities 134; GLF 148; great leap forward (1958–1961) 137–8; in health endowments 142–5; health institutions *140*; health resources 135; Henan Province 135, 145–8; infant mortality rate *140*; initial stage (1949–1957) 136–7; Maoist period *135*, 136, 148; Mean population *135*; national statistics 139–42; state of the health system 136
China Family Panel Studies (CFPS) 136
China Health and Nutrition Survey (CHNS) 136
China Health and Retirement Longitudinal Study (CHARLS) 136
China Institute for Income Distribution data-set (CHIP) 136
Chinese Communist Party (CCP) 136–7
Civil Service Code 81
clinical laboratory 21
clinical pharmacology 33
clinical trials 80, 82–7
Clínicas Quirón 187
clinics 4, 139, 141, 146, 155, 157, 159, 163, 166–8, 178, 179, 184, 187
collective entrepreneurship 8
collectivisation 138
Colonel of the Medical Corps 52
commercialisation 79, 87
communicable disease control (CDC) programs 137
communities of knowledge 8
companies, branch of health and burials 176, **177**
Comprehensive Statistical Data and Materials 136
Congrès des syndicats médicaux de France (CSMF) 124, 127
Conseil d'État (Council of State) 124
Conseil national économique (National Economic Council) 124
Conseil supérieur de l'Assistance publique (Senior Public Assistance Board) 115, 116, 128
Consumer Protection Board 79
Cooperative Medical Schemes (CMS) 137
Corporación Financiera Reunida (COFIR) 187
Covidien 49
criminal negligence 81
Cros (Spanish chemical group) 31–2
Cultural Revolution (CR) 136, 138–41, 143, **143**, 143–9, **144**, 145, 147–8
curving process 55
Cutter Laboratories 12
Czech Republic 34

Dade Grifols 28–30
Dade Reagents 28–30
Dainippon Sumitomo Pharmaceuticals 86
Davol Rubger Company 12
decentralization 109n4
demilitarization 109n4
democratization 31, 98, 109n4
denazification 109n4
density: nurses of **7**; pharmacists of **7**; physicians of **7**
dental care products 48–9, 59
Dermagraft 79, 83
Design and Construction of General Hospitals (book) 166
Deutsch Bank 35
developed countries: nurse-to-bed ratios **60**
developed markets, Grifols and Ferrer 34–6
Directorate General of Health *(Dirección General de Sanidad)* 178
Directorate General of Insurance *(Dirección General de Seguros)* 178
Distel 160
diversification 32
Division of Medicine and Public Health (DMPH) 105
DKV **185**, 187, 188
doctors 144–5, *145*, 148; allocation of *146*
Domin, Jean-Paul 15, 155
Donzé, Pierre-Yves 15–16
Draper, William H. 102
drug innovation 8
Dupont 31
dynamic imbalance 47, 48, 62

Early Access to Medicines scheme 85
economic and social inequalities 134
ecosystem 76

Einheitsversicherung 100
Ellerbrock, Dagmar 109n2
Enantia 35
entrepreneurship 4–5, 11, 78, 81
environmental sanitation 137
epidemic prevention station (EPS) 137
Eremkin 46
Espriu 181
Eugenics 101
Europe 20, 189n1
European firms 26
European Medical Agency (EMA) 77
European Recovery Programme 15
evidence-based medicine 10
extensive medicalisation 115
eyeless needles, MANI's products:
characteristics of **50**; Japan 45; long-term trends in sales *48*; making surgical needles from stainless steel 53–6; sales at home and abroad 57–61; SMEs 46; surgical needle supply chain 51–3; sutures to stainless steel eyeless needles 56–7

factory management systems 154
Faure, Olivier 155
Federación de Mutualidades de Cataluña 181
Federal Health Office (Bundesgesundheitsamt) 105
Federal Republic of Germany (FRG) 98–100
Fédération des syndicats médicaux de la Seine (Federation of Medical Syndicates of the Seine) 125
Ferdinand-Dreyfus, Jacques 122
Ferrer 21, 22–3, 34–6
Ferrer y Cía SRC 31
first movers, growth strategies of *23*
Fisscher 46
'fit': cell-based therapies 73; issue of novel therapies 72; in Japan and Britain 72; regenerative medicine 73–4
Fomento Nacional 190n14
Food and Drug Administration 27, 30
Fosdick, Raimond B. 102
four pests 138
France 4–5, 11, 25, 155, 159
Franco's dictatorship 26
French Bismarkian system 128
French health system 125
Fujikeizai 53
Fujimoto 53
functional hospital 155

Gansu Province 144
García-Canal, Esteban 14
GDF Gesellschaft für dentale Forschung und Innovationen GmbH 61
Gemeinsam gegen die Achsenmächte 110n25
Gendron Wheel Chair Company 12
Genentech 76
General Health Law 182, 184
general hospital *(byoin)* 158
general insurance companies 186, 188, 189
generalisation: access to care 115–16
gene therapies 77
Georges Cahen-Salvador 124
German Social Security 99–100
Germany 1, 4–6, **7**, 9, 11, 12, **13**, 14, 15, 24–34, 37, 74, 76, 97–108, 115, 121, 155, 159, **159**, 160, 174; after 1945 98–9
GlaxoSmithKline 76
global leaders 21
Goldmann, Franz 103
Governmental Reorientation Funds 104
GRAPO 187
Great Kanto Earthquake 162
Great Leap Forward (GLF) 137–9, 147–9
Green Cross Corporation 34
Gri-Cel 29
Grifols 21, 22–3, 32, 34–6
Grifols Blood Bank 28, 29
Grinda, Édouard 123
Groen 46
gross domestic product (GDP) 1, 118
Grupo Santander Central Hispano, 2001 34
Guillén, Mauro F. 14
Guizhou Province 140

haemophiliacs 81
hard stainless material ultra-fnely 54
Healing Democracy *(Demokratie als Heilmittel)* 109n2
Healios 86
health branch: and burial insurance 179, **180**; evolution **185**; insurers **182**; premiums **185**
healthcare 1, **14**, 74–6, 83, 99, 135, 137, 139, 142, 148, 189n3; Britain 75; demand 15, 114–29; industries 21, 22; Japan 75–6; legislation 99; United States 74–5
health care corporation *(iryo hojin)* 165
Health Care Finance Corporation *(iryo kinyu koko)* 168
Health Care Law 168
health contexts 74, 87
health economics 1, 2
health expenditures 1
health industries 1
health inequalities 134
health institutions 136, 139–43, *142*, 143, **144**, 148
health insurance 2, 4, 8, 11, 16, 23, 24, 74, 76, 82, 100, 101, 103, 104, 107, 137, 165, 174–89
Health Office *(Comisaría Sanitaria)* 178
Henan Province 15, 135, 136, 143, 145–9; number of doctors *147*
Hermann Distel 160
High Architecture *(Koto kenchikugaku)* 161
Hill–Burton Act, 1946 166
Histocell 35

Historical Statistics of Japan 157, 157, 158
Hoechst 31
hospital beds by country **13**
Hospital Organization and Management (book) 164
hospitals 4, 6, 8, 9, 11, 59; by country **13**; interwar years 160–3; operating room *167*
hospitals for patients 166
Hospital Survey and Construction Act, 1946 166
hospital system 154–6, 158; international comparison **159**
Howell, Joel D. 155
Hugues, Thomas 8
human cells 77
Human Fertilisation and Embryology Act 81
Hunan Province 143
Hundred Flowers Campaign 138
hygiene 137

ICI 31
igualatorios médicos 176–7, 179–81, 183, 188
imperial science 6
independent medical doctors *(kaigyoi)* 158
industrialisation 6, 9, 11, 117
Industrie-Unternehmungen AG (InAG) 12
industry cluster 62
infant mortality rate *140*
innovation scholarship 74
Institute of Psychiatry 80
institutional changes: *Conseil supérieur de l'Assistance publique* 116; expansion of assistance 116–17; expansion of insurance 117–18; Radical Party allies 116
institutional environments, United States, Britain and Japan **75**
institutionalisation 115
Instituto Central de Análisis Clínicos 26
Instituto de Bioingenieria de Catalunya (IBEC) 35
Instituto de Cirugías Especiales, SA 184
Instituto Nacional de Previsión or the Ministerio de Sanidad 23
insurance companies 2, 4, 16, 24, 76, 82, 174–89
insurers, health branch **182**
Intercytex 80, 84
International Health Division (IHD) 103
International Hospital Association (IHA) 160
internationalisation 21, 22, 31
Interprovincial Española de Seguros, SA 187
iPS cells 85, 86
Italy 6, 25, 34

Janus Developments 35
Japan 4–6, 20, 27, 76, 82, 156, 157, 162, 169; hospitals *157*, *158*; hospitals, interwar years 160–3; hospital system 156–60; number of hospitals and beds *51*; postwar reforms 163–5; public hospitals 165–8
Japan Atomic Energy Research Institute 57
Japanese Association of Hospital Architecture (JAHA) 166–7
Japanese firms 79, 81, 84–5, 87
Japanese Yen 45, 48, 49, 53, 59
Japan Federation of the Medical Worker's Unions 59
Japan Finance Corporation for Small and Medium Enterprises 47
Japan Hospital Association (JHA) 164–5
Japan Tissue Engineering (J-TEC) 81, 84–6
Jikei University Hospital 160
Johnson and Johnson (Ethicon) 38n5, 45, 46, 49–50, 61, 80–1
Journal of Architecture 161

Kanji Matsutani 47, 54, 55, 57, 58, 60, 61
Kassenarztgesetz 101
Kawakami 76
Kazuhiko Hagane 47
Keio University Hospital 160, *161*
Kimmel, Elke 110n25
Kipping 77
knowledge-intensive industries, advanced countries 36–8
knowledge transfer 15, 26, 27, 154–69

Labisch, Alfons 155
Laboratorios Andrómaco 38n9
Laboratorios Ferrer SL 31
Laboratorios Grifols 29
Labor Médica de Seguros and La Sanitaria, SA 187
La Equitativa 178
La importancia de las redes sociales 38n9
Länder (federal states) 106
Latour, Bruno 8
Laurent, Jules 122
leadership 62
Lindner, Ulrike 110n19
literature review 76
local government 138, 146
London Stock Exchange 80

Madrid Salud, SA 25, 186
MANI's products 45–8
Manuel y Francisco Ferrer SL 31
Maoist period 15, 134–49, *135*, 136, 139, 141, 142, 145, 147–8; China 148; health institutions **144**; hospitals **143**
Marrow-Tech Inc. *78*
Masamitsu Matsutani 47
Massachusetts Institute of Technology (MIT) 33, 79
mass migration 6
maternity 139
Matsutani, Masao 45, 47, 51–4, 61
Matsuyoshi 53
McGaw, Foster 12
Mead Johnson and Company 12

Medicaid 74
medical care system 108
medical imagery 8
medical innovation 8
medical instruments industry 46
medical insurance 118
medicalisation 115, 154
medical technical personnel 145, *145*, 148
Medicare 74, 83
medizinische Polizey (medical police) 101
Medtronic 45
Meiji Restoration 156
Menicon 81
Merck and Company 12
mergers and acquisitions (Grifols) 34–6
Merlin Biosciences 80–1, 84
Merlin Ventures 80
Mexico 58
Miami Pexaco Intl Corp 34
microfabrication 60–2
Millerand, Alexandre 122
Ministry of Health (MOH) 137
Mitsui zaibatsu 161
monoclonal antibody 77
Monod, Henri 116
Morikawa Iryoki 53
multinationals 8, 9, 11, 14, 20, 22, 24, 27, 31, 36, 186, 187, 189
Musée social (Social Museum) 116
Mutualidad de las Fuerzas Armadas 182–3
Mutualidad de los Funcionarios de la Administración Local (MUNPAL) 183
Mutualidades de Funcionarios de la Administración de Justicia (MUGEJU) 182–3
mutualidades laborales 180
Mutualidad General de Funcionarios Civiles del Estado (MUFACE) 182–3
Mutual Insurance System Charter 118, 128
Mutua Madrileña 187
Myanmar 61

Nasdaq 38n5
National Diet Library 47
national healthcare systems 76
National Health Service (NHS) 75, 106, 155
National Institute for Health and Clinical Excellence (NICE) 75
national insurance 100, 107
National Socialism 98–101
National Survey of Fertility and Contraception 136
Nature 77
Neary, Francis 8
needle-equipped sutures 49
neonatal tetanus 141
neuroscience 101
new organisational and commercial knowledge, United States and Germany 26–34
New York State Health Commissioner 79
Nichimen Enterprise 58
Nidec 84
NIF Ventures 81
Nihon byoin kenchiku kyokai 164–7
Nihonshoji Corporation 57
Nikkei Top Leader 47
Ningxia province 142
Nobel Prize Award (Yamanaka) 85
non-Western civilizations 6
North American Alpha Therapeutic Corporation 37
Novartis Diagnostics 35, 80, 83
NSDAP member 104, 106
nurses 56, 59

Occidental Hooker 31
OECD statistics 1, 2, 6, 12
Office of Military Government for Germany, US (OMGUS) 103
ophthalmologic knives 48–9, 59
Organización Ceyde, SA 184
Organization for Economic Co-operation and Development (OECD) 175
Organogenesis 79–81, 83; revenues and losses *78*
original instruments manufacturers (OEMs) 53
Ortho Pharmaceutical's Orthoclone OKT3, 1986 77

Page, Benjamin B. 110n46
Pamar, Inderjet 107
Parets del Vallés 30
Parkinson diseases 80
People's Republic of China (PRC) 136–7
Pérez, Paloma Fernández 14
Perkins, Barbara Bridgman 10
Pharmaceutical and Medical Devices Agency (PMDA) 77–8, 81
pharmaceutical company 14
pharmaceutical industry 4, 12, 14, 20–1, 25, 36–8, 77, 146
physicians compulsory law of 1955 101
Pickstone, John V. 8
Pierre Laroque 124
Pinch, Trevor 8
pioneering countries 4–5, 11
plasma industry 21
political systems 5
Pons, Jerònia 16
postwar reforms 163–5
Potts, J. M. 28
premiums, health branch **185**
prevention first policy 137–8, 141
Previasa, SA 187
Previsión Médico Social de Huelva, SA 186
primary wholesalers 53, 56
Private Health Insurance 189n2
private insurance law, 1908 176
Progil 31

Proteome Sciences 83
Provincial Archive of Public Health Records *(Weishengzi)* 136
public health: Hamburg 106–7; and medicine 97; and social insurance 99–101; transatlantic visits 105–6
public healthcare system 5, 84
public health insurance 184
Public Health Service 98, 101, 102, 107
public hospitals: model for 165–6
Puig, Nuria 14
punching 55

Qinghai Province 142

Rabro 32
Radical Party allies 116
Rahmenbedingungen 109n5
Rausch, Helke 110n26
recombinant DNA technology 77
regenerative medicine 77, 78, 80, 83, 85; first phase, 1970–2002 78–82; second phase, 2002–2015 82–6; United States, Britain and Japan 77–8
Reichsmark (RM) 100
ReNcell 83
ReproCELL 86
Research Center in Hospital Building *(Byoin kensetsu kenkyujo)* 160
Ribera Salud 188
Rockefeller Foundation (RF) 15, 25, 97–108; Hamburg 108; post-war Europe 97; and public health in Germany 101–5; Weimar Republic and National Socialism 97
Rosenberg, Charles E. 155
Russia 46, 76

Saiseikai Utsunomiya Hospital 52
Sams, Crawford F. 52
Sanitas 187, 188
sanitation 141
Sass 46
Scandinavian countries 25
Schellenberg, Ernst 109n14
schistosomiasis disease 138
Schleiermarcher, Sabine 15
Schlich, Thomas 8
Schneider, W. H. 107
School of Hospital Administration *(byoin kanri kenshujo)* 164
School of Hygiene in Toronto 105
Schools of Public Health 105
Schütz Dental GmbH 61
Scottish Widows 187
Seguridad Social de los Funcionarios Civiles 182
SegurosSegurCaixa 187
Self-Defence Forces Central Hospital in Tokyo 56
Senate's Finance Committee 121–2
Severo Ochoa Award 33
Shaanxi Province 143
Shandong Province 143
sharpening process 55
Shell 31
Shibasaburo Kitasato 161
Shire 83
Shumsky, Neil Larry 10
sickness insurance 175
Slovakia 34
small and medium-sized enterprise (SME) 46–9, 59, 61, 62
small clinic *(shinryojo)* 158
small firms, health care industries in Spain 23–5
small organisation 62
Smith & Nephew 79, 83
social component 101
social insurance 15, 99–101, 103, 107, 115, 116, 118–29
socialisation: contractual system 127–8; demographic crisis and its consequences 121–2; healthcare 126–7; healthcare demand 15; health issues 115–16; health system 118–20; regulated competition 120–1; social insurance 122–6
Social Market Economy 108
social networks 8, 38
social policy 116
social protection system 174
social security scheme 182
Sociedad General de Farmacia 27
Sociedad Interprovincial Española de Seguros, SA (INTESA) 184
sociology 8
Sojitz Corporation 58
Spain 6, 11; Civil War 188; health care 189; health insurance companies 175, 179–82; local and provincial initiatives 176–8; mutual insurance funds 182–4; OECD 175; private *vs.* public health insurance 184–8
Spanish-American Wars 9, 10
Spanish Civil War 23, 26, 175
Spanish health care industries 22–3
Spree, Reinhardt 155
stainless eyeless needles 57, 58, 60; *see also* eyeless needles, MANI's products
stainless steel eyed needles 53–4, 56, 60
Standard Oil 31
state government 138
Statistique Générale de la France (French statistics office) 115, 119
StemCells Inc. 83–4
stem-cell therapy 79, 81, 84, 86
sterilisation 57
Stevens, Rosemary 155
strategic alliances (Ferrer) 34–6
surgeons 56
surgical needles 48–9; supply chain *52*
Surugadai Inoue Hospital 160

Suzuki, Akihito 164
Switzerland 4–5, 11, 25, 160

Tadanao Kagimoto 86
Takahashi, Masayo 86
Takamatsu 160
Takanezawa 51
Takeuchi 46
tax deduction 191n41
Taylorism 154
technological capability 48, 49, 51, 59–61
Terumo 81
Testskin 80
therapeutic revolution 22
3i 80–1, 84
Tibet Province 144
Timmermans, Stefan 10
tissue-engineering technology 77, 79
Tochigi Prefectural Library 47
Tokyo 46, 165
Tokyo ishi kenchiku shinyo kobai riyo kumiai 163
Tokyo Stock Exchange 61, 86
Torrejón Hospital 187
Toshiba 58–9, 61
traditional Chinese medicine (TCM) 145–6
transatlantic transfer 105–7
TransCyte 79
TransScience 81
Trommsdorff 32–3, 37

Umemura, Maki 15
Unión Nacional de Entidades Sanitarias (UNEAS) 181
uniQure's Glybera 77
United Kingdom 4–6, 11–12, 25, 34, 155, 175
United States 4–6, 9, 10, 12, 20, 27, 31, 34–6, 52, 56–8, 76, 77–8, 81, 82, 86, 155–6, 160, 175
US High Commissioner for Germany (HICOG) 105
US Orphan Drug Act, 1983 77

vaccination 137
Versicherungsanstalt Berlin (VAB) 100
Vietnam 61
Vilar, Margarita 16
visitation programmes 15
Vogel, Morris J. 155

Wacker Chemie 31
Wadhwani 77
Weerd-Nederhof 46
Weimar Republic 104
Weindling, Paul 110n45
welfare protection 114
Welfare Section of General Headquarters (GHQ) 52
Wengst, Udo 109n5
Western Bloc 60
Woolgar, Steve 8
workshops layout 154
World Health Organization 2, 6
World War I 6, 12, 107, 118, 121, 127, 157–8, 178
World War II 6, 9, 11–12, 14, 15, 20, 22, 26, 27, 32, 37, 51, 52, 76, 159, 160, 162, 169

Xin Zhongguo Wushi Nian Tongji Ziliao Xupian 136

Yamazaki, Seiichiro 162–3
Yanagawa 47
Yokoyama, Chikafumi 86

Zemtsov 46
Zennippon byoin kyokai 167–8
Zhejiang Province 145